# RARE EARTH

Anna Khameneva is a respected scientist
expelled from her native Russia owing to her
controversial novel about a nuclear winter. She
can never return home: the KGB has
confiscated her passport and, in reprisal,
separated her from her only, beloved son.

Anna is suddenly alone in the West and at the
centre of world-wide media attention, courted
by diverse political factions who wish to claim
her as their figurehead. Hesitantly she accepts
an offer of support from one such group, and
thus begins a circus of notoriety, and an
intimate odyssey through America. But
underneath Anna's success is the sinister voice
of the political piper, demanding to be paid.

**About the author**

Mary Lee Grisanti grew up in Larchmont, New York and graduated at Smith College and New York University. She lives in New York City, where she is at work on a new novel.

# Rare Earth

---

# Mary Lee Grisanti

**CORONET BOOKS**
Hodder and Stoughton

**For Mom and Dad,
Chris and Paul
and Uncle Paul**

Copyright © 1986 by Mary Lee
Grisanti

First published in Great Britain in
1987 by Hodder and Stoughton
Limited

*Coronet edition 1988*

Printed and bound in Great Britain
for Hodder and Stoughton
Paperbacks, a division of Hodder
and Stoughton Limited, Mill Road,
Dunton Green, Sevenoaks, Kent
TN13 2YA (Editorial Office:
47 Bedford Square, London
WC1B 3DP) by Richard Clay
Limited, Bungay, Suffolk. Photoset
by Rowland Phototypesetting
Limited, Bury St Edmunds, Suffolk.

**British Library C.I.P.**

Grisanti, Mary Lee
    Rare earth.
    I. Title
    813'.54 [F]      PS3557.R53/

    ISBN 0-340-42150-9

This book would not be possible if Sasha and Elizabeth Gamburg, and their son, Elie, had not personally opened the heavy doors to the Soviet Union for me. They spent untold hours with me around their kitchen table, drinking tea, sharing their bittersweet reminiscences of home and family left behind, explaining cynical Russian jokes, reciting Pushkin and Mayakovsky. They opened their home and their lives to me and gave me a way to approach and appreciate a very large, very sad country. Their tenderness and trust and willingness to undertake difficult journeys of memory have informed every part of this manuscript.

I want also to thank Nina Kerova and Slava Tsukerman, Anya Von Bremsen and her mother Larisa Frumkin, and Olga Kogan, for their openness and help in so many of the details one must know in order to understand characters who have grown up on the opposite side of the earth to oneself.

Charles Mann read this manuscript many times and made many important suggestions. His experience as a journalist was invaluable to me, as was his sense of humour which got me over many a rough spot. David Smilow's gift for arriving at beginnings, middles, and ends as if it were the most natural thing in the world helped me bring the book to its final form.

My father gave me great help in researching the law on espionage and, more importantly, infused me with his own tremendous respect and love for the law. Armand Serfaty also helped me with the legal research and was always there with the most basic kind of moral support, without which no author ever finished a book. I must also thank Daniel Benson and Elliot Cohen for sharing with me their knowledge of federal prison and FBI procedure.

5

I want to thank my editor, Susan Schwartz, for her great perceptiveness, patience and care through each stage of the project, and my agent, Jeanne Drewsen, for her unfailing sensitivity, judgment and support.

To the private doors which must be opened in order to write a novel, Jeffrey Benson gave me the key.

Finally, I was sustained in every way by the love and concern of my family, in particular my mother, whose gift for life inspired this effort.

Personality is dependent on the world at
large, on one's neighbours. It defines itself
by reference to others and becomes aware of
its own uniqueness only when it sees the
uniqueness of everyone else. . . .

The thirties and the forties were the years
when ideology triumphed over everything else,
and the extermination of anyone who refused
to accept its propositions or – even more
important – its phraseology was regarded as
a normal security measure. . . .

Who cared about traditions offering only
personal salvation – of which there was in
any case no guarantee whatsoever?
– Nadezhda Mandelstam
*Hope Abandoned*

In all the universe, temperatures of equal heat are to be
found only in such transient phenomena as exploding
supernovae.
– Jonathan Schell, quoting
Dr Henry Kendall,
Department of Physics, MIT,
explaining how a
thermonuclear weapon
works
*The Fate of the Earth*

Learn from a star the meaning
of light.

> – Osip Mandelstam
> Voronezh, 23 March 1937
> *Selected Poems*

# Rare Earth

*This is the pencil that I managed to steal from Olga. She does not understand how much I need it or she would have given it to me freely. This is the paper that Marina passed to me when she died.*

*I want to be explicit, I want to confess. We do not steal from each other here. Can you imagine the day that we did? Perhaps here we have finally achieved perfect Communism; a communism of women and children only, the elderly, the sick and the dying! There is little labour here and fewer goods; our only abundance is of suffering, but I do not believe that any one of us is privileged to suffer more than the next. No, everyone shares equally. I have seen the sick give the dying their food, for each one we lose brings us closer to being alone.*

*I stole the pencil because I was afraid. Even one more day without trying to write it down and I think I would no longer care. I would begin to live only in this obliterating present and forget fully that there was any time that came before. The discipline of pain would control my imagination; I would never admit the possibility that something could come after. I am like the insane soldier at Hiroshima who, when the bomb had burst and the wounded howled around him, searched for his rule book so that he would know how to go on.*

*God bless you, Pasha – If only this were a letter! I cannot help writing as if there were some way that you could read it and know that I am alive. I am alive, Pasha. They moved us after you left.*

*Some of the women say that those who remained behind in the Moscow shelters were cooked alive underground; this happened in the last war. There is, I know, no way to be sure. Still, I have tried to point out that if the direct hits were there, the temperature would have been thousands of*

11

*degrees. Everything, including the militiamen and the old ladies (do you think they knew, for only the aged were ordered to remain?), would have been vaporised instantly. But I suppose because we have never seen anything solid vaporise before our eyes, many of the women refuse to believe it. They speak of the most horrible stewed and baked images. It would be almost funny – all the terror of nature and hell translated into the empirical evidence of the communal kitchen. But the children, who are always hungry, are tortured enough without this.*

*They don't believe that I am a geologist because I cannot tell them anything certain. A geologist after all is a scientist and scientists are supposed to know. I realised, going back in my own mind to find one thing that was still any good to me, that our methods must long ago have evolved out of fear. We restrict ourselves to the perceptible evidence because, quite simply, it is a comfort. And because they believe nothing I say, yet know I am motivated by the desire to comfort them, they have decided I must be a doctor.*

*This, of course, makes perfect sense; our doctors are most often women, abominably trained, and used to causing pain to people who cannot comprehend them. You cannot imagine the trouble this brings me – I know a few things about minerals and the earth, I know next to nothing about medicine. And I cannot refuse to help.*

*When influenza broke out among the children after the move East, we were in despair. I knew there was sulphur in the bedrock – but how to use it? We scraped it, burned it, mixed it with water, with water and ammonia. We fed it to the sick children in apple sauce made of dried apples; we made tea with it. Olga and I even swabbed her little boy with a rag wrung out in the cold tea.*

*The shelters smelled like the old-fashioned hell of the monks. Sulphur, fire, sickness. We prayed – no one said a word to stop us. The children were bright with their fevers, but it was deceiving, for radiation causes delicate red haemorrhages in the skin. Those who could fight the infection turned pale when we rubbed them with ice; those who were already dying remained ruddy. Towards dawn on the fifth*

12

day, the virus seemed to wane, but even as some children recovered, others began to bleed from their ears and eyes. Those with radiation sickness died by the end of the week – except for two who fought it off. I have no idea how, but I believe now they will recover completely. Olga's Misha was one – a beautiful boy. Is it possible that his ability to fight back has rendered him in some way immune to radiation? What an extraordinary child we shall have created, if that is true – a man whose descendants could own the stars. If he does not grow up sterile. That is the thing, isn't it? Though I wouldn't dare say it.

Olga now insists that Misha is partly mine – she gives me her son, how could she deny me the pencil? – but I cannot be proud. What will happen the next time? We are back in the earliest days of science: everything is fear and magic.

A few weeks ago one woman's husband came through with the volunteers from the South. He brought her what we all believed was the most marvellous present: a boxful of earth from Georgia. It was beautiful – black, moist, so fertile, it seemed to us, it smelled of milk. But not one of us had a seed to plant in it. Of all the precious things each of us had grabbed up as we left – a photo, a book, a piece of lace, even some peppermints – no one had a seed.

Finally someone had the idea to cut up a potato and plant that. Do you know we kissed that potato before it went under the knife? It was a ritual, we sang to it; the boxful of black earth was a shrine. We even burned candles in front of it – our holy icon of St Potato-in-the-Field! (Not merely out of superstition, however: it would not otherwise have had enough light here, underground. Even roots in the earth must still somehow sense the sun.)

But it did not grow. Now, after six weeks, we have finally dug up the mouldy pieces. Everyone blames the poor potato and wants some other patron saint. But I am afraid that it is not the plant that is dead, but the boxful of earth itself. The soil is a living thing, too; it is possible that the dirt in this box is just a lifeless corpse.

I'm crying – how stupid! You may be lying somewhere

13

*in pain or worse . . . but I am convinced – irrationally, I know – that I would feel it if you were.*

*There are women here who hide themselves when their hair falls out. Not because of vanity, as I thought at first. But because they are animals who want to be alone as they die. Or perhaps – though who's to say this is not what motivates animals? – they just want to prevent the little ones from looking on.*

*As for the children, it is not possible to talk about them. All talk about children is really talk about the future. It is no longer natural to think these things. It is cruel or insane. One mother began to speak, quite casually, about how her little boy will look more and more like his father as he grows up. Within a few minutes, she was incoherent.*

*And I cannot help crying over a boxful of dead earth. If you are alive, Pasha, and if you can hear me in your dreams, bring me a box of new earth. As large as you can carry.*

*And a seed.*

*More soon.*

# One

The empty avenue was quiet and dark with the elegant overhang of chestnut trees; the houses, enormous, elaborate, secretive. She recognised at once that this was where they would leave her.

The hotel was inside a courtyard; an old man read a newspaper at a table, a gardener pruned the boxwood hedge with manicure scissors. She knew from the awkwardness of the new leather chairs in the lobby that it had once been a private house. The modern decor sat badly on its surface like makeup on an elderly woman. It had an early-nineteenth-century stature and dignity that repelled everything alien to it – the teenaged bellboys smoking cigarettes, herself and the polished, taciturn Soviet attaché who accompanied her.

'*Madame la Professeur Khameneva,*' he announced at the desk. His French sounded exactly like Russian.

The concierge, stiff and slightly pink in a cutaway and tight silk tie, nodded.

'*Vingt-cinq,*' the concierge said to a bellboy. The bellboy took the key and picked up her bag.

'Follow him,' the Russian ordered her. He did not put out his hand. She knew that the time had not yet come for the official goodbye.

Room 25 was on one of the upper floors that was seldom needed and not refurbished. It was slightly dingy – the blue silk on the walls had faded to a kind of overcast grey – but still quite lovely. The graceful fruitwood armoire opened by means of a large iron key in the lock, from which hung an old, thin tassel. The room still had the same lopsided ormolu chandelier with half the rock-crystal balls missing that all the rooms had once had, and the same deep bay windows as all the rooms on the front of the hotel. Moscow had swallowed the price of a front room, no doubt, because this made surveillance easier. The only economy was that it was under the eaves. But to Anna, the low ceiling made it cosy.

She had been waiting in the room for almost seven hours. It was not difficult; the room was unlike any she had ever seen. And it was private – she could not hear another human being, not even a car. At that hour the only traffic was the occasional horse-drawn carriage, carrying newlyweds to their hotels. The sound of horses' hooves on the pavement made her feel as though she were eavesdropping on people living in a fairy tale and she sat listening for quite some time. When, at two-thirty in the morning, they still had not returned, she decided to take a bath.

For a Parisian hotel of that period the bathroom was really only ordinary. But like the bedroom, it had quaint French doors whose thick antique glass opened into the tops of the chestnut trees of the Avenue Hoche. She went out and stood on the balcony and listened to the water rushing into the tall porcelain tub.

Did warm water have a softer sound than cold? Certainly the night in Paris had a gentleness she had never expected in a Western city. It was in the air that carried the scent of burning leaves; it was in the lights, forbidden in that part of Paris to be any colour but incandescent white of a certain minimal wattage.

She watched the wind as it swayed the canopy of trees over the entire avenue down to the square. The square had once been named Etoile for the way in which all the streets of Paris seemed to radiate out from the Arc de Triomphe like the rays of a star. It was now named Place Charles de Gaulle. Thinking of the lovely square surrendering its name to politics filled her with sadness so sharp it was almost hatred. But it was useless hatred, she told herself. Why should she care what stupidities the people of a French nation performed? Their streets were not more beautiful than a thousand others that had had their fountains toppled and their names rehabilitated. And besides, the star would always be a star.

In the bathroom, she turned off the handsome bronze spigot which had been allowing water to course silently through the gorge of a ridiculous swan. The absence of the sound of water had made her aware that the deep tub was now brimming. It took her breath away: all this water, the enormous tub, the floor-to-ceiling mirrors, the blanketlike towels, the double sink, the bidet – all for her.

For a moment she let herself stare at her image in the half-fogged mirrors. The steam was flattering, like candlelight. Her eyes were smarting and dark with exhaustion, but in the fogged mirror the circles under them did not show. Her eyes were shadowy and enlarged, her cheeks were flushed with the heat rising from the water. The steam smudged the lines at the corners of her mouth, and her hair was only a deep smooth brown, the threads of grey lost in the condensation.

For a crazy moment she thought to get her camera – the Japanese camera that her son, Seriozha, had produced out of the dangerous nowhere of the black market two days before she left. She could photograph the bathtub and the balconies; she could send him a picture of the two huge beds. She pictured the men who were certainly across the street watching her room; she imagined their faces as she started suddenly photographing everything in sight. She began to laugh. Something to keep the 'neighbours' awake, she thought, and went to unpack the Nikon.

The suitcase had been Pasha's. It was leather and it was still good, though she would have taken it, even if it weren't. She riffled through all the new clothes, but she couldn't bring herself to handle them too roughly. She had never had such things before – American panty hose, an Italian silk scarf, a white lace bra, a black lace bra. She could not find an excuse for this last item. She had just seen it in the special-access store and wanted it. She had hoped the woman who had okayed the purchases would not notice. But she did, and smiled a smile that made Anna feel like an informer.

The camera was nestled safely in her bathrobe, an old rose kimono. This, too, was from before, yet it was rather

19

pretty. 'Madama Butterfly,' Pasha would say whenever she put it on. And knowing that he could still cry, awash in the sentimentality of that opera, she would raise her arms in a deliberate flutter and wrap the satiny wings around his head. She would breathe in the odour of cigarettes in his hair and feel him whisper to her breasts. The old robe was of East German synthetic gossamer; 89 percent of the fabric's production went to parachutes and this, she knew, made it infinitely less desirable than the real silk dressing gowns she had seen in the special store. Nonetheless, she had always had an absurd and happy image of grim paratroopers floating through the sky in something so beautiful, and she kept the robe because sleeping in it had, in a very slight way, eased the agony of sleeping alone after Pasha's death.

She took the camera out of its tender nest and hung it around her neck as if it were jewellery; indeed, it cost more than any piece of jewellery she had ever owned. She clipped on the flash attachment as Seriozha had shown her. Then she held it up and looked through the lens.

The blue tile sweated with steam and drops ran down to the floor. Flash! The light bounced all around the reflective surfaces of the tile, mirror, marble and water and the camera whirred as the film wound. Now she pointed the camera at the bronze swan, pressed the shutter, and let brilliant light glitter instantaneously on its stiff wings.

She shot the sink, the extravagant pile of towels, she even tried to get close-ups of the doorknobs, which were of amethyst glass. Later, in the colour prints, she would stare and stare at a nexus of prismatic lavender and wonder what such an amazing image could be, and who had put it in her camera.

On her knees, she realised she was losing control and she stopped. She stood up and put the camera safely on the bed. She carefully took off her new travelling clothes, now wilted and wrinkled, and sat for a moment, comforted by the satiny familiarity of her old robe.

In the tub, everything went out of her mind. To her

body, the water was vodka and the heat seeped into her bones like drunkenness.

Summer, she thought, at least they had left her summer. The light, the long days . . . Now that she lived without Pasha she was like a hibernating animal – her body came to life only when it was warm.

And summer was the only time that Seriozha was home. The University was closed and he went with her to the dacha, to keep her company and to write. He wrote most of the day, and at night moved a camp light out onto the porch. After a few minutes he would put the lamp out and sit in the dark watching for fireflies. You're not writing, she would say. Yes, I am, he always answered.

This June the word had come. For at least a decade the Société des Géologues et Métallurgistes – a small, but elite association of Western European earth scientists – had sent her a formal invitation to their annual conference held in Paris. She was, of course, never permitted to go. Pavel Leonidovich Khamenev was involved in 'sensitive' nuclear research; the government was afraid that he talked to her and she might talk to foreigners; in fact, she and her husband could not bring themselves to speak of it even to each other.

But since she had written the novel – her smallest book (none of the obligatory ideological chapters or the salute to the Supreme Soviet in the introduction), her least laboured (it had flowed out of her like blood in the few weeks after Pasha died) in a long career of scientific testimony – a number of unusual things had happened. The Société's invitation had not arrived in her University mailbox. She had instead been summoned to the office of her department head, Konstantin Kyrstov, who had tactfully insisted that she represent the Institute at this important conference in the West.

She had done research for him many years back; nothing special, she had thought at the time. She supposed he had asked her because none of the male students were interested in the electrical properties of the common elements known inaccurately as rare earths. Everyone was obsessed with heavy elements, radioactivity, anything to do with weapons, especially in those days. But the simple lanthanides that Kyrstov and Anna, then Anna Nikolayevna Petrova, had studied ended up leading to a great improvement in the first Soviet colour television sets. The elements could produce deep, true reds and greens – a pleasure that many people in the Soviet Union were still, twenty years later, unaware of. Kyrstov had taken credit for the work, and the press had lauded the genius of the Soviet scientific establishment. But for Anna, who knew as well as anyone else that American television could not have the colour capacities it was reported to have without such technology, the most important thing was that she had come to the attention of the Institute's star, Academician Pavel Khamenev – a physicist, a dreamer – the man she would marry and who would become the father of her only child.

This June, twenty-two years after she had met Pasha, and one year after his death, she had sat in the old-fashioned department office and stared out of the open window as Kyrstov collected himself. She watched the students sun themselves on the Lenin Hills beyond the University.

'Pavel Leonidovich would be proud of you,' Kyrstov had told her. He said it simply. It was true, in more ways than the one in which, if it was overheard, it was intended to be.

'Thank you, Kostia,' Anna answered. She had absently used the diminutive of the old days and suddenly wondered if he would resent it. He cleared his throat and offered her a cigarette. She refused it because she could never smoke after watching Pasha die. But she used the opportunity to search Kyrstov's face. His features had the loose expressivity of people who eat, drink and smoke too much, and she knew him well enough to glean at once the answer she was looking for.

'But, Kostia,' she pushed him, 'I cannot possibly speak for all of us as well as you. If anyone is to go, it should be you, the chairman.'

'Anna Nikolayevna!' His hoarse whisper betrayed more

emotion than he had shown even at Khamenev's funeral. 'Don't torment me! It is you who must go, of course it is you. Once there was time to change what you have done, renounce the book, perhaps come back to work at the Institute. But there is no choice now. Go and go quickly and thank God that the times have changed and this is all that is asked of you.'

All that is asked of you is to give up your son for your country, she thought. What a good Komsomol mother I could be.

'Don't upset yourself, Konstantin Dimitrievich. I don't know what made me argue.' She felt almost sorry for him; he was truly in a disgusting position. Why should she make it worse for him when the decision was not for either of them to make?

'It's not your fault,' she reassured him. 'It is what we all knew must come.' She did not say, 'I knew.' He noticed this, and knew the reason why.

'We all knew,' he repeated gently. 'It could not end in any other way.'

She embraced him when she left, and gave him the great gift of looking away from his eyes. Then she went home to tell her son.

Seriozha was now twenty-one and a writer of short quick verses like ax blows. He had not yet published a book, but everyone agreed that he soon could. He would be popular with the same not quite young people who managed to own jeans and Miles Davis records but were poor enough still to smoke Russian cigarettes. He was handsome, unlike Pavel; it was obvious that he was her child.

Their bond was the impenetrable understanding that exists only between a mother and a child and only in a place that is rich in deprivation. He belonged to her and he understood. She had been able to get on with it, make her preparations – getting the passport, buying and packing the clothes, receiving the few friends Seriozha knew could be counted on to restrain themselves, and in general, saying goodbye.

For although she was a full professor in the Institute of

Earth Science of Moscow University, one of the few women so highly placed in the faculty and the only one in her department, although she had done important research and won many academic awards, in her own mind she was really Pasha's wife and the mother of Seriozha. She was no different from the red-eyed girls who stand outside the school on the first day. She had been a red-eyed girl herself and cried in her husband's arms that first day, nearly twenty years ago, that the boy had disappeared into the children's *kollektiv*.

'No one has died,' Pavel Leonidovich had said to cheer her.

But a part of her had stepped smiling behind the new painted doors of Moscow Kindergarten 114 and that part of her had not returned. She was twenty-four years old and that morning was the first time she understood that one day all the events of her life would be subtracted from time and she would die.

The helplessness of being submerged in the huge French tub was exquisitely soothing; it, too, made her think of death. Because she had married Pavel Leonidovich, she had never had any other lover, but because she understood death, she knew what having a lover would be like. She could identify precisely with the wives who lived in tiny, smoky apartments where everything was covered in the utterly lifeless orange corduroy sold in the state stores. These were wives whose husbands drank but became silent instead of amorous, whose husbands' parents lived with them, sickly and reproving. She knew what it meant for such a wife to meet someone in a park, to see the anxiousness in that man's face – for her and only for her – to accept the gift of an orange or an apple too precious to be eaten but meant rather to be held in her pocket and once and again raised to her lips just to touch and to smell.

It was only because she loved Pavel Leonidovich more than life that she had been able not to want to kill herself in those last horrible years when he had not quite given up his fight against the Institute, the authorities and the cancer. And after he was gone, she had still disciplined herself not to feel the passion – for that is what it finally became – for feeling nothing. She could not betray Pasha – for his son's sake. But now that she herself was gone, how would she be faithful?

By the time the knock came, she was shaking with exhaustion and the water was cold. She got out quickly, expecting them to come in, and afraid they might see her, her gown not pulled closed, her hair dripping and almost matted.

But they waited and she rubbed herself hard with the towel in an attempt to wake up. Her fingers and feet were wrinkled from soaking for so long; she reminded herself of a drowned man she had seen once on a beach. She tried to force a comb through her hair, but the comb had not come from the special-access store and teeth broke and remained in the knots. They knocked again and she pushed her wet hair behind her ears. She felt ugly when she went to open the door.

'May we come in?'

There were three of them. The man who asked was the one who had brought her to the hotel that afternoon. He now wore a creamy wool suit and looked French though he spoke Russian. The other two wore skimpy black raincoats, cut in the same single-breasted style as those of the men who had met her at the airport. Can they really be so obvious? she thought. Even here, have they nothing to fear?

There was a grey light in the windows. She could hear the sounds of vans stopping at the houses along the street, delivering bread and milk. Houses where people woke up, today as every day, kissed their children, ate their breakfasts.

'Citizen Khameneva?'

His voice was quite gentle and she realised that just for an instant she had actually forgotten that he was there. She gave him her attention.

'Citizen Khameneva, you know why we are here?'

At the last moment, she was suddenly unsure.

'Please, will you show me your passport?'

25

He did not watch her when she turned her back to him and she felt this. She wanted to cover herself, to hide the soft skin of her neck that showed in the modest V of the robe, to pull the robe tighter across her knees in case it opened slightly as her steps swayed. Her feet were bare and they seemed white and hideous to her. She was about to cry.

She was embarrassing him; she could tell when he took the passport and then, without really looking at it, tucked it into his jacket.

'The news of your defection has been published in Moscow this morning.' He told her this quietly, without taking any pleasure in it. As with Konstantin Kyrstov, she found herself looking away from his eyes, excusing him, helping him to finish what he had to say quickly and cleanly.

'It is known that you have accepted a quarter of a million American dollars for the rights to your book.'

Now the tears came but she also began to laugh softly.

'Who will believe that such a book costs so much?' she asked him.

'You will,' he answered, 'when you have been here longer.'

She looked at him. He was thin and his skin was tanned. His light suit was sleek and cut close to his body. He did not look Russian at all.

'How can you love your country so little,' he asked her formally, 'you who have been given so much?'

Now she stared at him. She would not take her eyes away from his face. He waited for her to say something but seconds passed. Finally he let himself out the door and the two men followed. Only then did she look away.

'My son?' she called out as soon as she heard the door shut. 'When will I see my son?'

But she did not open the door and run after them. She did not even attempt to make them tell her.


'Tell me a story,' Christian demanded. He was wide awake. Lilianne would not be home for hours. Perhaps this was one of those nights when she would not be home at all.

'*Une histoire*,' he repeated.

Ian McDonough froze for a moment, then laughed. Why, when his major problem was that nothing seemed real, should his imagination have deserted him? He looked at the pale blue clouds printed across the wallpaper, then out the window to the sky beyond. He could see the lovely bell-shaped streetlights, even, in the distance, the Eiffel Tower. He tested his mind once more, with the same result; he was absolutely unable to make anything up.

'You don't have to if you don't want to,' Christian now said politely.

The utter diplomacy of this five-year-old broke Ian's heart. Lilianne's son by her first employer (a director who had turned over the chic apartment to her in exchange for being absolved of the duty to give the child his name), Christian accepted Ian as well as he had accepted a number of other temporary fathers, who were neither as young nor as genuinely likable as Ian. Christian would have done so had Ian made no effort at all, and Ian, whose own father had been home so seldom as he grew up, tried hard to be there for him.

Ian longed to know the right words to tell the child. A fiction that would be transparent, so that the child would not feel betrayed, yet strong, so that the illusion would truly comfort him. He took Christian's hand and suddenly the image – it was an odour actually – of the baby's hands pressed against the mother's face came to Ian from the Russian woman's book. He remembered all the ways, some fanciful, some frantic, in which she had tried to protect her child.

He raised Christian's hand to his lips. The boy let him but looked at him oddly.

'Once there was a boy named Nai,' Ian began.

'That's a strange name,' Christian interrupted. 'Is it American?' Ian thought for a moment. 'No,' he said, 'I think it's Irish.'

'How do you spell it?'

'N-a-i.'

27

'N-a-i,' Christian repeated. '*Il est un de tes parents, ce garçon?*'

'You're very smart, aren't you?' Ian said, smiling. 'Yes, he was related to me. A long time ago.'

Christian smiled, indicating that Ian now had permission to go on with the story.

'The boy lived in a country where the climate was very mild. It was warm and sunny. There were flowers and breezes.'

'Like the Côte d'Azur?' Christian inquired.

'Even better,' Ian replied, wondering in which of Lilianne's lives the child had been taken to the Côte d'Azur. 'And one of the best things about living in this land was that everyone was always outdoors. Not just to play and run around, but they went to school outside and ate their meals outside and at night they slept under the stars.'

'Right out in the open?'

Ian saw the child's anxiousness and hurried on.

'Well, to tell you a secret, Nai did not like sleeping outside very much. He was afraid.'

Christian nodded.

'He was afraid of all sorts of things. Of monsters. Of shadows – sometimes he thought the shadows of the trees were ghosts that would strangle him as soon as he closed his eyes.'

'*C'est ridicule*, commented Christian, sounding particularly Gallic. 'Everyone knows these things do not exist.'

'But all the same, you can imagine how he felt. After all, sometimes you are afraid to go to sleep, aren't you?'

Christian thought about this, obviously weighing whether or not he should admit the truth. Of course, that was what telling a story was all about. The boy hated to sleep and would only go off quietly when he was thoroughly exhausted and distracted.

'Well, that was a long time ago. Now it is different.'

'Why?'

Christian's lower lip jutted out.

'Tell me a different story. I want to hear a story about space.'

28

Space, Ian thought; he must have invented a hundred stories about space. But now he could bring no image to mind – increasingly, his thoughts seemed empty and airless. Khameneva's story was the first thing to penetrate that vacuum in some time; he could not stop thinking about it. He did not want to tell Christian that story exactly – but he wanted Christian, like the child in the story, to feel that Ian would somehow be capable of the most extraordinary feats, if it were necessary to protect him.

'I can't think of another one right now,' he said. 'Do you want me to finish?'

The child sighed and looked at Ian with his head cocked to one side. After a moment he decided he would trust him.

'Okay,' he said in English. It was one of the cherished handful of words Ian had taught him; even at five, he knew English was chic. Ian smiled and took his hand again.

'One day when Nai was playing on the beach, digging up the sand to make a castle moat, he saw something really strange. It looked just like a bit of broken glass but it glowed. And it was not just one colour, it was all colours, all at once.'

'Like the windows in Notre Dame?'

'No, more like the little crystals in the chandelier.' Ian nodded over his shoulder toward the living room. 'Except that it was very, very bright. As if it were alive.'

Christian considered the strange substance of the story. Watching the boy's pale hazel eyes flecked with yellow, Ian half believed he was seeing the coloured lights.

He took a breath to go on, but just as he was about to reveal the secret of the wondrous substance – that it protected anyone who looked upon it – he lost the thread of his story. He became conscious that he was telling a lie. Christian waited patiently.

Despite its grim subject, the book had comforted him, Ian realised, because he wanted the mother to be right, to save her child. He wanted, with something so male and so unreasonable in him that it embarrassed him, the child to survive because the father in the tale had given up his life for him.

29

But now he looked at Christian, who waited for the rest of the story, as Ian had resigned himself to wait the very next morning for the rest of a story fashioned by his own father; Christian listened to him, as Ian would tomorrow listen, only because he loved the teller of the tale. There was still something special, after all these years, about spending time alone with his father; something important about his father wanting to talk only to him, even though they had nothing to talk about.

'You are going to tell me the rest tomorrow night?' Christian asked. His combination of disappointment and tact was acute. It made Ian feel that no one in his whole life had ever loved him but this child.

'Yes, if you don't mind.' Ian couldn't quite look at his eyes and at that moment he felt the child disconnect.

'Come on,' he hastened, 'give me a hug.'

Christian allowed himself to be hugged, and Ian held him for longer than he knew. Through the light blue pajamas the child wore, the scent of his skin, warm from the bath, overcame Ian; Christian had used the same soap as Lilianne, with its poignant, sunny smell of summer grasses. He felt the boy's body quite suddenly but quite gently relax, and that palpable relaxation was so like the way Christian's mother sometimes dropped off to sleep when Ian was still inside her that it made his shoulders ache. He let Christian fall asleep in his arms, then settled him back against his pillows and pulled up the sheet.

For a moment the child struggled to wake up and Ian knew he did not want to be alone.

'Da?' Christian called him softly. It was the Irish word for father that Ian had taught him, without telling him what it meant. The boy thought it was a nickname, but still it pleased Ian to hear him say it. It was almost as if he weren't nearly thirty-three with no wife or child of his own, as if Lilianne could be true to him and he would never have to leave her – as if all the fatherly things that his own father had made impossible for him were somehow still real and still possible.

'Did you make that story up?' Christian asked with a sleepy air of finality.

'Only partly,' Ian said.

Christian did not respond, and Ian put his whole hand on the boy's silky head and felt him dreaming. He was sure he was dreaming, for his little head seemed incredibly warm and alive in his hand. He could feel life and breath in his soft scalp and in the satiny static of his hair as it clung to his fingers.

'Nothing will hurt you,' he heard himself say in a whisper. 'Nothing will hurt you.'

When the sun came up, Seriozha was still at the dacha. No goodbye could have been more meaningful, or more final, than his refusal to accompany his mother into Moscow. What could have been added in front of other people – in front of the KGB officers who had practically moved in in the last few weeks? Why they were needed he really couldn't say. The phones had been 'checked' at least once a month, 'to make sure the lines are in running order'. They had the best phone lines in Peredelkino; the only problem was they could never say anything on them. He supposed that the two men were there after all as the most basic kind of human gesture. That their heat and breath and footsteps should make their presence totally tangible and inescapable. The two men were like the political poetry he refused to write: hefty, humanoid symbols of social realism, realer than real.

No, breakfast had been the fitting goodbye. The jar of elderberry jam spooned out with the decadent excess that meant there was no tomorrow. Breakfast at six in the morning when the first light was dim and lacked any hue of the yellow that heralded the precious latesummer day. Yesterday, he had cried, but this morning as he sat looking into the shadow of the larches where it was cool and no sun ever penetrated, he realised that he had cried as much out of happiness for her as out of his own loneliness. He'd felt, in a way, much the same when his father died.

'Father is gone now,' she had told him. Had she used

the word 'finally', or was that in his imagination? Seriozha had stayed at home then, too. He had felt much closer to his father there in the house they had shared, where he could see his books and his pipes, his boots and his phonograph, than at the hospital where the tiny emaciated man, pale almost to the point of blueness, was not really his father but a terrible devil of suffering sent to make his father's last hours doubly unreal. What his father must have felt like inside, Seriozha could only imagine; but he knew that it was made worse by each person who came into the room and stared in confusion until they finally recognised him.

Recognition was something important to Pavel Leonidovich Khamenev, immensely so. He had been proud of the recognition bestowed on him – member of the Lebedev Institute of Physics of the Soviet Academy of Science, twice a winner of the Order of Labour, the Soviet Union's highest civilian award, for his work on the hydrogen bomb. And it was this recognition, as much as the nature of his work itself, that had made him quit the Institute and lay down the tools that he had, for a lifetime, used with more inspiration than anyone else of his generation. He wanted his refusal to work to be recognised, part and parcel with that other, earlier, official recognition. He felt that he owed it to society in the purely old-fashioned way he had owed it to fight in the Great Patriotic War, or to do the research in the first place.

When Andrei Sakharov had written his first letter of protest, and later when he had stepped down from the Institute, Pavel Khamenev had been deeply shaken. It was as if God had stepped from heaven because he could no longer bear to look down upon the beings he had created. Sakharov had, like the excellent colleague he was, delivered to Khamenev the proofs of his doubts; he left him no choice but to follow his example.

But for Anna Khameneva, things were different. She was not made of the same heroic stuff as Yelena Bonner, Sakharov's wife. Before Khamenev's act, she had devoted herself to her family and her work; she, like almost everyone else, had wanted a better world but believed really only in the world she could touch – her husband, her child. She had taken her stand simply because she loved Pavel. In all their life together, they had been one person.

In one year Seriozha's father and mother had both passed beyond the horizons of their suffering; his father was dead, his mother deported. He already thought of her in the same way he thought of his father: she was gone to a place where Seriozha would never again see her, a place, he was tempted to believe, that spelled the end of the sorrows of this life. Leaving here, she had died; arriving there, she would be resurrected. He wished only that he could give her the gift of forgetfulness, that she would not think of him left behind, without her. Failing that, he ought, he supposed, to give her his death as a present. For then there would be nothing to hold her back. She would finally be free.

But that was not allowed, of course. Though the two men had left with his mother, there were others. Who knew which neighbour stood at the kitchen window and watched Seriozha above the steaming dishwater? This one day alone was not to last, he knew. His mother was too valuable to give away for nothing. He was the collateral. It was only a day alone to think, perhaps to plan, on the wisdom of capitulating. It was the reason that he had stationed himself on the porch. The first person who walked over the rise into the yard, he believed with sickeningly strong instinct, the first person who volunteered to console him, would be his betrayer, and he wanted to meet him head on. He wanted to stare at him with expectation and courage. He wanted to welcome him.

But in the end, it was Katerina Grigorievna who came, walking carefully in her bare feet on the pine needles. She smiled when she saw him watching.

'Sergei Pavlovich, what are you thinking about all alone there? You're looking at me as if I were a ghost.'

'Excuse me, Katinka,' he apologised, using her nick-name with real affection; he had known her since Young

Pioneers. 'I am the ghost. I was thinking about death and pretending to be dead to see how I liked it.'

She stared at him solemnly for a moment and then shook her head and smiled. 'You're crazy, Seriozha,' she told him, 'but I suppose you have a right to be.'

'You're wrong,' he said. 'No one has a right to be crazy. It is a crime against the state. I know. Otherwise, I would be. I would think that our phones are tapped and that all the neighbours are watching me, and that you yourself have come over to listen to every paranoid word I say so that you can report to someone who will get you a vacation in Italy next winter.'

'Shh. Stop talking about ridiculous things. Someone may hear you. How can you say such horrible things to me?'

She sat down beside him on the porch step and lay her face against his shoulder. She had the same soft cheeks and turned-up nose that she had had as a child, characteristics of that kind of blonde Russian beauty which is girlish even in an old woman. Her hair was still cut in the old way, too; a straight, fine fringe across her forehead and loose and long in the back.

Since childhood she had not changed – only since yesterday. Yesterday she had held his hand and sipped stinging peppered vodka out of his glass while a few friends toasted his mother.

'Have I changed since the last time you saw me?' Seriozha asked her.

She looked at him, amused and puzzled, and lightly kissed the top of his nose.

'No, not really. Just a little crazier, a little sadder,' she said.

'You're lying.'

Her smile diminished steadily by infinitesimal increments and he could measure the effect of his words in her lips; now he was sure. He was about to tell her the truth, that he knew she had consented to inform on him, but then he stopped. Was it really possible that she didn't know he knew? He looked at her silently. And what of it?

34

There was nothing he could do for himself except try to rise with the flood. Why should he make trouble for her when it no longer mattered?

'I am not sadder,' he explained. 'Yesterday, before she left, I was sad, but today I am not. I'm glad she's gone and I only hope she will not waste her life missing me.'

Katerina relaxed. 'What a thing to say,' she told him, rubbing her cheek once more on his shoulder. 'She's your mother.'

George McDonough was accustomed to finding surprises in his suitcase. When the children were small, Kate used to tuck their toys – a fire engine no bigger than an index finger, a blue-eyed doll – in among his starched shirts to remind him to bring home appropriate presents. Later, she merely laid the already gift-wrapped packages on his bed the night before he left. It was years until he realised that this should have broken his heart.

Now her surprise was no longer a surprise. On his last several trips he had found the same colour photograph in a silver frame slipped in the folds of his pin-striped suits. The frame had been a wedding present, monogrammed G-McD-K, the improbable acronym of both their names wound together in the style that had been fashionable when they first set up house. But what was really improbable was the photograph itself. It was at least fifteen years old – Kate wore the bright Saint Laurent prints of the late sixties, Ian had the short, spiky hair of an altar boy and Mary Ellen was a baby.

The picture looked right on the Louis XIV desk. It made George feel yet more at home in a beautiful place which he liked to fantasise might be his true and inherent habitat. Only if he looked closely was he aware that he was not any longer the handsome young lawyer, squire of the pretty Kate, father of two ruddy Irish children. That was why Kate had taken to including the photo in his luggage – away from home he could take the time and privacy to unabashedly study the man in the picture and try to figure out what he had to do with the man he was now.

But when he thought of who he was now, he liked to think of himself more in terms of the small, constantly changing frames of a moving picture than in the sterling shrine his wife had picked out as a bride at Tiffany's. There had been a moment when retirement had seemed the definitive stopping of all movement, freezing a man's life in a way so palpable it made him feel stiff, cold and arthritic. But the Foundation had changed that, offered him a way, at nearly the last minute, of assuaging his private fears by going public.

The Naughton Foundation for World Peace, with its endowment of almost half a billion dollars, was not the largest of private philanthropic agencies, but it was one of the most effective. Its grants were awarded as carefully as its portfolio was managed, and George, as administrative executive of the Foundation's board, had steered the ship in what everyone agreed was quite a successful direction.

At a time when many of the country's oldest endowments were foundering in the shallows of social programmes that could not survive without federal assistance, the Naughton Foundation had been singularly adept at picking causes and individuals who could either count on continuing government support or get along without it. 'We're interested in what you're going to bring to the party,' George was fond of saying to prospective fellows. Those thinkers underwritten by the Naughton Institution for Freedom, its Institute for Defence Studies, or Social Policy, and its various other departments, were now among the premier idea producers consulted by the present administration. It all added up to a considerable kitty of political prestige and influence which allowed the Foundation to 'indulge' in its few, highly publicised, highly defined pro bono projects.

For George, running the Foundation as if it were a multinational corporation had paid off in terms of both the Foundation's ability to do good and his own ability to participate in the higher adventures of power. He never denied this or tried to make less of it; he enjoyed it and believed absolutely that these perquisites enhanced his performance. This was, at last, a popular point of view and he received a certain amount of reinforcement from everyone except his own family.

Whenever George was in the local office – the offices were usually to be found in elegant villas that, as tax dinosaurs in an increasingly socialist Europe, had been purchased by the Foundation from emigrating oligarchs – a residential apartment was put at his disposal. In Madrid he occupied the top floor of a small and impeccable baroque palace. In Manila, the penthouse of a smart new oceanfront condominium complex with a direct line to President Marcos. Though the phone flattered the little boy in him who had long yearned to know what it was like to pick up the famous 'red phone' – was there a dial tone? did an operator assist you? did the Supreme Leader answer the phone himself? – the ex-OSS man in him accepted that this was probably one of the simplest and most straightforward ways to bug his rooms.

Naturally, there was nothing so gauche in Paris. Here, the offices of the Foundation were in a lovely, late-fifteenth-century château situated in what could not quite be called a suburb. The land was rich and had been landscaped into *allées* and cunning, almost natural *bois* for at least four hundred years. Neighbours, like the Rothschilds, managed somehow to pay the taxes, and the only other tax-exempt retreat belonged to the ambassador from the Holy See. It was one of the more serene places one could imagine waking up in in the morning – he'd written this on a postcard to his daughter, Mary Ellen, in her final year at Georgetown. He hoped she'd take it the right way.

But George, too, had occasions to ponder the right way in which to bear the privileges that had come with his position at the Foundation. He was a policeman's son, and even after being a partner of the Wall Street firm of Gordon, Mahoney, O'Shea for over thirty years, he was still a bit queasy about the way such wealthy philanthropic agencies worked. He was no longer in the business of earning money, he had often to remind himself, but of giving it away.

He liked to think that he had been chosen because he was equally at home in the hovels of the poor and the haciendas of the rich; the Jesuit education that he had grown passionate enough about to insist on for his own children had inured him to such thoughts. It was the privilege of the hacienda to relieve the misery of the hovel – this he had said to his firstborn, Ian, the last time he had seen him, in a terse discussion about the Foundation's implicit support of the Reagan administration's policy on Central America.

'That's a laugh,' Ian had rebutted him at the time. But Ian's eyes were bitter and he spoke entirely without humour. 'Let's face it, Dad, you're more at home in the hacienda, and that's precisely why you're there. And in spite of your command of rhetoric, or more likely because of it, the business of the Foundation is largely to promote rapport with exactly the kind of regimes that most rigidly endorse the distinction between rich and poor.'

The whole thing, of course, was pure, pure Ian. The loaded words, dripping with liberal certitude: 'rhetoric', 'regime', 'rigid'. The slightly skewed and emotional syntax that made it look as if George's eloquence was the causative factor behind a handful of authoritarian governments. And right in the middle of it, the hurt eyes and little-boy appellation: Dad.

Who was crazier, father or son? George wondered. The child was now thirty-two years old, old enough to have made up his own mind; indeed it would be appalling if he did not have strong opinions of his own. Why then, when they spoke, did George somehow always swallow the bait? Why did he care anymore whether or not Ian admired him or his work?

The early-morning wind stirred and the leaves of the magnificent chestnuts outside brushed against his windows. Blights had felled most of the regal trees George remembered from the Europe of the war, and those in the villa *parc* struck him with the brave nobility of a last stand.

There was also something essentially French about chestnuts, George thought; their shade, so perfectly suited to the graceful Cartesian lawns of châteaux, was particularly cool and aristocratic. These trees had retained their bearing through many a changing of the guard, their limbs were solid and scarcely movable even in the strongest winds, their deep foliage rendered all the prestigious and petaled undergrowth of the garden precisely that: undergrowth, and trivial.

The phone rang. It was Françoise in the office downstairs reminding him of the day's schedule. Nine o'clock, a representative of a representative of Iran's Mujtahid. There was still grotesque suffering in Iran, though it was out of fashion to acknowledge it and the newspapers had gone on to more timely troubles. It was one of the silent amendments that George had made to the Foundation's charter, riding out the fashions in suffering. It was not his fault that simple consistency had now managed to bear him aloft on the current tide in Washington.

Ten o'clock was assigned to a conference call with the Swiss office. Twelve-thirty, to lunch, in town, with Ian. Better arrange it at some modest place, he instructed Françoise. He did not elaborate and hoped she would choose a bistro that was neither obscured by a line of limousines nor in a neighbourhood where the Foundation's own black Citroën would be in conspicuous bad taste. He had given up choosing the restaurant himself on his second-to-last visit with Ian. They had eaten in the lovely, mossy garden of the Hotel Plaza-Athénée under candy-striped umbrellas. Ian had glanced briefly at the prices and accepted only clear soup. At their very last lunch, however, in a cheap little restaurant of his own choosing, Ian had eaten the roast heartily and helped put away two bottles of wine. At least he was not a vegetarian.

Depending on how soon Ian and he got into an intractable argument, he would have either the end of the afternoon or the early evening in which to pay his call upon the Russian woman, Khameneva. That is, if everything had gone as his friends in Washington assumed it would. He

had not heard anything and accordingly prepared himself
to feel two ways about her: either he would be in a position
to offer her the aid and comfort of the Foundation in
resettling and, more importantly, in launching her book in
the United States, or he would not. If he was, then he
would see to it that she met people who could make the
way easier for her, help her adjust to the brisk, bracing
pace of life under capitalism, gradually instruct her in those
things her country had carefully omitted from her frame
of reference, especially in reference to itself. If not, then
there were more than enough Russian émigrés in the
world. It was practically a business in and of itself.

He had his coffee and the papers in the large panelled
library of the villa. Panelling, he reflected, now implied a
crude American kind of wall covering; probably a wood
derivative or composite printed with pecan grain and intended to cover Sheetrock and carcinogenic asbestos foam.
The wood of the library with its ruddy patina came from
the trees on the property which had been hewn and carved
by hand two centuries ago. An odd setting in which to
discuss hunger, he thought. But he had been briefed that
the Mujtahid was more concerned with media than meat.
And anyway, the purpose of the imposing offices was
to reflect the august and American magnanimity of the
Foundation.

He had finished *Le Monde, The Times* of London,
glanced at the *Herald Trib* and was halfway through *The
Wall Street Journal* when Françoise announced his old
friend of the Allen Dulles days, Lowell Christopher.

'You're not with the Mujtahid, are you?' George
laughed, shaking his hand. He knew why Lowell was
there.

'No, no, the Mujtahid is having coffee in the front room.
Sorry to disappoint you.' Lowell's voice was as Bostonian
as his name.

'Not at all. What can I do for you? Are you in Paris
long? Can we have dinner?'

'Thanks, but if you want to have dinner with me you'll
have to eat on Air France. I'm going back over to Brussels

at seven o'clock. You know they have me over there with the NATO team.'

'I'd heard. How is it?'

Lowell shrugged.

'As bad as they say? I hope at least you're getting out a lot. The restaurants in Brussels . . . well, suffice it to say, that is one place Kate hates me to go without her.'

'Yes, well, there's only so many oysters you can eat, but I'll tell you these Warsaw Pact people throw them down like there's no tomorrow.'

'Maybe there isn't; you ought to know. I just hope you'll give your old friends the word when it gets to that point.'

George smiled and they both laughed. It was for a moment amazingly like the old days. But there wasn't a war and Lowell Christopher's thick blond hair was white. George wondered how he looked to Lowell.

'How is Kate?' Lowell asked.

'Fine. You know she's got a job? She's a real estate agent. Works nights, weekends. Finagles government loans so that minorities can move in next door.'

They both laughed again. Lowell had been earning a dollar a year for as long as George could remember.

'How's your wife?' George couldn't quite remember her name. He remembered only that she had been sick for a number of years. He hoped suddenly that she wasn't dead.

'The same,' Lowell told him. He took the inquiry well; he showed only enough feeling to indicate that he was a good husband. This was because, as George and a few others knew, he was a homosexual, one of those who marry late and make determined and loving family men, distracted and a bit distant from their wives but wholly dedicated to their children.

'I see Ian's byline every now and again,' Lowell continued. 'He's a good writer, though I daresay his opinions must make your skin crawl.'

'Oh, it takes an awful lot to make my skin crawl anymore. What about your two, what are they up to?'

Lowell reached into his jacket and took out a slim

and elegant Mark Cross billfold. Out of it he pulled two snapshots of two girls.

'Julia is at Morgan Guaranty and Elspeth is still in school,' he informed George.

'Oh? Where? You know our Mary Ellen is down at Georgetown.'

'Good Lord, both children processed by the Jebbies. They'll be the scourge of your old age, George.'

'They already are.' George shrugged. 'I suppose you have sent Elspeth into the godless environment at Harvard.'

'You're damn right. Godless I sent her in, and God willing, she'll escape the Krishnas, the Communists, the Born-Agains, and godless emerge. But she's in Asian studies and she's so sympathetic to everything she reads. Do Buddhist women shave their heads, too? God, I never thought of it.'

'Not at Harvard,' George said, 'but I can understand your concern. She's very pretty.'

Lowell was quiet for a second and then smiled. 'Yes, she is, isn't she? All the blonde hair I used to have. The adage is right; youth's wasted on the young, though I shouldn't say it.'

'Quite all right with me. It's not half of what I would say if you got me started.'

'What would you say?'

'"How sharper than a serpent's tooth," and all that.' George shook his head. 'But really I can't complain. By the way, would you like some coffee? I can ring Françoise.'

'No, no, actually I just came by to say hello. I was talking to Arthur and when he found out that I was on my way to Paris he gave me a message for you: "The patient is in stable condition and will receive visitors tonight." Isn't that asinine? Imagine Arthur telling me to tell you something like this. Sometimes I think that people like your son are right; they are all quite mad in Washington. I hope you're not into anything serious.'

'Oh, he's kidding. You know how Arthur likes to carry on. I'm going to call on some peacenik expelled from the

Soviet Union; an author. I can't imagine any reason why you or anyone else shouldn't know.'

Lowell looked at him askance. It was an intimate, penetrating glance that suddenly, though gently, tipped George's equilibrium.

'Arthur must have a reason.'

'I swear. It's absurd. Arthur is crazy.'

Lowell laughed. 'You see, Ian is right.' He put out his hand. 'Take care of yourself, my love to Kate.'

They shook hands warmly and again the image in George's mind was of Switzerland during the war.

'Good luck with the Mujtahid!' Lowell said with a perfectly straight face as he left.

Ian met his father in a brasserie near the Jardin des Plantes, the botanical gardens where Ian liked to walk with Christian amidst the ratty cactuses and neglected palms. There were toy sellers in the garden who sold little furry monkeys on strings – some were dressed as soldiers, some as gypsies. The monkeys dangled convulsively on display from the rims of the vendors' umbrellas and there were always children gathered underneath, eagerly demanding the most spastic ones. Ian detested these monkeys and would never let Christian have one. The restaurant directly faced the row of umbrellas in the park, but mercifully his father had chosen a table inside.

The oak door and windows made of ancient green and brown bottle glass seemed promising; there was something primordial about European beer halls that to Ian would forever recall the depths of his first Saturday nights at college. At a remove of fifteen years, this was now a pleasant, bittersweet feeling.

His father was there, alone, for most people had chosen to sit in the warmth outside. He looked remarkably at home, in spite of his inevitable Brooks Brothers suit, button-down shirt and dark tie, the reddish colour of which would be called morbid, if that were a colour. There was already a glass of beer on the black glass tabletop.

'It's still good beer,' he said to Ian, standing up and

43

shaking his hand. They shook hands a second longer, but slightly less emotionally than old school chums might.

George picked up the frosty glass and raised it towards the sign above the bar which said 'Stella', under which stood the enormous Alsatian proprietress of the place.

'I used to think every barmaid in France was named Stella,' he said, and laughed.

Ian smiled. Stella Artois beer from Belgium was the Budweiser of Europe, proclaimed from every neon above every bar. But Ian was no longer sceptical of what he thought of as his father's World War II naïveté.

'She seems like a Stella if ever I saw one,' Ian told him. At that moment she shot him a hard glance, and to cover his rudeness, Ian asked for two more.

'You look good,' his father said, nodding encouragingly. Ian wondered whether the cheerful nod was because his father had expected him to look worse or because Ian had tried to dress up a bit – a rumpled Liberty cotton tie of tiny, English-looking flowers and a double-breasted navy blazer that was unbuttoned and hung obscenely open, the way unbuttoned double-breasted jackets do.

The beer arrived via a young girl who was the picture of the woman behind the bar, except that she was as dark and North African in colouring as her mother was fair and Germanic. She wore a necklace that spelled out the name 'Jocelyn' in intricate lettering that forced the reader to stare at it rather too long in order to decipher it. She let Ian figure out the word above her breasts and smiled.

'Well, she certainly likes you,' George said as the girl turned back towards the bar.

'She probably likes a lot of people.' Ian shrugged. 'But I wouldn't want to tangle with her mother.'

'No, I think not.' George laughed. 'By the way, *your* mother will be delighted to hear that you have shaved your moustache.'

'I'd forgotten about it.' Ian absently touched the clean-shaven space above his upper lip. 'How's Mom?'

'Super,' George replied, heartily endorsing his wife. 'She has a job.'

44

'Yes, I know. Does she like it?'

'She's raking it in. The only problem is that every time she earns a thousand dollars' commission, our tax bracket goes up and I have to pay two thousand dollars.'

Ian stiffened. 'Do you still resent her working?'

'Please.' George's voice was the caricature of boredom he affected when he was irritated. 'I'm just delighted that she's finally learned that being the wife of a busy lawyer wasn't all for naught. She picked up a few marketable skills along the way.'

'And you've always been in favour of marketable skills,' Ian said, referring to discussions which had dogged the beginning of his career as a free-lance journalist. The apprenticeships that Ian had served immediately after college – bumming around Europe and selling the odd magazine the odd feature – had not been his father's idea of adequate preparation for 'real life'.

'So how's your girl?' asked George.'The actress – are you still seeing her?'

Ian could guess what his father thought about his living with a French actress who had a child out of wedlock, and had therefore made it a point never to ask him.

'She's doing very well.'

'Is she working?' This was not an innocent question.

Ian closed his eyes. He had tired of pointing out that his father resented his mother's attempts to be a breadwinner at the same time that he despised Lilianne for allowing Ian to support her and Christian.

'Not right now, actually, but she is up for a good part in an American film. She should hear any day.'

George looked at his son. Ian realised that he had just paraded before his father's inner eye the spectacle of his son running around New York – eating at the Four Seasons, bumping into his parents' friends at the theatre – with a contemporary version of the classic 1950s French *sexe bombe*, blonde hair bouncing like breasts, breasts bouncing like basketballs. He laughed.

'If Lilianne became a sex symbol, the first thing she'd probably do is leave me,' Ian reassured him. George looked somewhat relieved; was this because it was so obviously true? 'And if she didn't, I still wouldn't bring her to your Christmas party.'

George tried to be amused but he was not. Ian took pity on him.

'Don't worry, Dad. I'm not going to settle down with her.'

Neither quite knew whether this was good news or bad. They studied the menu. It had been run off on an old mimeograph machine; the ink was purple, the paper damp and redolent of the grapey scent of the ink. They debated about switching from beer to wine and decided – it was the closest they came all day to a satisfying meeting of the minds – that they really preferred beer.

George ordered, and Ian felt a slightly drunken and primitive happiness – after all, you wanted your father to be the guy who knew how to order. His father was not pretentious. You couldn't really say that about him. It was more that he was a hypocrite. Ian knew his father would have drunk wine if there had been anyone else present; wine was the decorous choice in Paris, after all, and with *coq au vin*. But what was decorum, except what you did because you imagined others watching you? This was perhaps the difference between a man of conscience of his father's generation and one of his own. Ian felt alone inside his own mind, awesomely alone. There were no guardian eyes, no voices other than his own. His decision making took place in a landscape like Monument Valley; an empty waste with sudden terrifying upsurges of will like fire-coloured monoliths of sandstone.

But Ian was certain his father felt that he was being judged by a quorum of estimable figures inside his head – flawlessly dressed figures chosen from the same impeccable academic backgrounds as the scholars in the Foundation's famous think tank. Add to these judges Ian's grandmother – but not as she had been in life; rather, an austere and ideal mother dressed in Irish linen and lace, smelling of lavender powder. And a triumvirate of Jesuits – the first, the most important, the last. They would also be abstracted, like Bernini marbles, into masks of judgment and hidden wisdom.

Then there were the people who actually *did* watch him all the time – the trustees of the Foundation, the press, the politicians. This was the Inquisition for real, Ian knew, and he could not succeed in making himself understand why his father did it; why he gave up so much of his life for the ephemeral approval of shitheads.

Ian took a long swill of his beer and felt generous. The food came; they talked about the house in Greenwich, which seemed more a hotel than a home these days. They talked about Washington and his father even loosened up to the point of joking that the Secretary of Defense was so pro-Arab that the Pentagon cafeteria was closed during Ramadan. Ian took this to mean that the man had been earmarked for removal and he was now an officially approved target of humour. But he did not consider passing this tidbit along to a colleague who could use it; his father was working too hard to entertain him.

'Would you like dessert?' George asked him when the plates had been taken away. 'I think I noticed a gorgeous *tarte Tatin* when I came in.'

Ian smiled. 'Dessert? I thought you were into "lean and mean".'

His father looked disappointed.

'Only kidding – I'd love some,' Ian said. He knew that for his father to break down and eat sweets meant he was relaxed, that everything was going well. Suddenly he wanted to have dinner with his father, too. And maybe, after, go for a walk or take in a play . . . 'What are you doing later?' he asked him.

'I'm looking in on a dissident writer who has just been expelled from the Soviet Union,' George told him. 'A writer. We're going to give her a grant.'

Ian sat up. 'Her? You don't mean Khameneva, do you?'

George nodded. 'A heroic woman. No one who knows her story could possibly delude themselves any longer that the Communists want peace.'

Ian stared at him. 'You've read her book?'

'Only the excerpt in *The New York Review of Books*. I don't think it's been entirely translated yet – though now the KGB will probably bring out a flood of books just to kill her earnings.'

I've been away from America too long, Ian thought. 'I didn't know you read *The New York Review*,' he said. 'I have a press copy of the French edition, if you want it.'

'Thank you,' George said, refusing to take the bait.

'The Naughton Foundation is going to give *her* a grant?' Ian pressed.

George motioned to Jocelyn for more coffee and the check.

'We've given grants to a number of Russian dissidents,' George responded matter-of-factly. 'I take it you like whatever you've read of her book.'

The pieces still did not quite fit in Ian's mind. 'Come on,' he said. 'It's one of the strongest anti-nuclear statements to come out of the Soviet Union, an attempt to imagine what it would be like to live through "nuclear winter". Whatever you think of the book, it caused quite a stir there, or they wouldn't have kicked her out. When did it happen?'

George had taken out his wallet. He looked at his American Express card, then decided against it and gently lifted out several stiff franc notes the colour of rainbow trout.

'Late last night,' he told Ian, and went again over the notes, wetting his finger, making sure that none were stuck together.

Unbelievable, Ian thought. 'Thanks,' he said to his father.

'Hold on a minute,' George told him.

Ian looked at his father who looked at the money. Then Ian knew. He knew that his father had known all about Khameneva's expulsion before it happened. He also knew how and, more importantly, why; only Kremlin watchers of government status could have better methods of surveillance than the press. He stood up to leave.

'Sit down,' George ordered him. His voice was harsh and low. Ian tried to isolate exactly what it was in his father's expression that wrecked the symmetry of silver hair, blue eyes and heavy Irish eyebrows, and made his face seem alien, the wrong face for the man, or the wrong man for the face. People had always told Ian how much he looked like his father. But he was no longer sure who his father looked like, and, worse, he recognised that this was something that could and would happen to a man. You might look in a mirror one day and realise that you did not look like yourself anymore. Or maybe you didn't know you were still yourself and didn't care. Then who did your children look like?

'Why can't you give us the benefit of the doubt?' his father was saying. 'It's just a human act of helping and caring. These people are at such a loss when they come here, ignorant of everything –'

Ian knew the bitterness in his father's voice sprang from a cynicism concerning Ian and not those who had asked his father to make this offer.

'And so you will "educate" her? Point out the error of her ways?'

Ian's tone was casual and for a second George seemed ready to argue the merits of the case. But then he sensed the meaning behind Ian's too obvious meaninglessness and drew back, insulted.

'You're making a mistake,' Ian told his father. 'You underestimate how much she has suffered for what she believes.'

'And you underestimate the people who made her suffer. One assumes, however, that she is more realistic.'

'Thank you for lunch, Dad,' Ian said, and pushed back his chair a little more emphatically than he'd meant to.

'Don't write about this without checking with me,' George said.

Ian walked out. Across the street he saw the brightly coloured umbrellas of the toy peddlers. There were, for an odd moment, no children, and the monkeys simply swayed back and forth gently on the breeze like storybook dead men swung from gibbets. He headed for the nearest phone.

\*　　\*　　\*

'Harley?' Ian had dialled the number of an Australian photographer he occasionally worked with. If there was anything happening anywhere, Harley would know. He was a predatory animal and, like a leopard in the dappled shade of the jungle, he knew precisely where his next meal lay.

'Who is this?' Harley had just woken up.

'Ian. Listen –'

'Oh, hallo. You know, I got a great shot of your girl last night with a load of Americans at the Festival. Very nice; you never said a word. What – do you keep her locked up?'

'Obviously not, if she's at Cannes.'

'She was delighted to find out I knew you.'

'I bet,' Ian said.

'What?'

'Nothing. I want to ask you about something else.'

'Shoot. I hope I didn't say anything I wasn't supposed to. I was going to use her for page three but if you'd prefer . . .'

'It's up to her.'

'That's a boy. What can I do for you?'

'Have you heard anything about a new Russian dissident? A woman –'

'I was at the hotel this morning; decent place near the Arch of Triumph – La Chaumière. She won't let anybody in. I mean, she must think she's bloody Mick Jagger or something. She won't even open the door or you know her picture would have been in the paper. She's too upset by it all; you'd think she'd be thrilled. I'm going to try again tonight. You want to come with me? I'm sure Shitface will take something from you on it.'

Shitface was Harley's name for his Algerian editor. Ian had always thought that Harley's attitude was just the typically virulent Australian prejudice, but when Ian met Shitface he realised that Harley was referring to a unique and personal obsequiousness. Shitface would not only take his article; Shitface would beg Ian to make a series out of it. Ian would have to spend a lot of time with the woman.

50

He might be able to convince her to let him follow her around and see all the people she would meet in the next couple of days, even weeks.

'Yeah, that's great.' Ian thanked him. 'I'll call you in a couple of hours.'

He rang off and loosened his tie. He had put the tie on to have lunch with his father; now this made him angry. He took the tie off and shoved it into his pocket. If there had been the usual pile of Parisian garbage he would have thrown it away.

But the corner was unnaturally clean and gave him no correlative for his anger. The tidy surface of the street – there was even a picturesque old woman sweeping and smiling – rejected all spleen. For a moment he thought he wasn't in Paris, in a way not unlike the way he sometimes thought that Lilianne was not a woman.

Lilianne's son was probably still waiting at school to be picked up. She would have forgotten about him, or assumed that Ian was taking control, which was the same thing. When she came back they would not discuss it; there were always only the same two choices – leave things as they are or just leave. Her beauty was independence itself, rejecting all demands. Like the well-manicured street, all the dust, old news and overripe fruit of other people's lives were irrelevant to her.

He hailed a cab, eager to hug Christian and wondering how he would manage to get past the crowds of reporters around Khameneva while watching the little boy. But really, he thought as they pulled up to the school, it couldn't be more perfect.

He instructed the cab to wait.

No one had knocked at the door since midmorning. Then, she had sat very still, refusing to acknowledge there was anyone there. It was not something she did with any premeditation but with an animal instinct to be silent and dead in the face of loud and too curious strangers. They went away. The phone rang. They came back; the phone rang again and again.

But she remained as if unconscious. Actually, she was acutely conscious, concentrating on sensing every neuron in her body and extinguishing its action. Later it would seem to her a sign of the existence of God that one was not responsible for one's own heartbeat and breath, for if it had been up to her, she would have willed herself into absolute inertia.

But when it had been quiet for some time, she herself no longer seemed enough to fill the silence and she began to listen. There was a little street noise, barely audible cars and occasionally an earsplitting motorbike. There were sometimes footsteps in the hall, the sound of keys and, once, someone whistling through his teeth. She felt an urgent need to step out and see the whistler; it was a live, cheerful noise. But she was afraid to open the door.

She began to ridicule herself – she was finally in the West and here she was, keeping herself prisoner. She tried to summon up a feeling of hatred so intense that it would make her open the door out of spite. This exercise nearly worked, but when she went to dress, the starchy newness of all her clothes seemed so alien that she was defeated.

Now she heard another knock. It was a very small knock; such a shy, tentative sound that this time, almost without thinking, she found herself hurrying to the door.

When she opened it – at first only a little bit – she saw nothing. But when she looked again and opened it wider, she saw a small blond boy holding a large bouquet of wildflowers. Their Russian names flooded her memory – colza, blue veronica, swanflower, deep violet Ivan's tea. She hesitated to reach for them, but their quiet, musky fragrance overcame her. She took them in her hand and brought them to her face, deeply breathing in their message of nostalgia.

The little boy turned and looked down the hall with a question in his eyes. Anna saw a man standing perhaps ten feet off, and understood the child's question: should he hold his ground? The man did not advance. He watched Anna intently, waiting for a sign. When she continued to stare without speaking, he smiled weakly and motioned to the boy to leave.

'Please,' she said, somewhat shocked by the sound of her own voice. 'Come in.'

'*Spasibo*,' Ian said. His Russian was clumsy; it did not fit his tongue, the way Western clothes often did not fit the Russians who managed to own them. It was loose where it ought to be tight; he squeezed vowels that ought to be let out. She smiled.

'*Dit merci*,' he prompted Christian. She realised that French was not the man's language either.

'*Vous parlez anglais?*' Anna asked him.

'*Je suis américain*,' he told her. She looked at him carefully. She had occasionally been introduced to Americans at the University, but she had never known any personally. There seemed something giddy and auspicious about taking her first step out the door on her first day in freedom and meeting an American. She put her hand out and he shook it, less vigorously than she expected he would. Then the fear came back.

'Why did you come here?' she demanded in clear, if slightly slow English.

'I have read your book,' Ian said.

She knew that copies of the manuscript, typed by Seriozha, his friend Katerina Grigorievna and perhaps others, had made their way out of Russia. But until he spoke of it, the fact that her book had reached the West had never seemed real. After all, the manuscript was always only a folder full of smudged and fragile papers, the corners curling from being carried in the rain. Some copies were actually handwritten and it had moved her unexpectedly to see her own words in the intimacy of another's hand. But she had never seen it as a book – printed, with a cover to protect it, dated, with her name on it for history to read.

She looked at him, this stranger who had read her deepest thoughts, written down in the fresh grief of a widow. His expression made him seem not much older than Seriozha – he was handsome, his skin very clear and

53

shading to a true red across high cheekbones like that of a boy just come in from playing in the first sun-dazzled snow. But his black hair was shot with silver throughout and as he stood, half smiling, she saw the many fine lines about his mouth and eyes. She realised that they were all still standing in the hall, that her feet were bare and she still wore nothing but her beloved and wretched pink robe.

'You know much more about me than I know about you,' Anna said to him.

'My name is Ian McDonough,' he told her. 'And this is Christian Vallier.' At this point Christian surprised her with a lovely, deep bow. Ian explained that the five-year-old had for some reason recently been taught this gesture and the delighted laughter it always provoked in adults had reinforced it to the point where it was a permanent – in fact, incessant – part of his behaviour. Anna felt herself smiling for the first time in several days. It was a physical feeling of inactive muscles being involuntarily stimulated; it almost ached.

'Christian,' Ian prodded him, a little disgusted.

'He is charming,' Anna protested.

'Yes, well, too charming by half. He knows he is being cute. Don't you, Christian?' He looked fondly at the boy and then at Anna. He put his face closer to hers and lowered his tone. 'You know how children are when they meet someone new,' he told her.

'Yes.' She knew exactly what it was like to be small and dependent and alone in a room of tall, unreachable voices speaking of you in words you only half compre-hended.

She turned towards Ian and looked into his eyes, the way people do when they are not sure that they speak a language well enough to be thoroughly understood.

'Forgive me, but I have not eaten for more than a day now – I don't know Paris' – she began to falter – 'and I was afraid to go out by myself. And I don't want to stay in the hotel any longer –'

He interrupted her. 'That's why we came. Do us the honour of having dinner with us.'

'Thank you,' she said. She wondered at herself for being so rude, but she didn't really care anymore. She wanted to go out. 'If you will just wait one moment, I will change my clothes.' She smiled embarrassedly and pulled back through the door into her room, closed it and, after a moment's hesitation, locked it.

Now she turned back to her suitcase in earnest, wanting only to get out at once. But as she pulled apart the once-folded piles of clothes, everything was wrinkled, or unsuitable, too bright or too noticeable. Finally she decided on a crumpled off-white suit of raw silk. It was light, for the afternoon was hot, and its accompanying lace blouse was the very prettiest of all the new things.

The lace bra, the silk panties, the white slip embroidered with white butterflies along the hem; the soft blouse, the rumpled skirt and jacket. She pressed her hands down the skirt and pulled the jacket this way and that to try to get the creases out, but it was a token effort. What mattered now was being in the open air, walking on a crowded street, talking to another human being, eating a piece of bread.

She opened the door, conscious that her new suit was wrinkled yet still proud of it. The young man and the boy were sitting on the floor playing some game; various small French coins were arranged on the different colours on the carpet. The young man quickly stood up; the boy pocketed the change. She laughed.

'What a very nice suit, Anna Nikolayevna,' he said, using the respectful Russian patronymic.

'Thank you, Mr McDonough,' she said.

'Just call me Ian,' he told her. 'Mr McDonough is my father.'

In the Bois de Boulogne, dusk was gathering in the high trees, a pink, late-summer dusk, so subtle a colour that it made Anna think of the lilac-scented talc women wore in Cheknov stories. She and Ian sat at a small table in an outdoor restaurant; the heavy white tablecloth scarcely moved in the breeze, the dying sun made rainbows in huge crystal *ballons* of white wine. Christian was curled up on two chairs pushed together, Anna's silk jacket under his head.

'I'm afraid that's not very good for your jacket,' Ian said softly. But she could see he was grateful to her for slipping it between the boy's cheek and the wooden seat of the chair.

She waved her hand. 'My clothes are all – in trouble.' She had searched for a word she didn't know, and obviously not settled on the right one, for he laughed as if she were being clever.

She looked down at her plate. She had ordered simply a plate of fresh fruit – it had arrived a dazzling mosaic of orange and melon slices, raspberries and grapes. As the waiter had set it down in front of her with perfect, perfunctory insouciance, her eyes had nearly filled with tears. Nothing could have more clearly told her that she was a slave taking her first meal at a free man's table, for she had never been able to have such delicacies before in her life. At first she ate each morsel slowly – holding the raspberries against the roof of her mouth until they disintegrated like candy – but when the waiter returned to clear Ian's plate she nearly panicked.

Ian laughed again, but gently; he motioned the waiter to go away.

'Relax,' he said.

He didn't say very much. He let her eat. She asked a few questions and he answered them. He told her about the park, he fussed with the boy. It was all very quiet, almost normal.

'I'd be glad to show you a decent clothes cleaner tomorrow,' he offered. 'Don't use the one in your hotel. They're always thieves. I mean, it will be very expensive.'

She reflected seriously for a moment about her clothes – now the most substantial of all her remaining material possessions. Then she laughed.

'I have a whole new wardrobe,' she told him. 'To me, this is like owning a collection of modern art.'

'That's not so crazy,' Ian said. He hesitated. Perhaps he

did not want to insult her by acknowledging that she had never had such things before. Perhaps he didn't know. 'Especially here in Paris,' he assured her. 'Clothes really are *objets d'art*, everyone makes such a cult of them. The fashion shows are like grand opera – and cost twice as much to produce.'

'You think that is bad?'

'I suppose I do, really. It's too much and everything is so expensive. A family of four could pay their rent and live for a month for the price of one dress. In fact, some women practically go without eating in order to wear the latest fashion.'

'If I were young and living in Paris,' Anna said, 'I would probably do the same thing. People need beautiful things in their lives. They also need to be unique, different from one another. This is a very deep need; it is the same everywhere.'

'You would?' He sounded genuinely surprised.

She looked at him, amused. The rainbows in the wine had gone from the reddish end of the spectrum into the blue. Blue iridescence sparkled like waves across the table-cloth.

He followed her gaze down to the play of colour on the cloth and for a moment seemed to lose his train of thought.

'I suppose I thought, because you are a scientist, because of the book, that you wouldn't care very much about that sort of thing . . .' His voice trailed off, suggesting all the other things she might not care about.

'You thought that I cared only about saving the world.' There was suddenly a catch in her voice and she hoped her sarcastic words made it sound like a laugh.

At that moment the waiter returned yet again and this time set in front of Anna a small bowl of dark red straw-berries – each no bigger than the tip of a child's finger.

'*Fraises de bois*,' Ian told her. 'Wild strawberries. Try them.'

They had a deep, sweet flavour which pricked the tongue almost like pepper. She smiled and offered the bowl to him.

He shook his head.

'All for you,' he said.

'Who are you, really?' She turned to face him fully. 'Why did you come for me – how did you know where I was?'

He straightened up in his chair, but he did not meet her eyes. His lowered gaze might have been simply boyish and shy – or it might have been that he knew he was capable of seeming like a boy.

'I'm a journalist,' he told her. 'I knew where you were because one of the photographers who tried to see you this morning told me.'

Now the set of his face seemed grim.

'In fact, I called this photographer myself because I wanted to do a story on you. I've been covering what the editors like to call the "cultural cold war". To tell the truth, until recently I had to write a lot of articles on things like who still lives in the great houses of France, or where Princess Caroline's husband buys his neckties.'

He shrugged at her; she shrugged back at him. She smiled; he did not.

'But lately what's selling is Superpower confrontation, which is fine with me because I want to write about politics. What I am really good at is the portrait of the little guy, squeezed between the big, nasty bureaucracies with no place to turn. Mostly I interview ballerinas who won't get back on the bus. Sometimes somebody flies me to England or Germany to talk to kids who dye their hair green. Once I did five thousand words on a nineteen-year-old from Oklahoma who was seeing Italy for the first time by escorting long-range cruise missiles.'

'I always wanted to see Rome,' Anna said.

'I talk to these people,' Ian told her. 'They talk to me. They get to like me, they trust me. I write down everything they say. Then I rewrite it into basically the same one-thousand-, three-thousand- or five-thousand-word story that says the world is shit, excuse me, but there is still some hope. Without the hope, none of the American syndicates will pick up the story. You see, it has to be positive and uplifting, just like back in the USSR, only here we do it for money.'

He had finished his sentence with a false flippancy. She realised that his boyishness had begun as an attempt to manipulate her, to make her like him. But it was giving way before the uninhibited desire of a child to confess a lie.

'They do it for money, too,' she said.

'The more you care about the person,' he told her, 'the worse it is when they trust you. I wanted you to trust me.'

He said it as if it were the most detestable intention a human being could have had. It could be, she knew.

The air had stilled and was very warm; she noticed beads of sweat forming on Christian's flushed forehead. As if he were reading her mind, Ian got up and with his napkin very gently wiped the boy's face. For a moment he was no longer thinking of her or of what he had said. He was a mother.

'You are a very good father,' she told him.

He blushed.

'Don't blush.' She almost laughed. 'You'll make me feel old.' But it was a lie; that he blushed at her compliment made her feel young.

'He's not my son,' Ian said.

'His mother must be very beautiful.' She said it in kindness.

But Ian edged towards the child protectively. 'Yes,' he said, 'in a way.'

Anna looked at him. 'He's lucky to have you,' she said. She had surprised him.

'I do trust you,' she said. This statement surprised him more. 'If someone is going to write about me, it might as well be you. You have been very kind.'

He was embarrassed. She could see that there was a struggle; he wanted to thank her and let it go at that but he wouldn't let himself.

'I want to know you, Anna Nikolayevna.'

'I will tell you anything you want to know.'

'That's not what I meant. I'd just like to know you as a person.'

She had long ago trained her emotions to subvert their signals in the eyes of others. Her hands grew hot and she moved them from the table to her lap.

Christian stirred in his sleep; she brushed back a few strands of very fine blond hair from his damp forehead. It must be time for him to be taken home and put to bed. The little boy belonged to another life, as did everyone in the world except, today, Anna herself.

Ian tried to modify her silence. 'I will show you around or whatever, just until you get settled. Unless you know people it can be rather difficult.'

'I know the Société des Géologues et Métallurgistes.' She laughed in a small, hopeless way. 'But I've never met any of them.'

Her eyes filled suddenly. She was embarrassed.

'But if I trust you I trust you,' she said, nodding. Her words, her voice, her whole body was straining for assurance. 'I will be very grateful for your help.'

Ian did not look directly at her. 'You're doing me the favour,' he said.

She reached for her wine. Ian instantly sat up and added cold wine from the iced bottle to what was in her glass.

'Do you like it?' he asked.

'Yes. It smells like river water.'

'It does?'

'It does to me.'

He put his nose into the glass, breathed and closed his eyes.

'What river?'

'Not the Moskva.' Images came back sharp, clear, fragrant. 'The Moskva smells like Muscovites! Though to be fair it smells like grass and rain in the early summer.' Summer was when Seriozha came home. 'No, this wine smells like the Neva, in Leningrad, which mixes with the sea and tastes of salt and . . . 'And freedom, she'd nearly said. It was a thought from a poem of Akhmatova's which ran frequently in her mind, like a familiar melody.

But she did not want to think of poetry. Every September, Seriozha wrote poetry in their dacha of birch trimmed with sky-blue paint. The dacha which could no longer be there in a town that no longer had a name in a country that was over for her.

She put her hand on his hand.

'You should take him home to bed,' she said softly. Her hand was still on his and he did not move. She withdrew it.

In the cab coming back to her hotel, Christian slept in Ian's arms and from time to time she felt the sleepy weight of the boy shifting toward her. She let him lean; it was natural and for a moment soothed her gnawing need for the ordinary, the affectionate commonplaces of life which she had lost in one stroke.

When the cab stopped in front of La Chaumière, she thanked Ian. Then she kissed the bare back of the little boy's neck with an old-fashioned, murmuring kind of kiss, the way nurses kiss infants on their bellies.

Ian averted his eyes.

Lilianne was in the kitchen wearing a T-shirt of Ian's that claimed to be the property of the Federal Penitentiary at Alcatraz. This, he knew, was the equivalent of Christian's having learned to bow.

She wore no makeup and looked a bit sleepy. But she hardly ever wore makeup and her stock-in-trade was her huge, heavy-lidded eyes which had a way of looking at you as if you – you alone – had awakened her.

'Paddington.' She smiled at Christian, calling him after the little English bear in a yellow slicker that Christian loved.

'Ninon.' She smiled at Ian, calling him by a nickname she'd made up and kissing him on both cheeks. She kissed him before she kissed her son; after all, it was Ian who had done her a favour.

She spent some time with Christian before he went to bed – she scrubbed his face a second time, with laughing, maternal hardiness; she listened patiently for the $n$th time to Christian's account of his trip to see the new Siberian tiger at the zoo. But this time, when he announced, as he always did, that it was his intention to own such a tiger someday, she did not tell him, as she always did, that this was not possible, unecological and humanly contemptible. She smiled and said maybe he would. Her shift in strategy had an exciting, disquieting effect on the boy, as though he had deliberately done something to provoke a slap and received a kiss instead. Ian knew that children's lives depended on consistency, even though it was sometimes viciously boring. He knew that after Lilianne closed the door, Christian was not asleep.

Lilianne quietly made orange juice for herself and Ian. She went about this with an expression of loving concentration on her face, choosing the most unblemished oranges, squeezing them vigorously. She filled Ian's glass a little higher. He poured this excess into her glass, and refilled his own with vodka.

'Oh, Ninon, you're not happy,' she said to him. 'I'm sorry I didn't tell you I was going away. It's my fault, I know, but at the last minute they invited me to go with them in their plane  It didn't cost a thing.'

She had come up behind him and put her arms around him. He felt her small hard breasts against his back. She was not deliberately trying to be seductive; her body belonged to her as to a child. She expressed herself fully and unconsciously in her gestures, and breasts were sometimes for solace.

'Who are "they"?'

She proudly stated the name of an American director who had made a grand, horrifying film about Vietnam and put together his own repertory company full of young and desperately committed actors. Despite himself, Ian was impressed.

'How did you manage that?' he asked her.

She held her glass in both hands and studied it as she spoke. Since she did not let him see her eyes, he knew she would say something he wouldn't care for. Then when he relented – the eyes, his reward.

'I was in Fauchon a few days ago with Christian, I met the wife. She wanted to know about his school; they are here for several months' shooting.' She pronounced the word 'shooting' as if it were another word for what Rodin did when he took clay into his hands. 'So we became friends.'

And so they had had lunch and after lunch everyone just sort of flew off to the festival. It was all very disorganised and simpatico, very American, she reassured him. You know how Americans are, she said, teasing. Friends forever twenty minutes after you meet them.

Ian felt the back of his neck grow warm, but the vodka was already in his blood and Lilianne could not suppose she had embarrassed him. She referred to his first encounter with her; he'd taken her home from a party – the most beautiful girl at the party, the most beautiful girl in Paris, which was to say, in the world – and she had simply stayed. One night, then the next. It was only after a few days that he'd learned she had a son. To this day he didn't know who had looked after Christian at that time.

He felt suddenly that he belonged to a world of Americans trying to make instant friends with foreigners – his father, himself, a movie director's wife. He hadn't felt so American for a long time.

'She is my friend, really,' Lilianne repeated. 'She is going to teach me to play tennis.' At this she laughed and shrugged; Ian could well imagine a match between the Los Angeles wife, addicted to sweat and exercise, and Lilianne, whose waiflike body seemed to demand no exertion beyond a sort of protectionism – no smoking, no drinking, no staying up all night.

'She knows I'm an actress; I'm not hiding anything. She needs me as much as I need her. She's new here.'

Lilianne's tone was now as defensive as it ever got. Another word and the conversation would be upended and unsalvageable. If he would just relax, say something, the conversation would simply drift off into sleep and tomorrow morning would be moored in the same place as yesterday morning. Safe, reasonably watertight; his mouth would not be full of splinters, the seas would not seep up past his nostrils as he slept.

'Then everything is fine, then.' She didn't notice the spasm in his syntax and he had cleansed his voice of any timbre of challenge. She took his hand; they went to bed.

Alongside her, her thigh cool on his thigh, which was hot, he wanted not to touch her. But he also wanted to sleep. Her hands were thin and smooth, as if powdered; her mouth felt strangely refreshing and cool like the rest of her skin. Under her touch, he felt huge, clumsy, febrile.

Afterwards, he felt not relaxed, but hollow. He wondered if Christian had finally fallen asleep.

The same car went by the dacha twice. They couldn't see it through the trees, but they knew it was the same car by its slow, deliberate passage; the engine made itself heard in two long lento, legato phrases, one after another. After the second, Katinka got up and went in.

But Seriozha stayed where he was, sitting on the porch steps, lighting up cigarettes and drawing letters on the slate step with the burnt end of a match. When several minutes had passed and still he had not followed her inside, Katinka came out carrying a bottle of Johnnie Walker Red.

'Where did you get that?' he asked her. His voice was harsher than he had ever heard it.

She reacted with both surprise and cool. 'Somebody brought it yesterday.' She broke the seal on the bottle and raised it to her lips. Then she offered it to him.

He took it and said nothing. She stood there for a few moments, but when he wouldn't talk, gave up. He remained there until the bottle was nearly empty.

Though the afternoon was now dissipated, the light was becoming unbearably bright to him. He sat with his eyes closed. But this brought out the sounds: cars passing, a phone ringing – here or in a neighbouring house, he could no longer distinguish – footsteps, doors opening and shutting, loudly, quietly. It was the quiet movement that shocked him. The sense of stealth around him jolted him as surely and as silently as a measured voltage of electricity.

64

Enough to terrify a participant in a behavioural study, say, but not enough to kill him. Katinka had ceased trying to attract his attention. Now he merely heard her watching.

Finally he heard her rapping on a windowpane. He turned. She stood inside, naked, beckoning to him with her hand.

It was a deep and awful feeling to see her naked in his father's house. It meant it was now an abandoned house, where no one lived, where anyone might do anything.

He wanted to break the window, but at the last second he couldn't bear to damage the house. The glass, the wood, the chairs – all were dear to him, his last, his true, his inanimate family, the dead but eloquent artifacts of a past in which there had been love. It required great control.

And tears blinded him. Acidic, alcoholic tears, the sick tears of a dying animal in a trap. He went inside and carefully took the phone off the hook. Next to the open receiver he placed a small tape player, and in it he inserted an old and well-worn tape of John Coltrane blaring 'A Love Supreme'. The saxophone gasped and yawed, so loud it was hardly a sound anymore, but only a kind of percussive nausea. This might give him seven minutes until the car came back; the neighbours would give him a little longer.

'I'll fuck you for them, like you fuck me,' he told Katerina.

She did not move. 'You're wrong,' she said.

He hit her; he felt the butt of his hand meeting her jaw. His hand throbbed and she covered her breasts.

'You're wrong.' She was crying now, but only out of pain. Crying did not distort her voice; it was even and insistent.

'I'm wrong,' he sobbed. He had his arms around her and he bit her shoulder very hard; he felt suddenly that the animal in the trap was still alive. It had a minute left, a few seconds, he could tear her apart with his teeth. He felt her go rigid with pain. Then she kissed the top of his head.

Her shoulder bled where he had bitten it, her face

65

was white. His anger was turning into hate but this she recognised and accepted. The hatred was hot and pure, not different from desire – maybe purer. She gave herself to him.

Through the open door, they now saw men on the steps. Katerina shook her head very softly and they went away. Seriozha put his face again on her breast and let her take him to sleep.

At La Chaumière there was no breakfast for another two hours and Ian was shown into the bar. He felt certain that he would be the only person here at such an hour. But he was wrong.

Harley did not so much put his head up in greeting as raise his eyebrows in a friendly way; the way, Ian supposed, that a chimpanzee in the wild might establish species recognition with another of its own. Harley was drinking rye and Ian was sorry to see it. Drinking was something Harley claimed had caught up with him covering Vietnam. Certainly it was only talk of Saigon that accompanied Harley's heavy drunks; talk which Ian dreaded, not because it was repetitious, but because it served the recurring purpose of exorcising Harley's horrible visions, pictures that were worse imprinted on the mind's eye than on any front page. Harley's photos were famous not only because he had memorialised the bareheaded suffering of children but also because he had caught the consciousness of wrong on the metallic, anaesthetised faces of soldiers.

'Two great minds that think as one,' Harley said as Ian came into focus. 'We're the first ones here.'

'Is that your breakfast?' Ian asked.

'Dinner.'

Ian smiled grimly and ordered coffee for two. Harley accepted this gesture of being looked after.

'You were supposed to call me,' he told Ian.

Ian nodded. 'Something came up,' he said, unsure whether he was going to lie, or if he would have to.

'I see.' For a moment Harley's face reverted to an easy, drunken acquiescence, compounded by that same, slightly zoological expression of recognition – this time of gender. 'If I had something like that at home, I wouldn't have called me either.'

'I wasn't at home.' Oh God, Ian thought, what now? 'Listen,' he told Harley, 'I don't think she's as hot a story as we thought.'

Harley's eyes wavered unfocused for a moment, but when he turned towards Ian, his drunkness seemed entirely gone.

'Are you shitting me?' Harley said to him. His voice was hard-edged and Ian could taste the whisky on his breath.

'I don't want to do it,' Ian said. He knew that his voice was low and unconvincing and that Harley would think he was trying to cheat him. 'She's been through too much already; I can't do it to her.'

'You mean you already filed.'

'No – I really mean what I just said.'

Harley looked at him and nodded slowly. 'You came here last night, you're here at dawn today, and you think it's not a good story. If I didn't know you better I'd say you're a smarmy little cocksucker.'

'She's not up to it; she's as naked as a worm after a rainstorm.'

Harley now waved his hand up and down in front of his face as if trying to clear the air of a bad odour. He pushed the bottle of rye in Ian's direction.

'It's too early,' Ian said.

'In your case it may be too late,' Harley told him. 'Jesus Christ.'

Ian thought for a moment about taking the bottle, but his stomach was already sore and tired. He had not slept well; all night he had been conscious of Lilianne's body next to his. Suddenly that silky presence was a kind of hair shirt, an electric irritation that started him uncomfortably awake each time he grazed it. 'I love you, Lili,' he had repeated to himself silently. But the words rattled around in the emptiness inside him and finally he'd gotten up and left.

'Doesn't all this ever make you sick?' Ian asked.

'It makes me hungry.'

'That's a good sign.' Ian pushed the bottle back.

'I like to eat. I like to drink. I like a roof over my head. By the way, do you have any desire to see Sri Lanka?'

A vision of deep green tea plantations and dark thunderheads washed over Ian's head. Leaving town was not necessarily the worst thing he could think of at that moment.

'Yes,' he said.

'Rebels have been attacking the shrine at Kandy,' Harley told him. 'Bodies all over the temple. Blood and gold, literally.'

Ian closed his eyes.

'I take it you talked to her last night?'

Ian nodded.

'So what the fuck are you waiting for? Call her – it's just us. I'll shoot her and you can get her out of here until the crush is over.'

He shook his head. 'She trusts me,' Ian told him.

'Terrific,' Harley said. 'I owe two months' rent.'

'I'll loan you the money.'

Harley's eyes narrowed affectionately and for a moment he seemed drunk again. 'I worry about you,' he said.

But then that slight, slobby sweetness vanished from Harley's face and Ian felt a hand on his shoulder. He turned to see Anna.

'I didn't think anyone would be in here now,' she said in a small voice. 'I couldn't sleep.'

Ian stood up. So did Harley.

'Join the club,' Harley said, smiling and putting out his hand. 'Harley Arthur.'

Anna took his hand.

'Anna Nikolayevna Khameneva,' Ian said.

'I should have known,' Harley told her, pulling out a chair for her and looking at Ian.

'You have seen a picture of me?' Anna asked.

'No, from your face,' Harley said to Anna.

'He's a photographer,' Ian told her.

'And he's been drinking,' Harley said.

'Oh,' said Anna. 'I'll have whatever you're having.'

Harley laughed and signalled the waitress. 'Vodka,' he told her.

'I hate vodka,' Anna said. 'This is fine.'

Harley handed her the bottle that was still on the table and she took a drink out of it. Ian was surprised.

'It's going to be a long day,' Harley said.

Anna looked at Ian. Her eyes were teary from the harsh alcohol.

Suddenly Ian watched the scene come into close focus. He noticed that Anna was wearing makeup, lipstick of a too dark shade for her complexion and for the morning light which was just coming through the smoke-stained velvet drapes in startling shafts, like an illustration of divine revelation. He noticed that loneliness had chosen Harley's wardrobe – worn jeans, shoes that were expensive but stained, an oddly elegant black silk jacket that had once been Savile Row but which now made Harley look wanton, almost dangerous. And he noticed that Anna seemed to understand all this at once and now spoke to Harley easily and unafraid; she smiled and drank out of Harley's glass.

'What will they be like?' she was asking him. Reporters, she meant.

Harley looked at her. 'You should get out of here. Go someplace else for a while, until you're ready. Then you call them.'

She looked over to Ian.

'He wants an exclusive,' Ian told her.

'Give me a break,' Harley said. 'I've shot millions of refugees,' he said now to Anna.

Here comes Vietnam, Ian thought. God help us.

'And you've got the look.'

Anna was listening intently, as if, Ian thought, to a man complimenting her, describing her lips, her hair, telling her how she was beautiful.

'It's not pain, so much,' Harley said. 'It's really just surprise. I mean, shock is a word that seems to have pain in it. That's not quite it. Not yet.'

69

'You are right.' Anna nodded.

'Here,' Harley said, handing something to Ian. 'I can't stand it.'

What he put in Ian's hand were car keys. 'But first let me have one picture.'

Anna sat erect and still while Harley produced two cameras and a number of weird light attachments out of what looked like a dirty bag of laundry. He blew out the little candle that had been flickering improbably on the table long past dawn. Then he began to shoot without stopping. White light blasted from a silver-foil hood fashioned over the flash and Ian's eyes smarted. But Anna remained sitting formally, her expression unchanged.

'Here a second,' he whispered to Anna. She leaned her face toward him and he gently wiped off her lipstick with a Kleenex.

He changed cameras and started again. Now the bartender was motioning to them. Ian saw that hot light inside the back of his skull.

'That's enough,' he told Harley.

'That's it?' Anna asked.

'I said just one picture, didn't I? Go on, you two, get out of here.'

Ian took Anna by the arm and they left. The sun on the street was dizzying after the murk of the bar.

'You shouldn't trust people like him,' Ian told her.

'What about people like you?' she asked back.

'Nor people like me,' he said.

'Then I won't,' she said. But she was smiling and took his arm as they walked.

The road was hot; black-smelling heat came up from the tarry pavement as they sped along, the windows down. As far as the eye could see on either side were wheat fields, going in waves from a yellow midsummer gold to a bleached late-summer white gold. She could see the wind moving in the fields but she could not feel it inside the car. The little Renault was too noisy for conversation and Anna pressed back into her seat, accepting the heat as though it were some kind of wholesome but malodorous medicinal treatment. Ian wore sunglasses but she squinted in the sun, feeling it burn the sensitive rims of her eyelids, enjoying the burning.

'Where are we going?' she asked Ian.

'What?' Ian leaned over to hear her. 'Sorry,' he said, slowing down.

'Can we stop?' Her voice was nearly strident.

'Of course.' Ian pulled over.

There was total quiet. Anna now heard the breeze, a soft sound like women walking by in silk skirts. Bees appeared, floating over the wheat, sometimes borne backwards on the air, and she heard them, too.

'Where are we going?' she asked.

Ian looked at his hands on the wheel and smiled.

'I don't know. This is the road to Chartres. We could go there.'

The sense of open space in the fields, the emptiness and stillness blotted up Anna's thoughts. She could not help associating it with safety.

'There will be people there, no?' she asked him.

'Yes.'

'But not reporters?'

'No.'

'The only reporter I have to talk to is you.'

'You don't have to talk to me,' he told her.

The fields were in places platinum under the direct sun. The heat shone.

'It is all right to walk here?'

'I suppose so,' Ian said. 'I don't see why not.'

She was out of the car ahead of him, walking forward with a sureness that left a perfectly straight path behind her. Ian followed without speaking.

She stopped when she could no longer see the road and sat down. Ian stood above her.

'If you sit,' she said, 'no one can see you.'

Ian sat, cross-legged and a bit awkward, a measured distance from her. But she was not looking at him. Her face was up toward the light, her eyes were closed.

71

'We will stay here just a minute,' she told him.

'All right,' he said. But she did not open her eyes.

'It doesn't matter,' she went on. 'You cannot tell a minute here. It's like a lifetime, like my life since I left – I don't remember when. I don't know how long I've been here – it's like what they used to tell children to explain why they couldn't remember being born. God wipes away your memory so that you won't be able to tell anyone what heaven was like.'

'That's the first time I ever heard somebody describe the Soviet Union as heaven,' Ian said.

Anna looked into the distance. 'It was hell. Even Dante made hell too special, punishment too personal. What a notion – think of it now – that the punishment should fit the crime.' She laughed a low laugh. 'The crime is breathing, so they suffocate us.'

The air in the wheat was pure and sweet; it smelled almost of bread.

'But it was my home,' Anna said.

Ian reached out and touched her hand. She knew that he tried to make this merely a human gesture of condolence.

'I want to go back to the city,' she told him. 'I am supposed to speak to the geologists at four o'clock.'

'You don't have to speak to them or anyone, if you don't want to.'

'If I listened to you, I'd never make any statement at all. I'd live in total silence.'

Ian said nothing. In the absence of noise, she realised, the odour of the fields was stronger. Sun toasted the dry straw; the soil was ripe and well worked.

'That doesn't sound so bad,' Ian said finally. 'If you don't speak, you can't lie.'

'I have to speak,' she said. 'I didn't come from Russia so that I could have the privilege of remaining silent. And anyway, there's no point in living in fear of lies; no one can destroy the truth.'

She saw how much he wanted to believe her; she also saw that he did not.

'Let's go,' he said softly.

But instead of standing up, she lay down on the ground. Looking up, she saw nothing but light in the sky – not even blue – she saw only the blindingly illuminated emptiness that poets loved to call infinite and eternal. She wished it was, for it felt as though it should be. But her mind knew too well how finite, how particular and temporary a sky could be. Troposphere, stratosphere – it was a structure of circles more delicate than Dante's, and it held all life within it.

'I have so much to do,' she said suddenly.

She stood up too quickly and for a moment she staggered. Ian held out his hand to her. She was flushed and perspiring from the heat, but as she took Ian's hand, she realised that her own hand was cold.

The Société des Géologues et Métallurgistes met in a building off the Boulevard St.-Germain. Anna and Ian were welcomed in through a delivery entrance in the back to avoid the reporters who had been stationed in front of the building since the night before.

In a very elegant refectory, they were served an excellent Bordeaux by some of the most eccentrically dressed people Ian had ever seen. The men and women were dressed alike, and divided between those who wore colonial khaki and those who wore heavy English tweeds despite the sultry September afternoon. The men seemed to favour ties knotted as ascots, and the women, chunky jewellery that was reminiscent of ancient religious rituals. But their odd formality stopped with their sartorial effect. They had followed her struggle as colleagues and they greeted her effusively, even emotionally. They clustered closely around her, asking her questions and nodding sympathetically to almost everything she said.

Though the outside of the brick building had reminded Ian of a vicarage in a George Eliot novel, inside there was little domestic about it and nothing religious. It was, in fact, a monument to evolution, decorated with massive oak tables and thronelike chairs. All the walls were lined with glass-fronted bookcases which contained few books.

Instead, these cases were filled with geological specimens from all over the world – spectacular pieces of uncut topaz, jagged agates that seemed to have live flames inside them, a sixty-carat opal fashioned into a dagger, and the world's largest crystal ball.

'It was cut from a single piece of Burmese quartz,' Baron Alfred de Neufontain, the group's president, told them. He was a tall man with a small man's face; round, red, more genial than petulant but presumably capable of either extreme.

'Feel it,' she said to Ian.

He looked at her.

'The quartz,' she told him. 'Touch it. That is how you can tell that it is not made of glass.'

Ian laid his palm against the cool, translucent globe. It felt hard, of course, but somehow he imagined that it was the hardness of stone and not of glass. It felt cold, too, and it did not warm under his hand. He pressed his finger against the glass of the case to test it. In a few seconds the glass was hot.

'It's totally different, isn't it?'

It was, but he had no idea why.

'If you had held your hand on the stone longer,' she told him, 'it would have become warm, too. And now if you touched it again, it would still be warm, while the glass has already cooled.'

Ian smiled but the baron nodded, quite serious.

'Here is glass,' he said, drawing forth a smaller ball from the dark of a lower shelf. He handed it to Ian, and Ian held it up to the window. It was a lovely thing that seemed to gather up the light and make the room float in it upside down. Then the baron lifted out the crystal ball as if it were an awkward, impossibly heavy baby. He leaned back under its weight and settled it against his stomach; even against the dark blue serge of his suit it sparkled gorgeously. As the glass had seemed to trap light, the rock crystal seemed to generate it.

'*Vive la différence!*' he announced.

Ian, who had never heard that expression used to connote the difference between anything except men and women, noticed that Anna smiled sadly. She turned to him.

'You see,' she said, 'it is not man-made. It is chemically nearly identical to the glass, but not physically. Its structure developed on its own for thousands of years, turning this way and then that. No one could totally imagine each and every crystal in that rock, no one could design it.'

'Yes,' the baron agreed, 'she always surprises us.'

It was a moment before Ian realised that 'she' was the earth. By then they had moved to the end of the long room and opened the doors on a large, old-fashioned amphitheatre. Ian's first sensation was that it smelled like the Kiernan Latin Lecture Hall at Fordham Prep, where he had gone to high school. His second sensation was that five hundred people standing and clapping in a hard, sustained rhythm generated a physical force that felt like walking into a strong wind. He winced.

But Anna's face remained still, and sad.

As she stood at the podium, she pushed back the hair from her face with her right hand. She felt the strength of the applause, though she could not make her eyes focus on faces; the force of it affected her more than its sound, for her nervousness had made her almost deaf.

She had not prepared any speech – when would she have done it? Not in Moscow, certainly, where any stray piece of writing would only have complicated an already unendurable procedure. Not in Paris, where among strangers she scarcely recognized her own face in a mirror and her words in a foreign language seemed not truly her own. She had supposed that the society was a small and diffident group of scholars; such their slim ivory-paper publication had seemed each year to make them, featuring as it did quite technical articles on subjects like the paleobotany of the Pennsylvanian Period. She had expected to be among colleagues, certainly, the vanguard of her profession; she had not expected to be among friends. Though she had long ago accepted the utter lack of information about the outside world that the Soviet government imposed, it had never before struck her that the other side of this coin was that one day she would enter a room of people she knew nothing about but who knew everything about her.

Five hundred people continued to stand, and as she finally looked up at them they clapped harder. It was perhaps seven full minutes before they began to quiet and take their seats again. But as Anna steadied herself to speak, she saw each of the three double doors in the back of the auditorium open.

Now students were allowed in, one at a time, one after another, and kept on coming until all the aisles were filled. They were noisy, erratically dressed in their light summer clothes, flushed and living in their own worlds like students everywhere. But their faces were intense with expectation and respect and those closest to her stood stock-still and communicated this silence up and down the ranks. Finally everyone waited.

Anna breathed.

'Dear friends,' she began, 'you must forgive me. My emotions are not my own. I no longer know myself.'

The quiet was now reserved. They waited for a metaphor perhaps, for Anna to write a subtext beneath her words to make them less strange. But strangeness was what they were about.

'I find today that I am a simple person, far simpler than I thought. For even though I stand here among a community of scientists who are ample proof that we are all citizens of one earth, I feel, without my country, without, in fact, the street that I lived on, the rooms that held my photographs and my son's old clothes, that perhaps I no longer really exist. Even the things that three days ago I placed no value on whatsoever and threw away in the trash – a letter I could not finish writing, a broken blue pencil – seem dear to me now and I wish that I could touch them.

'On my old desk are a few things – are they still there though I can no longer see them? Forgive me, but I do not ask this as a philosopher. I assure you that the old question about whether the tree falling in the forest really makes a sound if there is no one there to hear it has always seemed absurd to me. I grew up in a place where everything humanly conceivable was done to convince us that no one individual is ever in any way at the centre of things. It never occurred to me to argue with this. I have never thought that life needed me to go on.

'But I was wrong. The truth is so obvious that I am ashamed to have to admit here in front of you that I did not realise that every individual is in a way at the epicentre of life. Now that I have been forced to leave my home and my country, it seems to me that life has somehow stopped.'

Now Anna closed her eyes for a moment, and for that moment the hall and all the people vanished. As clear as if she were standing there, she saw her great old mahogany desk, her green lamp, her papers, Pavel's picture in an American Lucite frame and several fine fossils.

'On my desk, I had several pieces of amber. You know, the little specimens one can buy even in a hotel lobby on a tour of Russia. Our amber is famous, we are very proud of it, very poetic about it. A small clear piece of amber with a tiny insect millions of years old embedded in it is a good departure point for a meditation on endurance, on surviving. This is how it was often presented to us as schoolchildren. I thought it would also be a way to talk about extinction.

'But I was told not to take the amber as I was leaving; they would have confiscated it at the airport. Again, the oddest things have a way of becoming valuable when you want to take them out of the country. And this is exactly what I am trying to say.

'I could bring nothing valuable with me, nothing at all. I have left everything behind. I am my own meditation on extinction.'

Though the entire hall was still, Anna leaned forward and raised her voice. The expression on her face was that of a person afraid of being interrupted.

'What does it feel like to be extinct? It is numb – it feels like nothing. And herein is the danger. We are, all of us

77

here, confronted by the loss of everything that we know, including our lives, and we simply don't feel it.

'My colleagues, you have seen some of the most beautiful things that the earth holds. And you know how mysteriously all the things of the earth – the micro-organisms which live in the soil and renew it, the molecules of only three atoms of oxygen which make up the atmospheric ozone, which is our vital shield from the naked sun – are bound together and can never be separated. There is nothing I can add to your great experience of what a precious web of life this planet is. I can only speak to you about my life, and in so doing speak of your lives. For it is not only because the earth is unique in our knowledge of the universe that we have come together today; it is because in each of our lives we have been the witnesses of this mystery. What sights we have seen! What miracles we have held in our own hands! What would the earth be without our love for it? What will life be without us?'

Though she did not know it, as she finished her voice had become progressively louder and louder, yet people strained forward in their seats to hear her. Those students in the aisles nearest her were now close enough to touch her and unconsciously she had been speaking only to them.

They followed her words, watching her lips like deafmutes. Her French was heavily accented – many people there must not have caught everything she said. But there was no one who did not take her meaning. The instant that she stopped speaking those who stood around her rushed toward her; those in the gallery seats stood and cheered.

She heard a young woman's voice call her 'Anya.' She did not see who spoke, but her head turned immediately to the name of her childhood. Those who saw this took it up and began to cry 'Anya, Anya,' reaching for her. The word spread until she heard it everywhere around her. They kissed her and touched her. The faces that pressed against her own were hot with emotion. This surprised her; what she did not realise was that her cheeks burned, too.

*     *     *

Apparently the Russian woman never answered her phone; George had no way of knowing whether she had received any of his messages. This annoyed him deeply, but when he saw the commotion of reporters, demonstrators and television cameras outside the geological society he could not blame her. He instructed the driver to pull up as close as he could, then changed his mind, afraid. They stayed parked safely on the periphery.

Suddenly, he felt an overwhelming sense of detachment that afflicted him physically like sleep. Safe inside the car, he was weariness itself; outside him – frenetic activity, mostly waged by demonstrators young enough to be his children. He stole a first look at the bar built in behind the driver's seat.

At the core of it all was the press. Most people owned their own story, he knew as a lawyer. But God forbid you do something public with your life, something for the public.

A thirty-year-old image of Marilyn Monroe, cornered weeping by cameramen, came back to him. She had just been released from a hospital after a miscarriage. Kate, along the course of producing their two children, had had two miscarriages. God knows, the last thing on earth you would ever want to stare at was a woman who has just lost a baby. He remembered the face of that experienced actress staring in utter lack of recognition at the cameras, as if they were some kind of torture device made to come up close to your face and suck the breath out of you.

In his time he had prepared a number of defendants to face the camera. He always told them to do what a ranger in Yellowstone had once told him to do if he ever encountered a bear: don't let it sense that you are afraid. But the sense of danger never left him personally; he kept out of the public eye. He had even lost his liking for that kind of immediate, public recognition, much the way a camper who has once woken up to see his gear torn to shreds and left next to his head loses his love for sleeping out in the open.

But in the end, it was not fear of publicity which won out; quite the opposite – it was fear of intimacy. He knew that Ian was probably somewhere in that fray and the idea of finding himself opposite his own son in public seemed painfully absurd. What on earth could they have said to each other?

A second look at the liquor. He opened the walnut-grained door of the little cabinet, discovering that it was not in fact wood, but very, very good Formica. At that moment, feeling himself fully the victim of his Neoplatonic education, this excellent imitation of a small piece of wood was the last straw. He withdrew a bottle of something that turned out to be Armagnac.

Formica and Armagnac; life on the verge of the twenty-first century.

'Who the hell is paying for this?' he wondered out loud.

'Sir?' The driver's voice came through an intercom even though he was sitting only a few feet away.

'Nothing,' George said, and turned off the driver's ability to hear him. Then he turned it back on.

'Try to back out,' he told him. 'I'm not going in.'

He didn't hear any answer because he had again turned the driver off.

*My mind's not right*, he thought. The words both nagged and soothed him; he had heard them somewhere. But he no longer remembered that they were poetry.

It had been a kind of party, really, and it was almost two in the morning before they were finally alone. Anna's room was filled with empty glasses, overflowing ashtrays, folded newspapers.

Most of the ruder paparazzi had been kept outside, physically restrained by hotel staff; the reporters allowed upstairs were from official papers, well dressed and well behaved. There was such a difference between these men and women and the ones who had yelled continuous questions in every language outside the Société that Anna immediately felt surrounded by the same kind of sophisticated intelligentsia she had known in Moscow. It seemed natural to play the hostess.

Though most of the guests were reporters, some were not. These others were émigré academics who had followed her story in the Russian papers, pacifists who sensed a new front opening, writers and reviewers who knew Anna as the story in a book. The Russian academics brought food – heavy bread and sausage that Anna would never have eaten at home but which now seemed the only thing on earth that she could really taste. They also brought wine and American whisky, which the reporters caught on to, finishing it off and sending down for more. The writers were the unending source of cigarettes, the pacifists of agreement.

It was not the wine that loosened her tongue; it was not that after the strain of the speech she had finally relaxed. It was the intoxicating intensity of the conversation, the ability to be understood in Russian, the knowing laughter in response to old Moscow jokes.

Twice Ian edged toward her on the couch where she sat, her stocking feet tucked under her, and touched her lightly on the arm. When she looked up at him, he raised his hand discreetly and lowered it again. Her father had used such a gesture when she was a child and played too loudly in the one room in which they lived and he worked.

She smiled and lowered her voice.

'Anna,' he whispered to her when the young French journalist she had been talking to got up to scrounge for a cigarette, 'watch what you say.'

Suddenly an old, familiar iciness pierced her lower abdomen.

'An informer?' she asked Ian.

He shook his head.

'What?'

'A writer, a reporter,' he told her.

'My God,' she said. 'You terrified me.' She sat back again. Thereafter, the party seemed louder and she did not enjoy it as much.

When they were gone, Ian tried in vain to open the windows wider.

'What do they all want?' Anna wondered out loud.

'You know what they want,' Ian told her. 'And you gave it to them.'

She looked at him. His eyes showed the same intense expectation that she had seen in the faces of the students, but not the same hope. And there was something intimate about the despair in his expression; as if he expected so much of her that actually there was nothing she could do but disappoint him.

'I'm nothing if not honest,' Ian said, almost apologetically.

'Were you always so honest?' she asked.

'No.'

It occurred to her, sitting there in the shadow where he could not see her eyes, for only the bedside lamp now burned, that honesty should not be something so abstract. It should be something you can touch. It should have skin, like a man. It should have hands that grasp your own when you reach for it.

'Is it all lies?' she asked him.

'Lies? In America we call it hype – something exaggerated, insincere, put on for the camera.'

She thought about it and then nodded.

'The Soviet press does not distinguish between hype and lies,' she said.

Ian faced out of the window. Passing cars illuminated his face every few moments. She closed her eyes and he seemed more present as a feeling in the dark than as an American image that came and went with the movement in the street.

'But it's not all lies,' he said. 'That's the hard part. Figuring out what is and what isn't.' He turned and saw her with her eyes closed. 'Does the light bother you?' he asked.

'I'm just tired,' she answered. He walked over to the bed and clicked off the little lamp. For a while they sat there, she in the chair, he on the bed, in the dark, not speaking. Then she heard him get up and come over to her.

'Your book is very beautiful,' he told her.

How can something so painful be beautiful? she wondered; then she realised that for an instant she had thought not of the book but of herself. She tried to see Ian more clearly in the darkness; however, he was now so close that as soon as she looked into his eyes she looked away.

'Who was the young man in the story?' he asked. His voice was very low.

'I don't know,' she said. 'He is someone I have never met.'

She heard him take a breath.

'I just want to touch your face,' he said to her. 'Just touch it.' She didn't move.

He reached up and touched her forehead. Then her cheeks, then her lips.

'I want to kiss your hands. That's all.'

She held out her hands and he pressed them to his face. She felt his lips against her palm; once, then harder. Then nothing.

For some time after Ian had let himself out, Anna still sat there, her hands pressed tightly together.

In her dream Pavel was still alive. They were young. Seriozha was a baby. He lay on the bed between them both – they had no extra room for a baby, but he would have slept with them anyway. Pasha's sleeping hand lay open, reaching for her, and she moved to sleep with her cheek in his hand, like a flower in a cup. The baby curled against her, huddled under her breasts as before he was born. But one little foot was extended, toes perfectly symmetrical like a dancer's, and touched the thick, curling hair of Pasha's belly. Life, she thought with the satisfying illogic of dreams, is something that can never die.

She awakened long before she knew she was awake. Dream hovered for a while on the brink of thought; then there was thought and, of course, consciousness. She lay staring up at the small, snow-like crystals of the chandelier

83

patterning the ceiling in cold yellow and blue as cars passed by on the street and remembered the night that Seriozha was conceived. She was certain of the date – it was the first night they spent in their own apartment alone, an ecstasy of privacy.

Those who have known privacy all their lives – their own houses, their own rooms – could never know the intimacy of lovers who are never alone. The others had been their skin, their faces; suddenly alone together, Anna and Pavel were raw and terrified beings. Left for the first time in the luxury of isolation, they wanted each other too much to make love. She laughed with anguish and relief. They could scarcely touch each other.

Towards four in the morning, they had awakened without knowing they had been asleep. It had snowed, the streets were softened under a blanket of milky blue; there was no sound except the barely audible abrasion of the hard, exceptionally cold crystals against the window-panes.

'Are we dead?' Pàsha asked her. He, so ugly and knowing, could ask this and not frighten her. He smiled; a pleased, childish smile – they were awake in the middle of night, it was silent and it snowed.

'Yes,' she had said. 'We're ghosts.'

And ghosts, they had finally come to each other, untroubled by their lack of human context. She lay very still; he shuddered like a woman about to give birth. Later he told her – he was in his forties when he married her, his heart strained in the war – that that night he had thought he might die. But at the time, she felt not the frailty of his health, but the strength of life inside him, and knew he had created their son, given him breath, as surely as she had. Her own labour and the actual delivery of Seriozha, under the unsympathetic and utilitarian conditions of an army hospital near Sverdlovsk, did not efface this impression. In fact, in that cold, tiled room she had been conscious of wanting to meet his bravery.

Then there was the child. Perfect, warm, of a loveliness that was in no other way a part of life, of their lives, twenty years ago in a military installation hidden in the Urals. Like the milk-lit, snow-heavy night whose quiet they understood because they were already dead.

When Ian got home at nearly 4 A.M., Lilianne was waiting for him in a terry-cloth robe. For an instant, Ian felt like accusing her of sadistic premeditation, but he knew it was instinct; he felt her instincts now. He felt his own.

And besides, all he wanted on earth was to be alone. Alone in a chair, with his mouth open like an old man, scarcely awake, unsure if life flowed in or flowed out.

'Christian couldn't sleep,' she told him. 'You promised him that you were going to tell him a story tonight.'

'I'm sorry,' Ian said.

'It took me a long time, but I finally got him to close his eyes. I had to sit with him almost two hours.'

'Good.' Ian nodded. 'You win the prize. Mother of the Year. You put your own son to bed.'

Lilianne did not look away from him; she measured him with her eyes as though figuring the distance of his anger, the way one counts the beats between the flash of lightning and the crack of thunder to know how many miles away the centre of the storm is.

'Would you like a drink?' she asked him.

Ian shook his head.

'Ninon.' The tone of pliancy in her voice made all the muscles of Ian's neck and shoulders go rigid. 'Ninon, what's the matter?'

'I'm sorry,' he said. 'Nothing. I want to go to bed.'

'Okay,' she whispered in English, and left him standing in the living room.

He remained there until he no longer heard Lilianne turning alone in the bed. Then he rearranged the cushions on the sofa and went to sleep.

*As if to punish us for destroying the balance of His Creation, God has chosen the perfect way to remind us that once we were women and not animals. He has sent us one man.*

*And this man has fallen in love with Olga.*

*He is young. He wears the uniform of a soldier but he*

has the bearing of an officer. He comes from the inner ranks – no one knows whether he was sent here on purpose or has merely got lost here.

Those in charge are unable to let him go or stay. They have no order to detain him here, and fear being in technical violation of orders which may have been sent but not, because of the circumstances, received. There have been executions for even minor disruptions of discipline; teenage girls have been asked to stand and were shot where they stood. Punishment has become the same as law.

So he stays with the women. At first, he was put apart by himself but it was intolerable to see him alone. They began to look the other way.

Since he came to us, every meal has been like a party! We have thought of amazing new ways to cook our few supplies – tinned sardines, potatoes, flour, powdered eggs. An old woman named Maryusa makes a bread of flour and water burned on a griddle that is actually delicious – a tried-and-true recipe from the siege of Leningrad, she told us. A few nights ago, a very pretty woman who was a manicurist before made an omelet with the fish and it was superb – we all swore that she had found garlic somewhere! Our soldier told her gallantly that if the war is ever over and it is possible to live aboveground again, he will still remember that omelet and ask her to make it for him. The least substantial, most trivial type of flattery, of course; in the outside world this manicurist would have told him to go back to the provinces. But here we actually grew misty-eyed and fell on him with affectionate pinches and kisses.

So you can see how fond of him we all were. But now he has singled out one of us to be his lover, and I am almost afraid that someone will kill him.

I am afraid because I can feel this anger in myself. I look at Olga and her cheeks have colour for the first time. Though we have all lost weight, she seems blooming; her face is no longer yellow and drawn, her breasts seem alive under her sweater. Then I look at my own empty hands and suddenly I am filled with such despair and envy that I can imagine hurting him myself.

*I can visualise perfectly ancient rituals of fertility in which a beautiful young man is torn apart by women and his bloody pieces carried away – secretly, held next to the skin – to be buried in the ground, a plea for the harvest, both agricultural and human.*

*But there is never to be another harvest. Not in my lifetime, which is the same to me as never. Pasha – where is my child? Why did you not give me daughters in whose wombs possibility might have survived? Why did we have only a son, a man and a soldier like yourself, a sacrificial offering in your own name.*

*How easy it is now to believe in gods. If I am not to live, nor you nor anyone I have loved, then I want to imagine a family of superbeings who look at us with the same unfeeling tenderness with which the healthy look on the dying in hospitals – beings whose daily lives are the cheerful, animated tales told by brave lying children to the aged.*

*His face is not like yours, my love. For in your face everything is to be seen as in the works of Pushkin or Shakespeare; every emotion at one time or another I have read in your eyes. Your face is a medium for life.*

*His face, though young, is ancient. It is an austere mask, like those used in ceremonial dramas or mythical tragedies, behind which my poor soldier can live and suffer without restraint. I have seen him look at Olga when only his eyes showed what his life meant to him. There was great pain there, but not the hot, human pain I have seen in your eyes; a cold pain, a consciousness of absurdity.*

*I can imagine his hands upon her. Do you understand – can you forgive me? I want life, too.*

*What kind of an animal have I become?*

'What have you done?' Seriozha asked her. His hands were in her hair.

Though it was about ten, the sunset was not yet complete, for in the summer the sky over Peredelkino takes a long time to empty.

Her eyes in the twilight were an intense blue, the colour of Chinese bowls, or the blueberries ripening under the larches.

'If you know everything already, why do you ask me?' Katinka answered him.

His fingers loosened in her hair. The blue of her eyes was the colour of love and simplicity. It was impossible to disbelieve such a blue.

'Can we listen to some music?' she asked.

Seriozha went behind his father's desk. There, along with his favourite painted birch chair, the old woven cushion still upon it, were his father's treasures. Books – not just the coveted Western books but also fine old editions of Russian books that his father had collected over the years – records and the family's pride and joy, a Panasonic stereo set. He chose Beethoven's Sixth Symphony. The air was suddenly full of a music that was like a flock of birds all taking off at once.

'That's more pleasant,' Katinka said.

He laughed at her. He knew that the music would not be pleasant to those whose job it was to listen to their conversation.

'I wish I were a dancer.' She smiled, suddenly opening her arms and turning in time to the music.

'I wish you were, too.' He smiled with only half his mouth, an irony that he had inherited from his father, but which was handsome, even seductive on Seriozha, while it had been merely sad on Pavel Leonidovich. 'But you have a classic Russian figure.'

'I do not!' Katinka objected. She was proud of her relative slimness.

'What's wrong with that?' Seriozha went on. 'Russian women – the best in the world.'

'You would know, I suppose,' she told him. 'I am in no position to compare.'

Before his father's refusal to work three years ago, Seriozha had through Komsomol been granted a job showing foreigners through the Lenin Library. It was a canned little tour of rare books and old manuscripts prepared for the English-speaking tourist, deadly boring but an enviable opportunity to meet people. This plum, of course, had disappeared at the very beginning of all their troubles.

Katinka, though she had studied English, French and German, had never been formally allowed to meet any foreigners.

He looked at her and thought of girls from New York, girls from London. To him these earnest travellers in their patent-leather pumps and trench coats had been as exotic as bare-breasted Polynesians in grass skirts. Much more fascinating, in fact, for he had nothing to talk about with a South Sea native, and everything to discuss with an American. But he hadn't had the nerve to approach these girls – not for fear of them, for they too readily approached him, but for fear of confessing later to Katinka, as he knew he would have to. He was compulsively honest. It had once made him an exemplary Komsomol member; it now made him a poet.

'I never betrayed *you*,' he told her.

'I want to stay with you,' she said. She looked all around the room as if there might be something there – a painting on the wall, a book – that could somehow explain this to him. 'I have to be near you.'

'And this is how you do it?'

'I don't know what to do.' She had begun to cry again, quietly, hard, making a sound that was more like a deep, dangerous cough than a sob.

The record stopped. The silence was huge and resonant. Seriozha turned the record over and they listened in pain to the *Allegro*.

'Not between us,' he told her. 'It cannot be.'

'They'll only use me against you in some other way,' she said. 'Don't you see?'

He followed her thoughts flawlessly, and they had the too perfect pattern of logic. Logic which excluded everything in him and, he had once thought, her.

'Through everything,' he said to her, 'even after his death, my mother never betrayed my father.'

Her face was soaked with tears like a child's, her expression a child's profound bewilderment.

'How do you know?' she asked him.

\* \* \*

89

Harley came over at twelve. Ian was sitting on the balcony in cut-offs. Christian pulled at the fraying edges to make the fringe longer and Ian pushed him away.

'Hello, tyke,' Harley said to Christian.

Christian stared at him.

'Tyke?' Ian asked.

'I don't know. What do you call them?'

'His name is Christian, but I usually call them children.'

'To their faces?' Harley snarled. 'My, we're in a fine mood this morning.'

Christian edged back, off the balcony and into the shadow of the living room.

'Hey, you can stay here,' Ian called to him. But he was gone.

'Sorry,' Harley said.

'It was my fault.' Ian brushed nonexistent lint off his chest and felt the beginning of a sunburn. Cars streaked by in the blazing streets below like multicoloured metal fish; in the distance, the river moved slowly.

'Listen,' Harley said, opening a folded canvas chair and leaning in very close to Ian. 'The pictures are sensational. I really made her look great. Look.'

He zipped open a flat black portfolio and out of it took several enormous black-and-white pictures of Anna.

'Eleven by fourteen? What for?'

'Look.'

Her head was tilted slightly back and she was smiling a little, more to please the photographer than anything else. Her eyes were wide, and though Ian knew that they were brown, in the photograph they had become the colour of the Seine with the sun glinting off it. But it was not that Harley had made her beautiful – it was that he had caught the fact that at that moment Anna lived nowhere but inside herself. Her entire existence was present in the emptiness of her smile and the overfull luminosity of her gaze.

'Have you shown these to anyone?' Ian asked him.

Harley looked at Ian as if he had lost his mind. 'Went out on the wire yesterday before noon, thanks to you.

Nobody else had anything until late last night. I ran on the front page in Sydney, London, New York. Great splash in New York by the way: "REDS EJECT 'ROCK STAR' IN GAY PAREE." Rock star! I love it; can you imagine how many bloody idiots bought that edition? Rupert and I made a killing yesterday.

'And Shitface is going to give us the Sunday supplement cover,' he told Ian, elated. 'All you've got to do is provide some text.'

Ian looked blank.

'Words,' Harley said. 'The shit they put around pictures.'

'Oh fuck,' Ian said. Heat shimmered over the copper roofs of the 16th arrondissement; certain stretches of the river were velvet and certain were hammered gold. How could he go back to Anna now?

Lilianne came out onto the terrace. It was such a small space that the entire mood was at once dominated by her. She wore a pink sundress with a halter, and where the fabric curved from her waist, Ian could see her breast almost to the nipple. He knew Harley could see it, too.

'Hello,' she said, picking up a photograph. 'Who's that?'

'A Russkie,' Harley told her.

'What's that?'

'A Russian. You know, the usual.'

'Oh.' She nodded. 'One of Ian's Russians. Is she a cellist?'

The last Russians that Ian had covered had been a string quartet that had defected *en quatre*.

'Yes,' Ian said.

Harley put the pictures back into the portfolio. He did not look at Lilianne.

'Well, are you going to do it or not?' he asked Ian.

'I don't know,' Ian said. 'I'll go down with you.' He went in to get his clothes. Lilianne turned to Harley.

'Thank you for the pictures,' she told him. 'They looked wonderful. Everyone says so.'

Harley shrugged. 'You look wonderful; I didn't have to work too hard.'

She smiled. Ian came back.

Harley shook hands with Lilianne. 'Good luck,' he told her.

'You're out of your mind,' he said to Ian as they went down the stairs.

Breakfast came on a silver tray. Anna laughed. The room was still a mess; the waiter looked around in dismay for a place to put the tray down and finally handed it to her. Anna recognised him as the bartender who had been solemnly and reproachfully French the day before, but today he caught her mood and smiled, too, lifting the little dome from her croissants with a flourish.

Apricot jam, honey, fresh butter, fresh cream. Steam curled up from the tiny cup of coffee and she tasted its odour with that hunger that makes anything delicious, and delicious things exquisite.

He left her the morning papers and a little bouquet of pink papers which turned out to be telephone messages. She settled the tray on the bed and opened the newspapers; the messages scattered on the floor like the petals of a flower. As she gathered them up, amazed at the number of them, and at the names, all of which were strange to her, she noticed that a 'Mr Micdona' had called twice.

Ian's name. For a moment she stayed motionless where she was, on her knees on the floor. Now the odour of the coffee seemed so strong that it completely took her appetite away.

The phone rang; she nearly crawled to it.

'It's me,' Ian said.

'Come up,' she said, ashamed that she could not make her voice any louder.

When he came in she invited him to have some of her breakfast, but he would not sit down.

'Have you seen the papers?' he asked her.

'Not yet,' she said.

He looked at the papers on the table and lifted out *Le Matin*. In the bottom right-hand corner she was startled to see the formal picture of herself that had appeared in

92

Moscow when she received the Abrasov Medal. But she felt no link to that young woman, her hair in a bun, her life a succinctly plotted graph ahead of her.

The caption read: '*Tendresse pour la terre*.' Inside, there were several more pictures – pictures of her with Seriozha as a child, pictures of her with some women in the University – it was a regular meeting of departmental members taking part in some annual 'volunteer' drive, the kind of thing that always got left to women – and amazingly, a picture of her with Pavel on vacation in the Crimea. It had been one of their last lovely times together, just before the troubles. It was a precious picture and she could not imagine how it had got into a Parisian daily paper.

'Where did they get these photographs?' she asked.

'What usually happens is that someone on the Soviet end arranges to sell them to a paper certain to abuse them and discredit you. Actually, this isn't so bad,' Ian told her.

'But it's all wrong,' she objected. 'It looks as though I were a dissident. That picture, where it says that I am "mobilising" other women; I was coercing volunteers for one of our fund drives. Something stupid that we always had to do, everyone.'

'Look.' He spread the paper out on the floor. 'You can see that this is just all pictures. They hardly say anything at all. What they say is basically not offensive, even if it's wrong.'

Now he laid out the other papers. The leftist *L'Indépendent* ran a complimentary article – with all the same ridiculous and irrelevant pictures – under the title '*Pas encore convaincue*.' It spoke in glowing terms about her reception at the Société, but quoted nothing that she said directly, except a phrase taken out of context to read: 'No individual is ever in any way at the centre of things.'

Her confusion started to give way to an anger which she felt in the roots of her hair.

'I can't believe that newspapers in the West have as little regard for truth as Pravda. All this has nothing to do with me,' she said, standing up and moving about the room. 'Why didn't they just print what I said?'

Ian didn't look at her. 'We're not finished yet,' he said.

He breezed through *Le Monde*, a centrist paper; its coverage was no more or less offensive than *Le Matin*'s. But then he opened *L'Humanité*, the Communist paper. There, buried on the eleventh page, was an article about Anna and her book, referring to the 'cattle market' atmosphere that supposedly surrounded the imminent sale of not only the book but Anna's life story. It spoke of émigré dissidents as a wily and successful breed of entrepreneurs – something like art dealers. It ended with the cynical and particularly xenophobic French note that it was likely that Anna would sell the book in America, where the stakes were higher.

'You don't have the right-wing paper, *Le Figaro*, because it comes out at night. But last night's edition ran a picture of all the demonstrators outside the hotel with the caption "*La prochaine frontière de la propagande*" – "The new frontier of propaganda."

'You've got to prepare yourself, Anna. It's going to be like this from here on in. Someone will be listening to every word you say in order to make copy, and they don't care, a lot of them, if they get it right or wrong. Even the ones that do care have their own agendas; they all have papers to sell.'

Instinctively Anna stuck her chin out. It was a small, immediate movement, but she felt as though her head moved because she had been slapped.

'The West,' Ian said. 'It's a Brave New World.'

Anna did not know the book; she thought Ian was trying to give her courage.

'Why don't they just print what I said?' she repeated.

Ian laughed. 'It's not like that.'

'Listen,' she told him, 'you're a journalist. I will give you a statement and you will print it.'

'I'm afraid it's not like that either; no paper would simply print a statement – you'd have to buy an ad. The hardest thing is to merely say something and get it reported accurately, the way you meant it.'

She realised that it was the first time she had heard him talk about his profession without bitterness.

'One of the papers I work for wants me to do an interview with you,' he told her. 'I'll ask you questions and you tell me what you think. It's not a very good paper and I can't promise that everything you say will be printed. I can only tell you that I'll do my best for you.'

'I should do this?' she asked him.

'It's your best shot,' he said. Though she did not understand the expression he used, she knew he was telling her to do it. She also saw that he was afraid of failing her.

'Is this why you called me?' Her words seemed ridiculously full of feeling and she was humiliated.

'What?' he asked.

She showed him the telephone messages.

'I didn't call you,' he said. 'That's not me.' He threw the papers out. 'I don't want you to have to deal with anyone you don't want to deal with,' he said. 'I think you should change hotels and register under a different name. No more phone calls, no more reporters. When you're ready, you can decide yourself who you want to talk to.'

She turned and opened the suitcase that lay on the chair.

'You can send for that later,' he said. 'Come on.'

She put her hand in his and let him pull her toward the door.

'Why are you so angry?' she asked him.

He didn't answer.

An hour later, Anna was registered under the name Anne Duval at a small *pension* on the Ile de la Cité. She understood why Ian thought it was charming; it was very old, a porcelain basin and pitcher stood on a stand next to the bed and hot water was apparently brought on request – as was the bathtub. The toilet was down the hall. She did not want to tell him how this disappointed her. It was like Russia.

Still, it was a relief to walk out into the street as though she were anyone else. They went down the Quai de la Mégisserie; it was full of people, and she walked slowly,

95

letting herself become part of the chattering swarm of tourists and shoppers who strolled this district of bookstalls and pet shops. She laughed.

'What's so funny?' Ian asked her. He had been fumbling distractedly with a small tape recorder that hung over his shoulder.

'I never thought I would learn to appreciate anonymity,' she said. 'I spent so much of my life resenting it.'

'Talking like a star already,' Ian said. 'Come here.'

He took her hand and pulled her towards him. He seemed to be studying her neck and stepped closer. She stepped back.

'Relax,' he said; his face was almost touching hers. 'I was looking for a good place to attach this.'

He held up a small microphone connected to the recorder by a thin black cord. She stood still while he fastened it to her collar.

'That will work, as long as you don't stray too far.'

They walked along next to each other, unnaturally close, yet not touching.

'So let's start at the beginning,' Ian said. At that moment two girls went by on bicycles, jingling their bells furiously to get people out of their way. Anna jumped in the opposite direction from Ian and the cord of the mike pulled taut. Ian grabbed her hand and steered her back.

'There's going to be a load of street noise on this,' he said under his breath. He did not let go of her hand.

'So what is the beginning, Anna? Where were you born? What were you doing the day the Americans bombed Hiroshima?'

She shook her head. She had been three years old when the bomb was dropped, but she had read a great deal about Hiroshima during Pavel's ordeal. He had not encouraged her to do so and rarely discussed this reading with her, but she had done it anyway. She had always followed his lead.

'It begins with Pavel,' she told him. 'My husband.'

For a moment she had no idea of how to go on; how would she ever explain to someone who had never known him who Pasha was?

'He was the great star of my institute at the University when I was a student, he was my teacher. I was in awe of him – everyone was.'

But it was not just awe; it was love. She had wanted to hold inside herself the same images that he saw in the nightmares that tormented him in the months before he made his decision.

'Were you at all involved in his work?' Ian asked.

She hadn't realised how long she had been silent. She shook her head.

'How did he bring you in to it, then?'

She raised her eyes from the cobblestones to look at Ian.

'You know what it means to love someone?' she asked. She shrugged. She expected no answer. 'It's nothing so extraordinary to feel the same joys and pains as the person you love. I shared in his feelings because I loved him – not out of political outrage, I'm sorry to say, not out of moral conscience. It began because I felt what he felt. It is that simple.'

They continued along quietly. Ian's hold on Anna's hand had become looser. She had forgotten that Ian held her hand; now suddenly she was again aware of it and it comforted her.

'That was the beginning,' she repeated. 'The second step came when he died. Perhaps this sounds stupid, but this is when I began to think about what death means.'

In the first nightmare days, when she had not been aware of time passing, she told him, her imagination had taken over. Then she was tormented by her inability to touch Pasha or see him – in reality, by her utter and ultimate inability to protect him and keep him. Though he had died in her arms, rigid and blue from the failure of his heart to supply oxygenated blood to his brain, she saw him die again, a thousand ways, in the unique and hitherto unimaginable torments of nuclear holocaust. It was a constant hallucination – Pasha deforming ceaselessly before her eyes; burning, melting, turning in a tenth of a second to a man made of ash and disintegrating on the wind.

She had tried to tell herself that she was being dramatic; finding a way to make her own suffering as a widow more important than anybody else's. Pasha had died from cancer; all his life he had smoked short, harsh Russian cigarettes. It was a death like many others.

Still questions plagued her. She remembered his stories of the early days of research in fission – days of poorly equipped labs, of procedures which were new and speculative, of sanitary precautions which were so crude and cumbersome that they were all too often hurried through or ignored. After he had died, she looked at his clothes in the closet, suits he had worn for thirty years, and wondered which pocket might once have harboured some tiny grain of radium. It was now known that even a few seconds' exposure to such intense radiation was enough to trigger mysterious and fatal cell mutations years later. But by the time the famous double helix of DNA was described – a discovery which opened all knowledge of the cell – Pasha had already finished the bulk of his research.

'Forgive me, Anna,' Ian broke in. 'Stop for a minute so I can put in another tape.'

She waited. He snapped in the cassette and pushed the record button.

'Not yet,' he said. 'Now.'

'They also say cancer can be caused, or worsened, by emotional suffering,' she told Ian. 'This, too, was a factor.'

There were the years of torment – first, the silent anxiety, the voice inside him that grew louder and more insistent every day until that day he had refused to go back to the Institute. Had he ever forgiven himself for his part in bringing the earth to the threshold of annihilation? In the end, she wasn't sure. And if she was not sure, how could he have borne that stress during the subsequent years of government persecution?

'You know what I am trying to say?' she asked. 'The causes of – the excuses for – his cancer were all too obvious. I looked for reasons, I found hundreds. But nothing changed the single most horrible fact: I was not able to save him.'

'This is what made you write the book?' Ian asked.

'Not out of guilt as a survivor, if that's what you mean,' she told him, 'but because his death showed me so clearly what his life had meant.'

When there was nothing of Pasha left in the world to love, except his son and the things that he himself had loved, she had finally understood. When the person that she loved most in the world no longer had any existence, but had become indistinguishable from sunlight, from music, from the air itself, she knew she had no choice. This is when she had begun the book.

'I wrote instead of sleeping,' she said. 'I was afraid to fall asleep. The nightmares were so real, much realer than anything else. Pasha dead was more alive to me than all the people around me every day.'

But after a time had passed, something new had happened. The nightmares stopped. She began to dream in a different way. She dreamed of Pavel alive.

'"I am alone here," he would say to me in my dream,' she told Ian. 'I knew I was dreaming because in life he would never have said anything to hurt me. But it was enough to see him standing there again.

'For a while, I was like a mad person; I saved little things to bring to bed and show him in my sleep. An acorn in the autumn, pussy willow in the spring. One night, in my dream, he smiled.'

She saw Pasha, his mild, sideways smile, the gentility of his dead eyes. She stopped for a moment and leaned against a wall.

'Are you all right?' Ian asked. He let go of her hand, and though she knew that he did it out of respect for her privacy, it made her sad. It had somehow been easier to speak of Pavel because Ian held on to her hand.

It was not something she could explain; this was how she had written what she had written, as deficient and awkward as she felt it was. This is how she could leave Seriozha and how she could stand in front of cameras and crowds and speak about life. Pasha's death had deepened her love for life, had shown her how precious everything in existence was, merely because it existed. It wasn't really that she believed she could defeat death, but she was determined that Pasha would never die again.

'Let's take a break for a bit,' Ian said. 'Just walk. Relax.'

They turned around and walked back in the direction they had come. He did not take her hand again.

She was struck by two things as they walked: the splendid abundance of books – books mounded like women in the dreams of satyrs, like jewels in the dreams of thieves – and the number of bright, loud birds in cages of all sizes.

'Kookoorikoo,' Ian said softly to a huge grey parrot. The parrot remained impassive.

'I guess it's too hot to talk,' he said. 'So what am I doing dragging you through the streets making you answer questions?'

Anna lifted the hair off the back of her neck. The slight breeze carried zoo smells and the odour of dust from the books. For a moment she felt she couldn't breathe.

'Are you sure you're all right?' Ian asked her.

Her eyes watered and she suddenly felt nausea creeping up inside her. In front of her birds seemed to swoop and dive and beat their wings against her nose and mouth. She smelled their wings but she knew they couldn't escape their cages. For a second she staggered and put her hand down on a bookstall to steady herself.

'*Attention!*' an irritable voice cried at her. A small shelf of old blue books slipped to the left like dominoes. She watched them hit the cobblestones one after another, knowing that if she bent to pick them up she would not get up.

The bookseller, a small man in a denim apron like a cobbler, picked up each book and brushed it off on his chest. He swore at Anna, but Anna did not comprehend and saw only that he seemed genuinely outraged by the injury to the books, like a mother whose child comes running home with two scratched knees.

'I'm sorry,' said Anna. 'I'll buy them.'

She did not ask how much they were but began to take all the money she had out of her purse. It occurred to her that the money had been given to her in a packet before she left Moscow and since she had not yet had an occasion to spend it she had no idea how much she had.

The bookseller stared at her. 'Do you know what these books are?' he asked her indignantly.

She stared back, her money in her hand.

'It was an accident,' Ian broke in. 'She doesn't understand.'

'What are you?' the man demanded furiously in English.

A small crowd was now forming around them – the bookseller yelling at the top of his voice, the pretty woman dazed, the American man, obviously younger.

Anna heard Ian tell the little man that she was Russian; there was no time to warn him not to.

'*Bon*,' said the bookseller sarcastically. 'And you are American. You think you can do whatever you want?'

A chuckle, a murmur of approval, a cluck or two of shame.

'Now wait a minute.' Ian was getting angry. 'She offered to buy the books.'

The man drew himself up. 'These,' he sputtered, 'these are the works of Victor Hugo – *signed by him*. And I will never sell them to *you*. Never!'

Now there was a small spontaneous burst of laughter and some derisory applause. Everyone waited to see what Ian would do.

But he only leaned toward Anna and said quietly, 'He's crazy. Let's go.'

They left and so did most of the others. Two boys with large, printed, short-sleeved shirts stepped forward to look at the editions of Hugo. One couple remained rooted to the street where they had stood and watched Ian and Anna walk away.

'I think they're Americans, too,' Ian explained to Anna, who seemed bothered by their staring.

Finally they sat in a café and drank lemonade. Anna added several spoonfuls of sugar to the lemon juice and mineral water infusion, but it continued to taste so sour that she gave up trying to drink it.

'Where's your little boy today?' she asked him, making an effort to be brighter.

'He had other things to do.' Ian tried to laugh.

'Soon he won't need you anymore,' Anna said. What a terrible thing to say, she thought.

'You know,' she said suddenly, 'I never made a decision. I never decided: today my life will be given up for this. If anything, a thousand times over, I told myself the opposite. That I would never give up anything of mine for another person. When my husband died, that was the end of that for me. My son was already grown.

'I loved my husband,' she went on. She drew her hands to her breasts as she spoke, twisting the fabric of her dress. 'When he died I lost everything. Do you understand?'

'Yes,' he said quietly.

But she did not expect him to answer; she was lost in the private narcissism of grief.

She sat, watching the pedestrians swim by like brightly coloured ducks through her tears. After some moments she heard Ian's voice.

'Anna Nikolayevna, these people want to speak to you.'

She turned to see the young couple who had watched her disgrace at the bookstall. They were, it turned out, not American but Canadian. And they had recognised her. She invited them to sit down, but they were shy.

'I have two children at home,' the woman told her. She seemed too thin to have ever given birth. The husband dutifully showed the snapshots of two toddlers in pink corduroy. One clutched a large woolly doll made to look like a lamb.

'How lucky you are,' Anna told her sincerely. 'I never had a daughter.'

The husband thanked her.

'You take what God gives you,' his wife said. 'But I just wanted to shake your hand.'

Anna put out her hand. The woman pressed it, and the couple went away, looking once or twice over their shoulders.

'Well,' said Ian.

Anna sat quietly.

'Did you want to finish what you were telling me?' he prompted delicately.

She shook her head. 'It was just that I always believed that my son would live after me,' she said.

On the terrace, the night was one of those extraordinary, pellucid Parisian sapphires. Lilianne was at home for the stunning third night in a row and Ian insulated himself behind the earphones of the tiny tape player. He had spent hours transcribing his talk with Anna, hours straining to hear her words over the street noise. Her voice wouldn't stop inside his head now and he couldn't bear it. He inserted a music tape.

The pristine piano notes of Schumann spread their net over his thoughts; between the clarity of the music and the clarity of the sky he felt that he disappeared.

He wanted to write. He had everything he needed for the story – everything he was going to have before the deadline, anyway. But words eluded him. He did not even attempt to touch the keys of the typewriter. The interview was not what he wanted to write.

He wanted to write a letter, but it was not a letter like any he had ever written before, he knew that.

*I want to touch you, Anna*, he began in his mind. Oh God, that sounded awful, ridiculous.

*I want these words to touch you*, he began again. But what he couldn't figure a way to say was that he wanted the words to be his fingers, he wanted his touch to be able to speak for him as he reached for her in his mute, too ordinary way.

He typed these words out and saw how little they said, how trite and unoriginal they were. Then the music broke off in the middle of a phrase. He looked at the machine and saw that Lilianne was standing beside him and had pressed the button.

'Why did you do that?' he screamed at her. It was a moment before he realised how loud his voice was but he was not sorry.

'You couldn't hear me,' she said, taken aback.

'Leave me alone.' He could not contain the sudden irrational hatred in his voice.

'I just wanted to –'

'Leave me alone.' It was bad enough that he could only repeat this stupid adolescent statement, but now his voice trembled and he knew she heard it.

'Ninon,' she said gently.

He closed his eyes and felt tears pricking behind his eyelids. While he kept them closed and tried to hold back, he heard her walk away.

He rewound the tape and then *Scenes of Childhood* began again. He had managed to swallow the tears, but they remained hard and indissoluble in the centre of his chest, as if he had swallowed a stone. He massaged the place with his fingertips and gave in to the piteous feeling that the pain in the centre of his chest was all that remained in the world of him, of the man he had once believed he would be. He realised how bad he was being to Lilianne and this made him feel worse.

He tried to think of Christian. He imagined him asleep – all vulnerability was represented by that small blond head. And then he despised himself for making Christian into something he was not; a symbol for a role that Ian might fill, a way to show himself that he was necessary.

I do love him, though, he thought. There were the mornings that he spent in the little boy's room, letting Lilianne sleep. Their special times, when they played astronauts and Christian sometimes let Ian hold him while he told him all his five-year-old secrets.

But do I love him for himself or for myself? Ian could not trust himself to answer this, and the pain in the centre of his chest intensified.

It seemed to him then that his only child was the lump of pain inside him, and like a mother animal with only one sickly cub, it became precious to him. He wanted nothing except to be able to explain this to Anna.

\*　　\*　　\*

Anna was waiting for Ian in the small salon of the *pension* when he arrived. She saw that he was surprised; he had always come directly up to her room since the first day he had introduced himself.

She felt awkward as well, her discomfort underscored by a hard imitation Louis XIV chair covered in an unnatural shade of turquoise. The entire room was a stiff façade, a theatre set meant only to be walked through and never lived in. Ian looked at her and remained standing.

'Why didn't you tell me that these messages were from your father?' she demanded.

'Do you want to talk about it here?'

She nodded.

The only other chair in the room had been stationed for the sake of symmetry at the opposite end of a swollen-looking commode. Ian looked at it despairingly and then crouched down in front of her.

'It's very complicated,' he said.

'Then explain it.'

'Anna, I'd hoped that by the time my father spoke to you, you would have had more time to adjust to things on your own.'

'Why?'

'Because then it would be less likely that they could manipulate you.'

She looked at his face – upturned, and open as it always was. She had trusted him so easily.

'You are manipulating me,' she said.

'No,' he said. He was genuinely distraught. 'You don't understand.'

'How can I understand? I only met you a week ago; I've never met your father. All I know is that he is offering me an important opportunity and you have apparently decided in advance that I should not accept it. Who gave you this right?'

'Anna, the Naughton Foundation is a very conservative institution with a very cosy relationship with the current American administration. They are not interested in the same things that you are interested in. They are interested in you for one reason: to them, you are this year's biggest and most photogenic victim of Communism.'

'And to you I am this year's most photogenic anti-nuclear fanatic.'

'You can think whatever you want about me,' he said bitterly, 'but at least I believe what you believe. They do not. They want one thing from you, and that is for you to endorse their policies toward the "evil empire" of the Soviet Union.'

'You don't believe the Soviets are evil?'

'That's not the point. Under the auspices of the Naughton Foundation, you will find it very difficult, if not impossible, to make any other kind of statement.'

She stood up. Ian tottered back for a second, then recovered his balance and stood as well.

'I have to judge this for myself,' she told him.

'I wanted you to have more to go on.'

'I trusted you,' she said.


When George stepped up to her in the lobby, she knew at once who he was. And it was a strange, poignant moment: she suddenly saw Ian's face thirty years hence – dry deepened, changed.

During their discussion, though, she suspended her initial discomfort. George asked her many questions, and he listened to her answers with an understanding that was not graver than Ian's but more experienced. George did not offer his friendship in two hands the way Ian did. Anna knew right away there was something of a business proposal about George's interest in her. In fact, for the first time since she had arrived in the West, she felt that she knew her way around a conversation. The rapport between them was not so different from a Moscow rapport. Cordial, sincere, and ultimately self-interested.

And it was obvious from George's choice of restaurant that he was most concerned that she respond favourably. They ate at Lasserre.

'This must have been what it was like to be invited to dinner at Versailles,' she told him. She tried to see the decor as a tribute to beauty only and not to power; she was determined not to be intimidated.

At first it seemed easy. The walls were covered in yellow damask and the chairs in a golden and rose brocade. Gladioli formed perfect sprays in delicate Ming vases, and the tables were so richly laid with heavy silver, crystal and Limoges that she did not even notice the centrepiece.

'Look,' George said. He directed her attention to an exquisite silver object in the middle of the table – a highly detailed miniature clock tower.

She held her breath.

'Marvellous, isn't it?' George said. 'There's a different one on each table; the owner collects these little *objets* from all over the world. Ours looks like Big Ben.'

She looked at the small silver tower carefully and a hot, uncanny feeling crawled up the back of her neck.

'It's not Big Ben,' she said quietly. 'It's the Spassky Tower. The chimes of that bell are broadcast over Soviet radio twenty-four times a day. It also marks the one gate in the Kremlin walls which is for official use only.'

George immediately signalled to the waiter.

'For personal reasons,' he said, 'my companion finds this *bibelot* offensive. Can you please remove it?'

'*Mais, monsieur, ça c'est le Fabergé, fait pour le Tsar Alexandre III*,' the man answered.

'Perhaps I did not make myself understood,' George told him. His tone of voice was so authoritative that Anna inwardly cringed for the waiter.

But the man only nodded wordlessly, picked up the lovely, hateful little tower and whisked it away. Several moments later a waiter arrived with another intricate silver miniature – this time of a knight slaying a dragon.

'That's better,' George said.

Anna sat very still, not knowing how to respond.

'Anyway,' George told her, 'I would feel dreadful if anything prevented you from giving your full attention to the food. Will you permit me to order for you?'

'Yes, of course.' She knew that he saw her relief.

The first course was *casserolettes de sole*, served in

pastries shaped like soup tureens – and including tiny pastry ladles. When the pastries were opened, the steam smelled of the ocean.

'I have rarely had fresh saltwater fish, except in Leningrad, or the Crimea,' Anna told him. 'Moscow is hundreds of miles inland and only the highest of the elite can gain entrance to the sort of restaurants where it is served.'

George nodded seriously; he questioned her about other deprivations.

The fish was followed by duck, sauced in orange brandy. This was accompanied by a lighthouse carved from a loaf of bread. It had been browned in hot oil, its details branded on with a hot poker. A small candle inside made it glow with a tender yellow light.

Anna laughed.

'I feel like the little Tsarevich who wouldn't eat,' she told George. 'His father decreed that anyone who could find a way to make him eat would be richly rewarded. People came from far and wide with just such creations. But nothing worked until finally an old *babushka* gave him some black bread with onions – it was the only thing he'd never had before.'

George smiled. 'But that's not quite the case here, is it?'

She looked down at her food. 'No,' she said quietly, 'it isn't.'

'Have more wine,' he suggested softly. 'We have a lot to talk about.' He laughed now and she accepted the wine.

'I don't drink very much,' she confided.

'Russians are supposed to be great drinkers,' George said.

'Not all. Some of us are so disgusted by the amount of drunkenness that we do not drink at all.'

'Not unlike the Irish,' he told her.

By the end of the meal she felt more in possession of herself. Perhaps it was George's slightly old-fashioned and utterly familiar gallantry which made her feel like a woman. Not as Ian made her feel a woman – young, pretty, desirable – but a woman of her own age, come into her power.

108

'This is all too much,' she said when the chocolates came. She wanted her tone of voice to indicate that she was not merely being pleasant; now she wanted to know the price.

'No,' George said. 'It only seems that way to you.'

'Your son is a very fine young man,' she said to him suddenly.

George betrayed no surprise whatsoever. 'Yes, well, his mother thinks so,' he answered. Again, the smile that was Ian's with the sting taken out of it.

'And you don't?'

'Of course I do,' he said seriously. 'But if you have talked to him, it can't have escaped you that he and I do not share the same view of the world.'

'This is natural.' Anna shrugged. But she could see that her words, meant only as innocuous everyday wisdom, made George feel old. How did he show this? She wasn't sure, but he made her feel it in the same way, moments ago, he had made her feel so special. Her instinct was to say something feminine, reassuring; she noticed this and remained silent.

'Well, anyway, we didn't come here to discuss our children,' George said with an answering shrug. 'We came here to talk about you. You are what we call a VIP – a very important person. Now that you are in the West, you are going to be faced with a number of choices, and I may be in a position to be of some help to you.'

Anna thought of Ian's words, so similar but, she already knew, so different.

'Mr McDonough,' she said, 'I've just left a country in which every choice one makes – every breath one takes – is fraught with political significance. Now that I am in the West, I do not wish to ally myself politically with any individual or institution. I wish only to avail myself of the political freedom that I have always heard about but never known.'

George smiled. 'A woman after my own heart.'

She looked down.

'That's an Irish expression,' he told her. 'It means simply

that I couldn't agree with you more. But perhaps you don't fully understand what the fellowship means.

'To begin with, we can help you take care of the immediate details – a place to live, a publisher to advance you some money on the English translation of your book.

'We can also help you get back to work in your own field, introduce you to the same calibre of professionals that you worked with in the Soviet Union. Some of our fellows are among the top scientists in the United States.'

He paused and looked at her as if to ask if she were following what he said.

'Go on,' she told him, and leaned forward to listen.


'I had dinner with your father last night,' Anna told Ian at breakfast. She had been afraid that he might not come this morning; she was not sure he should.

But the moment he had sat down next to her, handing her the morning papers as he had each day from the first, the distrust of the previous day seemed wrong and intrusive. Though she had known him for such a short time, it was now natural that he should be the first person she spoke to every morning. She felt weirdly at home reading the papers next to him.

Ian stopped reading but didn't look at her. 'He's a very charming man, isn't he?'

'That's just what he said about you.'

Now he looked at her. 'It is?'

She nodded.

'So they think you're the greatest thing since Svetlana.'

There was a breeze that morning, the heat had broken during the night. The air was fresh, and in her sleeveless blouse Anna felt cold for the first time since she had come to Paris.

'I am satisfied that it is an independent organisation,' she said. But she knew there was a slight defensive tone in her voice.

'Bullshit. That's how they get their hooks in you,' he told her.

'I am not as naïve as you imagine; I know something about how these things work.'

Ian shook his head. 'You still don't understand.'

'I understand more than you think.' She held his eyes when she said this but she saw that she didn't convince him. And then, suddenly, her words no longer referred to the Foundation's offer, but to what was between them.

'Don't do it, Anna,' he said very quietly. 'You don't need them; they need you. Your book is worth a lot of money, you'll be able to get along perfectly well without a grant. And other people will help you, people who believe in what you believe.'

She saw the intensity in his eyes: *I believe in you*, he was saying, *I will help you*. The only thing she wanted at that moment was to reach out and take him in her arms.

But the moment passed and she kept her hands in her lap.

'It's not just money, Ian,' she said. 'The Naughton Foundation is in a position to introduce me to the kind of people who can really make a difference – the scientists, the politicians. How can I turn away from that? How could I hope to reach such people on my own, an immigrant?'

Ian held his hand up to his forehead as if he were in pain. After a few seconds, he reached towards her but stopped in mid-air in a gesture of explanation.

'The Foundation is, of course, strictly speaking, independent. You are not wrong about that. And they can certainly make some things very easy for you.'

She waited.

'But they will make other things impossible.'

She had thought it over long and hard. 'What things?' she prompted him. 'How can they make anything impossible?'

'It's so hard to explain. Money and contacts make everything possible in America; once you've been given them it is very hard to do without them,' he said. His voice was low. Perhaps he had already conceded his arguments.

'It's not easy to criticise people who invite you to dinner, Anna, and should you make the mistake of thinking that the people in power in America are more interested in

111

allowing you to speak your mind about disarmament than the same people in Russia, they'll soon show you the error of your ways.'

She straightened in her chair. She was angry.

'Ian,' she said, 'do you think that in a few months they can change what it has taken a lifetime to make me?

'But think of what we are really talking about – there is so little time. I know that America cannot be that different from Russia or the rest of the world: it is the people in power who at this moment hold our lives – all life – in their hands. But at least in America there is a chance that by reaching enough people things can change.'

I am a fool, she thought. Why do I sit here arguing when I have already decided?

He leaned forward and took her hands in his. She was not prepared for this.

'Anna,' he said gently, 'you say that the powerful in America are not so different from those in Russia. That is truer than I think you know.'

'I am not a child,' she said, feeling suddenly small and absurd.

'Yes, I know,' Ian said. His eyes were so full of emotion; he could not have known how he looked, she thought.

'You don't know me very well,' she whispered.

He shook his head sadly, agreeing with her.

'There is nothing I can say to you, is there?' he said.

'No.'

He held her hands a moment longer, then let go.

'I have to do this,' she told him as she felt her hands grow cold. He stood up to leave but did not walk away.

'I think I love you, Anna.'

She looked away.

'It's all right,' he said. 'I'm sorry; I'll go.'

On the way home, Ian stopped in the elegant glass-and-steel florist where, only a few days before, he had paid an extravagant sum for a bunch of wildflowers for Anna. This time he bought roses, the obligatory crimson roses, for

Lilianne. This is stupid, he thought, but he bought them anyway.

At home, Lilianne was surprised to see him so early. She looked the worst he had ever seen her. Her hair was dirty, she was wearing the same clothes she'd worn the day before.

'I thought you weren't coming for dinner,' she said. It was the first time he had ever seen her look humiliated, and for a second he wondered whether she would look as embarrassed if he'd caught her with a lover as she looked when caught with dirty hair.

'Well, here I am.' What next? he thought. She looked so awful, he reached out and stroked her cheek.

'I'm sorry,' he told her. 'I've been a bastard.'

She looked at him and he saw how much she wanted to believe him.

'Would you like dinner?' Lilianne asked him.

If only life were normal, he wished. If only hot food and a glass of whisky would fix it.

'Sure,' he said. 'Would you like to go out?'

She shook her head. He hadn't seen her cry very often in the last several years, but she looked ready.

'Let me make something.'

'Okay.' He forced himself to smile. He remembered the flowers. 'These are for you,' he said softly.

She held them without unwrapping them.

'I'm finally losing you, Ninon,' she told him.

Finally? he thought. But he said, 'No, you're not.'

'You can't lie to me.'

It was true, he knew. She was the expert in lies, she would find him out because she knew all the lines.

'It doesn't matter, Lili. It's going to be all right now.'

She watched his eyes with a mixture of worry and acceptance. He remembered when her acceptance had made him feel like a man. Now he felt like an animal.

'Where's Christian?' he asked her. He wanted to change the course of the conversation, as if it were a car on a highway which could turn off in a new direction and end up at a new destination.

113

But it was not to be.

'I sent him to sleep with the Pleurys,' she said. 'I wanted to be alone with you when you came home.'

'He should sleep at home,' he found himself saying.

'So should you.'

'I've been sleeping at home,' he shot back. Was it going to work? There was so much anger.

'But not with me.' Her voice was so quiet that all the words he might have thrown at her slipped through his fingers like water.

She started to shake. Her tears always began this way. He took her in his arms.

Everything is so wrong, he thought.

'Everything's going to be all right,' he told her. 'Don't worry.'

'Nothing is right,' she said. Her voice seemed lost in his sweater. He felt her breath on his chest through the cloth. 'Why does it always have to be this way?'

'Shh, shh,' he said. 'It doesn't have to be this way.'

But she just cried softly.

'Lili.' He stroked her and held her close as he spoke. 'Lili, it's not too late. We can work things out.'

She raised her head and looked at him. He had never seen all of her feelings present as they were at this one moment. He had stopped looking very deeply into her feelings, it had been too painful. But the price was that he had also stopped looking into his own.

'Lili,' he said seriously. 'Let's stop this. Let's just make things different.'

She listened to him, he thought, as he had once or twice listened to a gifted teacher or politician. He was very nearly inspiring, he felt it himself.

'Look, Christian needs a real home. We need to stop kidding ourselves.'

She nodded and the tears continued silently.

'Let's give Christian the home he needs.' Suddenly he was begging her. What had happened to his splendid control?

'It's you who need a home,' she told him.

His pride was down now, and he breathed.

'Then give me a home, Lilianne.' He asked her this simply with all the strength he had left.

'I don't know if I can,' she said.

It was the truth. He recognised it. And for the first time in a long time, he really loved her.

*My home, my home. Now I know what mourning really means. It's not the loved one that you lose. But the whole life that went with love.*

# Two

Anna's ticket was first-class. The seat next to her was empty, but from time to time the stewardesses sat down to chat. They were friendly, blonde, their teeth were the most perfect Anna had ever seen – every tooth on every one of them. America, she thought. In Russia, orthodontics was a highly esoteric practice, known only to the children of generals and Politburo members. For the rest of Russian mankind, the evidence of dentistry was either gaping holes or ugly and serviceable lumps of steel – steel fillings, steel caps, steel bridges, steel teeth.

She listened attentively to the stewardesses, without really hearing a word they were saying, but trying to imagine herself an American. They were so relaxed, she envied them deeply. They wore so many colours of eye shadow it was as if they might become any one of a number of different women at any moment.

'So what's Moscow like?' asked a young woman whose fuchsia-dusted lids shaded to an iridescent green at the corners. Her eyes had an inhuman beauty like a lizard's.

It's haunted, thought Anna. But she saw the lovely yellow houses and churches which somehow dominated the grey stone and grey shadow of the centre of Soviet power. The golden city, it was called; she had been a child there.

'The Kremlin is very beautiful,' she said, feeling ridiculous.

The young woman looked at her, those chameleon lids motionless.

'One always thinks of the Kremlin as those old men,' she said.

'The Kremlin is an ancient citadel,' Anna told her, as if reciting from a guidebook. 'Painted every colour of the rainbow.'

119

The stewardess listened politely and remained long enough for Anna to exhaust a pleasant supply of architectural and historical data on the Kremlin. This stewardess was replaced by others. They were all intensely interested in what Anna had to say; they were all young and beautiful. Anna could not bring herself to tell them very much that was bad.

After about five hours, she began to feel that she was inside out.

What's important? she asked herself. But because she was at that moment so conscious of being Russian, of being forty-three, of having steel fillings – it seemed like a rationalisation, and made her more suspicious of her own inferiority.

It was the second aeroplane she had ever been in; all she had to compare it with was the Aeroflot jet she had left Moscow on. Russian air travel could be quite sumptuous – for officials who were able to commandeer and even outfit private military jets. But the way Anna had flown – on a grimy and crowded Soviet civilian plane, managed by rude and harassed flight attendants whose jobs were awarded only on the basis of political reliability – there was no comparison.

She was not, she knew, one of those stalwart souls who, having grown used to hardship, can never accustom themselves to comfort, much less luxury. Hardship had accustomed her to the luxuries of her own imagination, so flying first-class on a jumbo jet bound for New York did not rattle her. There was something deep and selfish – perhaps feminine – in her that believed that she deserved it. And she enjoyed it.

Why was it that mere luxury and comfort felt startlingly similar to love and security? Perhaps this something inside her was a spoiled little child, born in another century, or in another country. A girl who might grow up to experience nothing but warmth and attention, new upholstery and paid bills.

There was a way in which material security became so intertwined with emotional security that they could not be separated. She understood that the relentless materialism of the country she had grown up in was related to deep needs for stability and security that revolution, civil war and world war had exacerbated ruthlessly.

How many times had she longed – longed as one longs for either health or death when one has been very sick – for a life that didn't have so many sacrifices, so many second choices, so many disappointments and so few compensations? In that, she was no different from most women she saw around her. Some days it was no more than a sharp resentment that she had to buy sausage instead of beef, a pair of shoes that were her size but not the ones she wanted or a hat of rabbit fur instead of fox. Once upon a time, Pavel could have made her feel stupid for such a petty despair – she had a hat, after all.

But there were other days when the sacrifice meant that she could not be home with Seriozha when he was two and three and four. The full and equal employment of women mandated by the 'progressive' Soviet government (in actuality the severe shortage of technical workers) left her no choice. And Seriozha would look at her with that perfect soft face, the eyes that thrilled her with some primitive love because they were *her* eyes, as if to say: Mama, I shall never be two or three or four again.

It also meant that Seriozha was an only child. For her, no daughter. For Seriozha, no bluff, robust boy who would have been a foil. No other baby; this hurt her more than she would have thought possible. It was a hurt that began almost as soon as Seriozha was walking and it had never left her.

For a wild moment – perhaps it was that incredible in-flight sensation of being a scrap of metal nothing in the air – she told herself it was not too late. She could be a mother again. She was, after all, on her way to a new life, a new country; why not a new love and new child?

This sensation of possibility lasted perhaps four minutes. She felt her whole body becoming warmer until she imagined that she glowed like an icon and like an icon could bless those who looked at her and recognised what happiness is.

Then it was gone. She could start a new life, but she herself would still be the same Anna; the Anna that too much had happened to.

'Caviar, ma'am?' The stewardess whose white plastic name plate labelled her 'Joanne' leaned over Anna like a nurse over a patient. Her look of solicitude was so sincere that for a moment Anna searched for the words to tell her what she had been thinking.

'We're only two hours out of New York now,' the stewardess told her. 'We'll have dinner in about ten minutes and by the time you finish your coffee the time will have passed.'

It was a sweet thought, Anna knew, and she accepted the hors d'oeuvre. The time would pass, she would be full of food and wine, she might even fall asleep.

But then that time would never come again and the feeling of emptiness would return.

At Kennedy Airport, Sarah Davidoff took the flyers out of her briefcase. The briefcase was her father's – an old leather portfolio, too expensive, but dog-eared in an endearing way. The flyers were black, white and blue brochures printed overnight at the expense of the organisation she belonged to and had helped to found, One Earth. Below a quote from Einstein was a small and very inspiring photo of Anna Nikolayevna Khameneva. The photo was the best one by far of all those that had appeared since Anna's arrival in the West, and it had run everywhere, yet it had the look of a funeral portrait.

All around her she could see the blue band of the flyer, people read them and waved them; hundreds of tiny images of Anna moved in the hot, colourful crowd like the patterned pieces of a kaleidoscope. She believed that Anna would not really look like that picture. She also believed that she would intuitively know Anna when she saw her. Sarah had read the book – twice, once as a smuggled manuscript and again in the small Russian-language edition put out by the émigré press – and she had an indelible image of the heroine of the story.

From where she was standing, behind a glass partition that marked the entry to the flight gates, she could see people begin to flow thickly through the concourse towards her. These were the first-class passengers with their plastic shopping bags from the Orly duty-free shop, their small, simple luggage – a suit bag, a briefcase. They could afford to be in Paris for a short time. She did not look at them carefully, expecting to spot Anna within the package-laden throng of economy-class vacationers.

But suddenly voices were raised around her, and she was pushed forward. There was Anna – for a second close enough to touch – greeted by a smart young man in a seersucker suit and four or five reporters holding out their microphones. Then cameramen with portable video cameras on their shoulders moved in, connected by cables to the sound men, who carried microphones long enough to reach into a crowd and heavy enough to use as billy clubs. They were so aggressive and rude that people did not bother to argue with them, and instinctively got out of their way. But when the cameramen had pushed up as close as they could to Anna, there was a spontaneous reduction in the jostling and loudness; enough, in comparison with their first raucousness, to make it seem as though in the centre of that fortress of big men and big equipment, there was a stillness.

These types have no trouble sticking their lenses into the faces of people dying in hospital beds, Sarah told herself. She strained to see what they saw, but she saw only the looming cameras as they backed away just enough to signal a kind of animal respect.

A crowd *is* an animal, she thought. The respect of the cameras communicated itself distinctly. Suddenly the noise level became nearly polite, more like a big party. There was no more yelling of any kind. Sarah felt a restraint comparable to a guest at a wedding. She remained where she was; in fact, she receded into herself almost as if to make more room for Anna.

For Anna was indeed the woman in the photograph; slender, nearly haggard, but in a way that spoke of exhaustion rather than weakness of any kind. She had instead that kind of stark fragility that Sarah imagined women used once upon a time to command the centre of attention. Sarah reacted to it involuntarily, as did, she knew by the quiet, many of the others standing there expectantly. In a way, she resented it. She wanted Anna to be tougher; she wanted her to be stronger than she herself was.

Now Anna looked down and took a piece of paper out of her purse. Sarah could see a white handkerchief and a glint of gilt that was probably a lipstick. Then Anna raised her hand and pushed the hair off her face with a slow, deliberate gesture; a man might have faced the crowd and smiled directly at them as he waited for their eyes, every last one of them, to focus only on him.

'What is important,' Anna began.

'Louder!' shouted a man next to Sarah. As he strained to raise his head above the people in front of him, his shirt rose above his jeans and his stomach showed.

Anna smiled apologetically. Suddenly in Sarah's mind the two images were excruciatingly fused; this man's doughy, white skin and Anna's painstaking effort to raise her voice. Anna's softness was so disconcerting Sarah held her breath. Oh please don't let me down, she thought.

'What is important?' Anna repeated. This time it was obvious that it was a question. But was that because she was asking the crowd or because she lacked command of what she meant to say?

Now Anna smiled again, but this time a sharp, startling smile, caused by happiness, even pleasure. Sarah was taken aback.

'Can you imagine,' Anna asked, her voice still soft but quite clear, 'how I feel to arrive in America?'

She waited, watching the eyes of the people near her as if it were a personal conversation.

'I feel almost as if I were in love.'

There was laughter, but it was not derisive.

'My life is beginning,' she went on. 'Here and now. A

124

life that I never really let myself dream of is suddenly to become possible for me.'

The good old God bless America, Sarah thought, and took in the satisfied expressions of most of the crowd.

As Sarah expected, Anna next said several things about her husband, going on to talk about the life she had left behind. But she did not talk about this life as had many other émigré dissidents, describing persecution and constant fear. She spoke of these things, but she did not linger on them. What she spent most of her few minutes saying sounded almost like a description of the ordinary things Sarah and everyone else had done that day before coming to the airport.

What is this? thought Sarah, again looking around at the faces of the other listeners. Their expressions were intense, but that intensity seemed to come less from what Anna said than from uncertainty as to how to take it.

There was now an odd feeling in the air. The Khamenevs had been the heroes of many dedicated groups who kept their plight in the eyes of the public. Some of these people had just sweated through rush-hour traffic to meet Anna's plane. They expected something different from her, but what it was, no one was sure. The only thing that was certain was that they expected so much they weren't going to let her disappoint them.

Sarah was not sure that what she felt was disappointment. She had stayed up all night printing an airtight brief against nuclear armament so that she might support someone who would step forward hard and irrevocably in favour of her cause, and here she was listening to a woman speak effusively about nothing but her own life. Yet she strained to hear every word Anna said.

'I know why you are here,' Anna told them, again too softly. But her voice picked up before anyone could interrupt her. 'We are all here because we are in love, and because when you feel love, life – every minute of it – is precious.'

Oh God, Sarah thought, and covered her eyes with her hand.

'To a lover, to a mother or a father – to anyone who truly loves – the question "What is important?" has only one answer.

'To be alive and know that the one you love exists also in the world. At first you might think that you want more than this – that it is important, for example, to have your loved one near you. But ask any mother who has a son in the army; all she wants is that wherever he is, he is alive and well. She asks no more for herself.

'What we ask is just this simple. What makes us ask is nothing more or less than love. Love in its most basic and unchanging form. Love that has no other purpose than merely to exist.

'Nature is like a family,' she told them, 'many separate elements which work together to support life in such a way that the whole is always more than the sum of its parts. Scientists call this synergy. We now know that this synergy can also be turned against us – thermo-nuclear explosions can affect so many separate aspects of the biosphere that nature will no longer be able to support human life, but in fact will be hostile to it.

'I know why you have come here today; we love and our purpose is the same.'

Some people in the crowd began to clap. Half the cameramen instantly turned their backs on Anna and began to photograph the spectators. This sudden reversion to the business of the news vaguely disturbed Sarah. She could not bring herself to applaud – somehow the atmosphere, until that moment, had been too intimate.

She could not hear the questions that the reporters asked Anna as she was hastened out of the airport; she could not get anywhere near her. She noticed that it was a limousine that took off in the flock of cabs, and made a mental note to find out who had sent it.

It works, Sarah thought. She was surprised and she felt a certain cynical detachment – such emotional rhetoric was all the political rage right now. But there was about Anna an unprotectedness, even a tenderness, that was unnerving.

126

'A Gandhi-like presence . . .' she heard a reporter whisper into a small tape.

'Oh Christ,' Sarah said, a little too loudly.

The reporter heard her and looked up. He was not at all embarrassed; in fact, he acknowledged her comment with a smile that embarrassed Sarah and she walked quickly away.

'A Christ-like figure,' she heard him add as she moved out of earshot.

George had been invited to view the festivities in the White House press office. Despite the fact that he and Arthur went back a long time, if he wanted to see Arthur these days he had to catch him in orbit, as it were, and the orbit was now exclusively centred on 1600 Pennsylvania Avenue.

'Fucking Christ,' Luke Keller, the President's press secretary, said as he clicked off the television. 'How can we compete with a woman in love?'

'The trouble with you people is that you take television too seriously,' Arthur Orr told him.

The press secretary bristled. The room was packed with staff and interns who gathered there at six to watch the news. It was generally one of the more relaxed parts of the day; for the most part, their work was done. Now they got to see what the press did to them. It was also their one chance to talk back – and they were known to yell at the tube with complete abandon.

'Fucking right we do, and that's why we're here. A hundred million Americans spend eight hours a day in front of the fucking thing.'

Orr put his coffee cup down on the bare mahogany of Keller's desk. The desk was new, as were the chairs, the carpeting, nearly everything since the Republican administration had taken office. George had to restrain an urge to put a piece of paper under Orr's cup.

'The level of the English language in the White House staff is not what it once was,' Orr said drily. 'And the other trouble with you is that you treat the media with a siege mentality. You're always on the defensive. You are so busy trying to figure out how to keep them from screwing you that you screw yourself.'

George watched Keller, who tried not to let his irritation show. He wondered how Keller had ever managed to rise to the top of a profession in which the essence of success was the ability to dissemble one's feelings.

'You know the President has enough problems with his enemies on this issue,' Keller said to Orr. 'Now if his friends start coming into this office and telling us how to do our jobs, he's going to have real trouble.'

Orr did not seem to react. George had noticed it before; this capacity to deflect insults like mere raindrops on a windshield. It was a quality not of politicians, he had learned, but of their advisers. And in Orr it was coupled with a slightly nauseating, high-handed graciousness that came from simply being listened to by the President.

'Now, Lucky,' Orr said to Keller, using his nickname in such a way as to make the secretary feel he was really getting his nose rubbed in it, 'of course I haven't come down here to try and teach you people your jobs. I'm just suggesting that there are a number of ways to handle this thing. It might be that Mrs Khameneva, once she has a chance to see how life is here, is going to mellow a great deal on the issue of armament. In that case one would have every reason to keep the doors open for her. She may come around – these defectors often do once they realise they don't have to wait in line for shoes. She is in a position to be very useful to us, if she is handled properly.'

'What do you mean, keep the doors open? You better tell me exactly what you mean,' Keller said. George looked away politely.

'All I'm saying is that the day may come when this woman is anti-Soviet rather than anti-nuclear. You might have a female Solzhenitsyn on your hands.'

'Look,' Orr said. 'You're a smart man; you don't need me to go into detail about these things. I imagine you could teach me a great deal.' He smiled and George watched Keller's facial muscles tighten.

'I don't mean to step on any toes,' Orr continued kindly. 'The President feels real compassion for Mrs Khameneva and for all the others like her. America has always been a sanctuary for such people and we feel that this administration is naturally part of a great American tradition in welcoming her.'

'Are you speaking for him?' Keller asked tersely.

'Would you like to call him? I can appreciate your concern.'

Keller slumped a little. The score was too low and there were too few minutes left of play.

'No. We'll get a statement together right now. Are you going to be around? Where can I reach you?'

Orr looked at his watch, a heavy gold apparatus designed for sailboat racing. There were so many little dials on it that George had more than once wondered how Arthur ever knew what time it was.

'I'll call you in half an hour – can you manage?'

Luke Keller nodded and shrugged at the same time. There was a very restrained sigh from one of the young women on the staff; the first sound any of them had dared make since Orr had come in to watch the news.

It was not the first time that the thought occurred to George that the real game was fought in the locker room of the winning team.

The candlelight was very romantic, but made it nearly impossible for Seriozha to follow his own words on the page. A storm had knocked out the electricity in Peredelkino. Now throughout the larches he caught the flickering gleam of candles and for a moment felt a certain love for all the other people living in those wooden houses. The darkness seemed to take everyone back into time, back into an innocence and vulnerability; he imagined women singing infants to sleep, men raising glasses of wine, little boys holding their fingers close to the flames so that the light burned through their skin with a weird orange glow.

Katinka had fallen asleep, or was merely pretending. Her arm was thrown back over her eyes and her breasts were bare. He got up softly and touched her nipple; it was warm with the startling warmth of sleep – obviously she had just pushed back the blanket in her dream.

He took her nipple gently between his lips, her warmth came into his mouth, and he began to suck like a child. She moaned a little in her sleep and he stopped. He did not want to wake her.

He wanted to drink in her dream, to swallow it at her breast. He felt something like the hunger that the baby of an undernourished woman feels; it was not enough to make love to her, he needed the essential nutrients of her illusions for himself.

'Seriozhka,' he heard her whisper.

'I'm here,' he reassured her.

'Did you write a poem?' She asked him this often, with the seriousness of a salesman's wife.

He laughed. 'Yes, I did. I think I did. I can't read it in this light.'

'What is it about?'

She asked the same questions, with the same lack of self-consciousness, nearly every day. The only thing that made him feel more foolish than her questions was his repeated attempt to answer them honestly.

'It's about the parts of you that are silk and the parts of you that are velvet.' As he spoke, he ran the flat of his hand across her stomach and felt her tremble involuntarily. He loved this; the momentary surge of power that it gave him never left him. It was like the first – the only – time he had ever held a gun, the gun of his childhood friend Vanya, who was in the army.

But then she lay very still.

'You are so stupid.' Her voice was quiet, but flat, not a whisper. 'You say you love your freedom so much but you are not willing to sacrifice anything for it.'

He took his hands back and let them die in his lap. The life that her skin had given to his fingers ebbed slowly; he didn't speak as he felt his hands growing cold. He didn't speak until he couldn't feel his hands at all.

'I can't help it,' he said.

'Nonsense.' Now her voice was bitter. 'You'll help it when the only job they'll give you is in a factory.'

He wondered about this. It was true that if he went on writing love poems, ignoring the necessity of establishing himself as a writer of 'political responsibility', then nothing that he wrote would ever see the light of day. And more importantly, when he finished his studies he would not have the choice of going on as a writer. They would merely put him wherever they wanted him. That was if they even let him finish.

But nothing seemed to matter. He tried to picture himself on an assembly line, perhaps fastening a bolt to whatever bolts were fastened to – actually he had no idea. The very vacuity of it seemed preferable to the fulsome 'challenge' of writing even one political poem.

Katinka looked at him with genuine pain. He knew that she loved him. She would work for him, rather than see him give up writing. She believed in his talent perhaps more than he did. It held a different, more public place in her life than in his.

'Let me read it to you,' he offered soothingly.

She pushed her lips together, determined not to cry.

'I don't want to hear it,' she said.


The pleasant young man in the seersucker suit, an administrative assistant from George's office, hardly spoke to Anna for the length of the ride from the airport to the McDonoughs' home in Greenwich. He proudly offered her vodka – Russian, Stolichnaya – and was offended when she could not hide her distaste.

Then, in an effort to cover his malaise, he switched on the small colour television that opened like a glaucous eye out of the seat behind the driver.

It was 6:10. Anna was on every channel.

'Fantastic!' said the young man.

Anna suddenly felt as hot and ashamed as when one of Pavel Leonidovich's superiors had once told her she was beautiful.

'An impressive debut,' commented a very handsome

reporter into his mike. He was facing the camera, and though his words seemed to describe the first performance of a young pianist, his smile was almost quivering, as though he had witnessed a birth. Anna couldn't take her eyes off him.

It was all coming back. The way they had treated her in the last few weeks before Pasha had died. Not the authorities – they were blindly, perfectly consistent. Their cruelty was to be expected and was never a surprise. Having seen her father hounded under Stalin, she was not taken aback to be served with warrants in hospital waiting rooms or hauled away from wedding parties. But the press, the few foreign reporters who were so kind and who guarded her friendship so bravely – now she began to suspect what she had truly meant to them.

'You must be delighted,' the young man said to her. 'You couldn't have gotten better coverage if you paid for it.' He himself was so genuinely happy that Anna could not respond.

'If people see through to the purpose,' she equivocated politely, 'then I suppose it is good.'

'Oh yes,' he said. 'I'm sure they will. You'll probably get picked up at eleven o'clock, too.'

Anna guessed that he was referring to the next edition of television news, and realised that he did not concern himself in the least with what she was really talking about. He was too young to be so insincere, she thought, and she sat quietly for the rest of the trip while he flipped through the channels.

The car exited the highway at the Byram section of Greenwich, Connecticut, and Anna noticed that the distance between the houses grew larger and larger. The smell of salt water hung in the humid September air.

The lawns were large enough to be taken for meadows, the trees old enough to cover the lanes with leafy vaulting, the houses voluminous enough to have sheltered in decadent privacy the enormous nineteenth-century households of Tolstoy's novels.

When the car finally turned down the gravel drive of a

huge old Victorian, Anna was lost in the vast and aristocratic world of *War and Peace*. A wide porch wrapped the McDonough house; there were wooden rocking chairs and barrels of pink hydrangea. At first glance, Anna imagined that the two young women who walked across the grass in antique white dresses were Natasha and Sonya, but when she got out of the car, they introduced themselves: Mary Ellen McDonough and her friend Karen Cleary.

'What beautiful dresses,' she told them. 'Did they belong to your grandmothers?'

Mary Ellen blushed a little. 'No, we bought them.'

The blood that rushed into Mary Ellen's face lit up her summer tan with a fresh pink light like a paper lantern hung in a garden at dusk. It was the same quick, revelatory colour that had struck Anna in Ian. Now she wondered how much of Ian's self-conscious intensity might spring from the same source – because he was not at ease with privilege.

At that moment the huge, polished oak front door of the house opened and Mrs McDonough came out. Anna saw at once that this woman was the mother of this girl, as she had seen that George was the father of Ian. Yet it affected her in an entirely different way. It gave her pleasure to see the incipient woman in the girl; she saw the way that the experience of the woman would bring into relief the round, benign beauty of the girl. But there was something else – the mother had been beautiful as a younger woman; now that beauty had been redrawn by pain and become insistent instead of merely inviting.

'I'm so pleased to meet you,' Mrs McDonough told Anna, taking her hand. 'And I want you to know we're delighted to have you. I told George I thought it was very important for you to spend a little time with an American family; I do think so, but selfishly, I wanted very much to meet you.'

'Thank you,' Anna said, and laughed. 'I am very happy to be with you.'

As she spoke, Anna noticed that Mrs McDonough listened to her very carefully, her head tilted slightly forward, her eyes serious. For a second, Anna felt foolish; why hadn't she said something more articulate, more grateful? It was a sensation she was beginning to have often now, for suddenly people were listening to her – listening with frightening, absurd intensity. This attention created a kind of hollow echo in Anna's mind, in which she was painfully aware of the smallness and paltriness of her own words.

'Come in, come in,' Kate McDonough now told her, reaching down and picking up Anna's flight bag herself. Mary Ellen and Karen, powerful and long-legged despite their fragile dresses, carried in all the luggage from the car. The young man in the seersucker suit spent the entire time making telephone calls from the back of the car.

'You can come in,' Mrs McDonough kidded him. 'We'll let you use the phone in the kitchen.' The two girls giggled and Kate turned to Anna. 'I hope you don't mind we're just women here; George won't be home until next week.' Her eyes seemed to want to explain more, but she only smiled.

Anna smiled, too. The thought that it would be just the three of them was immensely relieving.

'Tea?' Kate McDonough asked when they were seated in the kitchen. The kitchen was everything that Anna had ever dreamt about America: it was larger than the first laboratory she had worked in, cleaner and better equipped. The walls shone with painted tile, overhead lighting had been arranged to illuminate each individual workspace, there were so many cabinets and so many electrical appliances Anna had never seen before that she wondered if in fact the kitchen were also used as some sort of business.

'Mom,' said Mary Ellen with a sudden insight into Anna's staring, 'let's make tea in the microwave.'

'That's ridiculous,' her mother said.

But Mary Ellen went ahead and took four teacups out of a cabinet and pressed each against a lever in the refrigerator door.

'Cold water,' she explained to Anna.

Then she put a tea bag in each cup and placed them inside a dark glass cabinet, and pressed a button.

In exactly thirty seconds a bell rang and Mary Ellen removed four steaming cups of tea.

'In spite of all the miracles of modern science,' Kate told Mary Ellen, 'in this house, you still cannot get away without saucers and napkins. Use cloth napkins, please.'

Mary Ellen grimaced slightly, but arranged a tray in the way her mother directed.

'What's the point of saving time making tea,' Mary Ellen complained, 'if you're going to waste time with needless extras like saucers?' She glared at her mother, but Anna saw right away it was a friendly, mocking expression and that the present conversation was part of a comfortable mother/daughter ritual. Suddenly she was struck by a feeling of acute alienation, and she felt the blood drain from her head.

'Sit down,' Kate told Anna. She did.

'Here.' Kate put the teacup directly in her hand as if she were an invalid and Anna held the hot cup up to her forehead. The heat bit into her skin and shocked her to attention; then the warmth spread itself over her forehead and relaxed her. She had not known until that moment that her head was aching so hard that she had been keeping her jaw clenched; she smiled and felt exhausted.

'Are you okay?' Mary Ellen asked her. Suddenly the girl's face was very close to her own and Anna realised that everyone had seemed to be behind glass. She could not say for how long this had been; it was only now that she was struck by the fact that Mary Ellen's face was just there and she could sense the heat of her sunburn.

'You remind me of my son,' she said finally. 'I never win an argument with him. He is always so reasonable and logical, there is nothing I can say.'

'Children do seem to have a terrible logic of their own,' Kate said, and laughed. 'It's based on a principle of getting their own way in as short a time as possible.'

Anna shook her head. 'No,' she said. 'It is because they see through conventions and hypocrisies that we are used to. It's a kind of genius, really, to see things always as if it were the first time. My husband was like that, too – it is what made him brilliant at his work.

'My husband's birthday was the tenth of September,' Anna told them helplessly. It was now the thirteenth. 'It is the second birthday we have had without him.'

We? she thought. It tasted like a lie on her tongue.

'That's very hard,' Kate said. Her voice was low.

'We always had wonderful parties. So many people loved him, you understand. We would still be in the country then, it was still warm, still light in the evening. The house would be overflowing by three o'clock in the afternoon. Everyone brought food. Tatiana Alexandrova – she was one of his oldest friends – brought him a carrot cake. He hadn't been able to eat anything like that for months but he did that night. Everything made him happy.

'Tatiana Alexandrova is one of the most highly placed women in Soviet science,' she told them. 'She shared a Lenin Prize in medicine – you have heard of her?'

They hadn't but they were impressed.

'She cooked for him,' Anna went on. 'She loved to! He affected people like that. On this last birthday, three violinists from the Bolshoi orchestra came and played for him. It was very brave of them to do it – their careers could have been taken away from them in the blink of an eye, and they knew this. Do you know what it means to give up such work? To musicians, their instruments are a part of their bodies; and yet they came. They did it for him, they took that risk, because he had done it for them. He had given up his work. They knew what it meant for him to be alone, with his work only inside his head.

'He bore it so beautifully.' She turned to Kate now, and felt tears come painlessly, almost joyfully, cathartic like laughter. 'You know what it means to love such a man?'

Anna saw the sorrow in Kate's eyes and knew that it had nothing to do with being Russian or American but only with being a woman.

'I don't think so,' Kate said quietly. 'But it doesn't matter.'

'You're right,' Anna agreed. 'When you love, it is all the same.'

'Why don't you come upstairs,' Kate said gently. 'We're going to put you in my son's room.'

Ian's room was white. The curtains blew back into the room on the evening breeze, which smelled of fresh-cut grass and the tide coming in. Mother and daughter had kissed her good night gently, as though she were some very old aunt come home to die; Kate had even come back with some roses from the garden for her night table.

But Anna was conscious that apart from the roses and the few things that she had brought with her, the room very much belonged to someone else. The shelves were filled with strange books, there were school photographs on the walls, a map of pre-World War I Europe, a diploma, a graduation card. The drawers of the dresser had been emptied, but only one drawer of the desk – the others were stuffed with spiral-bound notebooks and old letters. In the closet, some tweed jackets had been pushed to one side and a lone blue tie hung on the hook.

She went over to the bookcase and read all the titles. On the lowest shelf there were some large, worn books with broken spines. These she pulled out; they were Frank Baum's series *The Wizard of Oz*. The first book fell open to a picture of a house spinning through the sky, casting a house-shaped shadow on corn fields below. She took this book to bed with her, but did not read it. She studied the pictures and the large, childish handwriting on the book plate: 'Should this book wander off and roam, please pick it up and send it home. Ian George McDonough.'

She held the open book on her lap for a long time, but her image was not of Ian as a child. It was of herself.

Finally she turned out the light, and stared out of the open window. The nearest house was too far to see, but every so often she heard a burst of laughter and loud talk. Occasionally the wind was also scented with the odour of food being cooked over a wood fire. This odour was reminiscent of childhood feasts in the country with her mother and father and grandparents, and still other feasts at which Pasha had presided. It made her ravenous. She sat very still and thought of the people eating this food the way, she imagined, a wolf might. Though it was not their meat she craved, but their happiness.

It was only a little after sunrise when she heard Mary Ellen's voice outside the door. Anna felt, not that she was waking up, but that she was being called from far away.

'Anna?' Mary Ellen asked in a whisper.

'Come in,' Anna said.

'There are people here to see you,' Mary Ellen said through the door.

Anna got up and pulled her robe around her. The memory of the *gebisti* who came at dawn to the hotel in Paris made her move like a prisoner called from his cell – she looked around quickly, involuntarily, to see if there was some last thing she wished to take with her.

When she opened the door, Kate McDonough had joined her daughter. They both stared at Anna fearfully.

In the driveway was a car with two men sitting in it. They were young men, dressed rather sloppily, as far as Anna could see; she knew at once who they were.

She opened the door and went out onto the lawn in her bare feet. The grass was wet and cold – in her anger it was electrifying.

'Please go away,' she said.

The man on the left jumped out of the car with a camera.

'We will go away, if you just answer a few questions,' he said.

'Please,' she repeated.

'Come on,' the man said. 'You've got to understand our positions, too. People want to know about you.'

'I said it all at the airport yesterday,' she said.

'What are your plans?' he asked.

'I don't know yet,' she answered.

'How do you feel about leaving your family behind?'

She put her hand up; he raised the camera.

'Leave me alone,' she begged him, 'just for now. I want

138

to talk to you, but I'm exhausted. It's only my first day here.'

'Do you feel guilty about leaving your son?' he pressed. 'Are you afraid of reprisals from the KGB?'

'Didn't you hear what I said?' she asked him. She felt her voice rising.

The camera clicked, the man held his ground.

'You're worse than the KGB,' she told him.

'Come in, Anna,' Mrs McDonough called. Her voice was high and controlled.

Anna turned towards the house and saw Mary Ellen was standing barefoot on the lawn right behind her. The light September wind pressed her nightgown against her thin body and suddenly Anna wanted to protect her from having her picture taken, too.

'Go in,' Anna said to her.

'I will if you will,' Mary Ellen said. She was starting to shiver. Anna looked at her gratefully.

'All right,' she relented. She turned her back on the reporters and started up the steps behind Mary Ellen. By the time they reached the porch, a van was driving up. A young woman jumped out as it was stopping; behind her was a man with a huge microphone.

'WOR-TV,' the woman said. 'I'd just like to ask you a few questions.'

Mary Ellen closed the door and locked it. It was 7 A.M.


'We just want an interview,' Zalessky said. He laughed and turned his face to the right as if posing for a camera. He looked the part of a Western journalist, his blue cotton shirt open at the neck, his English shoes scuffed and down at the heel.

'You make a very convincing journalist,' Seriozha told him. 'Too bad I know you.'

'Just last week,' Zalessky told him cheerfully, 'I went to the computer show with two women reporters from Paris. I told them how electronic mail is already loosening the flow of information between news agencies. They loved it. They even took my picture. My picture's been to Paris.'

'So can the rest of you be far behind?' Seriozha asked. 'Your bosses must realise by now you're something special. So in command of details. No regular KGB would ever let his shoes get so run-down.'

'You noticed? You're good; you always had an eye. Forgive me, Sergei Pavlovich, but you would be great at this. Really shine. You can appreciate the humour involved.'

Seriozha only smiled.

'For instance, we're going after the technology now,' Yuri Zalessky said. 'You wouldn't believe the hoops they jump through. At Novosti, you know, we have a room with French computers for French visitors, Jap computers for Japs, and even a room with American computers to keep our side happy.' As he said this he gestured upward with his thumb, indicating to Seriozha that it was all part of the Great Joke, intended, like all effort, for the approval of someone above.

'*Yob tvoyu mat*,' Seriozha said agreeably. 'You guys think of everything.'

'So let's get this over with,' Zalessky said abruptly. 'I'll see that someone drives you back in the morning. You won't even have to take the train.'

'I'm sorry,' Seriozha told him. 'Moscow can continue to get along without me. I have a lot of work to do out here. The blueberries are ripe now. I can't leave Katerina Grigorievna here to make all that jam alone. Can I, Katinka?'

He looked over his shoulder to where Katinka sat on the edge of her chair. She stood up to come to him, but he forbade it with his eyes.

Seriozha sat back in his chair and waited. The uneven wooden floor of the dacha seemed hideously fore-shortened; it seemed to slant towards Zalessky, who seemed too big and too close. In the days when his father was still alive, though barely, and he had first met Zalessky, he had seemed to be smaller, slighter. He was funny and sharp; the others had been archetypally humourless and dull. His father used to joke that the Committee on State

140

Security carefully cultivated that type to maintain a consistent and reassurig image; in changing times, the KGB had to be the one thing you could count on – more stable than the ruble, as characteristic of a good party as vodka.

His father had almost liked Zalessky and was the first to call him Yura, an affectionate diminutive that one might use with a child. He had been attracted to the young man's sense of humour. He had thought that it meant there was a chance that he could still feel shame.

He was wrong, of course.

'Sergei Pavlovich,' Zalessky said, never erring in his courteous tone, 'I have been sent because they' – again the upward gesture with the thumb – 'are getting very tired of seeing the people they send you spending the state's money to drive out here and back for nothing.'

'They took everything I wrote for the last two years,' Seriozha said tonelessly.

'Like, I said' – Zalessky shrugged – 'nothing.'

'They like to do nothing, you know that,' Seriozha told him. 'I just try to make it easier for them.'

Zalessky smiled and nodded; he could appreciate a good line. 'I know how much you want to make our lives easier,' he said. 'But does it ever occur to you that we would like to return the favour?'

'Sergei,' Katinka warned.

'Sit down,' Seriozha told her.

'Yura,' he said – this time, his use of the diminutive nickname sounded crass and derisive – 'if you want me to go down to Dzerzhinsky Square with you, you will have to kill me. Or at least beat me and drug me. You know what I mean; I'll leave the finer points up to you.'

'That's not my style,' Zalessky said in English. 'You know that.'

'I admire your English,' Seriozha told him in Russian, contemptuous of Zalessky's pretentious use of the language of the elite. 'But I don't give a fuck what your style is. That is the only way.'

'How silly,' Zalessky answered amicably. 'You study

141

poetics; you should know there is no one way. There is one goal, and many ways to approach it.'

'I'm sure you're more up-to-date on Marxist dialectic than I am,' Seriozha countered. 'But it always seemed to me that the whole point of it was to condition our poor, messy minds to accept the end of the era of ambiguity.' He turned to Katinka. He could see from her face that his own smile had passed the boundaries of civility; he wondered if his hands still belonged to him and whether they could still make fists.

'What it took Western civilisation eighteen centuries to achieve, Marxism undid in a few years,' he said to her.

'Seriozha.' She was nearly moaning, her hands twisted in her lap.

'So I, at any rate' – he turned to Zalessky – 'have concluded that if there is one surpassing goal, then there is one surpassing way of achieving it. This is consistent with our society, which, we all know, might have achieved Communism twenty years after the death of Comrade Khrushchev if only more people were like me. Dedicated to a single-minded way of doing things, I mean.'

Zalessky was red now. 'You've been drinking, haven't you?' he said quite loudly. Seriozha saw him looking around the room for the microphone contact points.

'What else is there to do in the country?' Seriozha responded.

'You asshole,' Zalessky said in a whisper. 'I'm trying to help you.'

Seriozha jumped out of his chair. 'Get out of here before I kill you,' he told him.

Zalessky looked at Katinka; she looked back helplessly.

'You're making such a big mistake, I can't tell you,' Zalessky said. 'The next time they won't send someone like me. Do you really think they give a shit? Do you think that they owe you anything? You're the type that ends up in a hospital, and let me tell you, you spend some time in there and you'll be the last one to think you should come back to society.'

'Fuck society.'

'It's hopeless,' Katinka said.

Zalessky stared at her and she did not have to say anymore. He picked up his Italian leather purse from the kitchen table and left.

After Zalessky had gone, the sound of the door locking behind him seemed to linger in the air for several seconds. Seriozha and Katinka sat quietly; listening, he supposed, to the sound of imprisonment.

'Do you want a drink?' Katinka asked finally.

'There's no liquor in the house,' Seriozha said. 'There hasn't been for days.'

She looked at him. 'You're not drunk, are you?'

He shook his head.

She got up and went over to him. He pulled her down on his lap; her hair fell over his face and he breathed in the scent of harsh detergent shampoo muted with precious French toilet water – his.

'You smell like me,' he said.

She smiled gently. 'I am you.'

He held her tightly.

'I want a child, Katinka,' he told her.

'I know,' she said.

'Now.'

She stood up slowly and remained in front of him. She pulled off her blouse, and freed her breasts from her bra. She laughed when he shut his eyes because it seemed funny to her that her breasts should cause him pain.

He entered her immediately, as she stood there, holding her skirt up to her waist.

He felt her suck him in with one deep, sighing breath. He stayed still.

'I will give you a son,' she whispered.

'I want a daughter,' he told her. His voice broke out of him loud and uneven, almost a sob. 'I want a daughter who will have daughters who will have daughters . . .' He was thrusting hard in her now and her face seemed to melt like butter under his lips.

'I love making love to you,' he told her. 'I want to people the world with you.'

Her sighs became deeper and deeper until his words were drowned in them.

On the plane, Ian plugged in to rock and roll. He'd bought his ticket at the absolute last minute and they had stuck him in the smoking section. But as he settled into the red, white and blue tweed of the Pan American 747, the beat was soothing; he turned it up loud and felt it in the pit of his stomach, the way he used to feel the firecrackers at the beach on the Fourth of July when he was a kid.

He did not take any of the newspapers the stewardess offered him. He could not bear to see one more column inch expended on Anna's supposed 'calumny' – her wounded retort to a reporter that he was worse than the KGB. It had been picked up universally, almost gleefully. It had swept her along from the page three features to the editorials. And there had been no repudiation – no statement at all – since. He pictured her now, surrounded by newspeople and yet more isolated than she had ever been. He did not know how he had let her go to the States alone.

There was only one reason he had not left the day he heard of it; it had torn him apart to say goodbye to Christian. Not because there had been any kind of scene whatsoever, but because the boy absolutely refused to accept Ian's going away. Neither he nor Lilianne had even been able to get him to acknowledge the idea that Ian wouldn't be home for dinner. Now that he thought about it, Ian wondered if that wasn't the telltale clue that Christian actually understood better than anyone. Separation was just so unthinkable, when you loved someone, that you could never think it. Even when it was happening, even after.

It wasn't real to him, either. He saw himself putting Christian to bed tonight, just like any other night. He had automatically scanned the newsstands in the airport for magazines with pictures of the space shuttle, just as if he could bring them home and spread them out on the floor like he always did. He still felt Christian's impossibly soft

144

cheek pressed hard against his own. That was the only image of separation he could contain. Of separation from Lilianne, he felt nothing – only the emptiness. The emptiness that had been there for so long, but which was now, somehow, emptier.

The man sitting next to him lit up a cigarette. Ian's first reaction was disgust, but after a few seconds he asked him for one. The man gave it to him amiably enough, but showed no inclination towards striking up a conversation.

Fine, Ian said to himself, inhaling too deeply and feeling for a moment like he might black out. Then the smoke surrounded him with its vaguely dirty, unhealthy scent and Ian sank back into his seat.

When he came through customs, his mother cried. She looked thinner than when Ian had left, four years ago, sharper and more elegant than when he had last seen her, eight months before in Europe.

'What are you crying for?' he laughed at her. But her tears warmed him. Although it was hotter and muggier in New York than in Paris, now, at nearly three in the afternoon, he felt cold inside his sweat-dampened shirt.

'You're exhausted,' she said, trying to pick up his carry-on bag. 'Do you want to eat breakfast here?'

Ian shook his head. 'I just want to go home.'

When he saw the slim grey Rolls-Royce in the parking lot, he had a sinking feeling.

'I don't believe it,' he told her.

'You know your father.' Mrs McDonough shrugged. 'Actually, it's not too hard to get used to.' She laughed and Ian tried to laugh with her but managed only a tired smile.

She handled the car very well; Ian sat back and found that even though he had not seen New York for such a long time, it was hard to keep his eyes focused. When the car left the grizzled brownstones of the Bronx behind and began to purr up the New England Thruway towards Connecticut, he gave up and began to listen to his mother with his eyes closed.

'You should have given us some notice that you were coming,' his mother now told him. 'We put the Russian woman in your room.'

'The luck of the Irish,' he said, too loud.

His mother reached out to touch his hand.

Ian just stared out the window. He did not want his mother to look at him.

'I feel sorry for her,' Kate continued. 'She can't even go down-town for an ice-cream cone without a reporter bothering her. And every day there's something new. Yesterday there was a picture of her son on the front page of the New York *Times*. Supposedly he refuses to leave their house in the country and return to Moscow for questioning. She's afraid they're going to arrest him.'

'They probably already have arrested him, if it's in the New York *Times*,' Ian said.

'That's what she said.' Kate glanced towards Ian now and caught the pain in his expression. She rightly perceived that it was not for Seriozha but for himself, though she wrongly interpreted the reason.

'For God's sake,' she reproached him, but her voice was tearful. 'You just got home.'

Anna stood for a moment on the porch and looked out across the wet grass to where Ian, Kate and Mary Ellen stood laughing. Their heads were tilted up at the sky and there was a deafening noise in the air. When she came out from under the roof of the porch, she saw that a white helicopter was slowly settling down to perch on the lawn like a huge, loud bird.

This strange bird sat on the grass for several seconds, its wingbeats blowing leaves off the trees like a hurricane. Then George McDonough emerged from its clear-plastic craw with his briefcase. As the copter took off again, he held his hand to the top of his head as though he were trying to keep a hat on.

'You're such a ham, Dad,' Mary Ellen told him. She was the only one who hugged him.

'Like to make an entrance, don't you?' Kate said. He kissed her lightly on the cheek. Then Kate stepped to one side, leaving George facing his son.

'Well, I was certainly surprised when Mother told me you were on your way here,' George told Ian. 'Are you on a story?'

'No,' Ian said. 'I'm home.'

'We've forgotten all about our guest!' Kate put in suddenly, grabbing Anna by the hand and drawing her forward into the group. But even as Anna felt herself being pulled closer she felt herself all the more separate and removed from them, as if they were actors on a stage and she a spectator who had rushed on during the play. They all stopped what they were doing – even what they were thinking – to look at her. But she was in no way a part of them.

'Please,' Anna objected. Kate had dragged her up to stand between her and Ian. Ian's eyes widened and she saw his hand move awkwardly at his side; his instinct was to shake her hand but some other instinct intervened. 'Please,' said Anna again. 'I don't want to inter –'

'Nonsense,' George interrupted her. 'It's marvellous to see you again. Are you faring well here?'

Anna did not understand his figure of speech but she saw right away that George was happy that Anna had suddenly been produced on the scene. In some way, it put him more in charge.

'Well,' he said, looking around the group as if he were speaking to a small gathering of the Foundation's trustees, 'I think we have something to celebrate here. We are honoured by having an internationally distinguished guest staying with us.' He nodded graciously to Anna and paused.

'And the prodigal son has returned.' Here he cleared his throat and looked at Ian, who at the last moment avoided his eyes.

'I'd say this calls for champagne,' Kate said.

'I'll go put it in the freezer,' Mary Ellen announced. Anna seized the opportunity.

147

'Let me help you,' she said, and followed her without waiting for an answer.

'I feel I am imposing,' Anna told her.

Mary Ellen squeezed her arm. 'Don't be crazy,' she said. 'They're really glad you're here. Otherwise the shit would be hitting the fan by now.'

Ian left his suitcases unopened and wandered out into the kitchen. Anna was sitting there with Mary Ellen, who looked up and smiled as soon as she saw him. Anna, however, deliberately kept her eyes on Mary Ellen.

'Well, you look good,' Mary Ellen offered amiably. 'You don't have a gut and you're not bald or anything.'

'Thanks.' Ian laughed. 'What were you expecting?'

'Only kidding,' she said softly, moving her chair to the left. 'Come here.'

He came closer and she hugged him around the waist. Her head was under his arm and he tousled her hair, noticing that it was cut short and stylish and streaked with blonde.

'My big brother's home,' Mary Ellen said to Anna in a baby voice.

Ian blushed and for a few seconds held her closer. She was so thin that, for a moment, he realised that he thought of her as much younger than she actually was. Her arms were too delicate, her eyes too large. But her face was so pink and happy.

'You've lost all your baby fat since I last saw you,' he told her. 'You're gorgeous; you look like a model.'

She beamed.

'How old are you again?' he teased.

'Free, white and twenty-one,' she said.

'Well, you're still my baby sister,' he said. Then he squeezed her head so hard she yelped for him to stop. They all laughed and Ian sat down at the table with them.

Perhaps thirty seconds passed in silence. Mary Ellen smiled cheerfully at Ian and then at Anna, Ian smiled awkwardly at Anna and his sister, Anna smiled into the space between them.

'Would you like some tea?' Anna asked suddenly.

'She knows how to make it in the microwave,' Mary Ellen told him.

'I think I'd rather have a beer,' Ian said.

'Now that's the best idea I've heard all day,' said George, who had come downstairs and was suddenly standing behind Ian.

'Hi, Dad.' Mary Ellen was again the first to welcome her father. 'What's up?'

'Nothing much,' he said. 'What's up with you?'

'CYO is organising a rally in support of Bikini at Fairfield University,' she said proudly. 'Anna said she'd like to go.'

'Bikini?' George asked.

'Bikini atoll,' Ian told him. 'You know, where we did atomic testing.'

George cleared his throat and looked at the tablecloth. Ian noticed that it was an old cloth of his grandmother's, printed with Hollywood-perfect bunches of cherries. It struck him instantly why his mother, who had a straightforward, bourgeois passion for everything new, should have set the table with this cheerful, faded cloth from the Depression. He got up to get the beer.

'Where are you going?' George asked.

'Just going to get the beer,' Ian responded neutrally.

George turned to Mary Ellen. 'It's out of the question,' he said. 'I know that your motives are good ones, but you've got to consider the whole picture; you've got to look at it from all the angles. Anna can't be seen at every fund-raising event for every cause; she's got to be very careful which ones she picks. Now, she's here as a guest of the Foundation, and with the special permission of the State Department. This particular cause is not really the right one for her to choose at this moment. Can't you think of anywhere else to take her?'

Ian stood motionless next to the table with four bottles of beer. Mary Ellen blushed, but he saw that she was determined to hold her own.

'Dad, it won't be like that. It's just a student thing.'

'Nonsense,' George said. Ian remembered too well how

149

short his father's fuse was and handed his sister a beer. He put the other bottles in the middle of the table.

'There aren't very many angles from which to look at Bikini,' he said without looking at his father. 'We blew up their homes and lied to them about it. Their rate of cancer now is something like twenty or thirty times that of even the Americans who were exposed to aboveground testing in the West in the sixties. All we can do is try to make them more comfortable.'

'Ian,' Mary Ellen said hotly, 'will you please keep out of this?'

Ian was stung, and for a moment George looked vindicated, but Mary Ellen raced on.

'First of all, Dad,' she said, 'this is going to be very low-key. It's just to educate people.

'Second of all, she is interested in it. And third of all, she doesn't know anyone here and there are going to be some good people there for her to meet.'

'Don't use a pronoun right in front of someone,' George told Mary Ellen.

'What?' she asked, momentarily thrown. Ian bristled.

'Don't say "she" when Anna is sitting right in front of you. And I'm sorry, it's just not as simple as that. I've had a lot of experience in these matters and I'm telling you Anna cannot just go wherever she or you please. You've got to use your common sense. You can't expect Anna to understand these things right away.'

It was on the tip of Ian's tongue to tell his father that what he was now doing to Anna was much worse than Mary Ellen's innocent use of a pronoun, but he saw how his sister sat on the edge of her chair, waiting for her chance to interrupt and he held it in.

'But –' Mary Ellen began.

'This is very serious,' George cut her off. 'I'm sorry but when you've been through these things as many times as I have you'll know what I mean.'

'Please,' Anna intervened suddenly. Ian watched his father and sister looking at Anna in nearly the same way, each expecting her agreement.

'If you think it is a very bad idea, of course Mary Ellen will not take me there,' she said. George eased back into his chair a bit.

'Don't you think that it's really up to Anna?' Ian asked tactically.

Ian knew that his father did not for a moment think that it could be left up to Anna. But Ian had thrown his father a curve and it might deter him long enough to get Mary Ellen off the hook.

At that moment Kate walked into the kitchen.

'Hail, hail, the gang's all here,' Ian began softly, knowing he could blame the heat and the beer. Then he noticed that his mother's eyes were quite red.

'Change of plans,' Mrs McDonough announced abruptly. 'Dad has got to go back to Washington tonight, so we'll have the champagne tomorrow night. I guess I'll make dinner reservations at the club. What do you think?' She was asking Ian and Mary Ellen only; she politely avoided Anna and deliberately ignored George.

Mary Ellen looked at George, surprised; then she looked out the window.

'Thanks,' she said softly to her mother. 'I promised to do something with Karen later and I don't really feel like getting dressed up.'

'I don't myself,' Kate said, much too loud. 'Ian, why don't you take Anna over to the club for dinner and we'll all do something when you get back.'

'Listen,' George started, 'tomorrow . . .' But Kate had already left the room.

'Excuse me,' George said quietly. He stood up and walked out after his wife. But Ian heard the screen door open and shut; then he heard the car motor. He knew that his mother was alone upstairs.

'Same old shit,' Ian said to Mary Ellen, trying to be light.

'What do you know about it?' she shot at him. Her face was red and her voice out of control.

Quite a lot, he wanted to say. But he let her push out

151

of the room, even caught her chair as it toppled backward behind her.

Anna looked at Ian; obviously, she wanted to soothe him.

'That's the price he has to pay,' she said gently. 'To have such a job, to give you all this.'

She leaned her head back and looked around the room. He tried to see the gleaming kitchen, the picture window, the sunlight on the hedges the way she saw it. It was still and opulent, like a movie set.

'Anna,' Ian said to her, 'he's not doing it for us.'

'If not for you, then for whom? For what?'

'I don't think he knows the answer to that.'

She turned away from him and leaned on her arm on the back of the chair. Outside the window, his mother appeared in the garden, carefully cutting russet chrysanthemums.

'Things are never the way they seem to be, are they?' she asked.


'It doesn't seem important anymore,' Ian said. There was a pleasant stinging of lime in his mouth; he had already finished two gin and tonics. The sun seemed to be taking too long to set.

Anna looked out over the water. She did not ask him what no longer seemed important.

'You grew up with all this?' she asked.

He nodded.

'How could you bear to leave it?'

Ian laughed a sad laugh, deep in the back of his throat. 'It was more like I couldn't bear to stay.'

The late-afternoon sun glistened across the water of Indian Harbor. Large, spotless yawls, outfitted for ocean-going, rode tall at their moorings; smaller racing yachts bobbed around them like chicks. The air was filled with the crisp, bell-like music of stays clapping against steel masts.

Across the lawns of the Indian Harbor Yacht Club little girls in organdie dresses ran with boys in navy blazers and miniature bow ties. The children were tanned and blond, their voices clear and high. Their parents strolled languidly behind them, drinks in hand. The American flag and the insignia of the club flapped hard in the stiff breeze. A piano was moved out onto the porch.

'Why did you come home?' she asked him.

'For many reasons,' he told her. 'I'd come to the end of the road.'

Two small boys came up cautiously to touch the piano as if it were a large black animal with a row of polished, musical teeth. Anna watched them with an indulgent, almost envious expression.

'What about your work?'

'It's time to move on.'

'The Foundation's clipping service sent me your piece; I liked it very much.'

'It was the most difficult thing I've ever written.' He wanted her to face him so much it was all he could do not to stand up and walk in front of her. The children were banging on the piano now; he wondered if this was why his own voice seemed so low.

'What about your family?' she asked.

He stared at her for a moment, not sure what she was asking him.

'Your little boy,' she said. 'His mother.'

'They are not my family,' he said.

She turned towards him finally and touched him for a moment on the top of his hand.

'What will you do now?'

He shook his head and looked around. The children had been made to leave the piano and a man in a white dinner jacket sat down on the bench and began to play.

As Ian turned towards the music, a man in a red jacket recognised him and waved. It was someone he had gone to high school with. Ian was conscious that the waiter had just passed and he had, for the moment, lost the chance of another gin and tonic.

'How the hell are you?' said the man in the red jacket as he came up. He looked genuinely delighted to see Ian

153

'Very well,' Ian said, instantly aware of his formality.

'Look great.' The man nodded. 'You've been in Rome or something, haven't you? With one of the wire services, isn't it? No – of course not. You're in Paris, on your own, isn't that right?'

Ian was amazed that his old friend knew so much about him. He could remember nothing about what his friend might have done recently; in fact, for a few seconds he blanked on his name.

'Gordon White,' the man said, seizing Ian's pause to introduce himself to Anna.

'Gordy White,' Ian repeated gratefully, 'Anna Nikolayevna Khameneva.'

Anna smiled. She seemed too tired to talk, Ian thought.

White shook Anna's hand with gusto. 'I saw you on the news the other night; I thought you were very brave. If you don't have a press agent, these people will eat you alive.'

'Yes, I know,' Anna said.

'Listen, why don't you join Nancy and me for dinner?' White said, turning to Ian. 'We're with Bill Allyson and his wife – he's at Ogilvy now, you know. I'm sure he would know ten people who could help you out.'

'Thank you,' Anna told him. 'Not tonight. But thank you.'

'Well, perhaps later for a drink? There's going to be dancing on the terrace.'

'Love to,' Ian said. When his old friend had walked away Ian turned to Anna.

'He's not so bad,' he apologised to her. 'I'm sure he really did want to help you.'

She smiled again. He had never seen her look so exhausted, not even in those first trying days in Paris.

'Tell me about him,' Anna asked. Her voice had a light, pained quality; he thought of Christian asking him for a bedtime story.

'I went to high school with him,' Ian said. 'We were on the debating team together.' They had been pretty close, as Ian remembered it; but that did not mean that Ian really

154

knew him, he realised. He cast about desperately in his mind for more to tell Anna.

'He has his own brokerage now,' Ian continued somewhat bitterly, remembering how he and Gordy had once excoriated the other Catholic school debating teams with their condemnations of corporate America, which was symbolised by racism, Vietnam, Kent State, and the anti-abortion, anti-birth control dictums of their own arch-diocese.

'He probably has ten kids by now. He can afford them.'

Anna looked at him, the pain still tense around her eyes.

'I guess,' Ian told her, 'that he is exactly what I did not want to happen to me.'

They both looked down the veranda to see Gordon White standing and pulling out a chair for a pretty young woman in a light blue dress. She smiled up at him as she sat down and he tousled the top of her hair as one might a child's.

'I don't understand,' Anna said.

For about ten seconds Ian felt a dull but very intense ache in his chest. He held his breath.

'I don't either, anymore,' he said. 'Well, I do, but it's harder.'

Anna waited.

'They didn't question anything,' Ian told her. 'We were always being caught between the way things are here in Greenwich and the way things really are. It wasn't as if they didn't know how things are; they had to justify themselves all the time.'

'They?' Anna asked.

'Our parents,' Ian heard himself say. 'People like my father.'

'No one wants to grow up to be like his father,' Anna said, looking out at the harbour as she spoke.

'I thought everyone wanted to,' Ian answered.

'I never wanted to, until now.'

'What did your father do?'

'He was a poet, though the only book of his that was published was a highly edited translation of Jonathan Swift.

155

I wish I had that book now – I was too young to read it when he was alive, and after he died, the family convinced my mother to get rid of it. All I know of it is what he used to read out loud when he was working on it. And he didn't read it out loud for us to understand anything; he just wanted to hear the sound of the English words.'

Ian suddenly saw Anna as a little girl. He saw her face grow smaller and smaller until her eyes were everything; he saw her lips babyish, plumper, pouting. And he imagined her listening with a child's perfect intensity – for in his experience children were capable of extraordinary concentration on those things which captured their imaginations – to the bitter hero of Irish nationalism.

'"We ate when we were not hungry,"' Anna quoted, '"and drank without the provocation of thirst." Which book is that from?'

'I really have no idea,' Ian told her, '*Gulliver's Travels* is the only one of Swift's books I've actually read.'

'As a very young child I thought that this was absurdly funny,' Anna went on. 'I couldn't imagine how anyone could make himself do such a thing. When I was old enough to go to school and learn about the "great historical inevitability of revolution", it was explained to me how this symbolised the cruelty and decadence of capitalist societies. But soon enough I noticed that this was all anyone lived for – to eat without being hungry and drink without waiting for a thirst.'

'Welcome to Greenwich,' Ian said, 'your perfect embodiment of capitalist decadence.'

Anna gestured towards the children on the lawn with their parents. 'This is what I dreamed of. But I dreamed of the women in long satin gowns and the men in tuxedos with medals pinned on them.' She laughed, but it was such a tired laugh it was almost a sigh. 'And this is what you wanted to escape from.'

She inclined her head towards the Sound as she spoke, and as if to give dramatic impact to her words, a line of little yellow electric lights suddenly went on around the perimeter of the lawn. The sea had disappeared into shadow as the sun had set; now there was nothing but the sound of it lapping against the boats and the yellow lights glowing in the salt-scented emptiness.

The pianist, who had been quietly playing popular songs, vigorously struck up a ragtime waltz and a few couples got up to dance.

Ian and Anna watched them without speaking. Anna's expression was a child's expression of delight and envy; Ian remembered the parties of his parents which he had watched from the top of the stairs.

'Would you like to dance, Anna?'

'I haven't danced since before Pasha was sick,' she said.

He saw that her hands trembled.

'Would you like to now?'

She nodded without looking at him and he walked without touching her onto the dance floor. When she was in his arms he turned the conversation back to her father.

'Why do you want to be like your father?' he asked her.

She put her mouth against his shoulder momentarily. Ian felt the ache in his chest return, but not hard this time; soft, as if the pain burned itself away and melted.

'Of all the people who lost everything,' she told him, 'he was the only one I knew who was happy.'

He held her closer; she was rigid. After a few moments, though, she relaxed and he looked down into her face. She was staring off past the yellow lights. She was not thinking of him, he told himself. She had relaxed because her thoughts were far away from this moment, and his arms around her.

'Do you want me to take you home?' he whispered.

'No.' She shook her head and he felt her breath on his neck.

'Is there anything I can do?' Ian asked.

She stopped dancing and looked up at him. She smiled but it was only with her eyes; her mouth did not move.

'I cannot explain it,' she said, 'but I am happy. Happier than I have been in a long time. And it hurts very much.'

'You don't have to explain,' he told her.

\*　　\*　　\*

157

She was the daughter of his law school friend who had died the youngest. He had to see her, George convinced himself, quite depressed.

Dan Davidoff had been the first Jew that George was close to and he had looked very Jewish in some way which George realised only now was actually indescribable. It was not in his colouring, which was dark, or in his gold-wire glasses or in his expression, which was tense and intelligent. George remembered him as handsome, though in fact he was not; he had looked old when he was still in graduate school.

But they had been raving anti-Communists together and the memory of that sheer, undiluted political passion was pure in George's mind, like the memory of the face of the first woman he had ever loved. It was only her face he'd loved in those innocent days, but one of the benefits of physical deprivation, he liked to think, was a certain succulence in the mind. Perhaps Dan also stayed a bit perfect in his mind because Dan had never really outgrown his idealism, eschewing the graduation offers of Wall Street law firms to make his career in the Justice Department. Many people had been startled when he abruptly turned against Nixon early in the Watergate scandal, but not George. Though he didn't see the reason for such drama himself, Daniel's act had pleased him; it made him feel young.

When Sarah walked into his office, he saw nothing of her father in her. She was beautiful in the way that his secretary was beautiful. Her hair was light, her eyes hazel. She was dressed out of a Talbot's catalogue. Her voice had been moulded by Rosemary Hall and Smith; it was as if she had never heard her father speak – there was no trace of that Eastern European inflection of a perpetual question.

It wasn't until she came to the point of their meeting that he saw his friend in her and it hurt him inadvertently, like swallowing a small, sharp bone.

'The reason I asked you to see me,' she said, 'is because of the Russian dissident to whom the Foundation has recently given a grant. She is someone with whom I would very much like to work.'

George could see how intense the girl was; he thought of her as a girl even though she was nearly Ian's age. She had spoken to him about a small press – he supposed it was one of those publishing houses that felt they had a mission to bring to light the soul-searchings of every Jew that got out of the Soviet Union.

'I don't believe she's Jewish,' George said.

Sarah blushed. 'No, she isn't,' she said. 'That's not why I'm here.'

George stared at his own hands spread out on the blotter in front of him. The blotter was dark green leather, his hands were tanned. He turned his hands up and noticed that his palms were more creased than the fine leather. When did I become an anti-Semite? he asked himself.

'I'm sorry,' he said.

She wouldn't let him go on. 'The Foundation has done so much to help Russian Jews,' she told him compassionately. 'It's entirely natural that you would think that that's why I'm here.'

He was struck by the earnestness of her insincerity. It both flattered and wounded him.

'I'm here because of an organisation which I have helped to found. I don't know if you have heard of us. We're called One Earth and we are devoted to educating people about nuclear disarmament.'

The word 'devoted' was the giveaway; her compassion had not been aimed merely at him. She was her father's daughter.

'What do you do when you're not doing this?' he asked her.

'Do you mean,' she countered, 'what is my real job? This is.'

George smiled. 'Your father and I used to go in for this kind of thing,' he told her, 'though we also had to support families.'

Why was he doing this to her? he wondered. She hesitated.

'Listen,' he said, leaning towards her. 'I'm sure there is something we can do; I can probably arrange for you to meet her. But I can't tell you what she'll do; she is very independent.'

'Thank you,' Sarah said politely. 'I appreciate it.'

'I hadn't seen your father for five or six years before he died,' George said suddenly. She looked away from him then and as she did he noticed that her eyes in the light were a molten gold.

But he couldn't stop.

'They told me he suffered terribly.'

Dan Davidoff had died of atherosclerosis; his brilliant mind had begun to disintegrate in his forties. The last time George had seen him, their conversation had skipped weirdly, but Dan's mind was so fast that George had believed that he himself was just too distracted by ordinary thoughts to keep up. When he had finally understood, the slight way in which Dan's words had been off haunted him.

Sarah nodded. The golden light continued to brim in her eyes but she was not crying. 'It was very strange,' she said. 'That disease seems to make a special travesty of each person it afflicts. Father could no longer read or write or recognise us, but he remembered perfectly whole passages of Latin that he had memorised in high school.'

We rot, George thought. 'What you must have gone through with him,' he said.

'We all went through it,' she said.

Her words were gracious; she seemed to include brothers, sisters, mothers, grandmothers, aunts, uncles, even George in this suffering. But the tone of her voice betrayed the absolute loneliness of her grief; she must have adored her father.

'I'll speak to Mrs Khameneva for you,' he told her. His throat was a bit tight and he realised that it made his voice sound dry and far away.

She got up quickly to leave. 'Thank you very much,' she said. 'I'll call you in a few days.'

'Thank you,' she said again.

'Maybe we could have lunch,' he suggested.

160

She smiled and shook his hand. When she left he reminded himself that her eyes were actually hazel and not gold and that she was the daughter of an old friend. He would ask his secretary to make the follow-up call.

The day of the party in her honour, Anna had retreated in defeat from the morning papers and sat in the cold sunlight at Ian's desk. Even after several weeks, fresh accusations still grew out of her remark that the press was worse than the KGB, but she continued to refuse to speak to reporters. She responded only to letters; it was the last vestige of control she could exert.

Four or five came now every day – requests for interviews, invitations to speak, offers to publish, but some private outpourings as well, often as not from other émigrés who had followed her odyssey in the Russian-language papers. When she had first noticed the beloved Cyrillic lettering among the envelopes, she had torn them open right away – carefully, so as not to disfigure those fragile and familiar characters which spelled out the name she had, until now, known herself by.

But lately she ached when she saw those handwritten envelopes, and pushed them to one side until she had read the rest of her mail. They were, nearly uniformly, pleas for her to use her new celebrity to call attention to the horrors that they had lived with in the Soviet Union.

The letters were full of pain, anger and hatred, and it did not surprise her that of those emotions the one she felt most deeply herself was the latter. Parting from Seriozha had largely cauterised her ability to experience the pain of parting at all; the graciousness of her new life in America had – inevitably, though faster than she could account for – dulled the intensity of her anger. Perhaps it was because anger was so exhausting; she simply did not have the energy to allow that anger to burn and do anything else.

But the hatred she now felt was as expansive and sustaining as love. It was much more than what she thought of as the natural and 'physical' anger she had felt as she had watched the authorities drive Pavel to his death. Then she had actually had to restrain herself from slapping policemen or throwing herself savagely on the KGB officer who had been responsible for Pavel's case. A million times over she had imagined choking the breath out of that sallow young man. She could feel his death in her hands; it was a palpable tension that ran up her forearms as matter-of-factly as the sensation of working with the large, stiff dough of black bread.

This hatred was nothing like that. It was no longer a sensual thing, the expression of which brought some measure of physical relief. It was as abstract and immortal as her soul, invisible, yet real like the forces which hold matter together at its most ineffable and most essential. She understood without thinking how hatred of the Soviet Union gave life to these letter writers, even more than their love for those left behind, or those with whom they had started anew. And she wished to let them know this, just as a person who is in love cannot bear to conceal it.

But the fact was, she could not. As strong as the hatred was, it rarely penetrated to the centre of her attention anymore, as love did not. It was not a choice; living – going forward – preoccupied her. It was a blind, animal thing; it was survival.

As she folded the letters and replaced each in its proper envelope, there was a very deliberate knock at the door.

'May I come in?' Ian asked her.

'It's your room,' she said, embarrassed.

'I wanted to see if there was anything you needed for tonight. I'm going into town.'

'Come in,' she said, beckoning him all the way into the room and shutting the door.

He came towards her awkwardly. She motioned for him to sit down. The bed was clearly the only place to sit since she occupied the desk chair but he sat on the edge of his own bed nervously.

'Relax,' she told him. 'If you knew how many apartments I've lived in that had no other furniture than a bed, you wouldn't feel so improper.' But the protective camaraderie of Paris was gone; she herself was acutely conscious of how big, how American, how showered and shaven he was. His sweater gave off a manly woollen scent of camphor, his skin of plain talc.

He smiled briefly. There was something about the fragility of that smile – the fact that he didn't want to smile, or was afraid to – that made her want to hold his face in her hands. She pushed her chair farther back.

'Ian,' she said, 'the press is killing me.'

'Yes, I know.' He tried to smile again. 'You can't hide from them forever, and saying they're like the KGB was the worst thing you could have done.'

'They are.'

'No, Anna, they're not; they're doing their jobs.'

'So are *gebisti*.'

'You've got to understand what freedom of the press means,' he told her. 'They have a duty to their readers to find out as much about you as they can. You only make it worse by running away.'

'I didn't expect you to defend them.'

Then she saw that she had hurt him; his face reddened as sharply as if she had slapped him.

She looked down at her hands.

'I had hoped that you would write about me.'

He didn't say anything. She felt him look at her, but she did not raise her head.

'I can't, Anna,' he said. 'I don't want to.'

'You didn't want to in Paris, but you did.'

'I won't do it again,' Ian said. 'I want to be free and clear with you – and I want you to be free with me.'

Freedom, she thought; but what she felt was like a hand on her throat.

'How can you be free if you give up your work?' she asked him.

'I'm not giving it up; I want to do better, more important work.'

'But you were doing important work,' she said.

'Maybe,' he said. 'Important in the way that some of the people you will meet here tonight are important, but not really.'

'What is important?' she asked.

'Not very much,' he said.

She stood up and walked towards the window.

'I have a choice to make,' she said. 'Several newspapers and magazines have asked me for interviews and I have decided to choose two.'

He nodded.

'Of the newspapers, I've narrowed it down to the Washington *Post*, the New York *Times* and *The Wall Street Journal*.'

'Can't go wrong with any of those,' he said.

'My instinct is to choose *The Wall Street Journal*. What do you think?'

'*The Journal?* Why?'

'They seem to be fair.'

He shook his head. 'They may be, but their readers are certainly not your natural constituents.'

'That's particularly why I want to reach them,' she said.

'You're not making it easier on yourself,' he said. 'But it's up to you. What about the magazines?'

'I want *Playboy*.'

He stared at her. 'You amaze me. Why them?'

'They'll pay me.'

He laughed. 'I doubt it.'

'I asked them.'

'You asked them?'

'They paid William Buckley; I read it in his book.'

'You're going to be just fine,' he said. 'You're going to fit right in at this party. And I can just imagine where you got a book by William Buckley.'

'In your father's library. He has about twenty books by him.'

'Yes, I know,' Ian said.

'The Russian government detests him,' Anna told him. 'I recognised his name, but naturally I'd never been able to read anything by him.'

'You might meet him tonight. They don't live far from here.'

'Really?'

164

Ian nodded.

'What do you think this is all about?' he asked her softly.

By seven-thirty that night, every light in the house was lit. The furniture gleamed – not so much with wax, Ian thought, as with the attention it had been given. On every table, flowers had been arranged with an autumnal insouciance that belied hours of his mother's time; she had even brought in stems of coloured leaves from the yard.

Caterers, in the person of twelve college students, had taken possession of the first floor. The girls wore antique white lace dresses; the boys wore pin-striped shirts and red braces.

'I'm going to throw up,' he said to Mary Ellen.

Mary Ellen, looking slightly red and scrubbed about her eyes, said nothing.

'Forget it,' Ian told his sister. 'You look lovely in Mom's dress.'

He looked at her, so pale in her mother's black dress, her lower lip trembling. He knew how she felt. Despite the fact that for once he knew he was utterly correct in his rented tuxedo, he still felt like a child, or worse, a poor relation; in his father's world, he was both.

Now the doorbell chimed. It seemed to ring throughout the house like the reverberation of a church organ. He heard the staccato of his mother's heels across the bare floor of the foyer. The door opened and a couple entered. Ian recognised Carter Bond, chairman of the board of the Carter Cable Network.

The doorbell rang again, then again and again. Suddenly the hall was overflowing with women and men. Sharp, provocative perfume drifted forwards on the draught of the open door; there was a prismatic flash of diamonds under the chandelier as women removed their coats.

He watched his father enter from the dining room with Anna. Her face was white, her eyes were huge. Her arm was linked with his father's and there was something strangely naked about her hands.

'Ian,' a voice carried towards him.

165

He saw the elegantly rotund form of Harold Beligrotsky, editor of *The New Review*, wearing a Macdonald-plaid cummerbund – a dazzling red and green slap in the face of the never too thin or too rich company which surrounded them. It was not something he would have worn, Ian noted, in the years before his reactionary journal had passed from merely reactionary to the new state of grace known as 'neoconservative'.

'Hello, Harry,' Ian greeted him.

'Do you know Beth?'

Ian shook hands with Elizabeth Donnerstag, whose essays on Cuba in Beligrotsky's magazine had catapulted her into the circle of the President's academic cabal. He realised that Beligrotsky was telling him that he was no longer to be considered a journalistic confrere of Ian's, but rather a colleague of his father's.

'There's Jerry,' Donnerstag said to Beligrotsky. She pointed with her little finger at the director of the New York City Public Library.

'Off with you,' Beligrotsky told her. She actually pinched him on the cheek and then turned on her heel without speaking to Ian.

'The Library's doing some benefit,' Beligrotsky confided, 'and Kissinger was to be the guest of honour. But somebody screwed up, luckily for Beth, and he's supposed to be on television the same night. She was on that Latin American commission, you know.'

Ian nodded. Back in the US of A, he thought, where special commissions investigating death squads in Central America are a sub-route to central casting.

'Who wasn't on that commission?' Ian said. 'The whole room is lousy with "special ambassadors".'

Beligrotsky gave him a naughty smile. 'You're so mean,' he told him, 'but so right.'

One of the stripe-shirted male caterers came by with a tray of brimming champagne glasses. Ian handed one to Beligrotsky and instructed the waiter to bring him a scotch. The young man got rid of his tray and returned with Ian's drink immediately.

'I'll have one of those, too,' Beligrotsky decided 'I see there are some perks attached to being your father s son,' he said to Ian. He laughed.

Ian ignored him. A few feet away, Anna had been introduced to an undersecretary of state specialising in US – Soviet relations. This man was now elaborately retelling the latest joke making the rounds in Moscow. Her face was rapt and it was obvious that she was in awe of the undersecretary's access to information. This infuriated Ian as immensely as it gratified the bureaucrat.

'I've heard that one a hundred times,' Beligrotsky complained sotto voce. 'Some poor jerk tries to crash Chernenko's funeral and a guard stops him at the door. "Do you have a ticket?" the guard asks him. "A ticket?" the jerk replies. "I have a subscription for the whole series."'

'Funny,' Ian told him. Anna was laughing.

'You know, she's got to be KGB,' Beligrotsky said. Ian stared at him, dumbstruck. 'She's too good-looking to be your average female Russian.'

Ian felt something break inside him, breaking cleanly in large, even pieces like a dish that slips out of someone's hands onto the floor. He knew he should walk away.

'You know the old joke about Russian women?' Beligrotsky asked. 'You don't?'

Ian waited.

'There's this international ladies' underwear show in Moscow. Lots of silk and satin and lace. An American woman visits and buys seven pairs of little panties – one for each day of the week. A French woman goes and buys five pairs – one for each day, except Friday and Saturday, her days off, shall we say. And the Russian woman goes and buys twelve pairs – one for each month.'

'If this weren't my parents' house,' Ian told him, 'I would punch your fucking face in. Excuse me.'

He turned to join his father, Anna and the undersecretary. He was shaking. He did not dare look back at Beligrotsky. Instead, he made an effort to smile at his father.

'Arthur has been detained in Washington,' the undersecretary was saying.

George tightened his lips together momentarily.

The man shrugged. 'You know Arthur,' he said. 'He can't be everywhere.'

An instant passed in which Ian was conscious that the reins of the conversation had been dropped.

'I'm sure he'll make every effort,' the undersecretary continued. 'I know how much he enjoys being with both you and Katherine.'

'I've been given the word that dinner is served,' George announced, and formally offered Anna his arm.

Ian watched them go, his hands dead at his side.


One of the young girls in lace, her hair braided across the top of her head, opened the double doors to the dining room.

The dining table had tripled in size. Small tables had been set up in the corners of the room. Silver sparkled; there were so many glasses beside each plate all Anna could think of was that if each were filled to a differing degree with water, somebody with the right talent might have been able to play the Ninth Symphony.

'Right here, next to me,' George told her, and stood behind her, holding out her chair. She saw that Ian was seated with his sister at one of the other tables.

'So what do you think of all this?' an elegantly dressed man on her left asked her. He wore an acid-blue silk foulard which a small golden dragon on a stickpin kept in place. The dragon held a ruby between its claws.

'I can't quite believe it,' she said. 'It's wonderful.'

'That's not what you'll say by Christmas, when you've been to one of these every night.'

'You're wrong,' she told him.

The man opened his eyes, amused. 'Not all parties are as interesting as the ones George and Kate give, my dear.'

'I'm sorry,' she said. 'It's so new – I'm still in love with it.'

'You fall in love all the time, if one is to believe your press statements. How marvellous.'

George leaned towards them.

'Anna, let me introduce Tripp Thomas,' he said. 'There's a good reason why I foisted this fellow on you.'

'I'm CIA,' the man said. He did not smile and Anna looked to George.

'Behave yourself,' George said to him. 'Tripp runs a rather small but rather nice publishing company.'

'It was rather nice,' he said. 'Until Global Petroleum got a hold of it. This year, our top book was *Boy George's Beauty Secrets*.'

'Who's that?' Anna asked.

'You tell her,' George said to the publisher.

The man waved his hand in the air.

'Wait until you see the movie,' he told them.

'You're kidding?' George said.

Thomas shook his head and turned to Anna. 'At any rate,' he said, 'you can see we have a real need to upgrade the list. I wonder if you can help us.'

'If you agree,' George told her, 'you'll be in good company. They've published every Nobel Prize winner for the last twenty years.'

At that moment, Kate came up behind George and tapped him on the shoulder.

'You're wanted on the phone,' she said.

'Excuse me,' George said, and got up from the table. Kate took his seat, slipping her arm across the back of Anna's chair.

At once, people turned towards Anna to fill in the conversational gap. She was invited to speak at a benefit for the March of Dimes, to play bridge with a group of Sovietologists, to attend a wine-tasting party. She surprised herself by finishing all the champagne that had been poured into her glass before anyone else's; she wondered if Ian was drinking champagne and whether it tasted the same in his glass as hers.

Then George returned. She knew from the way he looked at her that something was wrong.

He smiled at her but his smile was insincere in an entirely kind way. It terrified her.

'Arthur Orr has just called from the White House with a message for you from the President.'

The table talk died. George began to read from a piece of paper.

'Anna Khameneva, you, and your late husband, stand as shining examples in the struggle of individuals against tyranny. America has always been a sanctuary for people who cannot live and work under the oppressive political conditions of their native countries and this administration welcomes the opportunity to extend to you a great American tradition. We wish you happiness and health, and all the best that life in the United States has to offer.'

There was a courteous burst of applause. Anna was uncertain whether she should stand to acknowledge it, or whether it was really intended for the President.

But George continued to look at her unhappily and she did not move out of her seat.

'Tell me what's wrong,' she said.

He paused, then put his hands on Anna's chair, suggesting she get up. 'Excuse us,' he said.

'Tell me now,' she said. He saw that she meant it.

'It appears that your son has been arrested,' he told her. 'But we cannot confirm it. He hasn't been seen for two days.'

For a long moment she saw nothing. There was only the blankness of denial.

'Anna,' George said quietly, 'are you all right?'

She nodded.

'Everything is being done to obtain reliable information,' he said. She wanted to cry but the tears coagulated in her throat and her eyes burned dry. Everyone was now silent. She glanced at Ian; he was staring at her. She stood up.

'As you know,' she told the group, 'my husband was a physicist. He helped the government develop their first atomic weapons at the end of World War II. In Russia, he was very famous for this.

'But after a time, when we had moved away from the

170

war, and he saw so much of the country's resources being burnt up to make more and bigger weapons – weapons so large and so numerous that their force is never encountered within the earth's atmosphere but only in deep space – he refused to work on them any longer. They had more than enough bombs to blow up the whole world many times over. He saw no reason to make more – to make them more accurate, faster, whatever. He was of the generation who had given birth to this enormous power of destructiveness and he quite simply believed that that was the very thing that prevented it from being used. Being equals, each side would fear the other and this fear would hold the world in balance. He was a very clear thinker, a very logical man. He could not account for a day when we had all simply lived with that fear so long that we no longer felt it.

'But he lived long enough to see that happen. He saw the ultimate danger that he had helped to create, believing the healthy fear of this danger would discipline our leaders – which it did, for a while – become meaningless. And he felt responsible.

'He used to tell me: "I am like the old peasant in the fairy tale of the bears."

'In that story a woodsman lives deep in the forest with his family. One day he accidentally kills a mother bear and he brings the cub home. His children play with it and raise it; it is their pet and they love it. Sometime later, he takes his little son with him into the forest and they come upon two bear cubs splashing in a stream. Before his father can stop him, the little boy races up to pet them. To his horror, the woodsman sees the mother bear rush out and kill his child. The child gives the father one last look of surprise and betrayal. You see, because the father had let him have a bear cub as a pet, he no longer had any fear of bears, he had forgotten the danger.

'The peasant in the story died of a broken heart,' she said. 'In the Russian storybooks it says: "His heart cracked."

'Sometimes we say in Russian that someone dies because

171

he was too good to live; God likes to keep such good ones near him.'

'The Irish say that, too,' Kate said softly. Anna felt her words touch her like the whispers at Pavel's funeral, those sounds meant to comfort that she never really heard but only felt like ashes in the air as they brushed her face.

'My husband built these weapons and he knew that he could take them apart again,' she continued. 'It was his belief that a very few weapons and the readiness to manufacture them if treaties were violated was the only way for his country and the world to be safe. He submitted plans to the leaders, detailed, technical plans to effect such a situation. But they considered him a traitor. It was only because he was a hero that he did not die in prison.'

Now she no longer saw the guests; the tears were softening in the back of her throat and her words came of their own accord.

'Pasha,' she said, 'tonight your son is in prison; he has finally collected his patrimony. You thought you left us nothing, but you were wrong. You left us the ability to feel shame – shame that makes merely tolerating certain things impossible.'

She heard her voice rise and felt anger back up her pain with strength. She straightened her back and picked up her glass.

'To my son,' she said. 'To everyone who fights simply for the right to live with dignity as a human being. To Seriozha.'

'To Seriozha,' George said, raising his glass.

'To Seriozha,' repeated all the voices in the room, some vibrant and defiant, many subdued and soft. 'To Seriozha.'

Towards one in the morning, she found Ian and his sister sitting in the dark on the porch, smoking cigarettes.

'I didn't know you smoked,' she said to Ian.

'I don't, really,' he said. 'Someone left these here.'

The two small circles of smouldering red moved away from her and she sat on the steps between them. She felt Ian put his hand on hers.

'I am so sorry about your son,' he said.

She didn't answer.

'Aren't you cold?' she asked Mary Ellen.

'I don't feel anything,' the girl said.

'I know what you mean,' Anna said. She put her arm across Mary Ellen's shoulder. She felt her stiffen.

'I felt like a spectator at my own party,' Anna confided to her.

'Story of my life,' Mary Ellen said.

'Mary,' Ian said. There was tenderness in his voice, but also a reprimand. The girl stood up and went into the house.

'What's wrong with her?' Anna asked him.

'I don't know. She seems incredibly depressed.'

'The rally she wanted me to go to was today,' Anna said.

'I think what's upsetting her is more than a rally.'

They both sat silently. Ian lit up another cigarette and offered one to Anna. She waved it away.

'It's very hard to feel useful,' she said.

He didn't answer.

'Where were you tonight?' she asked him. 'I hardly saw you.'

The wind stirred in the trees; the leaves were already dry and made a sound like the ocean. The air had a cold, brittle smell of salt.

'Why did you really come home?'

'You know why,' he said.


He was awakened at eight by the cleaning lady; the package had arrived special delivery.

The handwriting on the address label was his own – he had spelled his name large and black. For the return address, he had clearly printed out Christian's name, 14 Rue de la Beaumarle, no. 2, Paris, France. He lay back in bed and balanced the flat package on his chest. He watched it rise up and down as he breathed.

Lili, he found himself thinking, how? How could everything we've been through not mean anything anymore?

And in perfect repetition of the pattern they had enacted for so long, he felt no answer from her in his heart, but only the physical memory of her hands moving over him, silencing him with his own deafening desire.

He thought about not opening the package at all.

But then he heard Christian. Like a melody that has been imprinted on the brain simply by being heard again and again, he heard Christian talking to himself as he did almost all the time – playing, eating, watching television. He caught snatches of the mad, little singsong dialogue that the child had continually with himself, in which were reflected all the strangenesses and fears of Ian's adult world.

He opened the package by cautiously prying off the staples that held it closed. As if ensured by his own deliberate fear of it, one of the staples pierced his finger under the nail and a drop of blood beaded up. He licked it off; it tasted like tears. He knew this because he had many times tasted Christian's tears, holding the boy during a tantrum, or after one or another of the real and imagined injuries of childhood. But he had not realised that he knew the taste of the child's tears until the moment that he tasted his own blood.

Inside the package there were three paintings that Christian had made. The paper was rigid with thick, children's watercolours; coloured powder shook out of the mailing envelope when Ian held it up to shake out a note. But there was no note, no message at all, only the pictures, which were signed by Christian with huge, lopsided C's, and titled neatly by some adult hand – not Lilianne's – on the back.

The paintings were blue and white, yellow and red, and green and black, respectively. There were only bold slaps of colour, nothing in the least representational. As Ian read their titles, he understood.

The blue painting was 'Voie Lactée' – the Milky Way. The yellow and red, 'Gare Interstellaire' – star station. The green painting, the biggest, was 'New York.'

He tried to replace the paintings in the mailer, but they

began to break at the corners. Then he was ashamed of himself. He had got out of bed and was holding 'Star Station' up to the wall to see how it would look there when Anna came and stood in the doorway. When she saw the pictures, her whole face shimmered.

'Your little boy!' she said.

Ian sat down on the bed and couldn't look at her.

She came in and closed the door behind her.

'Don't cry,' she told him. 'You will have another child.'

Her face was set and hollow. But unconsciously she stood hugging herself, and her arms were trembling.

'Oh, Anna,' he said. His voice was so low he was unsure whether he had actually said it aloud. The absence of feeling in her face was terrible; it panicked him.

He wanted to stand and take her in his arms, but instinctively he knew she would not allow it. Without really knowing why he did it, he sank to his knees in front of her, holding her to him, pressing his face against her closed arms.

At first she stood shocked and rigid. But then she opened her arms and held Ian to her. He felt her breathing against his forehead; he felt her pulse throbbing against his lips.


George took Sarah to lunch at the Harvard Club. The autumn sun streamed through the high windows into the dark oak room, smoke turned blue and then vanished in those perfect beams of light. The talk seemed loud, and George could hear football being discussed at the two adjacent tables.

How easy, he thought, to have at your disposal such a strictly defined universe as football. He looked at his empty plate; he looked at the girl across from him. Her food had hardly been touched.

'Don't you like your fish, Sarah?' he asked.

She shook her head in polite disagreement. 'Oh no, really, it's fine.'

Then the loud quiet returned. George signalled for more water. It came and the waiter made a small production of pouring it. It was the third glass for Sarah; George was drinking the wine.

'I have the impression,' he began, wondering if he was being foolish, but overcome by his sudden, ridiculous need to know, 'that your father would never have treated you like a child. Am I right?'

Sarah Davidoff blushed a little, and then, in giving his question serious thought, relaxed.

'You're right, actually,' she said, and smiled. 'That was one of the most marvellous things about my childhood. I never realised I was a child.'

Her hair, which was too long for a woman of her age, had been pulled back in a flat white bow. He wondered if she knew how much she looked like a child.

'You're about the same age as my son,' he said, immediately regretting it.

She stared at him, uncomfortable.

Several moments passed. At the end of the room, George noticed a man he knew who had once been in advertising. He was now retired. At his table, a very beautiful young blonde toyed with what appeared to be cheesecake. She handled her fork coyly, but George saw through her. The man he had once known sat back confidently, exuding that mysterious quality that can be described only as the 'upper hand'. Envy stole over George like a migraine.

'You have spoken to her about me?' Sarah asked quietly.

'I'm sorry?'

'Have you spoken to Mrs Khameneva about me?'

'Yes,' he said after a pause. 'She's willing to meet you. More than that I can't guarantee. She is very unwilling to ally herself with any group or movement; she really hasn't come out for anyone yet. And she might not at all.'

'I can't say I blame her.'

'Naturally – you never blame anyone except conservatives.'

Sarah was surprised. George laughed.

'I can just imagine how she feels being here,' Sarah said. 'In the Soviet Union there is no such thing as an individual

– it would be impossible for anyone to speak only as himself. Even Sakharov has been continually forced to act as an "official" spokesman for an organised "movement" of dissidents.'

'You're very well versed in things Russian.'

'Of course, my family came from Russia, you know that,' she told him. 'Though we're Jews.'

'I should think that would make you detest the Soviet Union. And here you are, heading up a so-called peace organisation, trying to convince people that our government should soften its hard-nosed policy towards them.'

He had finally managed to engage her. Her eyes were golden again, this time the goldest things in an oak room full of Tiffany cuff links, Cartier wristwatches, Dunhill lighters. George wondered if the man at the end of the room had noticed him as well.

'I can't hate someone I never loved,' she said, too curtly. It was as though she had touched him lightly – perhaps on the inside of the wrist.

'And anyway,' she continued, 'to me, it's not a US–Soviet issue – it's a human issue.'

George leaned towards her. 'Come on,' he said. 'How can you possibly not think of Russia? I mean, I am not an idiot; I can understand the point of just wishing to reduce the number of nuclear arms in the world, but we wouldn't have all these weapons if it weren't for them.'

'That's debatable,' she answered. 'There are a significant number of important thinkers both inside and outside the government who argue that our present rate of defence spending and armament is really quite independent of the Soviets. The Pentagon is a huge bureaucracy; the heads of its departments, like the executives of a corporation, constantly compete against each other and their power is measured by the size of the budgets they are awarded each year. Only, unlike in a corporation, they do not have to justify their spending by being profitable. What they are selling Congress – us – is something they call national security.'

'Well, I'm glad to hear that you are such a believer in a

free market,' George said. 'At least you're a capitalist. But you can't know as much about the Soviet Union as you do and not know that they have been spending fully twice the percentage of their GNP on defence that we spend.'

'Their GNP is roughly half of ours.'

'Exactly. They have a much stronger commitment to arms than we do.'

'But, Mr McDonough,' she said.

'Please call me George,' he reminded her.

'The ways that we arrive at our estimates of Soviet defence spending are specious,' she told him. 'We base everything on what we spend – what it would cost us to build a jet, or what we pay personnel.'

'It probably costs us less than it costs them,' he joked.

Sarah did not see the humour. 'In the sense that they cannot support both a military and a consumer economy, it most certainly does.'

'That shows you what it means to them,' George said, 'since they are still ahead of us.'

'The CIA's own reports,' she responded, 'show that our estimates of Soviet military strength have been grossly distorted.'

'That report is known to be a forgery.'

'Known by whom?' She was incensed.

'He's right, I'm afraid,' a deep voice put in politely. George turned to see Arthur Orr standing to his left.

'Arthur,' George said, standing up and shaking his hand. 'Let me introduce Sarah Davidoff. Sarah, this is Arthur Orr. If anyone can put this argument to rest, he can.'

Sarah's eyes widened involuntarily. She was quite smooth and it was an almost imperceptible thing. But George caught it and he was pleased.

'Knew your dad,' Orr offered amiably.

'I thought you were a Yale man,' George said.

'I was. I didn't know him from school, I knew him from Justice. That was quite a few years ago. I was also in Internal Security. You were the Russian scholar, if I recall.'

She looked at him, surprised.

'Oh, he was very proud of you, you know that. Pictures of you everywhere in his office. You'd won some kind of school prize at the time. He was pleased as punch.' Arthur Orr smiled at her, and after a small delay, she smiled back. George sensed Sarah's discomfort and searched for the right way to steer the conversation away from her.

But then Orr turned to him. 'So,' he said, 'how's the Russian at your house? Doesn't it sometimes seem we all have Russians on the brain?'

This last quip was intended for Sarah, but she did not know how to take it. George stepped in.

'There's no new information, is there? I haven't seen anything in the papers.'

'Let me make another call on that,' Orr said. He looked levelly at George, and George was not sure that he should say anything more.

'But everything is going well?' Orr asked again.

'Things are going quite well,' George said. 'I spoke personally to Jay Gessup at Cravath – he's a neighbour of ours – and we're going to see what we can do about *60 Minutes*.'

'Marvellous,' said Orr, nodding. 'I knew Greenwich was the right place for her. Maybe if I come visit for a while, I can get on TV, too.'

'I'll see what I can do.' George laughed.

'Do that,' Orr said. 'Nice to meet you, Sarah.' He turned to go and then stopped.

'By the way,' he asked George, 'what's happening with her book?'

'She hasn't decided yet,' George told him. 'I think she's still a little overwhelmed by it all.'

'I don't blame her. These publishers are sharks.'

'Not all of them,' Sarah said, offended. 'Why do you say that?'

'You can ask your friend over here,' Orr said, nodding towards George. 'We used to see quite a few libel cases, didn't we?'

'That's right,' George said.

'What she needs,' Orr continued, 'is someone she can

talk to, preferably someone who speaks Russian. She should choose a translator first, then a publisher.'

'That would be the way to do it,' Sarah agreed. 'You seem to know a lot about publishing.'

'Some of my best friends . . .' Orr kidded her. 'But seriously, through the years, a number of my clients have published books.'

George knew that Orr had had movie stars, gangsters and politicians as clients; as interesting and maverick a practice as it was possible to have. He also knew that he was twice as bright as Orr – he had gone to Harvard on a fellowship from a Catholic college when those awards were seldom available; Orr had glided into Yale on the strengths of football and his family. If George had not had a wife and children so young, he thought, he might not have stayed with his firm. But the truth was, he could not ride out the nauseating dips in altitude that one takes in business for oneself; he knew this. His sensibilities were too finely tuned, too acute, he told himself; he was not thick-skinned in the semi-bovine way Arthur was, able to flick away creditors like flies.

Now Orr smiled at Sarah. 'You speak Russian; you ought to translate her book yourself,' he suggested lightly. 'Get your friend over here to arrange something.'

'That's not a bad idea,' George said.

Sarah looked from one to the other. George wondered if he dared bring her to Greenwich.

'Well, it's an idea anyway,' Orr said. 'Good to talk to you again, George, Sarah.' He shook their hands.

'I don't suppose that you had considered that,' George said to Sarah when Orr had left. 'Perhaps you should.'

She sat very still, thinking. She looked at him for a moment, as if she were going to ask him a question. But then her face resumed its private expression of thought.

He found it impossible to speak to her as she sat there, so obviously turned inwards. He waited.

'I didn't know that you knew Arthur Orr,' she said finally.

He resisted the impulse to retort smartly; he knew he didn't have to. He merely smiled.

She looked off again. The lunch hour was over and the room was emptying. There were not enough busboys to clear the tables as fast as they were left and George began to feel oppressed by the refuse of other diners – beer bottles, still-smoking ashtrays, the dirty plates with their sausage ends, lamb chop bones, half-eaten baked potatoes.

'I very much enjoyed our conversation,' he said, unable to be silent any longer. 'I hope that even though we're on opposite sides of the fence you'll consent to taking the discussion further.'

She heard him and looked into his eyes. For an instant he saw her as a father; a lovely child who did not know she was a child.

'I'll set something up with Anna and call you in a few days,' he told her.

She nodded absently and did not say thank you. He stood up and came behind her chair. As she stood, she shook her head.

'Is something wrong?' he asked.

'That was so weird,' she said. Her inarticulate choice of words struck him after her eloquent diatribe.

'What was?'

'Oh, I'm sorry,' she said. 'Meeting Arthur Orr like that and hearing him talk about my father and what he said about me.'

'He's like that.' George shrugged. 'A prodigious memory for details. That's why he was such an outstanding litigator. He also enjoys being charming to attractive young women, if you hadn't noticed.'

She laughed politely. 'I guess so,' she said.

'You are very attractive,' George said; he felt his voice was suddenly stupidly low and small.

She looked down quickly. 'Thank you for lunch,' she told him, 'and for being so kind.'


It was Anna who met her at the train station.

'I'm Sarah Davidoff,' Sarah said, a bit thrown. 'Did you drive here yourself?'

Anna shook her head. 'I took a taxi; it will return for me in one hour.'

Sarah was entirely unprepared for the brusque tone of Anna's voice.

'I wanted to meet you on my own terms,' Anna told her. 'There are several questions I have to ask you.'

Anna directed her to a small coffee shop across the street. They were served tea in plastic cups with cheap tea bags that merely coloured the water. It was cold in seconds.

Sarah watched Anna dip her tea bag in the tepid water several times and then push the cup away. She could not reconcile this deft, impatient woman with the Anna who had spoken about love at the airport.

'Mr McDonough's secretary sent me your résumé and the samples of your translating,' Anna said. Her voice was all surface. 'Your command of the language seems very good to me. I have also seen the brochures your organisation puts out. Why are you here?'

Sarah was too taken aback to answer immediately. 'I don't understand,' she said. 'You know why I'm here.'

Anna's eyes narrowed.

What's going on? thought Sarah.

'What's wrong?' she asked.

'Why are you here?' Anna repeated.

'I'm here,' Sarah began slowly, incredulous, 'because of you. Because of what you stand for . . .'

But her words seemed to have the opposite effect on Anna that she intended. Anna was not flattered or even attentive, she was withdrawing completely, almost recoiling.

'There must be some mistake,' she told Anna. She looked around the room for a moment. There was a plastic sign above the counter with slide-on plastic letters. There was a lemon meringue pie with one piece cut out of it. The waitress behind the counter took a pack of Kools out of her pocket. The rest of the world was normal.

Anna didn't answer. Sarah felt a knot form in the back of her throat.

182

'Didn't George speak to you about me?' she asked.

'No,' Anna said. 'His secretary said he had asked her to forward your material.'

Sarah was too disturbed to be angry. Anna began to look like she had been painted by Van Gogh; her face was thick and yellow. Sarah wondered what her own face looked like to Anna.

'I can't imagine what I have done to offend you,' Sarah told her. Anna remained impassive.

'I'll go,' Sarah said. She was conscious that she had no real reason to be defensive but suddenly she was afraid she would cry. She stood up.

'Sit down,' Anna said.

Sarah looked at her. Suddenly Anna's face was clawed by an emotion Sarah recognised but had never felt with such intensity – fear.

'My God,' Sarah said, instinctively reaching out and touching Anna on the arm. 'What is it?'

Anna put her head in her hands.

'Six days ago I heard through friends of Mr McDonough in Washington that my son has disappeared. Ever since then I have expected someone. Every hour, I have waited for them to send someone to me.'

Sarah questioned Anna with her eyes, but before Anna could answer she understood. She knew who Anna meant by 'them'.

'You were sent to me. You speak Russian. If you translate my book you will have occasion to be with me, to watch me, almost all the time.' Anna looked at Sarah with shame.

After what she's been through, Sarah wondered, how can she still feel any guilt for suspecting the worst? She sat down.

'*Gnida*,' Sarah said with disgust. The word translated literally as 'lice', but it was used to describe people whose behaviour was repulsive. Anna nodded.

'*Mandavoshka*,' Sarah continued.

Anna gave a small, tired laugh. The word meant 'pubic lice', and was used when the other word did not adequately

183

connote the loathsomeness of the character in question. It carried the added dimension of dishonesty, surreptitiousness.

'Anna,' Sarah said suddenly. 'I want you to know that I am willing to resign from my organisation in order to work with you. I can understand that you may feel it would be better for you and your book to have no affiliations and I can accept that.'

'How can you accept it when you have worked so hard?'

Sarah leaned towards her across the uneven little table. 'I read your book six months ago. My father's sister works in Rome; she helps Soviet Jews emigrate to Israel. She always asked for news of your husband, before he died. After he died, she started to hear about you. More than one person managed to bring your book out of the country – how, I can't imagine. She sent it to me.'

Now Sarah felt her eyes fill with tears and though she was embarrassed, she forced herself to go on.

'I dreamed about you, Anna,' she said. 'Or rather I saw myself as you were in the book. I saw myself with a baby – just the warm, naked thing next to my skin and no way to protect it –'

She spoke in a very low tone to control herself.

'How can I even think of bringing a child into the world, if I'm not willing to do this?' she asked. She wanted to say more but her mouth trembled and she didn't trust the words to come out.

'Shh,' Anna said. 'Stop. You're ruining your makeup.' She was smiling.

Sarah dabbed the corners of her eyes; her finger came away black. She shook her head and laughed.

'No wonder George didn't mention you; you're too pretty,' Anna said. 'We all would have been suspicious.'

They both laughed now.

'Save yourself,' Anna said to her gently. 'We have a lot ahead of us.'

On the weekend, George was home and the house reverberated with tension as he deliberately pursued his week-

184

end métier – 'lord and master', Mary Ellen called it under her breath.

But to Ian, his father seemed more like an unhappy child and was obviously anything but at home in his own house. The idea of homelessness was beginning to obsess him – he ached even for the thin, furtive cats that roamed silently over the neighbourhood lawns, even for stray bees left in the garden at dusk. He saw the way that Anna watched them.

Ian steered clear of his father and kept an eye on his mother, who was relentlessly good-natured. Elaborate food appeared every few hours; there was always wine on ice. But if Kate prepared a steak, George complained that it was too heavy, that he was trying to lose weight. If the next meal was a salad, he fretted because he was hungry. Yet they did not fight. Kate would clear away the uneaten food on the pretty Meissen plates and George would lock himself away on the phone.

By eight o'clock on Sunday evening no one in the McDonough house felt at home anymore.

'Let me help you with the dishes,' Anna said to Kate. The two women went into the kitchen wordlessly.

Mary Ellen looked exhausted.

'Do you want to go get ice cream?' Ian offered.

She shook her head.

'Dad wants to talk to you,' she said.

'What did he say?'

'He didn't say anything,' she told him.

'Then how do you know he wants to talk to me?' he asked.

'I know.'

Ian put his arm around her. He knew what was coming. He'd been home almost three weeks now; he had made exactly three phone calls about work. He had not even begun to look for an apartment.

'I don't want you to move,' she said.

'You'll visit. When I go away you can bring your boy-friend.'

'You know I don't have a boyfriend,' she said.

'Why don't you, Mary?' he asked.

'I don't know.'

'It's because men are stupid, tasteless and blind,' he told her.

She smiled. 'You ought to know,' she said.

He hugged her tightly. Then he went to his father's study and knocked on the door.

There was no answer; he let himself in. George was on the phone and immediately lowered his voice and turned his back. Ian's first impulse was to leave, but he forced himself to stand his ground.

His father hung up.

'Washington,' he apologised.

'Don't bother,' Ian said. He knew his father did not whisper to anyone in Washington.

'Sit down,' George said.

Ian sat down.

'What are you up to?' his father asked.

Ian recognised that the casual diction was an effort to be calm, but he knew there was nothing relaxed about the inquiry.

'About six foot three,' Ian said.

'I asked you a question.'

'If you're asking me if I have a job, the answer is no, but I have a couple of leads and I should be out of here by next week.'

'Journalists without jobs can hardly afford to go around insulting editors of magazines,' George said now. 'I'd like to know what happened between you and Harold Beligrotsky.'

'Nothing,' Ian said. 'Beligrotsky said something disgusting and I took exception to it.'

'This is my house,' his father told him, 'and as long as you are in it, you better know enough to keep a civil tongue in your head.'

'That's just what I told Beligrotsky.'

George did not respond and in the silence Ian let his eyes wander over the bookcases. He noticed that two shelves were now taken up by his own college books. He got up and pulled out *Civilization and Its Discontents*.

'I'm still talking to you,' his father said.

'I'm sorry,' Ian said, and took his seat again.

'I've seen your article on Anna. It's not one of your better pieces.'

'I'm sorry,' Ian said again. He fanned the pages of the book in his hand.

'I think you let your own political prejudices stand in the way of talking about a rather special person.'

'I tried to let her do the talking,' Ian told him.

'She has a chance now to meet people, to enter academia and society. She should not be handicapped by being strapped to issues she could not have fully explored before she got here.'

'You better tell her that.'

'She's a smart woman,' George said.

Ian focused his eyes on an open page of the Freud. He carefully read the sentences he had underlined as a sophomore. He read them twice.

'I also question,' his father was saying, 'whether you should be relying on your relationship with me for subjects for your writing. I think you ought to ask yourself if that isn't just a little too easy.'

On page 38 Ian found the sentence he remembered. Once, it had seemed a noble and tragic inspiration for a career; now it mocked him. *Writing has its origin in the voice of an absent person*,' he read. He looked at his father.

'Don't worry,' he said. 'I have no intention of ever writing about Anna again. Her public persona is up to her.'

'That's as it should be,' George said.

'Yes,' Ian told him, 'it is.'

On Monday morning, when the house was empty and quiet, Anna and Ian took their coffee cups and sat outside in a small patch of October sun.

'It's time for me to leave,' Ian said.

'It's better that way,' she told him.

He knew she was sending him away.

'Well, in one way certainly,' he gave in. 'I can't stand to be here and watch what my parents do to each other.'

She smiled at him, a slow, broken smile. 'You are still a child,' she said. 'Every man has his demons.'

'Did your husband?'

But she wouldn't answer him. She held his eyes until he was forced to look past her. The waves seemed so cold that he could taste them; he wanted to wash himself in their clean, cold colourlessness – to scour himself, to rinse his mouth out with the clear, biting brine. His head began to ache.

'When there is no other freedom,' she said, 'love is more accommodating.'

He slumped for a moment and looked at the ground. They were sitting in lawn chairs and he was suddenly aware of how tender and fragile and green the grass was. It was vulnerable and unnatural; not the hardy yellow sea grass that should have grown so close to the water, but a delicately seeded lawn, nourished with a formula of fertiliser diluted in water, like some kind of vegetable baby.

When he looked up he saw only her profile, erect and still. He wondered what she would do if he touched her, if he took her in his arms.

'You're testing me, Anna,' he said. 'Why?'

He was right. She turned to him and her mouth gave her away, as though she were an unfinished portrait, the artist unable to capture her smile. Her lips were mobile, uncertain. How he had never kissed her, he didn't know.

'Freedom,' he told her, 'is all what you do with it.'

'Oh God,' she said. She shut her eyes. 'I never knew what a torture it would be.'

She turned her body towards him hard, abruptly, awkwardly. Her movement was so sharp and she was suddenly so close he was almost afraid.

'I want everything,' she told him. 'And here, it is possible to have it.'

Desire was so intense in her eyes that he felt empty; he was nothing compared to the limitlessness of her need.

'"Everything",' he said, 'is relative.'

She sat back in her chair and faced away from him again. 'Yes, it is.

'Here, I have not only the freedom to speak out but the chance to choose to do so or not. Can you imagine how much I would like to stay here and stay silent?' She looked back at him again and gestured out over the silky lawn to the hedges where tough, spiky September mums held up their stark white heads.

'Can you imagine' – her words came fast now but suddenly she stopped and breathed and reached for him – 'how much I want to lose myself . . .'

And she was lost; her hands stopped in the air, in mid-gesture. Instead of looking like she was reaching out to touch him, she looked as if she were protecting herself from blows.

'Yes,' he said.

She put her hands down. 'My child is in prison,' she said.

'Maybe not,' Ian ventured.

'If he is not in prison,' Anna told him, 'then he is somewhere worse.'

Ian had only one image in his mind of the mental hospitals in which the Soviets often held political prisoners – it wasn't even a visual image so much as a sensation. He had read that one way they had of punishing and controlling the politicals was to wrap them, swaddle them, in wet canvas. As the canvas dried, it shrank. It squeezed them so tightly that they could scarcely breathe and their circulation stopped. Sometimes prisoners subjected to this lost fingers or toes. More often, because it was combined with psychotropic drugs, they lost their minds.

'There is only one thing I can do for him,' Anna said. 'And that is nothing – not to alter my life in any way. If they think that they can use Seriozha to get to me, then there is no limit to what may happen.'

'You are going to be very famous, Anna,' Ian said

quietly. 'You are what we have all waited for – a mother fighting for her child. It's strange how we can't seem to find the energy to fight for our own lives, but you have somehow made us conscious of the lives that depend on our own.' He paused. 'You are also, I'm afraid, a perfect media image.'

Anna looked at him. It was the first time, he thought, that she had ever looked at him entirely without hesitation, without reservation, without any kind of fear at all. Then she smiled, that smile that never touched her lips and was only in her eyes.

Though he was about to leave, he was suddenly happy.

But after a few seconds, the smile waned, like a light on a dimmer.

'What is strange to me,' she said, 'is that I am a mother fighting for a child, but my own child is dead.'

'Anna.'

'It is the same,' she said. 'Don't you see? For me, Seriozha must be dead.'

I wish that I could be your child, Ian thought, and reddened. He stood up.

'It's not the same,' he told her. He spoke standing above her and she had to look up at him. 'You yourself said that when you love, you ask only that the person you love be alive and well, wherever he is.'

She took his hand and held it to her cheek.

'You are a good man,' she told him.

'You just said I was a child.'

She said nothing but rubbed her lips back and forth once across the back of his hand. It was not a kiss, it was more painful than a kiss could have been.

'You are not alone, Anna,' he told her. 'Maybe it doesn't mean very much, but I'm with you. I want you to know that.'

'It means a great deal,' she said. 'Did you think I didn't know?'

Now she gave his hand back to him and looked into his eyes.

'You are not a child,' she said.

'Maybe I am,' he said, 'if being a man means loving anything more than I love you. This is what I cannot understand about my father.'

His face was too serious; he could tell by her face, which was taut and vulnerable.

'I can't help it,' he concluded. 'Suddenly I have the most incredible sense of how short life is, how precious. There is so little that really means anything, when you come down to it.'

Fear came back to her face. She stood and for a moment took both his hands in hers. Then she walked quickly back to the house, turning only once, when she already had her hand on the door.

The day after Ian left, the house took on a hollowness that made her restless. Mary Ellen had gone back to school; Kate was out on an errand. Anna wandered from room to room in the sad stillness of the upstairs. Eventually, she discovered the attic.

The McDonoughs' attic ran the length of the house. It was a huge vaulted space. Oak beams held in place pale spruce planks, still dry and clean as the day the roof had been raised. The bare cleanliness of the wood, its painstaking, ordinary perfection reminded her of the raw pine cathedrals she had seen once or twice in the Russian countryside. This impression was enhanced by Kate McDonough's orderliness, for almost nothing was kept in the attic – suitcases of summer clothes, the children's old toys, several boxes of Christmas ornaments.

Yellow light slanted in through a fan window at the opposite end of the stair; this light cascaded like bounty from a cornucopia in the wooden emptiness. The emptiness, with its old-fashioned smell of cedar shavings, was delicious.

Even though she had become accustomed to the spacious privacy which was as inherent to the McDonough house as electric light and running water, the hollow silence of the attic intoxicated her. She nearly lost her balance on the top step; it was physically disorienting to suddenly find herself alone in such an enormous, quiet space.

I have never been so far from home, Anna told herself. And she realised as she thought it that she did not mean home, the home she had had with Pavel, in which Seriozha had been a boy, but the home she had lived in as a child. That, too, had been a wooden house, with staunch, scrubbed pine beams. It was in one of the forgotten parts of Moscow, an old cottage with painted cutout trim that was too pretty to survive postwar progress.

She remembered thinking as a child that the bare wood boards were horrible and cold when she woke up in the morning. That was before she had lived in a new apartment with a cement floor. She remembered, too, loving the old iron bed that had been hers – ornate as a valentine, and painted white with a cheap paint that sometimes powdered her hair during the night. The mattress was ruined and sank in the middle; there she would curl up like a hibernating cub, pulling the blankets in on top of her. Years later, when she had learned to sleep in Pavel's arms, the taste of those childhood sleeps came back to her; the taste of warmth, of safety – a fresh neutral taste like water – and the taste of dreams – a sweet and spicy taste like Christmas candy.

Perhaps it was the scent of cedar which recalled the cinnamon or allspice in those Christmas sweets; suddenly she saw her father. Her father as he had been in that house. A big man in a small house, his knees making the writing table rise when he was excited, his voice too low for a tall man. His voice, which was in reality a deep one, vanquished.

Unlike the very best poets, he was not arrested in the wave of 1937. But he had been silenced, nonetheless. The camps might have meant a kind of mental release to him; if he knew where he stood, his voice, at least in his own mind, might have boomed out in its natural timbre. The warnings, the interrogations, his wife, who was an official's daughter, his own daughter, who was born during the war when Stalin was the Father of the Fatherland, the Friend of Children, and Hope of Mankind – all these combined to tie his tongue so utterly that as a man of forty he actually began to stutter.

He had this stutter until the end of his life. The only time he was free of it was when he sang – as a young man he'd been a baritone; he'd even sung Mahler – but when he spoke, she never heard him complete more than a sentence or two before that humiliating hand grabbed his throat and throttled his words into syllables.

If you wanted to communicate with him, she caught on quite early, you had to write. As a schoolgirl she would leave notes around the house for him. As soon as she was old enough, she left the notes in English. It was their secret language; her mother spoke nothing but Russian.

*Dear Papa*, she would write, *if I only had pink ballet slippers instead of black, my feet would fly*. This was the kind of thing that was safe to say to her father, who understood and might draw big pink shoes on his good white paper and give them to her with a magic rhyme to make them dance. Her mother would scold her for asking for things they could not afford.

The scolding was justified. Since no one could hire Papa, it was Mama who provided for all of their material needs. Her mother worked incredibly hard as a chemist in a pharmaceutical plant. Her hands were always raw from chemical burns, her clothes smelled of formaldehyde. But she managed to obtain nail polish, which she meticulously put on and took off on the weekends, and her clothes were always smart and well cut.

It was this very determination to behave as though they were not poor that made Anna acutely sensitive to what they lacked. Only her father, who had lost everything and had no hope of ever having anything again, could make her feel that they were rich and special, that they had something of value that no one could take away.

Now she recognised that feeling again; it was love. A feeling of value. And a secret. Something which only one other person knew that you had and which no one could ever take away.

When the sun no longer hit the attic windows, Anna realised that it had been some time since she had heard the car pull into the gravel drive. But it was incredibly hard to make herself leave this huge space in which absolutely no one lived which was somehow like her small first home.

If only she and Pavel had had such an empty space when they had first fallen in love; but it was a desire edited by all the years that had passed since that event. In those days they would have been keenly embarrassed to have so much more than others. And love needed no space at all to grow, she knew. In fact, the less that you allowed it, the more virulent it became, the more determined to wrap its roots around you and survive until it took all the air out of your lungs.

It was with a knotted feeling in the back of her throat that she went down the stairs. Several times, under her breath, she said the word 'Papa.' But maybe it was 'Pasha.' By the bottom step it was only a slight sound, stymied by the memory of stuttering.

'It would be like a prison cell, without the window,' Sarah apologised.

Anna looked out of the open window to the Hudson River. It was a wide, Russian-style river, flat and dark; on the cliffs beyond it, small lights twinkled in the shapes of houses and churches.

'It's beautiful,' Anna told her. 'It makes everything seem quiet.'

Sarah looked at her for a moment, digesting what she had said.

'You're right, you know. There's something peaceful about it. When I look at the river, I don't hear the street noise anymore.'

Anna turned back to the interior of the tiny apartment. There was a studio bed, two unmatched chairs, a desk and a coffee table, on which was spread the Russian manuscript of her book.

'My father was a translator,' she told Sarah.

'I didn't know,' Sarah said. 'What did he translate?'

'Jonathan Swift.'

Sarah looked at her.

'How did he obtain the originals?' Sarah asked her.

'My father's books had been in his family. I can't tell you how much I wish I had them now.'

'What happened to them?'

Anna's gaze returned to the dark window. 'I don't know,' she said. Sarah did not press her. Instead, she got up and went into the kitchen.

'May I help you?' Anna asked.

'You couldn't fit in here.' Sarah laughed. She came back into the room with a teapot. The smell of good black tea infused the air.

'Sugar or jam?' she asked Anna.

Anna sat back in her chair. 'Okay,' she said, 'jam.'

Sarah pushed a large jar of raspberry preserves towards her. Anna took a spoonful of it and stirred it into her tea.

'Take more,' Sarah said.

'Thank you,' Anna said. Her voice was suddenly small.

'I want you to feel at home with me,' Sarah told her.

For a moment they were both silent.

'Why did your father choose Swift?' Sarah asked. 'He must have known there was almost no chance that they would publish it.'

'My father was a poet,' Anna said. 'Under Stalin, he was "encouraged" to turn his talent to more "educational" themes.'

'I wondered,' Sarah said thoughtfully, 'where your book came from. Forgive me, you know what I mean. Most scientists couldn't write something like this.'

Anna studied Sarah sitting there on the edge of her chair. Her face was white and tired; her hands, thin and slightly smudged with ink or newsprint, actually reminded her of her father's hands.

'Russia is a country where almost no one has his first choice of careers.' She shrugged. 'But don't misunderstand me – precisely because my father was a poet, I never wanted to write. I love rocks.' She realised how silly this sounded and began to smile. 'I really do. I love rocks and

195

dirt and fossils because they are the opposite of words. They simply are what they are. They tell us about the earth without interpretation. I detest words.'

Sarah spread her long, pale fingers on her knees. 'That's hard to believe,' she said.

'You know why I became a geologist?' Anna said, suddenly leaning towards Sarah.

'Why?'

'To study volcanoes,' Anna announced. 'All my life I've loved volcanoes. I've never seen one – though there are many on the eastern coast of the USSR. That's a military area and I was never allowed to go there.'

Now Sarah sat back. 'Would you rather have brandy than tea?'

'Why not?'

Sarah took out a bottle of Grand Marnier and poured it liberally into two brandy snifters. She held her glass out to Anna and they hit their glasses together, a little too hard. Then Anna drained hers while Sarah took a small sip.

'I knew you'd do that,' Sarah said; she drained hers in turn.

The brandy burned a delicate path down the back of Anna's throat. Now she began to feel warm. She reached out and touched Sarah's hand.

'Do you know why I wanted to study volcanoes?' she asked her.

Sarah shook her head.

'Because a volcano is the earth in convulsion,' she said. 'There is nothing you can do to stop a volcano. It is the earth angry and unappeasable.'

'Interpretation,' Sarah charged.

Anna laughed. The brandy was so warm it was like affection itself.

'You're right, of course. I always wanted to *be* a volcano.'

Sarah refilled their glasses.

'Now it turns out,' Anna said, 'that the smoke and ash emitted by volcanoes is one of the few phenomena we can

196

study to try to predict what would precipitate nuclear winter.'

Sarah's smile disappeared.

'Anna,' she said quietly, 'sometimes I think that it's inevitable.'

Anna swirled her brandy in the bottom of her glass. When she raised it to her lips, the fumes were strong and biting.

'Let me tell you why I wrote what I wrote,' Anna said. 'I was afraid, I am still afraid. But at the time I could see nothing but what I was afraid of.

'And it was worse because my husband had just died. I was alone. Without him, I suddenly felt like a child in a crowd whose parent has let go of his hand. I remember quite distinctly the feeling of being physically small and defenceless, and everything was big and hard and rushing around me. There was nothing I could do. Pictures of horror invaded my mind, hundreds of them, and I couldn't stop them; it was as if my mind's eye had become a mad, preprogrammed camera lens, opening and shutting sixty times a minute. The photographs were always of war, of burning, of melting – sometimes of nothingness, cold, like a fog.'

Sarah's eyes were open. She was listening without hearing. The camera in her mind flashed on continuously, too; she had the expression of an eyewitness.

'All this,' Anna said, 'was when I felt nothing but fear. I wrote down the photos in my mind because if I had kept them inside I would have killed myself.

'What I did when I wrote my book,' Anna said, 'was express my fear. What I am trying to do now is to act upon it to survive.'

*I have no patience left. I am not even afraid anymore.*

*I don't care what's out there – I want to get out, I have to get out. I can't stand the wet cement in here, the constant echoing noise, the smell of antiseptic over the smell of human flesh decaying. It is an odour like rubber burning overlaid with the fake innocence of pine.*

*I want to breathe real air. Empty air. Air that is invisible and carries only a scent of rain.*

*I want to be alone again.*

*In the last several weeks, the survivors have begun to arrive; those who were caught unsheltered. Generally we see people from the East only, rural people, protected by the dismal wastelands they had lived in and the chance of the wind patterns.*

*They have herded us, the healthy ones, into huge, low indoor pens. There are metal rails which keep us divided into packs of twenty or so. You have to become insane before you can sleep; a still rational person vibrates with irritation and cannot shut his eyes.*

*The state geniuses who designed this shelter decided in their god-like wisdom that it would be unwise to create any windows. I have no idea how far underground we are. Sometimes I hear noises on the other side of my wall and am sure that the world is right there, that all I would have to do to touch the real world again is to break through that cinder block.*

*The sounds I hear are sighs that might be the wind or might be the wounded. I hear scratching, which might be insects and animals – or it might be those desperately irradiated souls who have been turned away at the entrance to the tunnel.*

*They say that past the lead doors, where the commandant and the officers are housed, there is a periscope. If you pay, it is said, you are allowed to have a look. It is not to be believed, of course – what does money mean now, even to them? And if it is true the price of a glance is considerably more than hard currency; I have never seen any ordinary person who passed through those doors come back.*

*I thank God it is not true, because I know that I would spend my life as quickly as a paper ruble even for one look at the sky.*

*My imagination won't work. I can't see anything inside but what is outside. All I see is the face of the woman next to me in unutterable detail – each pore, each pockmark, all of her expressions, a sigh, a half-sigh, a smile that makes* her look like a child, another that deforms her mouth like a tulip dying and curling in upon itself.

Of the others, I see their still bright shoes, I see the stupid patterns of their ochre-coloured shirts. Can you believe it – nine out of ten of our stalwart citizens got dressed in their best clothes when the sirens sounded and they were called to the shelters!

With my eyes closed these images are only sharper. I see things that I no longer notice with my eyes alert. It is only then, for example, that I remember that little Misha has one bent finger, for I love him and his hands are soft and perfect to me.

Misha has taken to Olga's soldier. It does us all good to see the child make a father out of him.

But what will happen next? Each day I am given a white coat and taken with the other surviving members of Medical Committee 20 to the sick wards. Medical Committee 20 originally had seven members; now there are four of us. None of us are doctors. We are:

A pharmacist (Arkady)
An agriculturalist specialising in poultry diseases (Sonya)
A chemist (Dmitri)
A geologist (me)

Arkady was well trained and is a dear person. Sonya is a hopeless idiot, but as you may imagine, she comes from the country and has what we used to call a 'big heart'. Living on a collective farm accustomed her to a high degree of physical discomfort and a low degree of expectation, and this enables her to give comfort where we better-trained city dwellers are likely to despair. Dmitri's prewar specialty was gasoline-substitute research, so that gives you an idea how useful he is. Although to be fair, he is extremely handy with equipment and has more than once fixed the generator (which has resulted in his being given extra rations of potatoes, which he shares with us).

A note about our white coats: there is a small laundry which functions on the other side of the lead doors for the nomenklatura. We registered a formal complaint as medical personnel about the waste of water this entails. Someone

199

called Sub-Commandant Karensky took the time to write us a brief memorandum explaining that while our concerns were appreciated, the interests of morale and discipline were better served by presenting authorised personnel in uniform. And indeed, it seems our uniforms soothe the need that everyone has to believe that someone is still in control.

The three members that we lost were the only real medical technicians among us – Lyuba, a pediatrician, and Illya and Semyon, two nurses. Due to the overwork, and the lack of anything approaching adequate nutrition (even with the cod-meal cakes mandatory for all health personnel), Lyuba caught pneumonia and died practically overnight. She would not stop working until her chances of recovery were so uncertain that Chief Medical Officer Shalamov would not permit the use of precious antibiotics. To my mind it was a form of suicide, and a scandal in a doctor. But I have heard that the suicide rate among the medical staff is quite high and of course I can understand the reason.

Shortly thereafter Illya was called behind the lead doors to the officers' quarters – Little Kremlin they're calling it now – and we never hear a thing about him. Semyon, who was very patient and good, has replaced a sick doctor on another ward and comes back to visit from time to time. Apparently where he works is closer to the outside than we are – it may be right next to the tunnel leading out – and it is the last stopping place of the living. It is a travesty that they have placed a person of Semyon's quality there, where all he can do is little more than comfort the dying, but the prejudice against country people continues here below. Semyon has that broad, blond, yet nearly Asiatic face; they will not admit that it harbours an incisive, diagnostic mind – as if, somehow, the better Semyon's mind is, the worse and more specious theirs will seem. And in this regard, they are, again, quite right.

It is my only thought now to be transferred to Semyon's ward, where – if it is true that it is the last chamber in the channel towards the tunnel opening – I shall, without any regret, escape.

If I am going to die of dysentery, I'd rather it be because

of radiation than poor sanitation. For two reasons: one, radiation is something no one can really do anything about as opposed to poor sanitation. To live under such medieval conditions, to die of diseases that were controlled or eliminated generations ago, infuriates me; it makes it only more apparent what a stupid, disastrous experiment of a species we were.

The second reason is that in order to become irradiated I would have to breathe the outside air, see the sun in all its naked, ultraviolet grandeur, touch the brown earth once again – I want it so much I could eat it!

This is what the destiny of human beings – the most intricate and beautiful of all God's creations – has come to: the choice of what kind of dysentery to die from.

It was early June when the emergency broadcasts swamped the airwaves and sirens sang out in their nauseating treble from every street corner in Moscow. My lovely American calculator watch suffered a heart attack at the moment of the Electromagnetic Pulse, and has recorded the hour, minute, second and millisecond of our tragedy as once it was supposed the eyes of a murder victim retained the photographic image of the murderer.

By my calculations it is now the end of August. You wonder why I would have to calculate the date in a government installation – formerly everyone was so date-, so deadline-conscious; every door lintel in every factory proclaimed the number of days left to fulfill the quota. But you reckon without those peculiar social geniuses, the planners, who – I know this for a fact – determined that it would be better for us to lose our sense of time. We may have to be here a long time, they reasoned. It will be better for us not to be too aware of each hour, each day as it passes.

On our side of the lead doors there are no clocks and no calendars. In fact, an old woman had a small, glass egg timer – the kind that are miniature hourglasses – confiscated and she herself was threatened with several days 'on the table', as the prison here is called. It is called that because offenders are made to lie flat, one right next to the other, on the floor in a room the walls of which are only four feet high. There are very bright lights on all the time. The planners figured out that this is the optimum way of breaking a person's resistance in the least amount of time. Indeed it takes only four or five days at the most to reduce the most violent and independent sort to a raw-eyed embryo, with no other concern than to be shielded from contact, sound and, above all, light.

Since last I had time to write, I have witnessed the deaths of 234 men, 167 women and nearly 300 children. I lose count of the kids because they are so alive right until the moment when they die that I never think of them as dead. As well, their little playmates continue to speak of them, though they accept their passings, saying they will visit them, that they will make sure to share the toys next time, that they will eat cake together. Nearly every child I have treated remembers cake! The children have the most remarkably vivid memory for the good things that we have all left behind – cake, Christmas, new shoes, snow, fresh eggs rather than the pale powdered ones we are privileged to have from time to time. What do eggs taste like? I asked a seven-year-old boy from the Ukraine. They taste like daffodils, he told me. He meant that fresh eggs, no doubt cooked in butter, taste the way daffodils look when they first break the snow around Easter. I carried that image with me all day. It was the only beautiful thing that I have seen since I came here.

I am not sure about the size of days, not accurately anyway, but it seems to me that it is just one week since I was moved to Semyon's ward. It is horrible beyond telling. The terminally ill lie on wooden slabs covered with thin beaten metal and gouged in rivulets so that the blood and feces can be hosed off and run into a kind of irrigation ditch that divides the ward into four sectors. These people are considered so sick that they are not on the ration list for morphine or any other of the precious painkillers. They are scarcely fed. Why we are not allowed to kill them mercifully I cannot understand; but it has been decreed that they must be custodially cared for by the same people who have decreed that the ward floor must be scrubbed five times a

202

day. More energy and concern is expended in keeping the floor of the ward clean than in keeping the patients clean or even tidy.

The nights here are more than the dreamers of the Apocalypse ever glimpsed. The moaning is weak and minimal; at times, the only sound is the grotesque gurgling of the bloody stream of wastes moving out through the ducts. Energy is conserved by burning only the dim red directional and door lights. Sometimes, when the ventilators are overworked and the air is hot and humid, one sees the small red lights glowing in a hellish haze of moisture and one feels sure that the person bending over the next bed is not the doctor but the devil. Don't ask me what it smells like here – God is merciful and I, like the rest of the staff, have lost my sense of smell. I am not the only one who thinks I have met the devil in this ward. The most common conversation is this:

Patient: Doctor, when will it [the pain, the war, the human race] end?

Doctor: The devil only knows.

How much I have learned about my primitive, my ancient Motherland by hearing this old familiar phrase repeated here below! In English, I know, people say 'God only knows'! In Romance languages it is the same. But we Russians cherish a personal devil as the Western countries embrace a personal God. We have suffered so much that the devil is our prayermate; we are capable of desiring to be delivered from life by despair if there is no other way. It is the devil who has a face for us, and a willing ear and a ready tongue. I myself find that there are often times when I am so bloated with disgust and spite that I absolutely cannot envision a God who would listen to what I have to say.

Where is the God who will understand the last fifty-six hours? I know that it is fifty-six hours precisely because the first twelve hours I counted by seconds and minutes according to the pulse of my dearest friend. Now I cannot block out that throbbing measurement from my brain.

Yesterday they carried Olga here, dying of complications from a low radiation dose that, by itself, might have been nothing. You see, sometimes a person absorbs such a minimal amount that we don't really even register it – the scanners we use here are obviously very crude, they serve only to provide some sort of cutoff point. That person will seem completely normal until suddenly he begins catching every sort of infection and not responding to any treatment or drug; soon his system is quite out of control.

I stayed by her. I held her head up so that she could feel herself die with some dignity – you cannot imagine what it does for the dying to see something besides the damp, mildewed ceiling as their last sight of this world.

I promised to say goodbye again to her soldier and her baby, Misha. He's not a baby, of course, but as she died and spoke on and on (they all do, it's their last chance and it's piteous because no one listens; in each bed a monologue goes on; each row is a low, rumbling dissonance, the entire ward a tragic cacophony), she spoke of him as if he'd only just been born. Sitting there, listening, I saw the long, feathery hair she had been too nervous to cut until he was three. I heard the bumbling bubbles of his first laughter and his first words.

Olga died mercifully after only one day's agony. Semyon managed to allow the soldier, whose name is Nikolai, to slip in wearing a doctor's coat. All three of us could have lost our lives – Semyon for being responsible, Niki for doing it, and me just for knowing. None of us cared.

She didn't know any of us when she died. She kept asking for Niki, imploring that he should be told to take care of her son. No matter how hard he tried, he could not make her understand that it was him, right there, holding her, kissing her, until he was covered with blood himself.

For when they die of radiation sickness, they bleed from every opening, sometimes right through their pores. Her eyes were bloody, her ears bled and naturally she vomited blood until she was quite exhausted. It's quite different to see someone vomiting up his life rather than his last meal. You realise that it can never stop until they are dead.

How Nikolai bore it, I don't know. It's one thing to see people you don't know go through this – but someone that *you love . . . I wished my own eyes would bleed and blind me. Only the thought of there being no woman to hold Misha afterwards prevented me from breaking down altogether. When it was over, Nikolai and I washed in the Scrub Room; because we were so bloody, they insisted on following regulations to the letter. We were stripped and hosed down and our skins rubbed all over with a fine – though not fine enough – metal brush. After that, raw, bleeding, our lips and eyelids swollen from both the brush and the strong disinfectant detergent, we left Semyon's ward – or Kolyma as it is called, after that part of Stalin's gulag from which so few people returned. Actually, the whole wing is Kolyma; Semyon's ward is Izvestkovaya, which was the last outpost of the Siberian labour camps, an Inferno of psychopaths and syphilitics, at which the average life expectancy of newcomers was – at most – a few weeks.*

*We walked back to the children's ward very slowly. The soles of our feet were throbbing. We were past tears; in any event, the disinfectant had dried up the mucous membranes of our eyes.*

*'I have to get out of here,' Nikolai said. He said it quietly, simply. 'I don't care what's out there.'*

*'There is a way,' I said.*

*He stopped and looked at me wildly for a second. Then he started to walk again and I did, too, so that we could talk without drawing attention to ourselves.*

*'How?' he whispered.*

*'With the dead,' I told him.*

*He laughed; it was a horrible laugh, full of relief.*

*'But what if they just burn them?' he asked.*

*'They do, but they have to take them out to do it. Don't forget we are underground; the amount of oxygen that it would take to burn the dead would overwhelm our ventilators.'*

*'But who could they make go outside to do it?'*

*'Think,' I tested him. 'The people who are already out there and desperate to get in. They'd do anything.'*

*He laughed that laugh again.*

'You must have been a terror in whatever it was you did before,' he said. 'What did you do?'

'I was an earth scientist,' I told him.

'You were wasted,' he laughed. 'With such an astute understanding of human motivation you should have worked for the Party. You might have become the first woman head of State Security.'

'Shh,' I said. 'Someone might hear you.'

We found Misha playing 'dinner' with two little girls. It is one of the favourite games of the children and consists entirely of imagining food and eating it. Naturally, they are all very good at it! One of the girls even slapped Misha's hand gently for holding his ice-cream spoon incorrectly! And it was true – in his ardour to eat his airy ice cream, Misha was holding his invisible spoon in his fist. Someone, before, had brought that little girl up well.

We played, too; Niki pretending to carve a huge goose and I stirring a big pot of soup like a witch, threatening to throw the children in head first if they weren't good! We laughed until tears rolled down our cheeks. Then real dinner came – oatmeal with 10 millilitres of cod-liver oil. I put morphine in Misha's bowl.

When he was unconscious, I demanded the right, as a member of Medical Committee 20, to bring him to the Central Medical Office. I had kept my MC 20 papers, luckily, for the Kolyma staff has no rights and privileges. Everyone prefers not to be reminded that we exist. They let us go.

Once in the hall, we slipped quickly back into Kolyma, where it was already dark. It is their one concession to mercy; they turn the lights out early at night. In the healthy wards the lights are always on for security reasons. But here, they are not afraid of the insurrection of the dying; no one is more cooperative than someone who is desperate to live. And, of course, we have no crime in Kolyma; our 'zeks' have not the strength for rape or murder; the only thing they covet they cannot possibly steal. Occasionally someone 'cashes in his chips' and ceases to be a productive citizen of the USSR, but since they have saved us the trouble *of punishing them, we treat them 'leniently' – allowing them the same cremation as everyone else.*

We waited in the dark for our moment; it came during the shift in staff. Then we climbed into our body bags – Niki holding the white, comatose Misha inside his own loose shirt – and lay down side by side on an unattended wagon.

'Who left these here?' I heard a voice bark. A guard.

I felt someone's hands moving over me and then picking up the tag at the top of my zipper to read the number.

'One zero four zero six,' I heard a familiar voice say. 'Move these out of here.' It was Semyon. He recognised the numbers because he had procured the bags for me and, I had once thought, Olga. He pressed his hand against my face for a moment; I knew he was saying goodbye.

I must have slept. I don't know how long we were in the morgue, but it cannot have been too long, for only two layers were stacked on top of us. This was not as terrible as it sounds, for shielded by the real dead, I could open my zipper a bit and breathe. As well, I was grateful for the weight of the bodies – and they don't weigh very much, our dead – for the room was obviously unheated. But this was a good thing, too, for I could tell by the frigid cold and the draught of air across my eyelids that we were indeed next to the opening.

How can I express to you what happened next? The world has ended and the definitions of happiness and pain have all been rewritten.

Doors opened; and men came in to move us by hand. They actually sang as they worked! Low songs, prison songs. They laughed and told dirty, disgusting jokes – I wanted to scream out with laughter at their loathsome humour, it was so alive! As it was, I tried to remain rigid when I felt a man put his arms around me and pick me up.

'This one's a woman,' he said.

'Great,' taunted one of his colleagues. 'Why don't you open the bag? After you die, we can use your prick as a Geiger counter.'

They laughed; I felt my man's muscles contract with revulsion.

'You're animals,' he told them.

'And you,' someone answered, 'you're a little Pushkin; if somebody insults your corpse you challenge him to a duel.'

More laughter. I was heaved into a truck; I knew it was a truck because for the first time in weeks I could smell. I smelled the exhaust from the engine, the acrid odour of gasoline against the frosty odour of snow. The real corpses were frozen and had no odour – or maybe I had just become immune to their odour from constant exposure to it.

And then, as the truck crunched to a halt and everything was suddenly quiet, I smelled a fire – a plain pinewood fire – the healthiest, most beautiful fragrance in the world.

It must have seemed wonderful to the workers, too, because for a long moment no one spoke. Then someone said: 'What a waste of a good fire!' Everyone agreed with this apparently, for no one spoke or moved. Finally there was the voice of the person I had come to identify as the Supervisor.

'Let's go!' he said.

I felt the men move towards us reluctantly. I was picked up and carried in someone's arms – maybe it was my previous romantic defender? – and laid down, quite gingerly, on the fire.

For almost a full minute I lay there, in an ecstasy of warmth. The canvas of my bag had been stiff with frozen moisture and now I was enveloped in steam. The steam penetrated my anguished muscles, my icy, brittle bones; suddenly I was deeply, deeply relaxed. All I wanted was to sleep.

Then there was Nikolai, pulling me up abruptly, the flaming canvas peeling off me as I stood.

'Move!' he screamed at me. He stood, black with soot, holding the child in his arms. Misha's wispy blond hair began to burn.

I moved. I picked my feet out of the fire and plunged my hands into the snow on the ground, grabbing handfuls of it and smothering Misha's head. The snow melted and his singed hair came off on my hands. He awoke and started to cry out with pain and terror.

'Holy Mother of God!' someone shouted. I turned to see a few terrified faces illuminated by the fire. Beyond the faces it was night and fresh snow was falling.

'Let's run,' Niki said. We ran, our feet sinking into the untrodden snow, our legs crumpling weakly beneath us.

'Stop, stop,' people screamed behind us.

'Don't,' Nikolai gasped at me.

But they were catching up with us.

'Don't be afraid,' I heard a voice say. I couldn't help myself; I turned to see who spoke. When I faced them, they stopped.

And then I stopped. The faces were full of anxiety and concern. They were human faces.

Niki stopped. Misha clung to him. He whimpered now.

'Where will you go?' a face asked us.

Nikolai and I looked at each other. It was pitch black. Now that we were standing still I could see how thickly the snow fell.

'Come,' another face said. A hand was held out. Then another and another. But no one moved towards us.

I walked towards that hand. I don't know why, but with everything in me, I knew that I could trust that hand, it would never hurt me.

I reached the hand and I touched it.

'You're alive, aren't you?' the owner of the hand said. A man or a boy, blackened with ash, his pale blue eyes ghostly in his dark face.

It was not really a question. He said it tenderly. He was telling me I was alive, the way one tells a child who wakes up during a nightmare that it was only a dream.

We all stood there motionless in the freezing cold: these terminally ill, irradiated workers; a woman and a man in burnt rags; a bald child.

'What time is it, what day is it?' Niki asked.

They stared at him. He repeated the question.

'Do you know? Do they let you have a clock so that you know when to go to the tunnel?'

*It was such a sweet, normal thing to want to know. I smiled. But the faces around us were grave.*

*'We have a clock,' a deep voice answered him. 'But it doesn't matter. It's always like this.'*

*We looked at them and looked at the sky. There was no moon, there was nothing above us, only the thick snow.*

*Clouds of ash have blotted out the sun, I realise. And if this is true, then there must be a consequent cooling effect.*

*'Where are we?' I ask. I am shivering, but not from the cold – from fear.*

*'Near Cherkessk,' I am told. In the Caucasus Mountains. One of the southernmost points in the Russian SSR. It is August. And it is snowing. Huge, eerie flakes, so hard and so cold that they don't melt when they touch the skin.*

*I went and stood next to Nikolai and we pressed the child between us. Thus embraced with love and warmth, Misha finally calmed down and reached out above our heads to grab at the snowflakes.*

*'They're dancing,' he said. Perhaps he had been taken to the ballet, before.*

*'Can I touch him?' a short worker asked politely.*

*I nodded.*

*The worker gently touched Misha with just the tip of his finger. Misha allowed this. In fact, he smiled.*

*Then others came up, wanting to touch the child, wanting to talk to us about what it was like below. We walked back to the fire with them gratefully; we are with friends.*

It was about ten days before New Year's. It was the first time in weeks that Seriozha had had any idea what the date was and he wept with relief. He knew that he was right because today was the first day he had seen workers trudging up the snowy walk to the November 7th Psychiatric Hospital dragging *yolkas* – Christmas trees.

How human the trees made everyone look! The trees were impossible to manage unless they were well tied – and if you were lucky enough to be able to buy one you weren't going to browbeat the seller into tying it up for you. You had to have carried your own twine. And if you hadn't, then you managed, your hands sticky as the pine resin melted in your grip, cursing when the frozen needles pierced your gloves.

When Pelageya Isaayevna, the day nurse, came in with his lunch – *shee*, plain cabbage soup glistening with bacony-smelling pork fat – Seriozha inhaled it appreciatively and asked her if she had a tree.

She set down the metal tray and looked at him. Then a smile slowly worked its way to the surface of her face.

'Sergei Pavlovich,' she said. 'You're feeling better, aren't you?'

He nodded, soup already dripping down his chin and soaking the front of his shirt. She took a cloth from her pocket and dabbed his wet face. He stayed still and let her. He smiled at her – she was so fat and lovely today!

'If you are good, you know,' she said, 'you may be allowed to come downstairs on Thursday and see Grandfather Frost.'

When is Thursday? Seriozha thought. Is it tonight? And what will Grandfather Frost bring to the inmates of November 7th? Toy Kamchatka trucks? Toy Kalishnikov rifles? Or only blue plastic bottles of bubbles?

'I want a gun,' Seriozha confided in her.

She frowned. 'Sergei Pavlovich,' she said quietly, 'please be good.'

He was being good.

'Do you have a tree?' he repeated.

'Yes,' she told him. 'A nice one, too. As tall as you are.'

'Can I taste it?' Seriozha asked her. He remembered very well the luscious odour of Christmas trees, and the flavour of pine, candles smoking, roasted meat, the first vodka he had ever tasted, burning his lips from his father's glass.

Her face returned to its usual November 7th impassiveness. She cleared away his bowl – he had spilled most of it and had forgotten to be hungry as he thought about brittle red glass ornaments and coloured lights.

'Come back, Pelageya Isaayevna,' he said as she closed

the door, tray in hand. But he didn't say it with any force, and she ignored him, as she usually did.

So now it was just another long day, to be devoted to staring out the window and imagining what books he would be reading, if they'd let him have any books. In the last several days he had imagined reading Tolstoy's *Resurrection*, but he always got only as far as the first few opening pages, which were a description of spring in the country. There, he would lose himself remembering pussy willow and cherry blossoms. He imagined lying perfectly still, stretched as if dead on the pungent, thawing earth, with blossoms raining from the trees like a soft, early snow, covering him, hiding him. And under this blanket of tender, pale pink blossoms, safe from everyone's eyes, he dreamed.

He dreamed of Katinka. He held her very gently in his arms and sang to her. In his imagination he had an extraordinary voice – like an opera singer – it soared and whispered, his whole being evaporated and materialised in its tone. He wrapped her in his voice, he intoxicated her. He had had to abandon any hope of ever seeing her again once he had been carried through the doors of the November 7th; otherwise they would have crushed him by now. But in his heart of hearts – the heart they knew existed, but could never touch – he cherished only one hope: that he had managed to make her pregnant.

And lost in thoughts of babies, their milky skin, their breath like the grazing of those falling petals, he drifted in and out of sleep until Zalessky let himself in.

'Good afternoon, Khamenev,' Zalessky said. Since he used his last name, Seriozha knew that it was to be interrogation in earnest today.

'Happy Christmas,' he told Zalessky kindly.

'Happy New Year,' Zalessky corrected him. The New Year had replaced Christmas under the Soviet system. Religion was an opiate; delicious, as Stalin knew, allowing it to be dispensed only in official doses.

'Of course.' Seriozha nodded. 'Happy New Year. Do you have a tree?'

'Yes, indeed,' Zalessky said, softening in a way that was perceptible to Seriozha but not to Zalessky himself. 'Quite a good one, too. Major Petrov got me one from the special batch they get upstairs each year. A real beauty – you can smell the forest all through the house.'

Seriozha conscientiously reminded himself that Zalessky was a human. He had a nose, two eyes, a mouth to eat and speak with. He must live somewhere, have a table and a chair and a wife who probably was sad like any other wife when Zalessky didn't come home at night.

'What does your wife look like?' he asked.

'Not so young as your girl,' Zalessky told him, 'but tightly packed. You know, like a sausage.' He laughed and Seriozha gave up immediately.

'So,' Zalessky said heartily, 'did they tell you that Grandfather Frost is coming on Thursday?'

Seriozha stared out the window without answering. Snow was falling lovingly, delicately, like Bolshoi dancers in their white Tchaikovsky costumes intent on delighting the Christmas audiences of children and their mothers, who always cried. If you wanted to see young mothers at their sentimental best – before boredom and the suffocating demands of household, children and job had sucked all the life out of them – you could stand outside a kindergarten on the first day of school, or sell your soul to get tickets to the *Nutcracker*.

'Here,' Zalessky said, 'Grandfather Frost hands out some special presents. We make an effort to capitalise on the holidays, you know.'

Seriozha wished that he remembered how to laugh. Yes, he knew. In provincial factories, Grandfather Frost, warm in his red felt suit and white fur collar, sometimes had the keys to apartments in Moscow. In Moscow offices, he sometimes had tickets to Koktebel resorts. Maybe in the November 7th Hospital he had magic sleds that flew out over the city at night and landed soft in the snow of freedom.

Seriozha continued his silence.

Zalessky came over and stood next to him. He actually

put his arm across Seriozha's shoulders and stared out the window, as if what he saw, he saw with the same eyes as Seriozha.

'I saw your girl last night,' he said.

Seriozha looked up to where the snow began, a whirling something out of nothing, creating a pattern symmetrical and improbable as a man's destiny.

'I've never seen her look better,' Zalessky continued.

Seriozha stopped breathing.

'Maybe she's got something in the oven, you think?'

Suddenly the greasy soup that Seriozha had swilled came up in a wave. He vomited all over the windowsill, all over his blue hospital pajamas; he splashed Zalessky's shoes, which were no longer the scuffed English shoes of a disinformation regular, but the perfect Italian shoes of an officer who travelled in the Chaika lane, never having to walk through the wet streets.

'The devil take you!' Zalessky moaned. It gave Seriozha pleasure to hear an ancient religious expletive on the lips of this robot. He felt the pleasure in the pit of his sore, alien stomach.

Zalessky sat in the one orange vinyl chair without bothering to look at him. He picked up the phone that never worked when Seriozha touched it, and five minutes later Pelageya Isaayevna returned with the tasteless blue liquid that made Seriozha dream.

He swallowed it.

His stomach coiled into a tight knot – it was not really his stomach but a snake that lived inside him. And in a few minutes, the snow turned green and pink and sometimes floated backwards to the sky.

'You ass,' Zalessky told him. 'Do you think anyone really gives a shit about you?'

The snake relaxed and stretched out to its full length. If it were not so tired, it would have wound around Zalessky and squeezed until it flattened his lungs. But the snake had just eaten Seriozha's insides and was sated and slow.

'Keep it up as long as you like,' Zalessky said, irritated but again in control of himself. 'But it's a waste. We don't

214

give even half a shit about you. All we want is to be able to do with your mother as we wish. You don't matter at all. Fight or don't fight. Talk or don't talk. Write or don't write. For us, it's all the same.'

In his mind, Seriozha coaxed the snake to eat more, he tempted it with a finger, a cheek, an eye. He fed himself to the snake piece by piece, until there was nothing left.

A few days before Christmas, George drove to New Haven alone. He took the Rolls Silver Wraith and listened to a tape of Karajan conducting the Stuttgart in Corelli's Christmas Concerto. As he sped along I–95, the car reverberated with the throbbing of religious violins and violas. He remembered the same massive musical emotion from the Christmas service at Fordham when he'd been a student. Exhausted from exams (none of these 'reading periods'; they'd had to go through straight from their papers and courses to exams) and suddenly homesick, twelve hundred boys would participate in a very long, very solemn High Mass. The Mass was still in Latin, the incense still strong enough to make you faint on an empty stomach, the music still by Palestrina. It was music that George remembered in perfect, wholesome detail the way a child remembers. He had played the cello. It was the last time he had with passion done something that he wasn't very good at.

He noticed that there weren't any Christmas decorations of any kind in Jack O'Keefe's office, though someone had made an effort to stand up a handful of Christmas cards on the bookcase. One was a Flemish Nativity scene and George tried to recall where he had seen the original. When Jack's door opened and Jack's last patient, a nineteen-year-old girl with thin blonde hair and Dresden skin, walked out, he remembered. The painting had hung in the dining room of one of his old firm's London clients.

'That you, George?' Jack's voice came from the other room. 'Come in.'

'You won't get me on the couch,' George joked. But he went in as he spoke. In the room there was no couch, only

215

two very soft, old-fashioned leather chairs; Jack's desk, behind which Jack sat in a rather more modern chair; and a wall of bookcases.

'Haven't you heard?' Jack asked. 'We don't use couches anymore.'

If Jack had been anyone else, George would have kidded him about the Dean's having caught up with his amorous successes. It would have been the natural thing, between two men of their age, old class-mates as they were. But Jack was a Jesuit and this was a line that George would not go over, as he would not have gone over such a line with his own mother.

In the rigorous tradition of the Society, Jack O'Keefe had gone straight on to his Ph.D upon leaving college. Then he had gone to medical school. It had taken him twelve years to become a psychoanalyst, nearly seven of which had coincided with his own analysis. George noticed that the old photograph of Freud visiting Clark University in Worcester was still hung reverently behind Jack's head.

'She's pretty, isn't she?' Jack asked George, not missing his train of thought by too much.

George realised that he must have looked embarrassed.

'Do you know what her problem is?'

'I'm not sure I want to know,' George objected.

'It's not the confessional, you know,' Jack said.

George waited to hear something macabre, sexual.

'Her brother was killed by a drunk driver two years ago and she has become obsessed by drunk drivers. To the point where she can do nothing all day except drive around spotting drivers who look like they may have had one too many. Then she reports them.'

George laughed a slight laugh of relief.

'Just a good citizen, I'd say. We need more like her.'

'It's ruining her life, of course.' Jack had opened a drawer and taken out a bottle of Chivas and two glasses, the type shrimp cocktail used to come in.

'Poor child,' said George as he took his glass. Then he looked at his friend. 'How do you stand it?'

'Oh, well, it's always worst at the holidays.' Jack grimaced as the scotch hit the back of his throat, and exhaled. 'She's okay. I'll break her of it by spring. She's working hard.'

'Working?' George said sarcastically. 'I thought all you had to do was dream – rather, that you can't do anything but dream.'

Jack smiled the sort of prescient smile that George believed all religious people eventually developed. 'Some people's dreams are very hard work.'

'I daresay.'

That porcelain skin, thought George, feeling the liquor; merely the result of disturbed sleep and carbon monoxide.

'Do you really believe in all that?' he demanded, gesturing towards Freud's photograph as they picked up their coats to leave.

'It's a way of picturing it,' Jack told him with the earnest indulgence that he used whenever George brought up the matter, as he had perhaps once a year since Jack had gone in to it. 'It's a metaphor, not so different from the ones we were brought up with. Original sin. Father, Son, Holy Ghost. Christ, George, if you can believe what we were brought up with, you can believe anything.'

'You don't believe in that, do you?' George asked.

'It doesn't matter. Do you?'

'I don't know,' George said quietly. 'But I think that it does matter.'

The two walked out onto the Yale campus. A few students recognised Jack and waved. Some others seemed to know him but not acknowledge him. No one called him 'Father.'

'Why doesn't anyone call you "Father" anymore?' George wanted to know.

'I have enough problems.'

George nodded. Not for the first time, it was abundantly clear to him how his friend could have managed to sacrifice the joy of ever having children of his own.

They wound their way towards the pub where they always ate when George visited. They ordered hamburgers and more scotch. It was dark, and innocuous renditions of

Christmas carols oozing from too large speakers only made the atmosphere more desperate. Above the bar, gold-foil garlands glittered.

'What is it?' Jack asked very gently. They had been sitting there in silence for longer than George realised.

George took a deep breath and was conscious that to his friend it must have seemed a sigh.

'They're sending Mary Ellen home from school before her exams,' he said. 'She weighs ninety-seven pounds.'

'Oh Lord,' said Jack sadly. 'We see a lot of that here.'

'I thought you might.'

The two stopped talking as the waitress put the heavy burgers in front of them. George looked at the fatty, red juices soaking into the bread and felt anger choking him.

'What happens?' George asked. 'What do you do?'

Jack shook his head. 'That all depends,' he said, 'on the family.'

'Oh God,' George sighed. 'Is it my fault?' The words rushed out though he could hardly hear his own voice.

'Do you think it is?'

'Is it?'

'There's time for all that,' he said. 'But what happens next? Has she seen someone?'

'Only the doctor down there. Kate has gone down to get her and I have to find someone in Greenwich.'

'I can help you with that,' Jack said.

George forced a smile. He looked at his food again and again gave up. He picked up his glass and swirled the remaining scotch into the melted ice cubes.

'What do you usually do with this?' he asked Jack again without looking at him.

'They usually have to spend some time in the hospital,' Jack told him matter-of-factly.

George sat there, listening now to a synthesised version of 'Deck the Halls.' He felt completely lifeless.

'How's Kate holding up?' Jack inquired.

For an instant George pictured Kate – at the palpitating heart of crisis, committed, no demand too outrageous – and he was angry.

'She's doing quite well, considering,' George answered.

'There's always a lot of anger at a time like this,' Jack told him. 'These things are very tied up with anger – not just the kid's – everybody's.'

'It's hard to imagine where I will get the time to deal with this,' George said.

'Be careful of each other,' Jack said softly. Now, George thought, he sounded like a priest.

What have I done to deserve this? he wondered with anguish.

'It sounds like you caught up with it in time,' Jack reassured him.

For a second George drew a blank. He saw, not his daughter, but his wife. And then he saw, not the woman he had married, but a whole diorama of a life, cars to cuff links – daughters, diapers, lawns, fences, mortgages, miscarriages, sailboats, sons, Boy Scouts, Girl Scouts. It seemed something to be kept in a cigar box bound with a rubber band, safe in the back of the closet, with all the other artifacts that had been precious to him as a child.

Nine hundred people attended the Gala Christmas Benefit for the Smithsonian Institution at the Kennedy Center; its red carpeting and modern, snowflake-like chandeliers seemed to have been created just for their jubilant Christmas effect. Even the flags of every country which draped the two sides of the room seemed to lose the banal connotation of a gesture to the nations, and had become banners raised in celebration – a kaleidoscope of parti-coloured medieval standards hoisted to a fanfare of Renaissance trumpet music.

But Anna was still shaking. George kept his hold on her arm.

'Anna,' he said, 'tonight is a triumph for you. Don't let anyone cheat you out of it.'

'That's her *son*,' Sarah told him in a harsh whisper.

Outside the centre, attempting to block the way in, had been perhaps sixty demonstrators, most carrying placards that were enlarged photographs of Sergei Pavlovich Khamenev – Seriozha.

It was a grainy, tormented image, blurred and under-exposed. But there was no doubt that it was Seriozha; and it was the last evidence that anyone had seen of him since he had reportedly been taken to the November 7th Psychiatric Hospital several months earlier.

The demonstrators were mostly from a group of Ukrainian nationalists. Anna had received a number of tough, even threatening letters from them, which she had tried to respond to in strong and sympathetic language. But it was no use; there was no middle ground for them. They viewed her as a hypocrite and a traitor because she did not use her position to publicly denounce the Soviet Union.

In nearly three months of nonstop speaking engagements, it was the third time that she had been confronted with these pictures of Seriozha. They were always carried by members of émigré organisations; even the women rushed up to press the posters against the windows of the cars Anna rode in – perhaps the women carried the photos with more bitterness and urgency than the men. The first time it had happened, Anna had been so shocked that she could not speak at the meeting of Protestant clergy to which she had been invited. The second time it happened, she had tearfully stood her ground outside a New Jersey high school and tried to talk to the demonstrators. But her halting, thoughtful sentences had only maddened the crowd, and her host, the school principal, had had to pull her bodily into the building.

Tonight they had had to remain in the car while the police got the demonstrators behind stanchions.

But then a young man – dark, handsome, Seriozha's age exactly – rushed up and threw himself against the car.

'Tell them what it's really like!' he screamed at her. The police moved instantly to drag him off.

He kicked at them and threw punches wildly. They began to beat him back with their rubber sticks. Anna's stomach muscles clenched and she involuntarily shut her eyes.

'He must be drunk,' George had said.

'*Khuligan*,' Sarah muttered under her breath.

Anna stared at her. 'Hooligans,' in the USSR, generally acted on some official instigation. They were the taut, frustrated bowstrings that the Party played to its own tunes.

Sarah turned her back towards George just slightly. 'It wouldn't surprise me a bit,' she said. 'There are more than one or two people betting on what you're going to do next. The new year is an election year, don't forget.'

George had laughed. 'Your friend here advocates the violent overthrow of the government,' he told Anna.

And Anna had just smiled; Sarah was radical, expected the worst of the government at every turn and did not care for the Foundation's political bedfellows. But George had never done more than make a suggestion or two about where or where not to speak; she had never been pressured.

'Smile,' George said to her now. A flash went off and she was blinded.

'That's it, thank you,' he said to the photographer. They resumed their slow arduous press for the dais, fighting their way upstream through sequins, feathers and black gabardine. She was kissed by people she had met at the McDonoughs' party, and shook hands with two senators, an American Olympic runner and the Librarian of Congress.

She was seated between George and James Bradford, a geneticist, whose popular and searching essays on science she had been given to read by Mary Ellen. It absolutely astounded her that he was as delighted to meet her as she was to meet him.

He stood and held out her chair as she sat down. He was more than ten years older than she, but had the tanned, tense energy that she was beginning to take for granted in many of the successful Americans she had met.

'One of my oldest friends,' he told her, 'used to be the head of the Geology Department at Columbia. He heard you in Paris, when you spoke; when he came back to the States he was very impressed.'

Anna smiled. He was, she was certain, a much more interesting person than she was. He had travelled all over the world, including to the Soviet Union; he knew scientists everywhere. But she could not make him stop talking about her. She was embarrassed.

'He told me that you had made his lifetime of work in the field worthwhile. That's incredible.'

'Too incredible,' she said.

'You're wrong,' he argued. 'We have all gone along doing our work forever, you know, and so many of us have been very nearly overwhelmed by despair in the last few years. What were we doing getting mothers to think about nutrition for their unborn babies if those kids weren't going to grow up? What were we doing, in the case of my friend, figuring out substitutes for fossil fuels that will be depleted in twenty years' time, if in twenty years' time we are very likely not going to be here at all?'

George now turned towards them; he had been chatting with the woman on his right, whom he introduced as an editor with the National Geographic Society.

'Jim,' he said to Dr Bradford, 'aren't you going to let the lady have an evening off?'

'No way,' Bradford said. 'I'm depending on her.' He winked at Anna and she relaxed. A waiter came and refilled their glasses with champagne; another came and put small plates of smoked salmon in front of them.

'If the world ends tonight,' George announced, 'we won't even feel it.'

'We probably won't feel it anyway,' the doctor said, 'seeing that we're sitting here in Washington.'

'That's fine with me,' the National Geographic editor put in. 'If I have to go, I would rather be vaporised.'

'You have a point.' Dr Bradford nodded.

George raised his glass. 'Life is short,' he said seriously. 'It always was. Let us make the most of it while we have it.'

There was a prayer and then the director of the Smithsonian began the evening's speeches. Anna was aware that her champagne glass had not been empty all evening and that the crowd was responding happily to all that was being said. It was a holiday and it struck her that here in America, in this room full of the richest, best-educated and most privileged people in the country, there was the same under-current of desperate partymaking that attended the New Year in Russia. Except, perhaps, not as sincere – in a Russian gathering, people could be quite gritty and deter-mined to have a good time; here the desperation was present, but the determination lacking.

Dr Bradford spoke next. He recalled being a young child and being brought to Washington. He had thought, he said, that the cloud-white dome of the Capitol building, firmly lodged as it is in the blue of the sky, was where God lived.

He had experienced a physical feeling of the paternal authority of government, he remembered. As he walked around Washington, holding his father's hand and listening to the stories of Lincoln and Jefferson and FDR, he had felt the quintessence of childish safety and security. And pride.

Now, at fifty-seven years of age, he told the crowd, he still felt that way when he came to Washington. He couldn't help it. It didn't matter that now he was in a position to know personally a lot of people who worked in the government, to know that they were, like everyone else, human and capable of error. He still had a deep, uncon-scious ability to believe that those in power knew better what was good for the rest.

Maybe, Bradford suggested, there was something bio-logically inherent in human beings, as in many other species, which made them crave authority. He suspected that this must be true, for there was everywhere evidence of it in the ways society organised itself, whether around families, religions or even the rebellion against traditional institutions. It seemed mankind always wanted an idea to submit to.

Oh God, Anna found herself thinking as Bradford went

on, it's Christmas. She believed that what the doctor was saying was right – she had seen the willful transformation of men into animals at the service of what some Americans still felt to be 'high socialist ideals' – yet something in what he said bothered her and she couldn't isolate what it was.

There was a spotlight on Dr Bradford; she traced its path across the crowd to the podium. In its smoky light the occasional sequin fluttered, diamond rings glittered as women put their hands in front of their faces to whisper, tiny sulphur flames flared as men lit their cigarettes.

She knew that Dr Bradford was trying to rouse this crowd from their silk and satin sleep. He was trying to awaken them by telling them that in spite of their education and position they were animals like ants, like fish, struggling according to the same principles of life and sharing the same small oxygenated space. His words were beautiful and intense; she saw the dark blue shadow over the jeweled crowd as the murk of the sea, full of the silent flittings and fannings of satiny tropical fish. Then she felt the fear of an animal huddled among its own, camouflaged by its own brothers, and she knew what was wrong.

The applause was polite when Bradford finished speaking. He waited only a few seconds before introducing Anna. She stood up and walked towards him.

'I want to thank Dr Bradford,' she said into the microphone. Hearing her voice boom out over the crowd never failed to stun her and she paused a moment.

'He is one of those real men of science, of whom I have been privileged to know personally perhaps one other, my husband. My husband, too, was a man whose knowledge of the physical world filled him with love, with graciousness towards all living things, with patience.

'But I am going to try Dr Bradford's patience a little bit, because I want to take exception to something he has suggested.'

She looked over at him. He laughed and nodded to her cordially.

'My friends,' she said. 'It is true that we have a strong, even biological desire to live by ideas. But that does not mean that all ideas are equal. There have been in the history of human society few ideas which have proven so worth living by as those in the Constitution of the United States.

'In my whole life, I have never been so alive as since I came here. Here, not only a person but an idea can breathe. Here a person can speak, can be published, can even broadcast his own television programme. Here a vote is not an empty gesture, but a statement that can be heard not only in a congressional district, or in Washington, but around the world.

'You are the most powerful people in the world. I don't mean the American government, or the American military. I mean the people sitting here in this room, the people in every city and town, on the farms, even the children who are too young to vote but old enough to help in other ways to elect officials who they feel represent them. The fundamental idea of your Constitution puts very real power into your hands. This is what the government of my country really fears.'

Applause thundered down from all sides of the room. It electrified Anna; she felt almost that she was growing taller under its force.

'This is why there will never be a real election in my country,' she said. Even with the microphone she had to raise her voice over the crowd. She waited.

'In my country,' she continued, 'Christmas is not officially celebrated. It has been replaced by the New Year. The idea of God is yet another that the leaders of my country cannot risk.

'But people celebrate anyway. Christmas is a feast that predates Christ, it is a feast of birth. People seem to feel this and they stop, at the end of the year, to celebrate life. The Soviet government can't suppress it and maybe we celebrate that fact, too; that life is something that is always more than we can account for, more than we can know.

'We are here together, in this season, to reaffirm life. Because we have become, in our generation, the curators and custodians of every living thing – including those ideas, like freedom of conscience, which live and are life-giving.

The rest of the world looks to the people of America to protect life, because you are the only people on earth with the real and immediate power to do so. You must. Thank you.'

The crowd rose to their feet. The sound of the applause coming back to her was a deafening, drowning wave. After a few seconds, she could no longer hear anything, but only saw the scene as if it were filmed without sound.

She went back to her seat. Each person on the dais stood as she walked by.

'That's the ticket,' George said to her.

When she got to James Bradford, he put his arms around her.

'You're a genius,' he told her.

She laughed. I'm a mother, she thought. And for the first time all night she allowed the dark image of the photograph of Seriozha to fill her mind. She kissed the black circles under his eyes, she put her fingers on his bruised, swollen lips.

She sat on the dais, quietly, her fingers pressed against her own lips, listening to the rest of the speeches, not hearing a single word.

After the dinner had been cleared away and the last speech given, there was dancing. A large band, each member ensconced in a white box decorated with the monogram of the band leader, struck up a loud, happy song and everywhere people pushed chairs out of the way and moved onto the dance floor. Anna felt the trombones stretch themselves along her nerves.

'We can slip out through the private reception area,' George told Anna.

Suddenly hundreds of green and red balloons were released from somewhere in the middle of the room. They floated drunkenly above everyone's head.

'I don't want to go yet,' she said.

'It's just starting to be fun,' said Sarah, who had come up to join them on the dais as the rigid protocol of the dinner began breaking up.

226

George looked down the length of the dais. It was nearly empty; those important enough to have been sitting there had been the first to leave. They were important enough to have other engagements. Or, as likely, important enough to enjoy asserting their privacy in public. James Bradford was flying in a friend's jet that night to join his family in Big Sur. He had actually invited her to come for Christmas.

She glanced at the dancers, moving over the floor with perfect freedom, some showing off series of smart, complicated steps, more merely bouncing up and down to the beat.

'Would you like to dance?' George asked.

The physical act of dancing seemed suddenly something as far beyond her strength as pole-vaulting. She looked at Sarah, who sat there flushed in her demure black velvet, unconsciously kicking the side of her chair in a nervous rhythm.

'Why don't you dance with Sarah?' she said.

'Don't be chicken, Anna.' Sarah laughed.

'What's that?' Anna said.

'Never mind.' George smiled. 'Come on,' he said to Sarah.

She watched George steer Sarah into the throng of dancers. They were both sleek in black, but they moved stiffly compared to those immediately around them. They did not look at each other.

In the nearly twenty years that she and Pasha had lived together, she could not remember dancing with him more than a handful of times. He was a terrible dancer. For a physicist, a man who knew more about the secret rhythms of the world than almost anyone else alive, he had not much sense of the tempo of a fox-trot, a waltz or a samba. He clung to her on dance floors, a slight sweat broke out on his upper lip and he applied himself so diligently to dancing that she always took pity on him after about ten minutes.

He was what he was, after all; Pavel was not capable of being charming, of doing things merely because they pleased other people – no matter how much he wanted to.

But she had been so happy dancing with him! As he struggled in her arms, one foot laboriously in front of the other, she had adored him and felt for the millionth time that he was the man most deserving of love in the world. How simple life had been in its way; Pasha was good and she loved him.

His simplicity had shone so starkly in the layered, shadowy reticence of their society. Or was it only that loving her husband and son had given her a simpler role? She watched the patternless movement of the sparkling dancers under the dim light of the chandeliers and knew that she had not really had any idea how complex were the lives of men and women until she came to America.

Suddenly a gentle and familiar voice spoke to her. She didn't see who spoke and for a moment believed that she was still hidden in her reverie of home.

'*Zdrastvutye*,' the voice repeated.

She now turned all the way around in her chair.

There, pudgy and pale in starched evening dress, was Konstantin Kyrstov, the head of the Geology Department of the Moscow Institute of Earth Sciences. His eyes were watering and red. She was shocked to see that he was such an old man.

'*Zdrastvutye, Annichka,*' he said quietly. He reached for her hand.

'Konstantin Dimitrievich!' she said, truly astonished. 'I can't believe it's you.'

She stood and embraced him. They had known each other for so many years; he had been in Pavel's class at the University, he had walked behind Pavel's coffin. The fact that he had had to be the one who dismissed her from her post at the Institute seemed only one small fact put beside so many others. He was someone from home.

'What are you doing here?' she asked him. Despite his position he had never travelled outside Eastern Europe before.

228

'We are the guests of the California Institute of Technology,' he told her. 'There are fourteen of us.'

Since being expelled from the Soviet Union, she had absolutely no contact with any of the official visitors that occasionally travelled from her country. Such travellers were under strict surveillance; they would never have risked losing their privileges by seeking out someone like her.

'But . . .' She looked at him searchingly; she still held on to his shoulders and was conscious of how old and frail and flaccid he felt under her hands.

'I'm an old man,' he told her, smiling with real pain and self-deprecation. 'They'll retire me next year.'

To travel to America had been his dream as it was everyone's. The Party doled out visas only as rewards, and only when they were entirely assured of the traveller's loyalty.

'Besides,' he said, looking off and knowing that she knew what he meant, 'my children and grandchildren are all at home.'

'Oh, Kostia,' she breathed. 'How strange life is. To see you here like this.'

'I heard your speech,' he told her. 'You could always rouse the masses.'

She laughed. 'How would you know?'

She had always been docile and professional at the Institute. She had accepted that men like Kostia were in control of her career and she had made the best of it, developing to an art the skill of never going about anything by direct means. Until Pavel had died.

'I knew.'

She felt a sudden and unreasonably strong affection for him and kissed him quickly on both cheeks.

'Have you heard anything?' she asked him in a whisper.

He knew what she was referring to.

He shook his head. 'He is certainly in the clinic,' he told her. 'More than that I don't know.'

She must have shown the despair she felt; she felt that

229

she was going to sink to the floor and howl like a wounded animal.

'Shh,' Kostia said, putting his hand on her arm. 'I'll try to find out more for you.'

She grasped his hand and kissed it.

Then a tall, fine-looking man came up to them. He carried himself with the arrogant grace of a ballet star. He was one of the handsomest men Anna had ever seen anywhere.

'Comrade Kyrstov,' he said, 'I hate to pull you away from such charming company but we are leaving now.'

He did not even look at Anna.

'I have to go,' Kostia told her apologetically, embarrassed by the young man. 'Don't worry, I'll be in touch.'

Anna watched the two disappear among the beautiful crowd, the tall young man elegant and at ease, Kostia so lumbering and awkward. Her breath stayed knotted inside her. It was as if that fat old man, whom she had once found so stubborn and irritating, were the last remnant of her family. She instinctively ached to run after him.

'You dance now,' Sarah said. She and George had walked up to her; she had watched them without recognising them.

'Oh no,' she whispered.

'Shall we go?' asked George.

Anna nodded.

'Who was that?' Sarah asked.

'Only someone I used to know,' Anna answered, without meeting her eyes.

December 31 was a Sunday. Kate, Anna and Ian spent New Year's Eve at Atherton-Crowell, a private psychiatric hospital near Stamford, with Mary Ellen. There was a party of sorts on the adolescents' ward; it had started at four in the afternoon. Anna drank sweet grape juice spiced with cloves from a small white paper cup. Ian had brought McDonald's milk shakes for himself and Mary Ellen. The girl glowered at him. She had not spoken to anyone since she had been sent from school. Kate was drinking coffee and her lipstick had come off on the cup. Now her face was colourless and soft under the high hospital light. George was in Washington.

Anna watched the teenagers in their faded jeans and too new pyjamas. Her eyes felt old and hollow. There were no fewer than three other girls who looked like Mary Ellen, their strong, tall bodies gone unnaturally limp and gaunt. She herself had hardly recognised Mary Ellen when she'd returned; she no longer resembled the tanned tennis player of September. She looked as if she had died and come back as a ghost to haunt them.

There was, on this most ebullient of holidays, no laughter. The young people on this ward scarcely even looked at each other and they did not smile. Not for the first time, Anna realised that smiling was mostly something one did because other people saw it.

She saw Ian try gallantly to draw Mary Ellen into a conversation. He sat close to her, telling her some story, touching her on the arm and on the knee as he went along. But though she looked at him with intense pain and longing, she did not talk to him.

Anna had read many sickening stories about teenage suicides in the papers; she tried to remember the worst she had ever felt as a girl. But that was in an utterly different world. It was harder now to have the incentive to struggle for the sake of the future. Could anyone really assure young people that they looked forward to a future – merely a normal life – anything like that their parents had looked towards?

She shut her eyes. She did not dare imagine the hospital where Seriozha was not a voluntary patient in earnest need of medical help, but a prisoner. She did not dare imagine Seriozha. Since it was true that he was in the November 7th, then they might already have subjected him to drugs like sulfazine, which was a kind of chemical shock treatment, driving the body's temperature above 104 degrees Fahrenheit and bringing on wracking pains and convulsions. Her only hope was that they still cherished some plan for him – some disinformation role, some denunciation, even some convincing blackmail – that would force them to keep him reasonably healthy.

At about four-thirty Ian whispered something to his mother. She straightened up.

'Anna,' she said apologetically, 'I forgot what night this is. Please. Ian will take you home.'

Anna did not question her; only kissed her lightly on the cheek. She had no desire to return to the new apartment she had been given by the Foundation two weeks before – a lovely, anonymous place on the thirty-second floor of a building near the United Nations, where the beige carpeting was endless, the windows enormous and empty. She did not say goodbye and Kate did not notice. She kissed Mary Ellen; her face was both cold and moist. Mary Ellen looked at her briefly and then turned away.

In the parking lot, Anna stood shivering while Ian brushed the snow off the windshield with a folded newspaper.

'So tonight is the night they're going to air your segment on *60 Minutes*,' he said to her. 'This is a very big night for you.'

'I don't want to go home,' she said, conscious that she spoke in a small voice like a child.

'Okay,' Ian said, nodding without looking back at her. 'I'll take you to my place.'

It was nearly impossible to find a parking space in Brooklyn Heights in the best of times, Ian told her. Thank God for the snow and suspended alternate-side-of-the-street regulations.

'This is beautiful,' Anna said as they stood in the foyer of his apartment, stamping the snow from their boots. It was a large, old-fashioned apartment, full of books and chiming antique clocks. There were clusters of Staffordshire figurines which seemed to inhabit the unlit rooms – horn dancers, flower sellers, mythical gods and goddesses and, over the fireplace, a jovial, drunken-looking Shakespeare.

'It's a sublet,' he told her. 'A friend of mine who is a

232

professor is on sabbatical in Vienna. I only have it until next summer.'

Anna shrugged, as if summer were as far off in the future as the year 2000.

'I mean, it's not a real home, not mine anyway,' he said, embarrassed at how that must have sounded but unable to mitigate its meaning.

'A real home?' Anna repeated.

She looked at him and realised that it no longer seemed strange to her that a man of his age had no home and no family of his own. No stranger than the fact that she did not.

He turned on the television before he turned on the light. It was the end of the second segment; Anna would be next.

The *60 Minutes* crew had followed her around, off and on, for several weeks. They had lugged cameras into school auditoriums, Knights of Columbus halls, company cafeterias – all the myriad types of places where she had spoken in the last three months.

She saw herself as she supposed she must really be: impatiently waiting to speak amid the chaos and crowds of rallies; losing her temper and crying when she was cut off on a call-in radio show in Connecticut; paralysed with anguish when confronted by angry Russian anti-Soviet demonstrators.

Ed Bradley had interviewed her politely, even enthusiastically. She had found it easy to talk to him; he seemed to want to bring out the best in her, asking her questions she was eager to address, leaving her time to get the answers straight. It had all seemed quite natural, despite the fact that she knew she was on camera and speaking to the largest audience she had ever addressed, and probably would ever address, in her life.

Sarah had come and put on makeup for her, and she had to admit she felt a thrill when she saw herself sitting on the steps of the American Museum of Natural History – the place she had chosen, with the delighted approval of CBS – knowing she was not just talking to the well-informed and courteous man in front of her, but to the whole country.

And to certain people in Russia as well. She knew that there were offices in Moscow that existed only to monitor American news programmes via satellite. Simultaneous translators in slick Western clothes were no doubt that moment creating transcripts that would be copied any number of times – first and foremost for the file they kept on her.

The thought of one's file was a thought no American she had met had experienced. Yet her file was as much a part of her as her unconscious. Everything that she did and said was registered in that dossier and might surface at any time to affect her life in the most profound way.

'Are you listening?' Ian prodded her.

He was sitting on the edge of his chair. She was on the couch, wrapped in an afghan someone once had crocheted with love and leftovers of lavender wool.

She turned her attention back to the screen.

Bradley was now interviewing someone she had never met, a man with a very well-educated eastern accent who seemed to be speaking from the office of a university.

'We have to ask,' the man was saying, 'where she gets the money for all this travel. She is a very unusual case – most defectors coming to this country crave a certain amount of anonymity, and where they don't, they have been among the most outspoken supporters of America's tougher policies towards the Soviets.'

'Don't you think, Professor Whiteside,' Bradley asked, 'that her message makes her of more interest to average Americans? Isn't it possible that her enormous celebrity is due only to the fact that people respond to this?'

The professor shrugged. 'Personally,' he said, 'I don't think so. In my view most Americans are vehemently opposed to the Soviets' systematic violation of human rights and I find her notoriety suspicious. At least it raises questions which to my mind have not been adequately answered.'

'You mean,' Bradley suggested, 'that she might be an

example of what this administration is calling Communist infiltration of the peace movement.'

'Shithead,' Ian spat.

'Quiet,' Anna said.

Next, the screen showed the lovely brownstone headquarters of the New York chapter of a group of Estonian nationalists.

'The Estonians are a beautiful people,' Anna said, 'very dedicated, very courageous.' The camera lingered over the Italianate façade of the building. The interiors were rich with antiques and spotless, and the camera settled on an attractive young blonde woman who, from her dress, might have been a banker or stockbroker.

'We have written to Mrs Khameneva repeatedly,' the young woman said. 'But she refuses to speak out in behalf of any émigré group – even a neutral coalition of such groups. This has not been our experience with most of the other dissidents who seek political careers here.'

Then her own face reappeared.

'What do you have to say about the life you have left behind?' Bradley asked her.

She saw anxiety shadow her eyes as she thought about Seriozha. She watched herself dive deep into her mind for words, but those depths were muddy with fear and she came back up with only handfuls of silt and sand.

'It's hard for me to speak about that,' she said. 'I'd rather not right now.'

The camera lingered on her face interminably, and she watched herself painfully avoiding Ed Bradley's eyes.

During the interview, he had at that moment reached out and lightly touched her hand. The camera, however, did not show this.

The last scene was of Anna at a parochial school in Brooklyn. She was showing the little girls how to tie bows in their hair the way Russian schoolgirls did.

'Right now there are millions of little girls in Russia who look just like you,' she told them. 'Say hello to them.'

And they all waved furiously and then broke into beautiful, crystalline, childish laughter.

'Questions, or no questions,' Bradley said, now seated in the studio, 'Anna Nikolayevna Khameneva has touched a chord in Americans which continues to ring out in wider and wider circles.'

Now Christmas music took over the air and a commercial showed Santa Claus transforming an ordinary group of citizens into a trembling choir – all as they sat, food and drink in hand, in an immaculate McDonald's.

Ian stood up and turned the set off.

'Move over,' he told her.

She sat up and made room for him on the divan.

'Don't get up,' he said, and as he sat back, he settled her against him as she had been before.

Leaning back in his arms, she felt a soft blankness come over her. The troubling images of the television seemed to stay inside the glass box. They were pictures of someone else, not her.

'I don't know,' he told her. 'I don't know.'

She said nothing. She turned her face in towards his chest and he stroked her cheek gently. She shut her eyes.

After a while she heard him whisper her name. She opened her eyes. The room was utterly dark; she could see a transient glitter of city light through the fogged window as the wind blew snow on and off the pane.

'Anna,' he said, 'stay here. I'll take you back tomorrow.'

She realised she had fallen asleep.

'What time is it?' she asked.

'It's after midnight,' he said quietly. 'Happy New Year.' His voice was very near in the darkness, very comforting.

He helped her stand and walk to the bedroom. She lay down on the bed and he stretched out delicately next to her. His body was warm but tense; she hid her face in his shirt.

'I don't want to cry,' she told him in a whisper.

'It doesn't matter,' he said.

She cried quietly; Ian held her.

'I remember too much,' she said.

'Shh,' he told her.

It was a long, still sleep – a black, undisturbed lake of

dreamlessness like the old days. In the morning, even this, too, made her sad, and they did not speak of it.

*We sit around the fire. Everything outside us is dark; the opaque, impenetrable dark peculiar to snowy nights. We eat roasted meat. No one knows whether the animals which wander aimlessly around the countryside starving are dangerously contaminated – our group has no Geiger counter or scanner, even of the crude type used below in the shelter. The only standard we adhere to is that of blindness. If the animal was close enough to a blast to have seen it, and is consequently blind, we don't eat it.*

*But it is nearly impossible to care. Can you understand this, my darling, and forgive me?*

*As I sit here and watch the firelit faces – they are human faces, Pasha, beautiful human faces, full of suffering, and you should see how they smile at the child! – I think of only two things.*

*One, that you are alive. I know it. The part of me that is you is still alive, I feel it.*

*And two, I shall never see you again. I know this, too.*

*What is left of life? Only the fragments that we can see and sense of it in the dark. The dark may last for months or years. The cold will take many years to abate.*

*My parents gave me life. They taught me to live, to learn, to fight, to overcome pain.*

*But you gave me love of life. Because you loved me, colour infused the world like the sun rising. I saw for the first time. Not just shapes of things. But things as they really are. The tender membranes of leaves, the blue veins in a pale lady slipper; the dazzling white and red and blue symmetry of stars. I saw – actually saw – the beat of life in the child in my womb. I saw it with my eyes closed as one sees music in the dark.*

*There are no children here. No children survived more than a few weeks, they told us. Misha therefore is like a god. They cannot do enough for him and his every movement delights them.*

*Someone has swaddled his poor burnt, bald head in sable*

237

pelts, the devil only knows where they were stolen from. He is fed constantly. There are actually a certain number of good things to eat; the shelter authorities have given the group guns, which they use to pillage any town they can travel to. I have not seen them do it, but I know that it happens. The group keeps the authorities happy by offering them nice gifts – things like tinned goods, the occasional jars of preserved citrus, bottles of wine. These things are probably irradiated, but below they have sensors to determine that. Here we throw caution to the winds.

Can I tell you what it means, after the suffocating stench of the shelter, to hold a candied orange up to your lips, to inhale its sunny, sugared perfume? Does anyone care if eating that orange means he will die sixty per cent sooner?

Misha is asleep, but some of the group are singing; it's amazing, the life of these old prison songs which manage to express the blood and soul of yet another generation. I've taken Misha now under my coat – I have been given a Red Army overcoat, you know, which weighs as much as a house and keeps you as warm. There is something about holding a sleeping child that makes you think of the continuity of the world. Did pre-hominid mothers with their scrawny babies sit thus in firelight and imagine that the world might cease to exist if the fire went out?

We have wooden houses here, built from unstripped, unsanded logs. They don't budge in the hardest wind and the walls still ooze balsamy-smelling resin when the fire's strong. But though these are the nicest houses most of us have ever had, we spend very little time in them. We like to stay around the main fire, all together.

Is it possible that the world can end not once but again and again?

Something has been happening and we have only just now understood what it means.

First, the shelter authorities began to make requests – demands – for certain items. This meant that the pillaging which the group had done only when its own supplies fell

238

too low had to become a mercenary thing, done regularly and with much calculation.

And with increasing risk, for the group is now so hated by the remaining enclaves of survivors in the towns that we live in fear of being attacked. We have not yet left our pretty log houses, but we guard them night and day. Soon, no doubt, we will have to roam the forest like gypsies.

And their demands are sickening. In the beginning they asked for food – difficult items, say sugar and chocolate, but understandable ones. Now they ask for strange and disturbing things – rugs, artworks, even musical instruments. The Society of the Dead, as our group calls itself, was put in the position of confiscating violins at gunpoint. Niki claims that a man was killed for hiding a harp. Knowing the people in our group as I do, I refused to believe it, but when the instruments were unloaded here, I became unsure.

There were sixteen violins, ten violas, a cello, three clarinets or other similar horns, two flutes, one of which had belonged to a rich Georgian and was made of gold. There was considerable argument about whether to hand this over; after all, gold is worth much more to those of us left in the 'free world' than it is to the authorities. But the Supervisor, a huge, quite smart man named Mikhail, decided that it would be a fitting sign of our good faith. The nomenklatura, given such a valuable item, might become less suspicious about what the Society keeps for itself. This last is a problem which could soon reach violent proportions.

But then there was the harp. At least six feet high, made of wood carved with angels and lyres and gilded with real gold leaf. None of us knows how to play it, but there was no way we were going to lower that beautiful thing down into the shelter. It somehow touched something deep in all of us and we voted unanimously to give it to Yevgeny, who plays the balalaika. That was about four days ago and Yevgeny gets no peace from people loitering outside his cabin, listening to him practise, hooting him when he makes mistakes, applauding him when he does well, calling out requests for melodies. Others readily volunteer to work

Yevgeny's shifts and some even quietly leave extra gifts of food by his door, giving up their own allotments for the sake of nourishing our musician.

Oh God, what are human beings who will kill for harps and live for music?

Last night, the camp was full of whispering. All of those who work directly with the dead came together for a secret meeting. They are not by any means all of those who make up the camp; perhaps they are not quite half The others work as cooks, carpenters, mechanics for the trucks, and perform the various other jobs on which our village life depends. However, those who work with the dead, and this means dealing with the shelter authorities, are considered special, apart and, to a certain extent, above the rest of us.

This is not, I must stress, because they are our links to the nomenklatura, but because they are our links to the world beyond death. It is a work of incredible magnitude, in this world in which life is not even cheap but really worthless, to manage to preserve any shred of dignity for the dead. But there is something profound and primitive in us which will not permit the desecration of a dead body. We believe somehow that we go into the next life as we knew ourselves in this life. And in spite of death all around us, I have never seen any member of the Society handle any corpse except with simplicity and respect. Only members of the Society are allowed to touch them. It is probably this factor which has protected us so long from the outraged survivors we have been forced to exploit.

Nikolai and I sat by our fire. Misha played with a matryoshka doll, that stupid, tourists' symbol of Mother Russia which is impossible to hate since every child can lose himself for hours playing with its round, graduated figures. In each cabin, women waited quietly alone. As if by silent order, no one went to the communal fire last night, but all remained behind their own doors.

Today, at dawn, the members of the Society got in the trucks and went down to the shelter. Everything was quiet while they were gone. There was an awful expectation in

240

*the air; something had happened in the shelter but none of
us knew what it was or what it would mean.*

*At noon they came back. We stood by the cold charred
place where the fire burns, wood in hand, ready to begin.
It was strange that we had not already started the fire, but
some deep instinct prevented us. We had all waited, tending
our kindling, without speaking.*

*The trucks stopped where they always stop. The men got
out. They were slower and sadder than I had ever seen
them. They peeled back the canvas from the bed of the
trucks.*

*Then they helped down about twenty-five small, live
children who stood shivering in the snow. They were in-
adequately dressed; some, I could see, were already in the
preliminary stages of typhoid and diphtheria.*

*We worked without stopping, separating the sick ones
from the apparently well ones, creating dormitories of sorts
out of three of the cabins. We are not equipped at all to
have these children, and certainly not to tend to those with
infectious diseases. We have no medicine to speak of, only
the odd, stolen bottles, certainly not what we need.*

*And the word is out now. These children are only the
first. Two hundred children are to be 'evacuated' during the
next several shelter runs. Since the authorities believe that
these youngsters will survive at most a few months to a few
years in the conditions of the shelter – not growing
old enough to reproduce – they have been declared undesir-
able.*

*How did their parents part with them? The children tell
us that they were told that they were to be 'resettled' where
conditions were much better for children. Mothers lined up
and begged the officers to take their sons and daughters out
first!*

*How could the authorities expect that our members would
agree to 'dispose' of the children? They held out the irresist-
ible hope of survival. Right then and there they accepted
three men into the shelter and promised to take more.*

*And without judgment, the men of the Society of the
Dead drew lots and three went down, including our Super-*

241

*visor. The rest quietly took the children to the trucks and brought them here.*

*Did it cross their minds to stop in the frozen forest and leave the children there, too far away to hear them calling? They would have died within hours.*

*I am absolutely certain that it did cross their minds. They must have thought of the fact that the children would surely die anyway, and perhaps more painful, protracted deaths. They could not have helped thinking, too, that our food supplies are just as limited as those of the shelter – in fact, the shelter increasingly relies on us.*

*But given the time it takes to drive to the tunnel, to get the day's instruction, load and leave, it is obvious that they did not stop, but indeed drove back to the camp as quickly as they could.*

'She's here,' Zalessky told Seriozha. 'She's in the next room.'

Seriozha made no movement at all. He kept his eyes shut.

The door opened. He heard her take a breath – it was not a gasp; she would not have allowed herself that.

'*Bozhyemoy!*' Katinka said. 'My God, my God, he is so thin.'

'You can talk to him,' Zalessky said. 'He can hear you.'

She began to cry quietly. 'Seriozhka,' she whispered, 'you've got to get out of here.'

His eyes would not open. They were made of paper, painted eyes with tissue lids. They might rip if he tried to look at her.

'What is it that he must do?' she asked Zalessky in despair.

'To start, he must eat,' Zalessky said. 'Otherwise, they tell me, they'll have to open his jugular and put a tube in.'

Seriozha felt Zalessky's hand on his throat and he let his head fall back. It was a cloth head, stuffed with old newspaper.

'What do you want?' Katinka repeated.

'Look,' Zalessky said. 'You are a sensible person, even

if you are not much help. We understand that it is not your fault. We have had him here for six months now and I think enough is enough. I have to tell you that this is my own opinion. Not everyone feels the same way about this. I've had to fight for him.'

*Katinka, Katinka*, Seriozha called. But he had known for weeks now that his words were only letters marked on dry paper; his voice had no sound. *Take me home.*

'But now,' Zalessky told her, his voice measured and warm, 'we are going to have to fight for him together.'

For the first time in six months Seriozha felt Katinka touch him. He felt her small hands cold on his knees. She had knelt down in front of him. He could feel her eyes on his face. She, he knew, had real eyes, full, liquid eyes the colour of the irises that now broke the earth along the hospital wall.

'I'll do anything,' he heard her say. He felt her words on his face.

'Oh, you don't have to suffer so much, little mother,' Zalessky said with real kindness in his tone. 'It's all going to work out very well, if we can just start by getting him back to health.'

There was a silence, then a chair scraped the floor. Seriozha felt Katinka's hands leave his body, and though her hands had been cold, the place where she had touched him was warm and he moved his own hands to cover it.

'You see,' Zalessky said, 'he hears you.'

'Tell me what to do,' Katinka said.

'All right,' Zalessky said. 'The future can be very simple. No one wants to see him ruin himself over this. A lot of people, here and abroad, expect Sergei Pavlovich to go on to do great and humanitarian things. Consistent with the traditions of his family and with the traditions of the Party. We would, in fact, like to see Sergei at the very forefront of our peace movement, as his mother now seems to be at the forefront of the American movement.

'The Soviet people, guided by the wisdom and experience of the Party, have long led the world in the desire for peace, for restraint in armament, for realistic and dedicated

243

negotiation. All over Russia and the other republics, in factories and offices and farms, groups work night and day to realise this ideal. Sergei could reach out to these people, he is eloquent. And he could reach beyond them to the West.'

'You want him to speak?' Katinka asked incredulously.

'Yes,' Zalessky said, his voice rising. 'We want him to speak, to write – even to travel, eventually. There is no more important issue at hand and he – and you – are in a position to play a very important role.'

'Give him to me,' Katinka said.

Zalessky hesitated. 'He's really in no shape to leave the hospital,' he told her sympathetically. 'But I think with your help . . . As well, before he leaves we will need certain assurances . . .'

Seriozha felt Katinka come up to him again. This time she stood before him. She stroked his hair and put one finger gently under his chin. He saw her finger quite clearly with his eyes closed; soft, plump, the colour of milk and fresh apricots.

Then he felt Zalessky pick up his own dead hand and hold it limp in the air for a second. Then he felt Katinka's belly under his hand. It was huge and hard. Zalessky pressed down with Seriozha's hand; something inside Katinka moved, almost struggled. Katinka stood still.

'Think of this fragile life, ' Zalessky said. 'Then think: it is not just your own child, but all children. It is not just this life, but all lives.'

I am not paper, Seriozha thought, but ash. And I will disintegrate on the wind.

Zalessky let go of his hand, and moved away from them. Seriozha kept his hand where it was. He opened his eyes and saw the iris eyes of Katinka. But they were not blue. They were colourless. When she saw him look at her, the blue fluttered back for a minute, like a blue jay trying to fly through a closed window.

She leaned her face close to his ear.

'Shh,' she told him in a whisper. 'I'll kill myself first.'

*Take me home*, he told her soundlessly. He could not even move his lips.

She kissed Seriozha's lips very lightly; still, it hurt.

'You are a criminal,' she said to Zalessky. 'You are a Nazi.'

He stepped back, insulted.

'I have really tried to do my best for you,' he said to her.

She shut her eyes. When she opened them again, the impassive softness had returned to her face.

'Please forgive me, Yuri Andreyevich,' she said. 'I know.'


'Ah, well, you can't expect any better from them,' Arthur Orr said. The subject immediately at hand was the NATO allies and George was inclined to agree.

Orr sat back in his chair and the waiter suddenly appeared with two cigars. Orr broke into a smile.

'Andrea,' he said, 'you are absolutely the best in Washington, no one touches you.' The waiter, dressed not in the standard tuxedo-like uniform but in a fine merino suit, bowed just slightly and left the men to their brandies.

'Look at this,' Orr told George, 'Montecristo. They get them from Canada. The finest Cuban tobacco.'

They lit up their cigars delightedly, holding them away from their faces momentarily like children, watching the opalescent smoke whirl into the air.

'It's a good thing you two aren't *elected* officials,' a jovial voice kidded from a table nearby.

George turned to see Senator Henry Brooker, Republican of Wisconsin; a former political science professor who had published his most influential books through the Naughton Foundation's Center for Defense Studies.

'Hi, Hal,' Orr said.

'Henry.' George nodded. 'You look like life is agreeing with you.' Henry Brooker had just been moved into his first senior committee position, on the Senate Foreign Relations Committee.

'Just back from the Philippines,' he told them.

245

'Ah well, yes,' Orr said. He looked off to the side theatrically as if Brooker had just said that somebody's wife was having an affair with the postman.

'What a mess,' George said. He thought of Luis Alvarado, who ran the Foundation's office there. He had gone to Choate and Williams; his wife was from Spain. His contacts with the government were impeccable; they had always been guests of Mrs Marcos at her children's birthdays. A year ago George had talked him out of resigning. Now he was in and out of the hospital with migraine headaches so vicious that it had come back to George that Alvarado was suspected of being dependent on morphine.

'I have a piece of news for you,' Brooker said. 'You know our friend Huggins?'

Charles Huggins was a wealthy Democratic congressman from Long Island. He was third-generation Wall Street money, a high-profile liberal with a house on the ocean in East Hampton. George and Kate had represented George's law firm at fund-raising dinner dances on the terrace there, once upon a time, when Huggins Sr. had tried to mount a gubernatorial campaign.

'Mr Freeze,' Orr said.

'But not Mr Nonproliferation,' Brooker said. He and Orr laughed.

'We got that one away from him,' Orr told George.

George smiled. Nuclear nonproliferation – refusing to sell nuclear technology or raw materials to nations that didn't yet have a nuclear capability – was the well-packaged sellout of liberal Republicans to the anti-nuclear movement. One had to admire the sophistry of such swing voters as Brooker, who had the difficult role of co-opting the liberals at their own game.

'Huggins is putting through a little sweetheart bill to bypass Immigration and Naturalisation for your Russian. Declare her an honorary American,' Brooker told them.

'There's no end in sight, is there?' George said. He smiled but neither Orr nor Brooker was looking at him.

'I thought we might do the same thing on this,' Brooker said.

'I don't think so, Brooker,' Orr said.

A moment passed. Brooker nodded.

'Well, good to see you,' he said to George. They shook hands.

'Keep me posted,' he said to Orr.

Orr nodded.

'You were quite right,' George said to Orr. 'She's the hottest thing since the USO shows.'

Orr seemed not to hear him. 'She's joined a Democratic coalition to tour and speak at major defence contractors' plants,' he said. 'I assume you didn't know.'

George looked at Orr. Orr was looking at the cigar smoke which he had just exhaled; it was a way, George realised, of ignoring him.

'I didn't know,' George said.

'This is just the sort of thing the press adores,' Orr said. 'They've got every sort of celebrity signed up. Paul Newman and Joanne Woodward. Meryl Streep. Linda Ronstadt. Bruce Springfield.'

'Springsteen,' George said inadvertently. He knew the name because the one time that he had managed to get Mary Ellen to talk to him in the last eight weeks she had asked him to buy her a record by this person. She had written it down for him and he had bought the record for her and the tape for himself so that he could listen to it in the car on his way to see her next Saturday.

Orr was irritated.

'I think you should have a talk with her,' he said.

How often had Kate said this to him. But Mary Ellen had been so easygoing, so trouble-free. Ian had exhausted his fund of fatherly anxiety; Mary Ellen had always tactfully understood that what he wanted was his freedom. He loved her for this.

'I hope you're not going to give me any crap about the integrity of the Foundation's board,' Orr said.

At first George registered only the word 'crap' and the tone of Arthur's voice, which he found crass.

'Arthur, please,' he said. 'You can't be serious. First of all, publicity is good for the Foundation; frankly, public relations are much more important to my board than ideological consistency. Secondly, my muzzling her is exactly the kind of thing the press would love to get hold of. And thirdly, we're committed for the period of the grant, which is a year. If she doesn't come around by then, that's a different story. I thought the point was defectors do that – come around.'

'I don't want your jesuitical rationalisations, McDonough,' Orr said to him. 'This is not what one would expect of a tightly run organisation. The whole thing has not gone the way we would have liked to see it go. It surprises me that a man of your experience is not on top of all the ramifications here.'

George sat in stunned silence. His cigar had gone out.

At that moment, the waiter came up and discreetly whispered to Orr that he was wanted on the phone.

Orr stood up and looked down at George. The customary benevolent expression had returned to his face; George had once thought of it as a smile.

'See what you can do,' he said.

George nodded. It was a slight, hardly perceptible nod, but at any rate Orr had not waited to see it.

Now George looked at the empty table and his cigar, which lay nearly intact in the ashtray. Something deep and powerful, something from childhood, grabbed him inside and he thought for several seconds about how to take the splendid, still unburned cigar home with him. But he was too embarrassed. He left the table without touching it.

At the coatroom, the sleek waiter quietly took him aside.

'*Signore*,' he said apologetically, and handed him the bill.


'This is one of those absolutely authentic Mafia restaurants,' Larry O'Neill told Ian. 'I heard about it from a writer of mine who hung out with a gangster for three years to write a book on him. Amazing. The things he witnessed, I don't know to this day how he can hold any food down. And you know what the New York *Times* reviewer said?'

'What?' Ian asked. An old friend from Fordham, O'Neill had given up the rough-and-tumble of free-lance reporting to become an editor at *Esquire;* he had never published any of Ian's European pieces, but Ian had always thought he might.

'He said that my guy didn't succeed in winning our sympathy for his gangster. I'm telling you, this gangster was a pig, absolutely disgusting. Evil. That's an old-style New York *Times* liberal for you.'

'What finally happened to him?'

'He's writing a novel.'

'I mean the gangster,' Ian said.

'Oh,' Larry said, and smiled. 'He cooperated with the feds and they gave him a bundle of cash and an entirely new identity. He started life over somewhere else.'

'Shit,' Ian said. 'Where do I sign up?'

Larry laughed. The waiter came with menus but Larry wouldn't take them.

'The eggplant parmigian,' Larry told Ian with the air of a broker delivering a hot stock tip.

'Sure,' Ian said. He had a vision of thick bread crumbs, thick tomato paste, processed cheese the taste and texture of wood shavings. For the hundredth time that week he cursed himself for leaving Europe.

'And your wine,' Larry told the waiter.

The waiter returned with a pitcher of purply-red wine and poured it into small tumblers.

'Actually,' Ian said, tasting it cautiously, 'this is quite good.'

'I think they make it in the basement,' Larry said.

'I wish you hadn't told me.'

They both laughed.

'So cut the shit,' Larry told him. 'Why haven't I seen anything of yours since you got back?'

'I haven't had any ideas you guys would use,' Ian said.

'Bullshit. I read a lot of the stuff you did for *Rolling Stone* and I can use stuff like that. Sort of.'

'Well, I'm not doing stuff like that now. Sort of.'

'What are you doing?' Larry asked.

'I've only done one article in the last six months.'

'So it must have been a good one – how did I miss it?'

'Well,' Ian said, 'I didn't do it under my own name.' Ian noticed that Larry perked up a bit; no doubt, Ian thought, he thinks I'm on to something interesting. He felt embarrassed.

'It was an article on anorexia that I did for *Cosmo*. They paid me pretty well but they wanted it under a woman's name.'

Larry sat back in his chair and stared at him.

'Come on,' he said.

'No, it's true,' Ian told him. 'And the reason that I'm even telling you about it at all is that I have been doing a lot of thinking and I'd like to write a different kind of article about it now.'

Ian saw Larry look around the room, as if to check that he was really there. There were only two other tables of diners, and from the tense, quiet conversations that were going on at them, Ian was willing to believe that the restaurant was indeed a Mafia hangout.

'I can see you're serious about this,' Larry said.

'The thing is,' Ian said, 'that a lot of the young people who get anorexia had older siblings who were in our generation. Typical sixties radicals. These kids were caught in the cross fire between the troublemakers and their parents. They grew up determined to be good kids. We rebelled against the generation gap; they were literally trapped by it.'

'I remember the generation gap,' Larry said. 'I also remember go-go dancers and pet rocks.'

'Listen,' Ian told him, 'these kids are conservative. The ones that everyone says are only concerned with going to law school, medical school, business school. They want –'

'Everything that we hated. A decent nine-to-five job. A house with a white picket fence. Golden wedding anniversaries. Savings bonds. Does it occur to you, Ian, that maybe we were the ones who were crazy?'

'About two hundred times a day,' Ian said, and laughed.

The food arrived at all the tables at once. Ian enviously watched the men at the neighbouring tables dig into mounds of fresh squid and pasta. His own eggplant was an extravagance of melted cheese, crisp eggplant, fragrant garlic. As soon as he looked at it he thought of his sister.

'I've seen it happen before,' Larry told him kindly. 'Hey, you know, you get to be our age and you're not married and you can't even *imagine* it and you do start developing a few harebrained theories about the American family.'

Ian laughed. The laughter felt a little loose in the jaw.

'This wine is strong,' he said. 'But seriously, I think there is a political angle to all of this.'

'You have to stick with the women's magazines on that one,' Larry told him. 'Or sell "The Politics of Bulimia" to *The Nation* and pick up the fifty bucks.'

Ian looked down at his food. The more he wanted it, the more he wanted to be able to give it up for Mary Ellen. It was so hard to explain; he felt stupid and irritable.

'Why should nurturing be the exclusive province of women's magazines?' he asked.

'If our readers have a question about nurturing, they don't pick up a magazine, they ask their wives,' Larry said. 'Look, I know this Russian defector lived with your family awhile. I could definitely take an article on her.'

'I can't,' Ian said. 'Family politics.'

'What about some more stuff on weapons?' Larry suggested. 'That's very big with us right now and your coverage of moving the Euro-missiles into Britain and Germany was fantastic. We could send you back there for a redux, if you want.'

Ian had lived for three days in a tent with the women of Greenham Common. He had met more women in three days than he had met in his whole life. He had met mothers and grandmothers, university professors and radical lesbians – the first lesbians he had ever known. One, Grace Harbus, had had a little girl Christian's age and watching her rapport with that child had perhaps been the beginning of the end of his fantasy of marrying Lilianne. Grace seemed to create such an aura of peace and safety around her daughter that even Ian felt calmer near her. She still dropped him a note from time to time; she simply had a gift for making people feel secure and cared for. That's what the National Security Adviser should be for, he thought drunkenly.

'You should eat something,' Larry told him.

'I'm okay,' Ian said.

'I could take an article on the Greens,' Larry suggested.

Ian shook his head. 'Trouble is that they're not selling what your magazine is selling. I mean it's not just you – it's America. Everyone wants to think of themselves as tall, rich, important, driver of a convertible, drinker of Napoleon brandy, member of a karate dojo. There's no percentage in acknowledging that you are small, vulnerable, not inclined to fight any battle for any reason.'

'Ian,' Larry said. 'Why not go back to Europe if you can't get something started here?'

Ian shook his head. 'That's what it's all about,' he said. 'Getting something started here.'

Larry poured out the dregs of the wine.

'And anyway, it's time for me to be home,' Ian said.

'Where's home at for you these days, by the way?'

Ian laughed again. 'Actually I have a sublet that I have to give up at the end of next month. If you hear of anything let me know.'

Larry took the bill and Ian noticed that suddenly the restaurant was empty. When they walked out onto the street, he saw that the street life – women sitting on plastic chairs on the sidewalk, children playing stickball, men standing around phone booths – had suddenly vanished. A police car rolled slowly down the block.

'Incredible,' Ian said.

'The Teflon suit syndrome,' Larry said, laughing. 'Everybody's got it these days. Write about that.'

'That's an idea,' Ian said.

'Seriously,' Larry told him, 'if you have an idea, run it by me.'

'Thank you,' Ian said formally.

'Look,' Larry said, 'we all need friends in this world.'

Mary Ellen was waiting for George outside the hospital when he pulled up. When he saw her, he didn't park the car, but drove up to her.

'Hi,' she said. Her voice was flat.

He tried to look away from the square of gauze that was taped to the base of her neck. It was discoloured and covered the wound where they had opened her jugular vein to feed her intravenously.

'Let's go for a ride,' he said. 'You don't have to check in until five, isn't that right?'

She nodded and got in.

'Like the car?' he asked. It was a little Mercedes convertible, green and tan, small and smart as a piece of fine luggage. Its purchase coincided with a directive from his accountant that a significant, business-related expense before the fifteenth of the month could move him into a slightly lower tax bracket. He travelled so much for the Foundation that a new car wouldn't stretch his luck with the IRS too far. But the tax savings did not account for the thrill he felt when he put the top down and opened the throttle on the Hutchinson River Parkway between Connecticut and New York City.

'What happened to the Rolls?' she asked.

'Mother has it,' he said. He was the only one in the family who ever called his wife 'Mother.' She had, in fact, never been Kate to him. He'd called her Katherine when they fell in love; it was such a beautiful, formal name, he had felt, so unlike his own pedestrian monosyllable.

'Where do you want to go?' he asked her.

'It doesn't matter,' she said. Her face was as blank and flat as her voice.

'Come on,' he said. 'I came all the way up here so we could have some fun.'

'You wouldn't have come if I weren't sick. You never visit me at school.'

'What do you want me to do?'

She did not answer.

He pressed the button to lower the roof.

Suddenly the late-spring sunshine and the brisk spring air slapped them full in the face.

'Isn't it great?' he asked her. She remained silent. He reached over and prodded her as if he were going to tickle her.

She smiled. It was the first real smile he'd seen from her in weeks and weeks.

He took the car slowly out of the winding hospital grounds and headed for the highway. When he reached it, he drove fast and carefully, passing every car and heading north towards the country.

'This air is just what you need,' he told her.

She looked at him and smiled again. It was a smaller smile and he could barely see it through her hair streaming in the wind, but it gave him the happy feeling of being right.

'Thank you for the record,' she told him.

He nodded. 'Look in the glove compartment,' he said.

She opened it, laconically – all her movements seemed slow now – and began to look through the handful of tapes that she found there.

Then she began to smile broadly. George had every Springsteen album on tape.

'You're such a ham,' she said.

He could never have begun to describe how this stupid saying of hers cheered him. He remembered when she was a baby, how he used to stand over her playpen and make ridiculous faces at her to see her giggle.

'Put one in,' he said.

She did. The sounds of drums and guitars throbbed through the speakers. He turned it up all the way. She was laughing now, as *Born to Run* rushed over them.

He took her hand and they drove through western Connecticut with the music blaring until he realised they had reached a halfway point and would have to turn around to make it back to the hospital in time.

'Let's eat something,' he said. He hoped that he had disguised all the hope in his voice.

'Okay,' she said.

'What would you like?'

'McDonald's,' she answered.

'That's easy enough,' he told her. He pulled off the main road and drove through the towns until he found one.

He brought their food to the car. He knew that she was making a real effort to eat. When he saw her faltering he pretended he was still hungry and asked if he could finish hers. She gave him her burger and french fries gratefully.

When they were ready to drive back again, he took his chance.

'I want you at home,' he said. 'I think that is where you belong now.'

He saw her joy disappear and her jaw tighten. She said nothing. He waited. He took a paper napkin and cleaned the dashboard for the second time.

'At least talk about it,' he said.

She was visibly angry and he felt trapped because it was the strongest emotion she had shown since she'd become ill. He wished he could cry.

She was white.

*I'm your father and I love you*, he wanted to say.

She looked at him. Why were children children for so long? he wondered. He couldn't blame her for being small and vulnerable but there was a part of him that wanted only to run from her need. That was his need, he knew this and he hated it.

He took her in his arms. She was absolutely still and stayed that way for several moments.

'Shall we go?' he asked finally.

She moved back to her seat. He started the car, she put another Springsteen tape in the tape deck.

When the tape was over they chatted innocuously.

'He's a very serious musician,' George offered. 'He doesn't use many keys, but those he resorts to he varies with considerable orchestral sophistication.'

She looked at him and shook her head.

'You're too much,' she said, but she was smiling. 'You hated it when Ian used to listen to it.'

'I don't remember Ian listening to this,' he said.

'You're going through your second childhood,' she told him.

She smiled but her voice was dry, nothing like a child's.

The church meeting hall was cinder block, but the inside was fresh with white paint and the women had incongruously hung starched white cotton curtains across the windows. These now lifted prettily on the breeze and Anna could see a field, and beyond a rail fence, an old, stunted orchard brimming with small blossoms which detached from their stems and floated like snow on the wind. Cherries, she thought, and held her breath; in Russia, spring in the country was synonymous with the fragile white and pink flowers that were once a symbol of Easter.

In Copper Hollow, Tennessee, the church hall – High Street Baptist Church – was the only place to hold a meeting of this size, except for the Synlab plant itself. But the company, whose yearly thirty-two-million-dollar contracts to produce detonators for neutron bombs were under discussion, had not made any of its facilities available.

The church itself was an old church; it had the fresh white clapboards that Anna had seen a number of times in country churches, and tall, clear-glass windows, shining clean. It was peaceful and modest in the green, rolling landscape. It was a church that was not an affront to God and made Anna sympathetic to the believers. The little building was a place of dignity, as the great cinder-block Synlab plant was emphatically not; it was traditional, a place where a man might feel part of the history of this particular place, as the prefabricated colonial homes of most of the workers were not.

The town – the Synlab workers – had shown up. There was to be a picnic and country music show in the evening, but even at nine in the morning the buses pulled up to the parking lot and the field across from it was full of cars and pickup trucks. She knew from past experience in little towns that after the country singers, she was the big draw;

as if she were a midget or a giant at a fair, people turned out to see the Russian.

In the local papers she was usually referred to as a 'defector'. This caused her a physical pain, like the one a parent feels when a child in a moment of rage turns on him and shouts: 'I hate you!' But she had long ago given up the hope of trying to explain how she could leave the Soviet Union and still love her country.

Their professor had once again exceeded his time limit. Anna felt the restlessness of the crowd. They were in their best clothes, most of them, the men in pressed red and blue shirts, the women in flowered dresses and patent-leather shoes without stockings. There were a number of small children there as well, handed whimpering from mother to father and back again. Occasionally, a girl would get up and walk back and forth in the aisle bouncing an irritable baby while still listening to the speeches. It was getting hot.

Tony Hamilton had now been drawn into the inevitable argument that always started when some amateur historian, sometimes cocksure, sometimes shy and worried, compared the present situation to Hitler's arms buildup before World War II. Tony considered himself a professional and he always refuted these arguments with painstaking detail; unfortunately, history being open to endless interpretation, he never got very far.

Anna smiled at a toddler in the front row. His mother picked up his little hand and made him wave to her. The three of them smiled.

Finally, the coalition's road manager, Judy Lowenstein, appeared from the back of the room.

'Professor,' she said politely, 'I'm going to have to insist that we break off here.'

There was some low laughter.

'We don't have too much time left, and Mrs Khameneva still has to speak.'

He shrugged and smiled a chagrined smile at his opponent and took his seat. The crowd settled down while they got a good look at Anna.

When she had been standing long enough for everyone to see her and become a bit impatient for her to talk, she smiled. Then she turned to Tony.

'You and I have the same argument all the time, don't we?' she said.

He nodded.

'I never win,' she told the audience.

The crowd laughed. Anna laughed. She looked at him again and he wasn't smiling.

'In my country,' she said, 'history is something absolute and concrete. It shows us *exactly* how everything that is now came from what is past. Nothing is left out. Everything is explained. Unfortunately, we are obligated to rewrite all of history every time we have a change in the government. Then everything from Creation to the atom bomb has to be redone to be coherent, consistent and correct. Thank God that is not the way things are done here in America, where history, like speech and religion, has the right to be free.'

There was a small, spontaneous burst of applause. They were listening.

She looked around the room and waited for a moment. She tried to find the little boy who had waved to her. Then she signalled to someone in the back of the room.

'I thought,' she said, 'that you wouldn't mind if I don't speak for the whole time allotted to me but take a few minutes to show a little film. It was made for British television and it is very short.'

She sat down and the lights abruptly went out. On the white wall behind the podium a gritty colour film began to appear. There were sounds of shuffling and disgruntlement; she knew they were afraid that she was going to inflict on them some budget propaganda about the effects of neutron bombs. But even if such a film could be made, this one was quite different.

It was a documentary about workers in the asbestos industry. It showed how men, women and children were devastated by the most horrifying and wasting cancers from even very limited – sometimes as limited as ten days

258

– exposure to asbestos fibres. It depicted the intolerable position of workers in whole towns who had no choice but to stay at work in factories that did not – and never could – respond adequately to safety requirements. It showed a little boy who was nothing but skin stretched over tender, damaged bone, whose parents could not even hug him without causing him excruciating pain. The mother cried and cried. The little boy had sickened and died within one year; his school had had asbestos tiles in the classroom ceilings. And again, pictures of the workers – worldwide – who had no other jobs.

When it was over there was silence. People were stricken and angered by what they had seen. Almost everyone had been moved. When the lights came back on, Anna was again standing at the microphone.

'What can – what should these workers do?' she asked.

After a few moments of quiet, there were various voices. She called on a young man in a light leather jacket.

'The unions should force the companies to comply with safety standards,' he said. Anna wondered if he was, in fact, an official of the Synlab workers' union. There were murmurs of approval.

'But one of the points the film makes,' Anna rebutted him quietly, 'is that asbestos cannot be made safe. Not to the people who mine it, or manufacture it, or use it.'

'Use the plants to manufacture something else or close them down,' a woman said. Anna thought she must be about her own age, but she was overweight and worn.

'In fact,' Anna told her, 'in England, workers have been able to force some of these plants to convert to other uses. The workers in those towns still have jobs. But you know as well as I do that what most companies would do is just close one plant and move it somewhere else. So that doesn't entirely solve the problem. And anyway, what about those people's jobs? Who's going to give them new jobs if they chase an industry out of town?'

There was total quiet now. Then the young woman who had waved her little boy's hand to Anna spoke from the side of the room, where she had gone to get a better view.

'It's better than dying,' she said.

Anna looked at her, and their eyes met. Anna had seen that look in the eyes of hundreds of young mothers, and they, she knew, had seen it in hers.

'That's it,' Anna said. 'It's a bad choice, but there it is. This is the situation we are in. Neutron bombs are much more dangerous to you and your children than asbestos. Not because your plants aren't safe – let's just assume they are. But because it is very possible that their use will annihilate not only us and our children but all life on earth. Here, of course, you only make detonators. There are no whole bombs. And anyway, what you do is necessary for the defence of your country.

'But the truth is, we thought asbestos was a necessary defence against fire until we realised how dangerous it was and forced industry – through the democratic process in countries like Britain and the United States – to develop other materials.

'No one can or should ask a worker to walk off his job, but we have a duty – we doctors, teachers, scientists and government officials such as are here today – to warn workers when they participate in an industry that is inherently dangerous.

'Scientists at places like MIT have looked at the various margins of error and measured them against the size of our present nuclear arsenals and they tell us that we are not very likely to live out our lives never finding out what nuclear holocaust really means. We have only a fifty-fifty chance. If you had only a fifty-fifty chance of winning a bet, would you put your job, or your house, or your life and your children's lives on the line?'

There was no applause. The hall was still, stiller, in fact, than it had been while she was talking.

Then three or four people began to clap and others stood up to speak to her. The young woman with the little boy was busy in the back of the room pouring coffee into white Styrofoam cups behind a table covered by a white paper tablecloth and paper plates of home-baked cookies, cakes and pies. People went and stood politely on line waiting to be served.

Tony Hamilton walked over to Anna. 'You did a job on me,' he said. He smiled but he was disturbed.

'You deserved it, Tony,' Judy Lowenstein told him. 'You never learn.'

'I'm sorry,' Anna said. 'I just think it's important for us to show that we respect everybody's right to have an opinion.'

'Don't do it again.'

'Come on, Tony,' Judy said. 'If you'd kept on it would have turned them off completely.'

The professor walked away, and Judy rolled her eyes at Anna.

'You're my kind of woman – person,' she said. 'You're not out to change the world, are you?'

Anna laughed. 'I just want it to last,' she told her.

The sound of country fiddles started up outside, careening through the sunlight, making the people on line in the church hall smile and tap their feet where they were standing. Children started dancing up and down, pulling their mothers by the arms.

'I wish I could just stop and stay here,' Anna said.

Judy looked out the high, open window to the spring sky. 'It's pretty,' she agreed. 'But I don't know if I could live forever in a place like this.'

What a luxury, Anna thought, to imagine living anywhere forever.

The tour wound its way to nearly every major defence contractor in the South. They did almost a city a day for a month. In each state, different people joined them, congressmen, senators, doctors, the occasional movie star, rock star or country singer.

In May, in Texas, at the end of a long day, there was a telegram waiting for Anna from Congressman Charles Huggins. It said only: WATCH SIX O 'CLOCK NEWS.

The House had voted. The final word on her immigration bill was: she was in. She was to become an American

261

citizen. She saw her face on the television in Judy's motel room.

Judy applauded Dan Rather.

The others started banging on Judy's door.

'Anna, Anna – it came through! They voted today. You're going to be a citizen!'

Anna sat very still.

'Leave her alone,' she heard Judy say to whoever was in the hall. They walked away.

She had been aware of the bill proposing her citizenship all along, but it was not something that she had sought out, despite the advantages of having an American passport; it was too much like leaving home again, and too final. She could not think about it too much, and had let the others thrust her forward. She did not know – and no one could tell her – if this made it better or worse for Seriozha.

As well, she had not really believed it would happen. It was not done very often, George had explained to her. The last time it had been done to expedite the use of a Scandinavian athlete on the US Olympic Winter Games team. Years ago, it had been done for Albert Einstein. George gave her to understand that since she was not in the class of either of these two people – 'extraordinary aliens', as they were referred to in the law – the bill amounted only to a very handsome gesture.

And exile had come to suit her. She comprehended exile; it allowed her finally to have a clear picture of herself. Russia was her home; she would never have a home again. She lived in the air between real places where other, real people lived. And in a certain way, only this drifting, homeless freedom could have given her the ability to dedicate herself to her work.

The phone was ringing.

'Should I get it?' Judy asked her.

'It's your room.'

'But it's for you, I know it.' She picked up the phone cautiously, listened for a moment, then looked at Anna. 'I'm sorry,' Judy said, 'I don't know where she is.' She hung up.

'Reporters?' Anna asked.

Judy nodded. 'Is there anything I can do?'

'No,' Anna told her. 'Thank you. I'd just like to go to sleep for a while.'

She went back to her room and sat by the window. They were in the Valentine Ridge Motel outside a town called Valentine in Jeff Davis County, Texas. It was the site of a plant where Minuteman missile parts were assembled. But the terrain outside the window, past the shallow parking lot and the road where huge trucks rumbled by all night, was amazingly peaceful. It was rangeland, covered with straw the colour of peach fuzz. It the long, late-afternoon sunlight, the shade of the straw across the low round hills made the land look soft.

By nightfall the motel was still. Everyone on the tour had gone into town for dinner; Anna could not eat. There was no one else there.

She opened the door and saw a thin line of red in the gentian sky at the edge of the horizon. It struck her as an image on a poster exhorting Moscow University students to take seriously their responsibility to give a month's work to the harvest on the steppes.

She walked out into the parking lot. There was a tiny gas station with one gas pump and a beat-up blue Ford with a 'for sale' sign. She stood by this car and wondered about all the places it might have been. She touched the huge left headlight that stared off in a slightly different direction than the right like a half-blind eye.

The screen door of the gas station swung out on its hinges and hit the side of the garage. A tall man in grey overalls walked slowly over, wiping his hands on a red rag.

'How do,' the gas station man said to her.

'Hello,' she answered.

They both looked out over the plain.

'How much is that car?' she asked him.

He looked at her.

'One hundred and fifty dollars,' he said.

'Can you wait a moment?' she said.

She went to her room and came back with her purse.

She took out two fifty-dollar bills and five tens. They were all new, crisp bills; everywhere she went she was a guest. It was nearly all the money she had.

'Key's in it,' he said.

'Thank you,' she said.

She had no American licence; she hadn't driven a car since before Pavel died. After his second house arrest, hooligans had destroyed their beloved black Zhiguli. There was no question of ever replacing it. She and Seriozha had ridden in the truck to the wrecker as if following a hearse. Seriozha's face had shone with jealousy and anger as the metal weights slammed the car into flat, shattered pieces; if he couldn't have the car, then no one would.

The door of the Ford was heavy and rusty and she caught her dress in it when she finally got it shut. She turned the key; nothing happened.

'Floor it,' the gas station man said.

She stared at him. He had grey eyes the colour of his overalls; his skin was creased and stained like the fabric. Then he smiled at her.

He came over and opened the door. He gently picked up her dress out of the dirty door hinge and got in beside her. He pressed down on the gas pedal a few times before he turned the key. The engine coughed and sputtered. He tried it again. It turned over. He got out.

'Thank you,' she said again. The car shook and she turned out onto the road very slowly.

'Watch yourself!' he called to her.


Ian's phone rang at one in the morning. It was his mother.

'Have you heard from Anna?' she asked him.

His heart dropped inside him.

'No,' he said.

'Oh Good Lord,' his mother said.

'What's the matter?'

'Apparently she's run away.'

'What do you mean?'

'She got in a car in Texas and took off.'

Ian's panic intensified.

'But why?' he asked his mother.

'No one knows,' she said. 'But it has something to do with her American citizenship. The bill passed today.'

Now he understood.

'She's okay,' he told her.

'How do you know?'

He had no idea why he was so sure. But he felt her in him suddenly; his heart seemed to push against the inside of his chest as if it were struggling to get outside his body. He took a deep breath. He imagined Anna running, running so hard and so fast that all at once she was lifted into the air.

'Don't worry,' he said. 'I'll call you if I hear anything. You call me if you hear.'

They hung up and Ian went to the refrigerator and took out a bottle of wine. Then he went to the closet and rummaged in an old raincoat pocket. He felt the too light metal of French coins and pieces of old bus ticket stubs. Finally he found what he was looking for; a crushed pack of cigarettes that had slipped through a hole into the lining. There were three cigarettes left.

Stale Gauloises, he told himself; to smother a heartache there was nothing like them.

He poured the wine and lit a cigarette and lay down on the couch with his head next to the phone to wait.


Even though it was dark, the road was hot and Anna's feet were hot against the floor of the car. She kicked off her shoes and felt the hard rubber coating of the gas pedal burn the sole of her foot.

She had the irrational conviction that everything behind her was on fire. Each car, each house she passed, she imagined bursting into flames.

Behind her the world was burning, ahead of her was the dark. Between them both she would disappear.

*We have had to burn our beautiful homes. Typhus, brought by the sick children from the shelter, has struck us and finally brought our forest world to an end.*

Between the sickness in our midst and the enraged survivors on our outskirts, we have made the decision to disband.

Of course, we all want to go together, but the food situation is such that we will have to go our separate ways. Like the too large and lonely gorillas of the jungle, we cannot live off this land together; we must shun the social advantages of a colony and travel in solitary families. We do not expect to find more than a few days' sustenance anywhere. But Nikolai and Misha and I will stay together; we are firm about that.

How is it, my darling, that losing my little forest home has brought back to me the tragedy of losing you all over again? Over and over I imagine that it is you I am parting from, your patient face that I will finally lose sight of. Last night I awoke in the middle of the night and I thought – I am home again, I am in our bed, I feel your fingers through mine, holding my hand in your sleep as you used to. But it was Nikolai's hand; he sat lightly on the edge of the bed. I had been having nightmares, he told me, but was too exhausted to rouse myself from them. I cried when I saw it was him, but he said nothing. He remained there quietly until I fell asleep again, I don't know how long.

Perhaps I spent three or four weeks sheltered in the piney houses of the Society of the Dead; leaving those houses behind now is like having a bone removed from my body.

And we have had to burn them. Typhus is virulent and can kill those of us weakened by radiation in a few hours. The children, you know, died as they used to describe young soldiers dying in war poems. They were mowed down like grass in a field – one after another, too weak to hold up their heads. They died so quickly that the disease had not even the chance to mar their perfect young bodies. As we burned cabins full of dead children I could not shake the horrible feeling that they were only asleep.

While they burned, Yevgeny played his harp. Its sound was so delicate that it could hardly be heard over the roar and crackle of the fire. Sometimes the music was drowned out completely, but sometimes you could hear a fluttering

266

of notes ascending, beating like the wings of birds above the acrid, black smoke. *It is the souls of the children escaping,* I told myself. For a moment I had the most beautiful vision – I was convinced that behind this flat sky of smoke and ash, there still existed the real sky, the Russian sky, the colour of cornflowers. And behind that sky – I believed this ardently in that moment – there still existed heaven, hung with white cherry garlands to welcome our poor dead children.

When the roofs and walls had collapsed and the fires settled down to finish their business, Yevgeny dragged the gorgeous golden harp up to the flames.

No one stopped him; we all have the feeling that we are leaving the best part of ourselves behind here. But I did not stay to watch it burn.

Niki and Misha and I have set off into the snow; behind us, the image of children sleeping in the flames to the lullaby of a burning harp. No one could bear to say goodbye. We shall never see each other again.

I leaned heavily on Niki as we trudged away from the others. I never think about how young he is; he never complains and I never question. His eyes were so tired that he kept them closed as he walked. We let the child choose the way to go through the trees – one way is as good as another. Misha, for all our travail, is, I am afraid, happy to be again the last child left in the world.

He sang as we lost sight of our last friend. One of those tuneless, patternless songs that children make up. The last music in the world.

# Three

Anna stood barefoot at the end of a sandy road. Across the street, there were several old steel barrels, painted bright orange but rusty now, and a small stand that said '*Fajitas*.' Three dark, dusty children were running in the road and screaming at each other. She did not understand what they were saying.

It was very hot and the sun was not very far up in the sky. It was the second time she'd seen sunrise since she left the motel in her car.

The first time had been on the highway. She had come out from behind some old broken mountains the colour of the shards of brown beer bottles that lay beside every road, even the most deserted. She had seen the sky go from purple-grey to milky yellow and stopped to see the sun itself.

It was the most enormous sun she had ever seen. It terrified her. She fell asleep for a few minutes, the dead wheel of the car in her hands. Then the sun woke her up like a loud voice that had been speaking to her for some time before she heard it, and she started the car again.

She bought gas all the time – every couple of hours – and had come to think of the soiled blue car as a kind of fatigued and thirsty blue horse; ugly, but faithful and companionable.

She did not stop anywhere to sleep. She bought fried chicken in a brown-paper bag from a store on the main street in a town where everyone was black and watched her quietly from the moment she stepped out of the car until she drove away. The car smelled with the sweet, greasy odour of chicken all night after that, and she stayed hungry. She had eaten the chicken, which was hot and salty and good, and drunk Coca-Cola to stay awake. But she was still hungry – it was a kind of hunger that eating would not fill, like the empty hunger mourners feed after a funeral. She did not stop again.

This morning the car had finally given up and laid down its burden in a tiny town on the West Texas border of Mexico. They couldn't fix the car there, she was told. It would have to be towed north to Ruidosa – which would cost two hundred fifty dollars, cash. The Mexican mechanic in the local gas station offered her twenty-five dollars to sell the car for scrap.

The Mexican lived in the gas station with his family. She could hear children crying and a dog barking and smell onions being fried. She asked him if there was someplace she could get something to eat and he pointed down the road where she now stood.

She crossed the street to the stand, bought *fajitas* – barbecued meat wrapped in a flour tortilla – and sat down on a rock. She was starving and could hear herself chewing like a dog. The children stopped playing for a moment and laughed at her. She imagined that her cheeks bulged with the tough beef and she started to cry. They backed away.

Finally she stood up and brushed off her dress and walked back towards the town to look for a phone.

There was a pay phone in the drugstore. She dialled Ian collect.

'Yes, of course,' she heard him say to the operator.

'Anna,' he said when the line was quiet. His voice was like rain in that dusty place, like sleep after grief.

'What time is it there?' she asked him.

'Six A.M., he told her.

'I'm sorry,' she said.

'Anna, where are you?'

'I'm all right,' she told him.

'I know,' he said gently. 'Where are you?'

'I don't know.'

'What's near there?'

'I think the next-biggest town is called Ruidosa,' she said.

'Give me your number and hang up. I'll call the operator and call you back.'

272

She read him the number on the phone.

'Hang up,' he repeated.

She held on to the phone and tears collected in her throat.

'It's okay,' he told her. 'I'll call you right back.'

She hung up.

The drugstore smelled of camphor and sterile gauze. It reminded her of an army hospital. The screen door slammed each time someone came in. By the cash register a radio played a mournful country song; the voice of the singer actually caught with quiet, dramatic sobs. She watched the minute hand of a big electric clock jerk each time the second hand went around.

It was nearly a half hour before the phone rang.

'You're in Las Hermosas,' Ian told her. 'And I'm going to fly into Marfa and rent a car and come get you. I won't be there much before dark – I have to change planes in El Paso. Is there a restaurant or a library or somewhere you can wait?'

Anna looked out across the street. There was a hardware store, a coffee shop and, farther down, the gas station where the blue carcass of her car still lay. On her side of the street there was the drugstore and the bank.

'I think so,' she said. 'A restaurant.'

'Just stay there, Anna.'

'Thank you,' she said. Her throat was dry and aching. She wanted to sleep so much she could have stretched out on the black-and-white linoleum floor of the pharmacy.

'Oh, Anna,' he said.

There was a long silence. She knew she would have to hang up and then she would be alone again in that dry, alien place with the sobbing music and the odour of sickness.

'Ian,' she said, 'I love you.'

'Oh God,' he told her. 'I love you, too. I love you dearly.'

Still she could not hang up.

'I'll be there, Anna,' he said. 'It's okay.'

\*     \*     \*

273

Ian walked into Nancy Ann's Coffee Shop quietly; his eyes ached from driving. It was dusk; lavender light had mixed with the yellow dust and seemed to move in the air like sheer curtains. He had seen Anna from the window, her head down on her arms on the table, and guessed that she was asleep. She had been gone two days, and from the distance she had covered, she must have driven almost every second.

He sat down at the table next to hers. The waitress seemed to have been waiting for him and came over. She was fat and blonde and wore a pink pantsuit uniform – a short dress and slacks – that reminded Ian of the stretch suits that babies wore. Her skin was young but worn and flaccid. She spoke to him in a whisper.

'She all right?'

Ian nodded.

The girl nodded her head, too.

'She's nice,' she said. 'But I thought maybe she was sick.'

'She's just been through a lot,' Ian told her. 'I don't want to wake her up.'

'Me neither,' the girl said. 'You want something?'

'Thank you,' Ian said. 'I guess I'll have some coffee.'

The girl looked again at Anna and went back to the counter. As she walked away, Ian could see her soft dimpled thighs through the candy-coloured nylon of her pants. She was a lot younger than he was, but probably already had one or two children. He liked her; her body looked the way he felt.

He stretched his back muscles, which were tight and sore, and relaxed. He watched the girl pouring his steaming coffee and cutting a piece of coconut-iced cake from a cake stand. He understood how Anna could have fallen asleep in the middle of this place in the middle of the day.

'Here,' she said, putting the coffee and the cake in front of him. 'Fresh this morning.'

'Thank you,' Ian said.

'On the house.' She shrugged. 'She's from Russia,' the girl said. Her voice was awed and even lower than it had been.

'Yes, she is,' Ian told her.

The girl stared at the back of Anna's head. How exhausted Anna must have been, Ian thought, to lie there with her face down, so still.

'Well, like I said, she's real nice.'

Ian smiled and the girl walked away gingerly on her crepe-soled shoes.

The coffee was too hot to drink. The fan near the door whirred with a kind of hushed beat like a far-off helicopter. Ian took a bite of cake and the dense sweetness of the sugared coconut seemed to coat not only the inside of his mouth but the inside of his brain, instantly making him sleepy.

He forced himself to swallow the scalding coffee. He felt it stream a boiling path down to his stomach and holding that heat inside made him feel cool for the first time since he'd got out of the car. He closed his eyes and sweat ran down between his shoulder blades.

'Ian?' Anna whispered.

He opened his eyes. She was sitting up and the left side of her face was flushed and creased where she had been leaning on her arm.

He smiled. 'Right here,' he said. He put his arms around her and she let her head rest heavily against his shoulder.

'Where's a good place to stay around here?' he asked the waitress.

'A decent place or a nice place?' she asked him.

He looked down at Anna, and gently brushed her hair out of her eyes.

'A nice place,' he said.

Church Rock Hot Springs was a hole in the mountains forty minutes off the road back to Marfa. When he finally saw the place appear out of the darkness in the headlights of the car, his heart sank. There was nothing about it to lighten the mood in any way.

It consisted of four tiny wooden cabins, the paint mostly scoured off the boards by sandstorms, with small yellow bug lights burning above the screen doors. Somewhere in the blackness beyond them was supposed to be a high-ceilinged cave hollowed out of molten lava millions of years ago, into which hot, pure water still flowed. It cost forty dollars to rent two well-scrubbed, well-worn cotton bathing suits, two towels and a cabin for the night.

'Well, that's the best bargain of this trip,' Ian told Anna. 'Do you have any idea how much it costs to get to a remote area of Texas in a hurry?' The clerk, a grey-haired lady, went back to get a key.

Anna shook her head.

'A lot,' he said. He heard his voice hurrying on, as if it were independent of him. It had become the desperately cheerful sound track of a romantic adventure that kept threatening to derail into some kind of sad documentary. Anna's eyes were depressed, though she had not let go of his hand, and Ian could not stop thinking of her husband. Her expression reminded him of the photographs that had appeared on obituary pages worldwide two years ago this summer – her eyes were hers, but her half-smile was the same as the dead physicist's.

'What makes a hot spring hot?' he asked her. 'You're a geologist; tell me.'

Oh Christ, he thought, I'm interviewing her.

'An inactive volcano,' Anna said tonelessly. It was the first time she had spoken in the last hour and a half.

The woman came back with the key. Ian wondered how you could lock a cave.

'Come on,' the woman said. 'I'll show you.' Her voice was almost gay and Ian noticed that she appeared to like them for no reason – perhaps she thought they were in love.

They walked across the parking lot, following the beam of the woman's flashlight. Between the first and second cabin, they went single file up a small dirt path.

'Watch your step,' she told them. She pointed ahead to a door built up out of the ground like an old-fashioned root-cellar door. It was padlocked.

When she had unlocked the door and opened it, she turned off the flashlight.

'Let your eyes adjust,' she told them. 'It's better that way.'

They all stood in the dark for several seconds, not speaking. Then Ian and Anna followed her down several steps and through utter blackness to emerge onto a wet ledge that was like a narrow, slate beach. They were standing in front of a small pool that glistened blue with the light of the night sky visible through an opening perhaps fifty feet above. In places, steam curled above the surface; the atmosphere was warm, humid and intensely soporific.

'It's beautiful,' Anna said.

Ian filled his lungs with the moist, comforting air.

'It's beautiful in daylight, too,' the woman told Anna. 'You get all these rainbows, especially in cooler weather. The Mexicans called the springs Arco Iris – Rainbow Springs – which is probably what the Indians called it. But somewhere along the line somebody decided to change the name to Church Rock. Make it more respectable, I guess.' She laughed and shook her head.

'Enjoy,' she said. 'I'll lock up when you're through.' She left them standing there, their awful bathing suits in their hands.

'What a great old lady.' Ian laughed.

'She wasn't so old,' Anna said. She walked off a little and stared up at the sky through the arched rock. 'It is a little like a church,' she said.

As she stood with her back to him, he undressed. She heard him, and did not turn around. He put his foot into the water – it was like stepping into a hot bath, except the minerals in the water gave it a silky, slippery feeling. He waded in up to his knees and sat down. The bottom was hard, smooth rock.

'My God, my God,' he said. The heat worked through his sore muscles as if it were dissolving them. He watched Anna watching him, outlined in the opaline blue light; the stillness was such that he could see her breathing. She pulled off her shirt and stood for a moment, her arms folded across her breasts. Then she let her arms fall to her sides.

277

When she reached him, her skin was as warm as the water; holding her, he could not tell where her body ended and his began. But when he was inside her, he held her face in his hands. Her open mouth trembled and he saw her say his name.

'The highway looks different now,' Anna told him. 'Farther away.' The windows of the rented Eagle were shut and air conditioning cascaded through the vents. Ian realised that Anna was shivering; the warmth of the night before had progressively diminished the longer they drove. He took her hand and rubbed it, but while she looked at him and smiled, he saw that he had not helped. The cold came from the inside.

He turned off the air conditioning and they opened their windows. The world was coming back. Even from the road he could smell heat and the raw, dry rock. Occasionally, in the flatlands, he could smell straw and cattle; then for miles the whole countryside would be steeped in that odour of fertility.

'This is a big country,' she said.

'Not as big as Russia,' he said.

'But I've seen more of it.'

Her voice was flattened by regret. He took her hand.

For hours the rugged West Texas landscape went by and Anna couldn't take her eyes off it. It was huge, hard terrain and he felt almost that he wanted to protect Anna from it.

'Close your eyes for a while,' he told her. 'Go to sleep.'

'I'll never really be an American,' she told him.

'I suppose that's the way every immigrant feels.'

He reached over and pulled the Avis map of Texas out of the glove compartment.

'I don't know Texas very well,' he said, 'but I bet it's not much different from everywhere else in America.'

He started to scan down the list of cities and towns. The print was tiny and the car swerved.

'What are you doing?' she asked.

'Look,' he said, starting to read out loud, 'Alpine, Boston, Edinburgh, Italy, Naples, Palestine – they're all the names of towns in Texas. Hey, how did I miss this? There's even one named Odessa; a city – it's got over a hundred thousand people. Anna, everybody here is from somewhere else.'

'Let me see that,' she said.

She read the map for several minutes.

'Weimar,' she said.

'See,' he told her softly. 'Everyone thinks of his old life when he starts over.'

She leaned her head back on the seat and closed her eyes finally. Tears ran silently down the sides of her face, down her neck, and wet the collar of her dress. But her face remained still.

'Don't worry,' he said. 'We'll go slowly.'

He kept quiet the rest of the way to the airport, and was conscious of the exact moment at which she fell asleep and let go of his hand again.

In the town of Sahd, Seriozha and Katinka got off the bus at the gate of the public garden which gave the town its name. In the eighteenth century, that *sahd*, or garden, had been a gift from the British ambassador to a Muscovy princess he had fallen in love with. The seeds of sweet williams and hollyhocks had travelled all the way from Devonshire.

It didn't really mean anything to anyone anymore – hollyhocks and sweet williams are among the commonest of wildflowers in the Russian countryside – and the garden had years ago been replanted with roses by the municipality. But to Seriozha, on the day that they began their exile in that closed town, the remembrance of seeds sent from far away was happy and buoyant. He renewed his hold on Katinka's hand.

She walked slowly. She had entered the ninth month of her pregnancy, and despite their best efforts to keep her rested and well fed, she was weak and usually exhausted. It was as if the long ordeal of Seriozha's imprisonment could only now take its toll; when he had been inside, she had been strong and tireless. She had gone every day

279

to the offices of State Security in Dzerzhinsky Square, bothering this secretary and that clerk, filling out an endless number of legal complaint forms, paying to have them stamped and certified. She never saw Zalessky there – he had seen through her initial agreement to inform; she had been of no help.

They had finally released him, Seriozha knew, not because they had a plan for him, but because they were too unsure of their plan.

Katinka was now as useless as Seriozha, only a minor bargaining chip in a game that no one had definitely decided to play. Sometimes someone – they would never know who – got bored of an evening and talked about playing in earnest. Somebody would be sent, to her or to Seriozha, to see that all the pieces of the game were still there, ready to be called into use. Then they would all go back to waiting.

It had been established recently that it was better for them to do this waiting in the town of Sahd, a town closed to outsiders because of sensitive biological research. Sensitive research in genetics, read the official story; research into biochemical warfare, it was said. The dusty June air near the garden, swarming with tiny early-summer flies and yet smelling of sweetish insecticide, made Seriozha afraid. He gave Katinka his handkerchief to hold over her nose and mouth.

The afternoon was too bright, too warm for that time of year. People walked languidly, gratefully. Cabdrivers left their cars at home and spent the day in the sun. Everyone moved towards the artificial lake in the park, which was huge and shady; they floated past Seriozha and Katinka in laughing groups of three and four, wearing bright summer clothes like dancers in a loose, modern choreography.

'Do you want to go and put your feet in the water?' he asked her.

She shook her head. 'I want to be settled,' she said.

They had a little trouble finding the apartment that had been assigned to them. It was in a project of seven-storey buildings, all exactly alike, built around dry, paved courtyards. Though the whole development was only a few years old, the courtyards were already cracking.

There were no lifts in the building. They walked up the stairs, stopping at each landing for Katinka to catch her breath.

When they opened the door, she began to cry. They had been told that the apartment was furnished. They had been unable to take anything with them from Seriozha's parents' apartment; the Khamenevs' things were considered state property until Seriozha's case was settled. Katinka owned very little and had sold what she owned in order for them to have some money starting out.

But now they saw that the apartment was virtually empty. A painted table and two mismatched chairs – one large, one small – stood between the alcove of the kitchen and the only other room. There, the wooden floorboards were dried out and uneven. A row of earthen flower pots stood next to the closed window; the plants were all shrivelled and dead. In the corner, a single folding cot had been opened. It had no mattress on it. Its coils were rusty and sharp.

'Here,' Seriozha said. He opened their one large suitcase and scooped out the clothes with both hands. He spread them on the floor. 'Lie down.'

She did, and he sat down next to her, lifting her head gently and placing it on his lap.

She continued to cry and he stroked her face, her temples, her cheeks and her lips, washing her face with her tears, wiping away the salty grime and cleaning his hands on his sleeve.

At about ten that night, he went next door and asked the neighbour to phone an ambulance. The neighbours were a couple about forty-five years old, suspicious and poor. No doubt they had been screened before Seriozha and Katinka were assigned the apartment; the man did not want to open the door. But when Seriozha told him that Katinka was about to give birth, the woman pushed her husband out of the way and went into Seriozha's apartment herself. The husband then dialled the emergency medics.

When they carried her down the six flights of stairs, all Seriozha could think was: she's too quiet. She was bleeding but the contractions were irregular and slow.

The medics who took care of her on the way to the Sahd hospital were two male nurses, older than Seriozha, efficient and comforting. He was sure that they did not know who he was. They put pillows under her back and under her legs and held her head up. They kept telling her to breathe. Once in a while one of them would look at Seriozha and tell him to breathe, too, then they would all laugh, including Katinka. But her laugh was so small that Seriozha would begin, unconsciously, to bite his lip and hold his breath again.

At the hospital, they knew who Seriozha was, and they made them wait. One of the men from the ambulance became furious and shouted at the receiving doctor, a woman with dyed black hair and green eye shadow. His partner tried to restrain him, telling him that it would only make matters worse. In fact, it resulted in the doctor turning on her heel and leaving them alone for nearly a half hour while other personnel tried to locate her superior.

The fetal heartbeat was lost at a quarter to midnight. At midnight, Katinka was admitted to an operating room and delivered of a stillborn boy. They had given her drugs to bring on labour and she worked so hard to deliver the dead child that she was prostrate with exhaustion at the end. The medic who had cursed the doctor cursed again. The other gave Seriozha some vodka in a paper cup.

'It's my fault,' Seriozha told them.

'That is not allowed,' a young woman in a white uniform said as the medic poured a second round of vodka, this time for the three of them.

The first medic tried to grab her.

'*Pozor*,' he hissed. 'Shame.'

'You'll lose your job, Yakov,' his partner told him.

But the girl straightened herself and said nothing more.

When Seriozha saw Katinka, she was white and there

were dark blue halos around her eyes. Her lips were livid and chafed from the anesthesia.

He took her hand, hoping not to wake her.

She did not open her eyes.

'It's not your fault,' she said. Her voice had been scraped hoarse by the anesthesia as well.

'Shh, sleep,' he said. I should have done anything, he thought.

They rolled her away to another room. The room he was left in was silent. He was aware that it was the middle of the night, and that though the walls had been painted sky blue, they were colourless under the fluorescent light.

It seemed to him that life itself had died with his son. He remembered that this was very close to what his mother had written and that this was why she had left him. In his despair, he had only one desire left – that this never happen again.


'Listen,' Ian told his father, 'this is bullshit.'

'If you want to talk to me,' George said, 'you'd better calm down.'

Ian had taken the subway to the Foundation's New York office – a neoclassical brownstone just off Madison on Sixty-ninth Street – as soon as he had got off the phone with Anna.

'I mean it,' his father said. 'You are in my office. Calm down.'

Ian wondered if the old idea of counting to ten when you were furious actually helped at all. He started counting. But at four, he lost his temper again.

'There's no question that it was pressure from the parent company,' he said. 'They dropped two other books at the same time – one on nuclear power and one that was a fucking nuclear joke book.'

'Welcome to the real world,' George said to him. 'I'm sure there are a hundred other publishers standing on line right this minute, waiting to snap it up.'

'Yeah, Farrar, Straus will snap it up for five thousand,

and she'll owe Thomas half of a seventy-thousand-dollar advance,' Ian said.

The light on the phone on his father's desk lit up. Ian looked at it. George looked at it. His father did not pick it up, but Ian saw how impatient he was.

'She's a full fellow of the damn Naughton Foundation,' Ian said, 'and a major New York publisher has just shafted her. Doesn't that concern you at all?'

His father's face was closed, as closed as he had ever seen it. It disturbed him and he looked away, over the surface of his father's desk, which was impeccably organised, the pencils in a leather holder, an obsolete picture of the family – Ian must have been sixteen – in a wooden frame, the papers under a crystal paperweight engraved with the thanks of some international rights organisation. He picked up the paperweight.

'The International Pen Club,' he read from the citation. 'I wonder what they will think about Anna's book being suppressed.'

His father exploded. 'Just where the hell do you get off?' he said. 'A publisher has a right to cancel a property that may interfere with its business interests. Her book will be picked up by someone else; she only has to pay Thomas back out of her earnings. These things happen sometimes.'

His father was so angry now that he was white and one vein stood out blue along the line of his throat. The sight of that fragile blue vein suddenly hurt Ian; he saw how soft his father's skin had become. Though he was thin and fit, his neck was beginning to be loose and crepey like an old woman's. This was all the sharper against the starched white shirt he wore, pinned underneath the tie with a gold pin. And the tie was silk, navy and crimson stripes. What care his father took to look well, Ian thought. In his stomach he instinctively recognised fear.

'I'm sorry,' Ian said.

His father nodded without looking at him.

'I am really upset about this,' Ian told him.

'I can see that,' George said.

The light on the phone went on again. This time his father picked it up.

'A minute or so,' he said, and hung up.

Ian stood up to go.

'I'm going to look into this,' Ian said. 'And I think you should, too.'

George nodded again, tired.

'Will you be at home for the Fourth?' his father asked.

Ian looked at him. 'That's the big day out at Huggins's,' he said.

'Oh, of course,' George said. 'We'll see you there, I guess.'

'Dad,' Ian said, 'I really am sorry. But I think something's got to be done about this.'

'Yes, Ian,' his father said.

As Ian opened the door to leave, a young woman jumped up from a chair and ran to the door.

'George?' she said. 'I'll just take a minute.'

Ian looked at her. In a white linen dress and leather sandals, it was Sarah Davidoff. At first he had noticed only that she had long blonde hair, held back by a tortoiseshell band like a schoolgirl's.

'Oh great,' Ian said, and left without speaking to her.

In the elevator, he kept seeing the dead photograph on his father's desk, in particular his mother's abstracted expression, part Antigone, part Revlon, and his own grossly long, frizzy hair. It had been 1969, and the boy in the picture, whose adolescent terrors had literally made his hair stand on end, was much too familiar, like a neighbour in an apartment building whom one always sees but never speaks to.

The three women sat in the stiff, barren apartment that the Foundation had lent Anna, talking about Anna's naturalisation ceremony as if it were a wedding.

'It sort of is,' Mary Ellen said. She was pale and emaciated, and this trip into the city to visit Anna was one of the first excursions she had made since she had come home. She was dressed in a green dress that reminded

Anna of a surgeon's gown. There was a small violet scar on her neck.

'She's right, you know,' Kate McDonough said. 'The congressman's secretary called yesterday to find out what colour dress I was wearing so they could pick appropriate flowers.'

Anna was embarrassed and looked down into her cup of tea. She could see her own lips reflected in the surface of the warm liquid; still, the cup was too sleek and alien, made for a robot with a tungsten mouth to drink from. All the dishware in the apartment was a futuristic glazed black pottery.

'Wild dishes,' Mary Ellen said.

'I don't know who picked out all these things,' Anna said.

'Oh, they just get some designer to do it all in these corporate apartments,' Kate said. 'Someone who has an eye for drama and glamour and doesn't have to live with the stuff.'

Anna glanced around the room. The furniture was all upholstered, all beige and cream, the carpet was the colour of oatmeal. The windows poured sun over everything like melted butter. There were times when she felt that she would slip off every surface.

'I like it,' Mary Ellen said. 'It's neat.'

They sat quietly and the air conditioner slowly swirled dust motes in the hot July light. The air-conditioning system was automatic; none of the windows could be opened. Perhaps this was because the apartment was on such a high floor. Between the beige anonymity of the apartment's interior and the swoony emptiness from the window to the street, Anna imagined that the idea of falling could catch up to you. You could get used to all that vacant-coloured space, and find yourself thinking that you already lived in the air.

Suddenly the phone rang, so loud in the bright silence that Anna started. She went into the kitchen and picked up the clean white phone from the wall receiver.

'*Zdrastvutye*,' a voice said.

286

'Who is this?' Anna asked.

'It's me, Kostia,' the voice said. Still, it sounded so slow and husky that she did not recognise it as his.

'There is some news about Sergei,' he told her. 'But I can't talk on the phone. You'll have to come here.'

Her hand shook. She looked out through the open space in the wall which divided the kitchen from the living room. Kate and Mary Ellen watched her and waited.

'I can't talk now,' she said. 'Give me your number and I'll call you back.'

He gave her a number and she hung up. But for several seconds she still gripped the phone. It seemed to her that the living room no longer had a floor – the pale carpeting was only a mist which hid a thirty-two-storey void. How would she make it across?

'Who was that?' Kate asked. 'Is everything all right?'

'It was someone from home,' Anna said. 'I'm sorry.'

They both looked at her sadly.

Anna managed to walk over to them and sit down.

'I'm glad that you are my guests, for once,' she told them. 'Please eat more cake.' The cake was tiny, made of ground almonds and decorated with candied violets. She had bought it from a French bakery that Sarah had told her was the best in New York and it had cost thirty dollars. Mary Ellen stiffened.

Kate reached past Mary Ellen to touch Anna's hand.

'Don't be so nervous,' she told Anna. 'It's going to be lovely.'

'I just want it to be over,' Anna said.

'Enjoy it,' Kate told her. 'The Hugginses have a beautiful home, and your friends will be there.'

'What are you going to wear, Anna?' Mary Ellen asked. It seemed to Anna that the girl's voice had never regained its normal volume. Now her words were always low, even when she was laughing.

'A white dress,' Anna said. The three of them began to laugh.

'Really?'

Anna nodded.

287

'And I always thought the next wedding I would go to would be yours,' Kate said to Mary Ellen.

'The next wedding I go to will probably be *yours*,' Mary Ellen said.

'That's not funny,' Kate said. But then the mother and daughter looked each other and began to laugh. Anna recognised that laughter – it relied on pain for its mirth, the way the wings of a plane rely upon the emptiness speed creates in the air for uplift.

When they were gone, Anna picked up the phone, and dialled the number Kyrstov had given her. Her mouth was dry with fear.

Seriozha; there was news of Seriozha. If she wanted to know what it was she would have to go. Obviously Kyrstov himself had nothing to do with it; he did not even have the ability to meet with her, for she knew he would have if there was any way he could. He was at the mercy of others who would not dare approach her directly.

A male voice, with a round, perfect American accent like a newscaster's, answered the phone. She said who was calling and was put on hold.

After a few moments Kyrstov came on.

'*Zdrastvutye*.' His voice sounded tremulous and far away.

'*Zdrastvutye*,' she said automatically. She didn't know what to say next.

'I can't leave,' Kyrstov said. 'What you must do is come out here to Glen Cove.'

He was referring to the estate which housed the staff of the Russian mission to the United Nations. Never, she thought.

If she went there, entered into the compound grounds, she would technically be on Russian soil again. They could do with her as they wished. She would never come out again. That was what they had done in her father's generation and to this day their effectiveness was based upon that fear more than any other. They called a person for 'questioning'. You never saw him again.

'Where is that?' she asked.

'Don't worry,' he said. 'They will send a car for you.'

'Absolutely not,' Anna said.

He was silent for a moment. Then she heard him ask someone named Sasha to come to the phone and give her directions.

The American voice returned to the phone and gave her directions via the Long Island Rail Road. All in native, distinctly Muscovite Russian. She answered his questions in English, but he continued to speak Russian to her.

He hung up without letting her speak to Kyrstov again.

After she put down the phone, she thought again of Kyrstov's words. *I can't leave. What you must do is come out here.* It was all pure Cheka.

He had been told to say that, taught to say it.

Of course, they wanted to hold out some kind of deal to her. She had expected it from the first. What she hadn't expected was that they would wait so long. That by the time they approached her she would be so desperate for even a single word. She didn't trust herself. What if, when she was there, it seemed to her that she could actually help Seriozha? What if they showed her that picture again, that blue, bruised photograph, and said it was real and that she had the power . . .

*I must not go*, she repeated to herself. She said it out loud. She said it in Russian and then in English and then in Russian again. She said it to the mirror. She tried to set her face hard and shut. She said it with her mouth closed.

Then she continued to say it silently, quickly, as she dressed to go, almost as if it were a prayer.

When she got off the train in Glen Cove, she found several private taxis waiting. As Sasha had instructed her, she got into one before she told the driver where she was going. He had been talkative and friendly until she told him. When she gave the address of the Russian compound he immediately shut himself off.

He drove off as soon as she paid her fare and left her

289

standing at the gate. She did not even have time to press the electric buzzer before a young man in uniform came out of the *butka*, the little guard booth, and addressed her by name.

'*Graszhdanka Khameneva,*' he said.

'I am no longer "citizen" Khameneva,' she told him. 'You may call me *gaszhpasha.*'

It was the word for 'Mrs'. But it derived from the antiquated expression 'milady'. It was no longer used within the USSR except for foreigners or by servants to address their employers. The young man bristled and walked ahead of her.

She followed him up a flagstone path underneath a canopy of whispering, fountainous elms, elms from a nineteenth-century engraving. Artfully cultivated wildflowers grew along the path, and she noticed that amidst their carefully weeded beds small cameras swivelled restlessly and tiny microphones – these were set in the succulents like minuscule metal seedpods – registered every sound. They entered an immense Tudor house that from the outside seemed like the set for a Mosfilm movie about decadent British imperialists.

But inside the floors were bare and glaring except for thin runners wherever pedestrian traffic was likely to be heaviest. There were file cabinets along the halls. Rooms that might have been salons, libraries, music rooms, were now offices with metal desks, hand-coloured photographs of the Politburo and the ubiquitous posters, exhorting the office workers to be mindful of the distinction between 'real' and 'materialistic' values. This meant, Anna knew quite well, that they were to bring their hard and precious American currency back home and deny the temptation to profiteer by buying stacks of Levi's and reselling them in Russia.

They had walked the length of the house to emerge on a terrace which faced a formal lawn and a pool. There were several white metal garden tables, shaded by umbrellas which flexed at different angles to block out the sun. A handful of women and men sat in bathing suits and tennis clothes, holding tall iced drinks. The sound of elegantly suppressed laughter mixed with the musical jingling of ice cubes and the deliberate murmur of refined Moscow speech. Kostia was there, sweating in a light-coloured suit. So was the handsome blond man who had accompanied Kostia at the Christmas benefit. He was wearing Bermuda shorts and a fashionably loose cotton sweater. He wore American boat shoes without socks the way Ian did and he stood up when he saw her.

'*Gaszhpasha Khameneva*,' he said cordially. 'I am Alexander Whittmore.'

She repressed a desire to smile at his name; he might as well have told her he was James Bond. She was grateful to him; just when she had been on the verge of being overwhelmed by the monstrous expense and pretension of the mansion, he had invited her to see how fake it all really was. But seeing how crude and thin was the veneer deepened her fear. She waited.

Kostia got up heavily out of his chair.

'Listen to him, Anna,' he said. He looked hot and awful. Again she thought: he has become an old man in such a short time.

'I have come here for one reason only,' she said to Whittmore. 'To find out about my son.'

'Would you like a drink?' he asked her. 'A gin and tonic, perhaps?'

'No,' she said.

'You won't mind if I do, however.' It was not a question. He was beginning to enter into sharper focus. She had been interrogated many times during Pasha's ordeal; she knew every type of Chekist. Whittmore was of the smooth, Westernised variety. He would be a gifted linguist, he would have a clever and most likely American sense of humour, he would be on her side, and remain there for at least the first half hour of their meeting. What this ultimately meant was that he did not have the last word He was the apparatchik who dispensed the decisions of someone above, someone without the need or the patience to probe the best way to persuade Anna, someone who

291

merely said, 'This is what we want. Get it any way you can.'

Whittmore summoned a butler in uniform. He called him Timofey.

Incredible, Anna thought, they have even brought their serfs.

'Please, sit down,' he told Anna.

He pulled out a metal chair for her. It felt cold as she sat in it.

'I understand that you are forced to choose a new publisher.'

She did not respond.

'Interesting,' he continued, 'how Americans do not seem to object to the very real economic censorship that they are subjected to. Nor to perceive that it stems from the very depths of their political system.'

He was testing her, she knew; he would tell by her response how cooperative or uncooperative she was going to be. He would then adjust his tactics. She decided it was wisest to force him to do the talking. That way, he would get to his point faster. And it was his point, after all, which determined what she had to gain.

'This may be a crossroads for you, Anna Nikolayevna. This might be the moment in which you reflect upon the advantages your country poses – which you yourself know better than most people – and decide if it is not wise to rise above a few mistakes which have been made.'

'Do not speak to me of mistakes, Mr Whittmore,' she said.

He sat down and pulled his chair up close to her.

'Listen to me,' he said. 'Here we are in New York, and certain things can be said which cannot be said closer to home.'

She smiled at his lie. He smiled back and she saw how white and straight his teeth were. It was probable that he was the son of someone quite high in the Party, perhaps in the Politburo itself. No doubt he had been educated abroad, received the finest medical and dental care that

Europe and America could provide; he had never in his life worn clothes made in the Soviet Union.

The butler Timofey, tall and placid as a servant out of Tolstoy, returned with the gin and tonic. Moisture beaded up on the cut-crystal glass and magnified the piece of lime inside into an icy, lime-coloured kaleidoscope.

'Are you sure you won't join me?' Whittmore asked again.

She was afraid to drink anything they gave her.

'No, thank you,' she said. She noticed that Kostia had walked down the lawn, away from them. He walked slowly, pendulously, weaving slightly in the heat from side to side.

'I hope Konstantin Dimitrievich does not have a stroke in this weather,' Whittmore said.

She looked at him. He was making fun of Kostia.

'He is an old man,' she said softly. Her voice was full of shame. Why had she let herself come here? There was a price for everything and she had only put herself in the stupid, and vulnerable, position of refusing to pay it.

'You know why I am here,' she told him. 'Come to the point.'

Whittmore sat back in his chair again and held his hands out in front of him, all his fingertips touching, making a sort of cage.

'You have suffered, Anna Nikolayevna,' he said. 'You and your family. Let's admit it; ours is a stubborn country, and simple, not like the United States. We have always felt that someone is with us or he is against us. There was no room for a man like your husband, who was for us on some questions and opposed us on others.

'But everything changes, even if it changes slowly. History has come to acknowledge that your husband had an important message, one that must not be denied.'

She noticed he said 'history', not the Party, not the leaders.

'We have searched for a way to build something positive upon the suffering of your husband, a way in which his contribution will not be lost to his people. A way in which

293

your contribution can be felt at home, among your own. Your son, too, must play his role in this.'

What he was saying, she knew, was that her life finally was of some value to them. They could use her for propaganda. If she agreed, she might even be able to go home one day; if she refused, it would be Seriozha who paid.

'*Pozor*,' she said. 'Shame. Do not speak to me of my husband. Do not even say his name.'

She felt her anger slipping out of her hands like a huge dog on a leash, lunging, dragging her along.

He drew back politely, looking away as though she would be embarrassed if he saw how emotional she was.

'It is entirely understandable that you feel anger,' he said. 'But where will it get us, Anna Nikolayevna? Is it not time to go on?'

She thought she would strike him. She stood up to go.

He looked up worriedly.

'Your son depends upon you,' he said.

Now we will get to the point, she thought.

'He is well,' he told her.

This meant that he had not been well. It was confirmation of the rumour that he had been held in the November 7th and subjected to torture by drugging.

'He is in Sahd, we are in close contact with him; he is waiting to know what you decide.'

Sahd was a closed city. He was in exile. Perhaps even under house arrest.

For a moment she wavered. She held on to the back of her chair and considered sitting down, accepting a cold drink, listening to every word that he might say about Seriozha, making him say them again and again.

He saw her fear and moved fast, instinctively; he was a predator.

'He is anxious to get back to Moscow, of course. You know what it is like in these provincial towns. No theatre, no ballet, the same sausage and cottage cheese in every store. And the medical facilities are not what they ought to be, though improving them has become a national priority.'

The sweat seemed to dry instantly on her forehead and upper lip. Gooseflesh formed on her bare arms.

'He is fine,' he reassured her. 'But unfortunately his girl had some problems – she was, as they say in America, "expecting" – and, well, these stupid provincial doctors did not manage to get to her in time.'

Her back suddenly ached as it had every day that she had been pregnant with Seriozha.

'She's all right,' Whittmore said. 'But the child . . .' He shook his head. 'It was a boy, I think. I'll check that for you.'

She turned away from him and began to walk back the way she had come.

She went through the house, dark now because of the brilliant sunlight on the terrace. She felt blind.

She went through the garden and up to the iron gate. But the man in the *butka* would not let her out. He had no order to open the gate. She held on to the wrought-iron bars.

'Anya, Annichka,' she heard. It was Kostia's voice. He was out of breath.

She turned towards him. His face was red and wet with sweat. She let him put his arms around her.

'Anna,' he said, 'it's not your fault. There was nothing you could have done.'

She looked into his eyes, begging him to convince her.

'You know how they are,' he said.

She felt her knees disintegrating. She leaned on him.

He took a thick envelope out of his pocket.

'You were supposed to take this,' he told her. 'Sasha told me to give it to you.'

'Alexander Whittmore,' she said, trying to spit the name out of her mouth like something horrible and spoiled. Sasha was the affectionate diminutive for Alexander – but who could have felt affection for such an animal?

Yet she clutched the envelope; Seriozha, she thought. She held it up to her lips and kissed it.

Kostia put his arm around her. His face was deformed

by pain, the wrinkles on his forehead and at the corners of his mouth, deep and carved.

A taxi pulled up to the gate of the Russian compound. The gates opened electronically. The cab remained where it was and Anna pressed her cheek against Kostia's.

'*Da svidanya*,' she said. She would never see him again, and in his deep-set eyes, shrouded in the shadowy grey flesh of an old man, she saw the dead eyes of the lost baby, more lost to her than her son, or even Pavel, because he had never had a chance to live.

'*Da svidanya*,' he said. He kissed her hand formally, but his lips trembled. Her last glimpse of him was as he stood there in the perfect garden, his huge suit a mess, his hands shaking at his sides.

In the taxi, she ripped open the letter that Kostia had handed her. She saw at once that it was not from Seriozha. Then she saw that it was not a letter at all. It was a meticulously prepared set of statements, numbered to the page, paragraph and line, that she was meant to fit into the English translation of her book. None of the statements was particularly offensive by itself, but taken together they amounted to a scathing condemnation of the American arms race, and a glowing encomium to the peaceful determination of the Communist Party of the Soviet Union.

When she arrived at Penn Station, she stood for a long time next to an enormous, vile-smelling metal dumpster, ready to throw the letter into oblivion. But one doubt haunted her – that there might be other, tacit clues to Seriozha's welfare contained in it. After nearly fifteen minutes, she refolded the letter and put it in her purse. On the bus back to her apartment, she realised that her clothes reeked of garbage, and she moved to the back where no one need sit next to her.

The heat shimmered on the lawns of East Hampton. The front porch of the Hugginses' house was decorated with bouquets of fire-engine red poppies, tight blue cornflowers and white sweet peas, tied to the railing by dipping sweeps of red, white and blue crepe paper. A Dixieland band played in a white gazebo, and the sunny sound of the brass zigzagged across the green grass to the dunes and the ocean beyond. The immense back porch of the Hugginses' mansion looked out over the bluffs to the Atlantic Ocean. On either side of the door were the American flag and the blue flag of the state of New York. Two banks of white folding chairs had been set up, with an aisle between them. The front row was cordoned off with a white ribbon.

There were perhaps seventy people sitting there, many of whom Anna knew or had met. She saw the Bradford family and was moved that they had all come in from California to be with her. She saw Sarah sitting by herself at the end of her row. Sarah was relaxed and wore a blue picture hat; she smiled and straightened her back when Anna looked at her. It was a message, Anna knew.

How will I get through this? she thought.

George came up to her and shook hands with Representative Huggins. He handed Anna his glass to drink out of; it was strong, ice-cold beer.

'Finish it,' he told her.

Its coldness seemed to wake her up, its bitterness wiped off her drowsy pain like a wet washcloth.

'Thank you,' she said.

'Smile,' he said. 'You're the star.'

She looked at him and in that moment she felt she saw to the root of his soul. She saw anger – anger stretching out in every direction like the hard blue Atlantic.

'When you're standing up there,' he said, 'just think: those bastards aren't going to win.' His eyes were wide open, he couldn't have known how loud his voice was.

Then the anger was gone, and he did not know that he had shown it to her.

'Thank you,' she said again.

He pressed her hand and took his seat next to his wife. Anna looked at Ian, who looked at her questioningly.

She took a deep breath and turned again to Huggins.

'Ready?' he said.

'Yes,' she said.

They sat down together on the white ribboned chairs.

Charles Huggins's wife, Claire, leaned over and touched her hand.

'We're so proud,' she said.

At that moment, a young police officer in white dress uniform came in and stood next to the American flag.

'All present, please rise,' he commanded.

There was a solemn shuffling of wooden chairs, and the judge came in, a man with white hair dressed in crisp black robes.

'Anna Nikolayevna Khameneva?' he called.

Anna stepped forward.

He read the small, terrifying paragraph that would change her in no outward way, yet as profoundly as if she had died and been reborn.

'Do you renounce the country of your origin and allegiance to any foreign country or person?' he asked her.

'I do,' she said.

'Will you defend the Constitution and the laws of the United States, pledge true faith and allegiance to the Constitution and, when required, bear arms or perform noncombatant service on behalf of the United States?'

'I will.'

'It is customary at this time to say a few words about the meaning of citizenship,' the judge said. 'I would like only to quote a small part of the law regarding naturalisation.

'"Admission to citizenship is, as it ought to be, jealously guarded and granted only to him – or her – worthy to become one in the great partnership which makes up the nation. The prime consideration is always the nation's welfare and not the applicant's, which is wholly secondary."

'Anna Nikolayevna Khameneva has demonstrated to a very unusual degree her commitment to the welfare of this nation and the world. I regard it as my privilege to welcome you into the American family.'

Now there was a spontaneous, though genteel, outburst of applause. Anna heard Mary Ellen's voice among those cheering her.

The judge smiled at her and reached out and shook her hand.

'That's it,' he said. 'How do you feel?'

Anna looked at Charles Huggins and his wife, and the Bradfords, all smiling as though she were their daughter. She looked at George, who leaned back, his arms folded across his chest, Kate, who held his sleeve, Mary Ellen, who suddenly had colour in her cheeks. She saw Sarah sigh.

Then she saw Ian, who watched her, looking as she had felt when she stepped off the plane – as though he were the immigrant, newly arrived on the shores of human happiness. She held his eyes.

'I feel safe,' she said.

After the ceremony the band played, and waiters who were tanned college students circulated with bottles of California champagne, oysters on the half shell, red caviar spread on tiny pieces of toast that had been cut in the shape of stars.

Tables had been set out under a tent on the crest of the dunes, and the white tablecloths whipped hard in the wind, as did the cotton skirts of the women. Almost everyone was barefoot.

The smell of charcoal smoke blew up from the beach and the children ran in and out of the waves in their clothes. Ian and Mary Ellen walked slowly along the shore. It was impossible to talk to Anna; everyone swarmed around her, kissing her, congratulating her.

'She has been really lucky,' Mary Ellen said. She squinted into the sun and Ian supposed she was talking about the clarity of the day.

'Sometimes I wonder if she hasn't been too lucky,' she said.

Ian looked at her. His skin felt taut and stinging across his cheekbones; he knew he had stayed out in the sun too long.

They walked along silently. The sun on the western horizon blazed through the breaking waves and Ian felt as if they were walking into the pure white light of Dante's Paradiso, that light which was the end of all questions, the absence of all doubt.

'You can see why people like to live in California,' Mary Ellen said. 'Have that in front of you all the time.'

'Are you thinking of going out there?' he asked.

'You went to Europe,' she said.

'Might do you good to get away from home,' he said.

'Ian,' she asked him. 'When you were away, did you have the feeling that home might not be there when you got back?'

He didn't know if he should answer her honestly. When he was away, he had imagined home where it always was, intact. When he got home, he realised that it had slipped off its foundations somehow, that in fact what he thought of as home was gone.

'In a certain way,' he equivocated, 'it will always be there, even if it's not.'

'That doesn't make sense,' she said. 'But that's what Mom says.'

'Well, she should know,' Ian said.

They laughed.

'Dad's hardly ever home now,' Mary Ellen told him.

'I gathered,' he said.

'But it doesn't bother me the same way. I want my own home now. Don't laugh, but I want my own place where you and Mom can come to.'

Ian put his arm around her.

'I'm not laughing,' he said.

'And Dad, too, of course. But he probably wouldn't.'

'He might,' Ian said.

'Ian, do you have a girlfriend now?' she asked him.

He thought it over.

'Yes,' he said.

She smiled the happy, naughty smile she had as a little girl. 'Is it Anna?'

'Yes.'

'Are you going to marry her?' she whispered.

300

'I don't think Anna will ever get married again,' he told her. 'She still loves her husband.'

Mary Ellen had stopped and wrote his name in the sand with a shell.

'She still loves Russia,' she said, 'but she's an American now.'

Ian wrote Mary Ellen's name and then drew a string of hearts after it.

'Let's go back,' he said.

They turned away from the setting sun and Ian's burned face suddenly felt cool. Mary Ellen walked faster than he did and he enjoyed seeing her ahead of him.

When the sun had gone down it was chilly and the heat rising from the wet sand turned to mist and curled in the air. People began to walk up towards the town beach to see the fireworks, carrying wool blankets and plastic beach chairs under their arms.

Anna walked with Ian along the edge of the wet sand. She could hear the surf close to her, and sometimes a breaking wave came up far enough to lap at her bare feet, but she could hardly see it.

She carried her shoes and a few stems of white snapdragons that she had taken from one of the table decorations. Ian, also barefoot, his pants rolled up and wet at the hems, carried a bottle of champagne. Every so often he offered her a drink from it.

'Anna,' he said, 'I've had my head filled with so much patriotic American bullshit today that I can't see straight.'

'That's the champagne,' she said.

He stopped and hurled the bottle as far out to sea as he could. They neither saw nor heard it land in the waves but they both stood there, peering out after it into the dark. The air was moist and dense, tasting of salt.

'Seriously, Anna,' he said.

'Don't ruin it,' she said. She looked away from him. He came closer and took her hand.

'It's just that I wish you would talk about it – I mean about what you really feel you're leaving behind in Russia

301

and what it's really going to be like for you as an American. Not all this "home of the free and land of the brave" stuff that's been flying around. You don't ever say very much.'

'What is there to say?' she said. 'My husband was killed in Russia; they tortured my son. He is in exile now.'

'Exile? Where? How do you know?'

'I can't tell you,' she said.

'You can't tell *me?*' he asked. She felt his hurt as if she had slapped him instead of spoken to him.

'You don't trust me,' he said. His voice was tremulous, disbelieving.

'I do,' she said. 'As much as I trust anyone.'

He took his hand away.

In the distance, the clouds were suddenly illuminated by a firecracker. They were lit from within with a dark theatrical red, which highlighted the fanciful outlines of the cloud bank, and then changed it. The red clouds seemed to boil in the sky.

Then there was the noise, like thunder rumbling across the water. Anna felt it in the pit of her stomach.

From the far end of the beach they heard the sounds of a crowd cheering. Nearby, tiny rockets burst in the sand and boys shouted.

A bottle rocket whined, and Anna felt both Ian's hands on her face.

'Look out,' he said. 'Those kids can't see us.'

A child raced by holding a green sparkler in one hand and a white one in the other. She almost ran into them but stopped, shocked for a moment, then laughed and ran the other way. For an instant she was close enough for Anna to see her face – round, pale, childishly drunk on the lights she held in her hands – then she disappeared into the mist. The sky again lit up – this time white and blue.

'How wonderful,' Anna said wistfully. 'I wish I were a child.'

Ian said nothing. They walked on a few paces. They heard the same boys shouting and saw several Roman candles spurting coloured sparks deliriously in the sand, like small, live springs from the earth's core. By one of the candles two boys stood, their faces alternately yellow, white and red in the spewing light.

Ian went up to them and then they walked away from the light and Anna lost them. For several moments she stood alone in the dark, staring into the empty space defined by the sparks. The clouds overhead were changing colour and the air reverberated with shock. When Ian returned, she clung to him.

He held her close and laughed.

'Don't worry,' he said. 'Look what I've got.'

He had a small cardboard box of rockets, sparklers and fireworks that he had bought from the boys. He took her bouquet and laid it on the sand. Then he put a sparkler in each of her hands and lit them. He moved her hands so that the lights left coherent streaks in the air.

'Write your name,' he told her.

Anna looked at him and then raised both hands at once like an orchestra conductor. She began to swirl the sparklers, then she turned and turned again, until she was spinning. She laughed.

Through the moving cage of sparks she created around herself, she watched Ian go about setting the other fire-crackers, positioning them carefully in the sand, lighting a match in his cupped hands, then igniting the fuses. He stuck each one in the sand like a candle into a birthday cake; they exploded into the air close above them and rained down showers of sparks. She saw him brush the confetti-coloured sparks off his shoulders as if they were dust.

Suddenly a green rocket tipped and slithered across the sand at her like an electric snake. She screamed and ran away from it. They laughed as they watched it head crazily up the beach by itself.

'Give me more,' she said to Ian, holding out the dead metal stems of her sparklers.

He put two new ones in her hands and lit them. She moved her hands above her head and drew white and golden half-moons in the foggy sky.

As she stood, her head thrown back, her eyes nearly

303

closed to protect them from the falling sparks, she felt Ian
come behind her and put his arms around her.

'Now you are a child,' he said.

She stood still as the white and gold fires in her hands
burned down into smaller and smaller circles. When they
were completely extinguished she opened her eyes and
saw the real moon outlined in the steamy clouds.

He turned her towards him and put his mouth on hers.
His closed lips pressed on hers gently, asking for nothing.
She put her hands on his face; her eyes were closed and
she touched him like a blind person.

'I'm real,' he said. She felt him laughing softly in the
palm of her hand.

They were both awake at dawn. Ian felt her hand in his
though they had basically kept to opposite sides of the
small motel bed.

'You're awake?' she asked him.

'So are you,' he said.

She was silent and he stared up at the acoustical tiles of
the ceiling. Probably asbestos, he thought.

She turned towards him and put her cheek lightly on his
shoulder.

'Why do motels always smell like this?' she asked.

'Like what?'

'Like the last person who stayed in the room died and
they have taken every sanitary precaution to prevent you
from ever finding this out.' She laughed and waited for
him to laugh.

He didn't dare look at her. He remembered her breasts
in the dark; they had seemed too soft. He'd been afraid
to let go, afraid of hurting her.

'I don't really make you happy, do I?' he said.

'It's not you,' she said.

She pressed closer to him and he turned to her and
cradled her. He covered her with the sheet so that he
couldn't see her nakedness.

'Is this my real life?' she whispered. Tears weighed down
her speaking voice.

He thought for a long time, holding her.

'I don't know,' he said. 'How can I answer you?'

She lay back and brushed the wetness off her face. Her face was red and Ian began to feel the stifling July heat of the day. He got up and opened the window. She threw off the sheet.

When he lay back down next to her, he put his face on her stomach. It was smooth and warm. He smelled his own body in her skin, like the peppered smell of the wet sand mixed with the wilting bouquet of white summer flowers that Anna had carried.

She put her hand on his face and stroked it. She outlined his eyelids, his nose, his lips with the tip of her finger. She touched him so lightly that he could hardly feel it. He felt sleepy.

'Forgive me,' she said. 'I am being Russian.'

He looked at her.

'Russians always cry at the great moments in their lives,' she said.

He took her hand and pressed it to the centre of his chest. The warmth of her hand eased the tension that was always there, melted the hardness a little, making it less jagged and painful.

'I want what you want,' she said. 'I want to go on. I want to live life.'

'Good,' he said. 'Let's eat breakfast. Breakfast is essential to life.'

She laughed and put her arms around him. He let her pull him down on top of her and he felt her laughter against his chest, fluttering like his own heart.


'By the way,' Anna asked him when the waitress put their eggs in front of them, 'where are we?'

'Montauk,' he told her. He was buried in the New York *Times*. He had bought the paper to find the coverage of her swearing-in party in two columns on the society page. There was a picture of Anna with the Hugginses, other pictures featuring the summer dresses and straw hats of the women and one of a wealthy local conservationist in braces and a straw boater.

305

But on the second page was the announcement of a Senate investigation into 'Communist disinformation and infiltration.' One of its prime targets would be the anti-nuclear movement. It had been called for by the President himself; it was an obvious sop to the ultraconservatives in his re-election campaign. To be headed by a rising star on the conservative horizon, Senator Henry Brooker, the commission intended to subpoena a number of major movement and media figures, actors, actresses, a number of the people that Anna had toured with.

'McCarthyism,' Ian said.

'What?' Anna said.

He looked up from the paper. She was happy; the happiest he had seen her in a long time. She was winding melted cheese from her omelet around her fork like spaghetti. When she saw him looking at her, she offered him the forkful of food and smiled.

Ian made himself swallow.

'What's the matter?' she asked.

He showed her the article.

She narrowed her eyes.

'Red-baiting,' Ian said.

She put her fork down.

'Many innocent people will be dragged through this,' he told her. 'These things are real witch-hunts. The people who start them are fanatics, the only people who can restrain them keep up their criticism in the press and there is incredible pressure to manufacture criminals in order to justify the whole thing. They can ask whatever questions they want to, in whatever manner they choose – there are none of the restrictive procedures that have to be followed in a real trial. Everyone is working for the camera.'

'And what happens if they find what they are looking for?'

'Then he or she goes to trial,' Ian said. 'This country is supposed to guarantee that the accused is presumed innocent until proven guilty, but the publicity surrounding hearings like these is so intense that it doesn't matter what the outcome of the trial is. Even if the person is acquitted,

306

his reputation is ruined. But this is ridiculous; they can't seriously expect to find KGB agents in the Freeze movement. They are doing this to discredit the work of innocent and dedicated people.'

'Ian,' she said. 'The *gebisti* have their fingers in everything they think might be a help to them.'

'How can you, of all people, say that? And even if they do, their involvement has got to be so minor compared to the number of people involved in good faith that it can't justify the investigation.'

'It doesn't really matter,' she said. 'They will get their scapegoat. They probably have him already, or they would not risk this exposure.'

'Anna, this may be especially dangerous for you.'

'No more for me than anyone else,' she said. 'I have nothing to hide.'

'It won't matter,' he said. 'If they want to get you they will.'

She looked at him, mildly shocked, as though he had suggested stealing the coffee-shop silverware. Then she smiled.

'Ian,' she reproached him. 'This is America.'

She stroked his cheek and he tried to smile at her.

When Ian dropped Anna off, late in the afternoon, the sun coming through the tyrannical windows of her apartment was long and saffron, and she felt happy to be alone.

She took her shoes off and padded around on the thick carpeting, thinking that it was remarkably like the beach, only softer, and forgetting what she was looking for. Her body felt fresh and young. She was sunburned. Across her shoulders, though she knew it was only the slight burn, she believed she still felt the young toughness of Ian's beard as he rubbed his face gently against her skin. It was a light, forgetful sensation, blotting out every other, like the first swim of the summer, when the water is fresh and you have forgotten completely what it feels like to be floating.

She floated around the apartment in her bare feet, locating a hairbrush, a fingernail file, choosing fresh clothes. Then the loud buzz of the intercom sounded in the kitchen.

She went into the kitchen and pressed the bar on the little television set in the wall. Into the screen loomed the darkened, distorted face of Kostia Kyrstov.

'Mr Kyrstov,' said the doorman's voice. 'Shall I let him up?'

'Yes,' she said into the empty space marked by a small speaker in the wall.

In a few moments, the doorbell rang. She had not been able to remember where she left her shoes.

When she opened the door, he came in quickly.

'I had to see you again before I left,' he said.

She took his hand.

'I'm sorry,' she said, pointing to her bare feet. 'I wasn't expecting anyone.'

He smiled and shrugged. 'We're old friends,' he said. 'I brought you this.'

He handed her a jar of elderberry preserves. It had been bought at an expensive Scandinavian delicatessen near the UN.

'Thank you,' she said. 'I don't think they have elder-berries in America. I haven't had this since I was home.'

'I thought so,' he said.

She went into the kitchen to make tea and he followed her.

'I am leaving in the morning,' he told her.

'I wish I could go with you,' she said.

He looked at her and nodded.

'You,' he said. 'Miss America.'

They laughed.

'I wish I could stay,' he said.

The water boiled and she poured it through the loose black tea in the teapot. The sharp, rich smell of fresh tea was biting in the air, like frost.

'You have such a good life here,' he said, looking around. 'I knew you did, but I had to see it.'

308

'It's a life,' she said. She poured tea into two of her gloomy black mugs, and they sat down at the kitchen table. Kostia dipped his spoon into the open jar of preserves and mixed the sweet purple jam into his steaming tea.

'No wonder they don't let us out,' he said.

'That's just what I thought, too,' she told him.

'I don't like all the cameras everywhere,' he said, 'but I guess if the Americans are going to give you all this, they're going to want to keep an eye on you.'

Anna laughed. 'Those cameras aren't for keeping an eye on me,' she said. 'They're for me – and all the other people who live here – to keep an eye on anyone who comes to visit. This is New York, don't forget.'

'Anya,' he said, surprised at her nonchalance. 'It always works both ways.'

She looked at him and saw that he was too old to understand anything but what he already knew.

'I want you to know,' he told her, 'that I think you are very brave. I know what it means to you to have left Seriozha behind, and if there is anything that I can do when I am back, I will do it.'

She put her hand on his.

'I know you will,' she said. 'Thank you.'

He stirred another hearty spoonful of jam into his tea.

'Let's talk of happier things,' he said. 'I don't have much time.'

'Why did they let you come, Kostia?'

'Oh, you know,' he said. Shame softened his sagging face even more. His skin was grey and looked as though it might come off in her hand if she touched him. 'I know that you won't do what they want, but I said I would talk to you anyway because I wanted to see you again before I left.'

She stared off past him to the small kitchen window.

'What will they do with him?' she asked Kostia softly.

He shrugged. 'I don't think they know themselves,' he said. 'Now that you're an American citizen you can bring pressure on them to let him out.'

She laughed – a short, bitter laugh; a frustrated exhalation like a sigh in reverse.

'They will never let him go,' she said. 'Once it suited their purpose to court the Americans. But people began to get the idea that life was better outside, that the sacrifices we made for "world Communism" were unfair and disproportionate. Now it suits their purpose to keep relations with America cold and hostile; when people are afraid of war, they are more willing to stand in line behind the *nomenklatura*.'

Kostia nodded.

'But,' he said, 'the American leaders are the same. It suits their purpose that the American people are also afraid and therefore allow them to spend whatever they want to on arms. The leaders are always the same everywhere – men entrenched in power and privilege. They will do anything to keep it.'

'You are right,' Anna told him. 'The only difference is that in America they cannot do anything they please. The leaders are accountable to the people.'

'Annichka, you amaze me. The American government manipulates the people in every way. Look at television.'

'They manipulate, but they cannot control. The American people have at least a chance to protect themselves from the madness and greed of their leaders. We do not.'

Kostia put his hand on the top of Anna's head as if she were a child.

'Since you are an American now,' he said, 'I hope you are right.'

Ian buzzed the intercom at midnight. She was sleepy and feverish from her sunburn, but when she opened the door she threw her arms around him.

'I should have let you get some sleep tonight,' he said apologetically. He was sunburned, too, and his eyes glistened like a child who has stayed up too late.

She shook her head and laughed.

'I'm glad you're here,' she said. She spoke with her mouth against his neck and she felt him shiver.

His hair was combed back, still wet from the shower. His skin was fresh and moist, smelling of American soap and the slight sweat of the summer night. She knew that he had hurried to her.

'You smell so young,' she told him.

He grimaced, but she smiled.

'Would you like something to drink?' she asked.

'No,' he said.

'Something to eat?'

He shook his head.

'Turn out the lights,' he told her.

She walked to each light and turned it off.

Ian went and sat on the couch. He was outlined against the huge windows, his hair highlighted by the white summer moon. She stood behind him, hesitating.

'Come,' he called her.

She moved closer. He took her hand and pulled her down next to him.

The city sparkled in front of them, coloured light scattered in unpredictable patterns, coaxing the eye to follow its trails into the invisible folds of night.

'Now I know what these windows are for,' she said. 'For us,' he said.

He put his face down and moved his lips across her breasts; where her skin was burned she felt cold, and she was conscious of raising her hands and touching his hair, as though her hands were a new machine, one made for that purpose but which she had never used before.

When he felt her hand on the top of his head he looked at her. He took her hand and opened it and kissed it.

What faith, she thought. What a gift.

During the night, when he had fallen asleep in her arms, she felt him shaking. She opened her eyes.

At first, she was afraid that he was crying in his sleep. She struggled to see his face in the dark.

But when her eyes had adjusted to the light, she realised

311

that, incredibly, he was laughing. Deep in some relieving dream, he was dissolving in laughter; his face was relaxed and smiling. She held him closer to her.

*Spasibo*, she prayed to the God who at the moment seemed clearly to inhabit the empty sky over New York. Thank you.


In the morning, Ian awoke because he heard someone outside the apartment door. He was instantly aware of his clothes jumbled on the floor.

'Who's that?' he asked Anna.

'Just the paper being delivered,' she said sleepily.

He lay back.

'I can't believe you get the paper delivered,' he said. 'What a life!'

She laughed and he felt her warmth define his body in the new, air-conditioned emptiness of daylight in her apartment.

The phone rang.

'Aren't you going to answer it?'

'You can if you want to,' she said.

He got up and found the phone.

'Hello,' he said as loud and authoritatively as possible.

'Who is this?' the voice on the other end said.

'Who is *this?*' Ian said.

'Ian?' the voice asked.

'Yes,' he said. And then he realised who he was talking to. 'Dad?'

George cleared his throat. 'Is Anna there?'

'Just a moment,' Ian said. He turned to Anna and held the phone out to her.

'Hello?' she said.

Ian watched her expression. First her smile died. Then her face became still and empty.

'One moment,' she said to his father. She covered the receiver. 'Ian, get the paper,' she whispered.

He opened the door a crack and pulled the paper in. He brought it to her and as she listened to his father, she quickly turned the pages.

'I see it,' she said.

Silence.

'Yes,' she said.

Now her face began to show fear.

'Do you really think so?' she asked.

Whatever it was, his father must have really thought so.

'All right,' Anna said heavily. 'I'll come in this afternoon.'

She hung up.

'What is it?' Ian asked.

'A Russian friend of mind was arrested yesterday and charged with being part of an espionage conspiracy. Apparently the FBI picked him up right outside this building. Your father wants to get me a lawyer.'

This is it, Ian thought.

'No,' he told her. 'I'll see that you get an independent lawyer.'

She looked at him with surprise and he watched her fear taking hold of her like a drug.

The Senate subpoena gave Anna less than forty-eight hours to prepare her testimony, and the phone rang constantly with people calling to give her support and sympathy. James Bradford even sent flowers – two dozen white roses. *The truth shall make you free*, the card stated. It was a lovely gesture, Ian thought, but he couldn't help remembering that this Christian quotation was engraved on the Langley headquarters of the CIA

The ACLU had responded quickly and sent an intense young woman who wore a tweed suit though the late-August days were still bright, and in the afternoon rather warm. She patiently drew out Anna's account of her movement activities, and continually reassured her that she had nothing to worry about. Then she turned to Anna's private life. Finally she asked Anna if she had ever been contacted by anyone who she knew worked for the Soviet government.

When she heard that Anna had visited the Russian

compound in Glen Cove, she counselled her to take the Fifth Amendment.

'I can't,' Anna told her.

'Let me explain it to you again,' she told Anna. 'You are not bound to cooperate in any way with your accusers; if they have something on you, they have to prove it. If they ask you something that looks bad for you, just don't answer.'

'That looks worse,' Anna said.

'If you're going to let them get into this,' the lawyer said, 'you are going to go to trial; I can tell you that right now.'

'Then I will be vindicated,' Anna said.

'Anna,' Ian pleaded with her, 'don't take a chance.'

'If I take the Fifth Amendment,' Anna said, 'then everyone will conclude that I have something damaging to hide.'

'They are not allowed to conclude this,' the lawyer said.

Anna's eyes showed kindness, but the rest of her face was set and grim.

'It doesn't matter,' she said. 'That is exactly what they will conclude. And from their point of view, when they find out about my conversations with Soviets, both at Glen Cove and at my home, they will feel justified. And they will find out.'

Ian knew that she was right. He looked at the lawyer, who only looked back at him.

'Listen to your friend,' the lawyer said to Anna. 'Even if the truth is on your side, you should avoid going to trial if possible. There is never any guarantee as to how a jury will find.'

Anna put her hand over her eyes. Ian was conscious suddenly that it was a gesture of his that she had picked up. He went over to her and rubbed the back of her neck.

'I think we're in for the long haul,' he told the lawyer.

She nodded. 'Okay, I'll get back to my office and see what we can do. I'm not in shape to handle such a major case; they're going to want to meet about this.'

By nightfall, Anna had received a call from the office of an attorney who was a friend of Charles Huggins.

He was a society liberal, Ian told her, he had handled one or two famous First Amendment cases. He had never handled an espionage case – but then who had? Until recently, very few cases came to court, Ian had learned, trying to find out about Kostia since his arrest. These things were handled by the State Department or by the respective security agencies involved. If someone caught a real spy, chances are they had their own spy in the other guy's territory and it made better sense to trade. The few cases that came to court seemed to be almost exclusively those with loud political overtones.

It's not going to go that far, he reassured her. But he himself did not believe it.

When it came to loud political overtones, Anna's case was deafening.

Miles Harding's office was in Rockefeller Center. Ian pointed out the murals on the walls and ceiling as they entered – paintings of huge, dusky workers, putting their broad backs to the work of rebuilding Depression America. The building's combination of structural affluence and pictorial socialism reminded Anna more than anything of a Moscow subway station.

On the eighteenth floor, Harding's secretary was waiting outside the elevator for them. She took them into an office that was quite small, but the view was opulent and the walls were hung with an eccentric assortment of contemporary paintings that had the distinct aura of a strong and private assertion of taste.

'Come in, sit down,' Harding welcomed them. He was a tall man, with thick, greying red hair and freckles. He looked like an exceptionally healthy, mature boy.

But Anna stood for a moment at the window. Below was St Patrick's Cathedral, Fifth Avenue, the small flag-festooned Rockefeller Square, where café tables would soon give way to the skating rink. To suddenly look down on the heart of New York City from this special office struck Anna the way opening her grandmother's jewellery box once had as a child.

'I would like to save all this,' she said.

Miles Harding looked at her strangely.

'She doesn't mean save it from nuclear holocaust,' Ian said. 'She means save it like a memory.'

'Which one of you is going to appear before the committee?' Harding asked. He laughed.

'Sit down,' he repeated.

'Thank you,' Anna said.

'I have been told that you refuse to use the Fifth Amendment privilege,' he said. 'Is that correct?'

'Yes,' she said.

'And you are aware that this means you are going to have to fight this thing all the way down the line?'

'Yes.'

'A lawyer is like a doctor,' he told her. 'We're going to have to talk about everything. You can have complete confidence that everything you tell me is strictly between us. I'm going to ask Mr McDonough to wait for us outside. Is that all right with you, Anna?'

'You mean Ian?' she asked.

'It's okay, Annichka,' Ian said.

He had never called her that before.

The door closed behind him.

'Would you like some coffee?' Miles asked her.

'No, thank you,' she said.

'Take a deep breath,' he said. 'We're going to handle this thing right, and they are not going to get away with it.'

'Mr Harding,' she said, 'I don't know how I am going to pay you for this.'

'First of all, please call me Miles. Second of all, let me start the ball rolling by being completely frank with you. We will start immediately to set up a defence fund for you. Your appearance is going to attract an enormous amount of media attention and this is one of the most important things that you and I are going to have to work on together. I expect that you will raise enough money to pay the court expenses; I don't need to be paid for this case and money is not my interest in it.

'I suspect that what we have here is not only an effort to undermine the most important grass-roots movement in the history of this country, but a flagrant abuse of power. Your case smacks of everything that is most repugnant to Americans – in fact, it would not be going too far to say that you are the victim of a Soviet-style campaign to discredit a dissident.

'But I'm getting ahead of myself,' he said. He put his hand on her hand across his desk. 'I just want you to know where I stand about this. I want to fight your case not just because I believe in your cause, but because I do not want your rights as an American citizen and a human being to be violated.'

He took his hand back.

'Now don't forget,' he said gently, 'you are going to have a few friends on the committee. Wallace Chapman, liberal Republican senator from Maryland; Louis Tucker, Democratic congressman from New Jersey – once held a chair in Russian and Soviet studies at Princeton; and maybe your best ally is going to be another Republican, a woman, Joan Fitzpatrick, representative from San Francisco. They were placed on this committee precisely because they balance the henchmen that Chairman Brooker has chosen. And Brooker's not so bad; he eats babies for breakfast, but he's normal at lunch and dinner.

'Come on,' he said, 'you were supposed to laugh.'

She looked at him but she could not smile.

'How are you feeling?' he asked.

'I can't feel anything,' she said. She was surprised that she had told him.

'You should be furious,' he told her.

She put her head down and covered her mouth with her hand. She began to cry, much harder than she thought she would.

'You are not helpless,' Harding said. 'They can't just do what they want with you. This is America. This is what the law is for.'

\*   \*   \*

317

The night before they were to take the 6 A.M. shuttle to Washington, Ian stayed with Anna. He made it a point to be up first and make tea. But he was shaky and off, and spilled the loose black tea into the pot. They were forced to drink tea with bits of leaves floating in it, and it preoccupied them so that they hardly spoke. Ian stirred his tea with his finger, trying to trap the little black specks; Anna sipped hers gently from the surface of her cup. When they got up to leave he noticed that she had hardly drunk any of it.

Miles Harding was waiting downstairs in a cab. He got out and let Anna get in. Ian took in Miles's grey suit, of a subtly woven gabardine, his navy silk tie, the requisite starched white button-down shirt. Ian was so reassured by this uniform that he was embarrassed. He shook Miles's hand gratefully.

The plane to Washington, even at six in the morning, was full. The passengers observed the unwritten rule of busy people; they ignored each other. Anna and Miles were left to talk quietly while Ian went through all the detritus in his wallet looking for a press card that would guarantee access to the hearing.

When they arrived at the Capitol, it was still only a quarter to eight but reporters and news cameras were already clustered around the steps. Beyond them Ian could see anti-Soviet hecklers, some with the dreaded placards of Anna's son.

'Do you want me to take care of this?' Miles asked Anna.

'No,' she said. 'I'll speak.'

She got out of the car and began to walk up the stairs. By the time she had gone three steps, Ian and Miles could not get close enough to touch her.

Everyone spoke at once. Ian heard only two questions distinctly. He realised that for the first time his identification with Anna was so complete that he hated the newspeople. They seemed inhuman to him – carnivorous birds that bore down, swooping and darting and tearing, and would then sweep greedily away to the next prey, leaving their victim ripped and bleeding but still breathing.

Anna kept her head down and pressed up the stairs. Then she suddenly stopped. Except for two photographers, she stood higher than the crowd.

'I wish I had the time to answer each and every one of you separately,' she said. 'There is a lot to be said today.'

Ian was surprised at the strength in her voice. It was loud; no one asked her to repeat herself.

The questioning resumed. Ian knew the trick; you had to be loud and you had to know how to stop this side of obnoxious. But Anna had no intention of answering any specific question. She was going to give a statement.

'The effort of the Committee on Disinformation and Infiltration to discredit the Freeze movement is a scandal of a type I am only too familiar with. It must wound all Americans to see some in their government resort to such tactics. But Congress has seen fit to make me a citizen of the United States and, like any other American, I intend to assert each and every one of my rights as a citizen to defy this abuse.'

Fighting words, Ian thought. A media insurance policy. She was going to have cameras following her like dogs if she kept on like this.

Miles took the cue to take her arm. He was tall and imposing and no one defied his progress up the steps.

'Very smart,' Miles said to her. 'From beginning to end. I especially noticed the "I wish I had the time to answer each and every one of you" line. That's just how you have to proceed.'

The Committee on Disinformation and Infiltration joint subcommittee on infiltration of the Freeze movement had been moved from the small committee room where it usually met to the larger Ways and Means Committee room.

'This is not a good sign,' Miles said quietly to Ian as they walked through the halls of the Capitol.

Ian nodded. The only reason to meet in such a large room was to make more space for the press. That meant they expected to drop a bombshell.

319

Indeed, cameras on tripods lined the back of the room like rifles poised for target practice.

The front of the room was defined by a large hemispherical table. On it were plaques bearing the names of each committee member and in the centre one which read merely: 'Chairman.' Each place had a plastic pitcher of water in front of it and a glass. How much do you have to say before your throat is that dry, Ian wondered. How mad do you have to be?

There were perhaps one hundred folding chairs, and most were already filled.

When the committee members filed in, it was not solemn, as Ian had supposed it would be. Except for one or two members, notably Representative Fitzpatrick from San Francisco, they looked as if they were businessmen ready to announce a new product. Fitzpatrick looked serious and determined. She smiled at a few of the newspeople and legislative assistants who knew her and settled her papers quietly in front of her.

The meeting was formally opened. Anna was sworn in.

'So help me God,' Ian heard her say.

God help you, he thought.


Anna began by reading a prepared statement which outlined her background. It started with her rise to prominence through her husband and his refusal to work for the Soviet government, and continued with the story of her book – all a chronicle of extreme antagonism to Russia. She described her parting from Seriozha.

Next, she recounted how the KGB had come to her hotel at five in the morning and stripped her of her Soviet citizenship. After that, she gave the events of her public work since she had come to America.

As she read, she was immensely conscious of her accent. She was aware that she spoke English very well, but that her accent forever branded her a Russian. If she met someone for the first time and they knew nothing about her, they would still be able to tell immediately where she was from.

From time to time she paused and Miles would hand her the glass of water which was always full in front of her. She had not realised until that moment why speakers drink frequently when they address the public. It was fear.

But she kept her voice steady. Especially when she spoke of Seriozha. Then the words seemed to speak by themselves, with her only watching them from far away.

She concluded with her swearing-in as an American citizen at the home of a member of Congress, as the result of a special act of Congress. The spectators applauded.

She turned around and looked for Ian. He must have seen her unable to find him and he stood up. He did not smile and neither did she.

Now Chairman Brooker began the questioning.

'Are you, or have you ever been, a member of the Communist Party?'

Anna looked at Miles. He was enraged.

'That is an improper and leading question,' he shouted.

'I will have to ask counsel to leave the room,' Brooker said, 'if you cannot control yourself. We are on a fact-finding mission here and this information is relevant.'

'If I may respectfully point out, Mr Chairman,' Representative Tucker of New Jersey intervened, 'almost all persons involved in advanced scientific or technical work in the Soviet Union can be expected to have pro forma membership in the Party. It is as meaningless and as indispensable as a driver's licence.'

'As I understand it,' Brooker responded coolly, 'only about six per cent of the Soviet population are actually Party members. This membership carries with it a number of privileges and rewards. Is that correct?'

Tucker's face was blank. 'Yes, but –' he said.

'Then I would like an answer from the witness to my question because it pertains to the issues at hand.'

Brooker turned to Anna and repeated his question.

'Are you, or have you ever been, a member of the Communist Party? Yes or no?'

'Yes,' she said. 'Yes, of course. It was necessary to obtain a faculty position at the Institute.'

He proceeded to question her closely about her status and her husband's status as scientists. Were they given a dacha in the country? Did they have a car? Would she describe their standard of living as well above that of the average Soviet citizen?

'Do you know a man named Konstantin Dimitrievich Kyrstov?' he asked.

'Yes,' Anna replied. 'He was the head of the Department of Geology at the Moscow Institute of Earth Sciences.'

'He was your superior?' Brooker pressed. 'You took direction from him?'

'While I was employed at the Institute, yes,' she said.

'When was the last time you saw him?'

'July fifth.'

'The day after you became an American citizen,' Brooker commented. 'And where did you see him?'

'He came to my apartment,' Anna said.

'Are you aware that he was arrested on that day, outside your building?'

'Yes,' Anna said. 'I read it in the paper.'

'And do you know what he was arrested for?'

Miles Harding's jaw was so tight that Anna could clearly see the veins of his neck throbbing. She could not turn back now. She could not pretend that she did not know what the charge was against Kostia; it had been stated in the New York *Times*. To give a truthful answer was to put her cheek softly on the block.

'I read in the New York *Times* that he was charged with espionage.'

The room broke into argument. Brooker banged his gavel on the table in front of him several times to restore silence.

'You read in the New York *Times*,' Brooker repeated mockingly.

Representative Fitzpatrick leaned towards her microphone.

'Mr Chairman,' she said evenly, 'this committee has already come under enough fire for its treatment of witnesses. I'm sure I speak for others here when I say that I would appreciate it if the Chair would confine his remarks to those necessitated by the testimony.'

'Do you know a man named Alexander Whittmore?' Brooker asked Anna.

'I have met a man who uses that name,' Anna said.

'How many times have you met him?'

'Twice.'

'And would you tell us where, and give us the subject of your conversations with him at the time.'

'The first time was in Washington,' Anna said. 'I had unexpectedly met Kostia – Konstantin Kyrstov – at a benefit for the Smithsonian Institution at which I was a speaker. Mr Kyrstov was travelling with a group of Soviet scientists and Mr Whittmore accompanied him. Mr Whittmore and I did not speak at that time.

'The second time –'

'Excuse me,' Brooker said. 'What was your impression of Mr Whittmore at the time? What did you think he was doing there? Did you think he was a scientist, too, travelling with the group?'

'No,' Anna said.

'Well, what did you think?'

'I thought,' Anna said quietly, 'that he was there to guard Mr Kyrstov.'

'To guard him?' Brooker asked. 'Like a prison warden?'

'Yes,' Anna said.

'Why?' he pushed.

'Because generally Soviet citizens are not allowed to travel.'

'And when they are allowed to travel, if I may follow your train of logic here,' Brooker said, 'they are kept under surveillance by the KGB. Is that more or less what you mean?'

Representative Tucker was angry. 'You are deliberately distorting common facts of Russian life,' he told Brooker, 'and parading them in front of the press with reckless disregard for how they may affect the reputation of the witness.'

323

A junior senator from Idaho, one of Henry Brooker's appointments to the committee, came to his leader's aid.

'Mr Tucker,' he said, 'it is precisely these so-called facts of Communist life that the public has an interest in seeing exposed before they have a chance to affect our way of life.'

Tucker waved his hand in the air as if brushing away a fly. Harding had briefed Anna on the backgrounds of all the subcommittee members; Tucker was a former economics professor and the junior senator from Idaho had been a farm-equipment dealer.

'Let's stick to the facts in the case,' Fitzpatrick put in.

'Was it your impression that Mr Whittmore was employed by the KGB?' she asked Anna.

'Yes,' Anna said.

'May I finish questioning the witness?' Brooker asked Fitzpatrick testily.

'Of course.' She nodded.

'And when was the second time you saw Mr Whittmore?' he asked Anna.

'In early July,' Anna said.

'And where was that?'

'In Glen Cove, Long Island.'

'At the Soviet diplomatic enclave there, isn't that right?'

'Yes.' she said.

Again, noisy discussion took over the room.

'Mr Chairman.' Fitzpatrick again interrupted. 'It is obvious that you have information that others on this committee are not privy to. I would like to know where this information comes from, since the Justice Department and the FBI have been, to my knowledge, cooperating fully with our investigation.'

'My facts come through an informant in the embassy,' Brooker said.

Miles leaned towards Anna. 'That could mean a lot of things,' he said. 'Wiretapping and other illegal electronic surveillance. That may give us something to go after them with, if we're lucky.'

Fitzpatrick bristled. 'I move that we adjourn this hearing

for a half hour so that the rest of the members can have a chance to see your records, Mr Chairman.'

This motion was heartily endorsed and Brooker brought down the gavel. The committee members retreated to an antechamber. About ten minutes later they were back. Brooker opened the meeting formally again with a roll call of the members. Then, clearing his throat ostentatiously, he addressed the room.

'Since perusal of the documents gives us serious reason to believe that the witness may be triable for conspiracy and espionage, we have voted to refrain from further public questioning of the witness and to turn over our files to a grand jury, pending further investigation.' He brought down the gavel again and the hearing was adjourned for the morning.

Anna had been there for less than one hour.


Ian made eggs for dinner. It seemed the blandest, most soothing thing he could think of. He cut up a late-summer tomato which was so ripe it was nearly bursting through its skin. Any other night, Anna would have taken real delight in something so fresh and simple. She did not even touch it.

He had bought the evening paper on the way home from the vegetable market, but he had thrown it away before he came upstairs. 'Khameneva Linked to KGB' was how the article started; with a headline like that he did not want to read the body copy, and he was sure no one else would bother either.

At home, the phone was conspicuously silent.

Now she will find out who her real friends are, Ian thought.

'You know something,' he told her in the early-evening stillness, 'I hate this apartment.'

She nodded.

'It's very cold and unwelcoming. When this is all over, we should move somewhere nice.'

She looked at him and he saw her eyes fill with tears.

'We don't have to talk about it now,' he whispered.

'No,' she said. 'Talk to me. Tell me where it would be nice to live.'

'Well, on Central Park,' Ian said. 'On the West Side, where the apartments are huge and old-fashioned. Or in the Village; we could live in a brownstone with a fireplace.'

He made her come and sit on his lap; she did so awkwardly, conscious that it was a childish thing to do and that by rights he was the child. But he ignored her embarrassment and whispered into her hair, making up houses they might live in, and lives to go with each house.

He felt her relax in his arms, and finally he stopped speaking.

'We could be happy,' she said. She said it to herself, and she spoke with the voice of a doctor lecturing a man who has lost both legs in an accident: you will learn to adjust.

He laughed at her gently.

'It might not be such hard work,' he said, 'being happy.'

'What did I do to deserve you?' she asked softly.

He hugged her tightly; he did not want to tell her that in those moments when he really knew that she loved him he felt a boisterous pride.

'You have a right to be happy,' he told her, 'just like everyone else.'

She leaned her face up to be kissed, and he kissed her but then he stopped.

'Why wouldn't you tell me that you had met Kostia and gone to Glen Cove?' he asked.

She pressed her cheek against his and spoke quietly. 'Isn't it obvious?' she said. 'I never knew at each moment what they might do; I didn't want to involve you. They might have tried to use you to get to me, or knowing you, you might have endangered yourself voluntarily. Now it turns out that I protected you not only from them but from your own side. If you had known about it you would be dragged into this, too.'

'But if anyone else had known about it, it would look better for you,' he told her.

'People will understand,' she said. 'I had to keep silent

326

to protect those I love. You understand that, don't you?'

'I understand why you did it; but it was the wrong thing to do. You should have told me, you should have told everyone you knew, announced it from the rooftops. That was the only way to be safe.'

She looked at him sadly. 'Ian, I think you cannot sincerely imagine what it means to live without laws, where those in power can do whatever they want to you, whenever they want.'

At that moment there was a sharp knock at the door. They stood up instantly and Ian went to the door and looked out through the peephole.

The small compass of the peephole was filled with men; he saw several faces, a shoulder, a back. They took up the whole hall.

'Who is it?' he asked.

'FBI,' one of them said.

Ian opened the door and eight well-dressed, clean-cut men came into the living room.

Without speaking, the men showed them their identification and a search warrant.

'You can't just show up at people's houses in the middle of the night like this,' Ian told the man, incensed. 'That's against the law.'

'Not in the state of New York it isn't,' the man responded. 'You'll have to stay right here,' he said to Anna. Ian wondered if only one spoke by regulation.

They began methodically to empty drawers onto the floor and to pick books off the shelves. They fanned out the pages to check in between them and hit the books on the table to break their spines and peer inside the bindings.

They took all the sheets and towels out of the linen closet and shook them out. They took everything out of the medicine cabinet.

Anna sat in the kitchen with one agent, her back to the others. She was silent but Ian was furious.

'You can't just take apart someone's house,' he yelled at them.

'You saw the warrant,' he was told.

He began to dial Miles Harding and realised that he did not have his home number. His hands shook, but Anna remained very still, her hands folded in front of her on the table.

'Excuse me,' an FBI agent said to Ian, motioning him to get out of his way. Ian stepped back.

The man tapped Anna on the shoulder and she looked up at him. He took handcuffs out of his pocket and put them on her.

'You have the right to remain silent,' he said to her. 'Any statements that you make may be used as evidence against you. You have the right to the advice of an attorney . . .'

She went with them without a word.

'I'm right behind you,' Ian told her.

'You'll have to take a cab,' the agent told him.

When Seriozha had taken the old cot downstairs to the garbage, it had cut his hands in several places like shrapnel. Now one of the wounds festered and would not close. It felt hot and itched inside the cloth that he had wound around it; perhaps he wound the cloth too tightly.

But he was not ungrateful for the pain. It kept him alert in a way that nothing else ever had or ever could. And it brought him closer to Katinka, whose illness he could not share in any other way. Superstitiously he told himself that when his wound closed, she would finally be herself again.

For weeks Katinka had stayed in bed; bed was a mattress that neighbours had given them and which they simply placed on the floor since they could not afford a bed frame. She had not recovered her former strength. He did not believe she would. She looked quite different; her colouring was permanently paler, her eyes were never teasing but always indulgent – in fact, forgiving.

She had applied for a sick pension from the state, but the application was held up interminably – a petty and faceless form of persecution. Meanwhile word had spread around the apartment complex as to who the young Moscow couple were; after all, it was not possible that

328

people born in Moscow would move to Sahd voluntarily.

People were suspicious, but Seriozha and Katinka received all visitors graciously. They were to a certain extent dependent upon the goodwill of their neighbours, since Katinka was not strong enough to work and Seriozha was denied work.

Ultimately self-interest triumphed over the tacit assumption that the young couple had done something to deserve their exile and all the hardships that went with it. People began to bring Katinka fabric and with her urban taste she was able to create dresses and skirts that could not be bought at any price in the state stores of Sahd, since access to the few hard-currency stores in Sahd was reserved for the provincial *nomenklatura*. Soon she had more work than she could physically handle, and generally she worked all day in bed next to the window. Sometimes she would fall asleep under piles of yard goods, looking like a small blonde child under a fantastic quilt.

But Seriozha had not been so lucky; expelled from the University, and unable to obtain references for the workbook every Soviet citizen is required to submit to employers, he finally showed up at five in the morning at the Department of Sanitation answering an announcement in the paper for street sweepers. The office manager assumed he was a drunk, but gave him the job anyway. There were not many people willing to work at that hour for thirty-six rubles a month. Thus he found himself from dawn until noon every day with a birch-twig broom, sweeping the square at the entrance to the public garden.

People made fun of him – the job was usually done by old women – but he was so quiet and passive that eventually the morning pedestrians who crossed his path concluded that he was ill or retarded and ignored him. Some were even kind.

And he was grateful for the work. He was outside. The summer weather had been mild and clear. There were birds, there were squirrels. Their unconcerned activities – stealing bread crusts from the garbage, chasing each other, climbing trees and calling in their cheerful, chirruping voices – delighted him in his solitude and he became quite attached to them.

In the afternoons he was free to sit at home with Katinka and write. He never told her what he was writing. She did not ask – it was not that she was not curious; it was that she knew instinctively what he was writing and did not question it.

He would sit there, his precious ballpoint staining his fingers with its greasy ink which smelled of a human smell like sweat, and watch Katinka sewing. Outlined by the late-summer sun in her yellow hair, pulling her needle with a calm and archaic gesture, she was like a painting by Vermeer.

Sometimes in the evening one of their few friends would come to visit. They had one friend in particular, Anatoly Krelnikhov, a low-level lab technician who lived in their building and who had heard of Seriozha's parents. He was short and his small, upturned, almost Kalmyk features gave him a perpetually happy, childish look. He always brought pastry for Katinka, whom he insisted on calling Katerina Grigorievna. He would tease her gently and familiarly about her smart city figure; you have no meat on your bones, he would tell her, warning her that one winter in Sahd would change her ideas about fashion. Katinka's customers treated her like a servant and she came to dote on him as if he were an older brother.

Seriozha knew that Tolya visited them because he was a decent human being. As well, working in a lab in a closed city meant that he had no companions but other scientific workers – there were no theatres to speak of, no nightclubs, restaurants, no music, no ballet. He was from the country north of Sahd originally but had been educated in Moscow. Seriozha could see by the way the man hungrily discussed life in the capital with him that he was starved for it. He looked up to Seriozha; Seriozha represented the world of the artistic and scientific elite, of which, as a student, he had only touched the sandal strap. But they never talked about anything more political than the state of Katerina Grigorievna's health, and it was only after many weeks of hesitant and inconsequential talk that Seriozha began to trust Krelnikhov at all.

One afternoon, after they had hot tea and small plum tarts that Katinka had made, Krelnikhov asked Seriozha to go for a walk with him. It was clear that he had chosen that moment to confide something in Seriozha; perhaps he thought he could, Seriozha afterwards reflected, because Katinka had that day exhausted herself baking for him. It was true that there was no one closer to them than Krelnikov in the city of Sahd.

Tolya told Seriozha that some workers in his lab were passing around a letter in support of Academician Andrei Sakharov. He spoke of Sakharov with something that surpassed awe; his voice became even gentler than it normally was. It reminded Seriozha of the kind of biblical reverence some men feel for their mothers. And it was obvious that Tolya was asking his advice about signing.

'I cannot answer you,' Seriozha said.

They walked in silence. Seriozha thought only of how he could run away and leave Krelnikhov alone in the street. He thought of Katinka, alone in the apartment, unprotected. He thought of her the way a mother animal thinks of her cubs, left defenceless in their den while she hunts.

They didn't talk anymore. Seriozha made the first excuse to turn back. Tolya was unhappy and embarrassed; his lips maintained their elfin, curved smile, but his eyes were dark and wounded.

He did not visit again.

Seriozha could not sleep. He kept seeing the expectation on Tolya's face; he had clearly wanted Seriozha to approve of him. If Seriozha had said the word, Tolya would have signed the letter proudly.

Ten days later, when summer had taken an unmistakable turn towards fall and the sunlight began to turn grey in the yellow treetops of the park by late afternoon, Seriozha decided to go to Krelnikhov himself.

He waited until the sun had set and he knew that Tolya would be at home eating with his family. Then he waited an hour longer because the fear was simply so strong that it took everything in him to control it.

When he knocked on Krelniknov's door, Tolya's family would not let him in. Tolya came out and they went downstairs together. They walked the streets for a while, quietly, each disconcerted by the other but unwilling to leave the other alone. Finally Seriozha asked him.

'Did you sign the letter?'

'Yes,' Tolya nodded.

Seriozha embraced him hard, and felt Krelniknov's arms around him, tighter than any woman's had ever been. He felt Krelniknov's heart pounding and it seemed to speed up his own heartbeat, making him giddy and happy. They went off to buy vodka and came home weaving at one in the morning. Katinka had been nearly hysterical with worry, but when she saw them together, drunk and delighted with each other, she wiped off their faces with a dishrag as if they were boys and listened to them sing until they fell asleep, just before dawn.

On September 22, the entire New York *Times* Op-Ed page was taken up by an agonising and haunting description of the life of a political prisoner inside Moscow's November 7th Psychiatric Hospital. The piece was unsigned but there was little speculation as to who the author was.

On the evening of the twenty-third, seven *gebisti* arrived at the Sahd apartment and began systematically to search through everything, knocking books off the shelves, holding every bit of paper up to the lamp, dumping clothes out of the closet.

Seriozha sat calmly at the kitchen table, refusing to answer questions. Katinka stood in the kitchen, quite literally guarding the small amount of food she had just put on two plates for dinner.

The search had been underway for about twenty minutes when Zalessky came in. He was tanned and dressed in a khaki-coloured suit – not a uniform, but a khaki gabardine suit of a stylish cut.

Seriozha looked at him and smiled appreciatively. He

wondered if *gebisti* had ever before encountered someone who was delighted to be searched. There was absolutely nothing in the apartment; his manuscript had been smuggled into the Moscow bureau of the New York *Times* by Krelnikhov four days before. He enjoyed the idea that they would find nothing; he enjoyed the idea that his high spirits should be absolutely unsuppressible except by violence. He could make them act like animals but they could not do the same to him; he felt such a strong feeling of release that it was almost joyful.

Zalessky caught Seriozha's air of superiority immediately.

'You may despise me,' he said, insulted, 'but you could at least ask me to sit down.'

It was on the tip of Seriozha's tongue to invite him politely to join him at the table but Katinka intervened.

'Never!' she shouted. 'You are not a guest in my house. I did not invite you here. Go stamp up and down in my living room like the Nazi you are, but don't you dare sit at my table!'

And with that she picked up both plates and brought them crashing down into the sink.

Zalessky winced, obviously relieved she had not thrown the plates at him. Then he recovered himself.

'You better watch yourself, Katerina Grigorievna,' he said.

She ran right up to him. 'Go ahead!' she screamed. 'Arrest me!'

He raised his hand to slap her.

'Yuri Andreyevich,' Seriozha said to him. 'Hitting a woman? I never thought I'd see you stoop so low.'

Zalessky stopped, his hand in the air, and looked at Seriozha with complete hatred. Then he turned around and went back downstairs.

They took Katinka with Seriozha to Lefortovo. They were told that Krelnikhov was already there.

Anna was taken to the federal prison, Metropolitan Correctional Center at 1 St Andrew's Place. She was

333

photographed, fingerprinted and subjected to a body search by a woman doctor her own age in the presence of a very young female police officer.

The stated purpose of this search was the same vague pretext that had been used to gain access to her apartment: she was suspected of having unspecified materials relating to national security, in this case perhaps hidden as a microdot or other miniaturised medium. The doctor touched her carefully and as quickly as possible, but Anna became quite dizzy and was afraid that she would vomit. The doctor held her head gently between her hands for a few moments, until Anna reassured her that the feeling had passed. Anna wondered if it was really possible to hate the doctor herself; she was not unkind, merely professional.

Her preliminary hearing was at eight o'clock in the morning. She would be charged with at least one count of espionage; since the investigation was continuing, the special prosecutor sent by the Justice Department in Washington argued that there should be no bail allowed. He cited that she might be able to leave the country with the exceptional help of a foreign security force or at the very least destroy evidence which pertained to national security.

Miles objected strenuously, stating her outstanding public record, and insisting that to be treated like a common criminal was unwarranted in the case and would lead to public censure as government harassment. The judge seemed more inclined to favour the prosecutor's arguments, Anna felt, but in the end compromised by setting bail at $250,000. The amount, Miles later explained, was lenient relative to other federal cases. Unfortunately, it was doubtful that her supporters would be able to raise it. The only redeeming point was that the bail seemed harsh enough to arouse sympathy.

Afterwards, Anna met with Miles in a small glass room that was like a doctoral student's carrel in a library. As always, he was graceful and assured in his impeccable grey suit. Anna wore the prison issue – iron-blue pants and shirt, essentially identical to those worn by the janitors in her building.

She was made to submit to maximum-security procedures mandated in cases of espionage, yet the FBI had found no material relating to national security in her apartment. They had, however, found the list of prepared statements meant to be inserted into her book. This they were keeping, Miles told her, as evidence that information had been overtly passed between her and Kostia Kyrstov. They would try to use it to link her to a conspiracy to steal indexed technical information of the calibre that Kyrstov had allegedly been caught with. At the moment, Miles did not think that the prosecutor believed that she herself had stolen or passed on any information. But in a conspiracy, he explained, every member – once it has been proven that he agreed to be part of it – is liable for the activities of every other member, whether he knew of those activities or not. The government was most interested in showing that, as an agent, she was used to disseminate disinformation; this would be enough to put her inside the circle.

But even if they could not link her to the conspiracy, her charge would still be a grave one: that of harbouring someone she either knew or had reason to believe was overtly engaged in espionage.

Finally, at about 2 P.M. on the day after she was arrested, she was taken to her cell. It was actually a small, not uncomfortable room, something like the rooms of snooping 'concierges' in Russian apartment houses – except that it had what would be for them an unusual luxury: a toilet and sink. There was a bed with sheets and a blue blanket, there was a table and a television. A window looked out on the blank cement wall of the Federal Courthouse next door. Her cellmate was a very small Colombian woman who had been caught bringing three kilos of cocaine into the country. She did not speak English and she seemed afraid of Anna.

The only good thing that she had ever heard about prison was the other people that you met there. In Stalin's days, when the jails and camps were packed with the intelligentsia of the country, many a young thug picked up a first-rate education, and emerged during the postwar Thaw a gentleman – speaking English, quoting Lermontov, able to identify Planck's constant.

She could hear other people talking but no one spoke to her. She could hear a radio, tuned to a Spanish music station; she could hear several different televisions at once. Before dinner, a Protestant minister came by, but she had nothing to talk about with him. He said something soothing; she agreed. He said something else; she could not remember what. He left her a can of Coke.

She tried to drink it, but it was fairly warm and she could not differentiate its flavour from the pungent odour of pine-tar disinfectant that emanated from the grey floor and walls.

She was brought dinner in her cell because, apparently, there was some doubt as to how a 'Russian spy' might be treated by other prisoners. When the food came she left it on the table and lay down to close her eyes for a moment or two. She was roused when a guard told her she would remove the tray in five minutes. Then she went back to the table, just in time to see sleek brown cockroaches scatter in every direction. When they were gone, her food still looked exactly the same. She ate nothing all that day and the next except candy bars that Miles and Ian brought her and she ate them in their wrappers, without touching them.

*We were lucky for a long time. We stayed on the face of the mountains; we found the tiny first growth of pine nuts frozen on the trees and ate them greedily with the tins of herring we had carried with us. We melted snow and boiled it for drinking. Sometimes we were able to trap a scrawny animal wandering disoriented in its own search for edible vegetation – a rabbit or a squirrel. We took one deer but we had eaten only about a quarter of it when the thaw set in in earnest and we were unable to keep the meat fresh. We cooked it and ate as much as we could stand, but after only one day we were forced to abandon the rest.*

*The thaw is much worse than the cold. At least in the cold and dark, certain things were hidden.*

*Now the sky is lighter. It alters over the course of a day, beginning with a regal purple in the morning and waning to a dull red after noon. We have strange sunsets, dark violet and indigo, occasionally shot with bands of orange and amber. On the high ground, the pines have died and there are always fires burning.*

*Even though it is warmer, nothing grows. Perhaps in the far north, where the plants were already acclimated to little light and low temperatures, photosynthesis has resumed. But here, even in the mountains, the plants lie dead on the ground, crushed first by the snow and now by the frequent floods, and unable, because of the lack of light, to pick themselves up again. And insects crawl over them, eating any and all of the little new growth.*

*I awoke this morning because there were insects crawling everywhere. Between my fingers, on my neck and in my hair, and yes, on my mouth and nostrils.*

*There is very little to be done about it; now that the temperature has started to rise, these prehistoric creatures, so stubbornly resistant to radiation, are reproducing at an unbelievable rate, and of course their natural predators, birds, butterflies, the more delicate insects, like most spiders, have vanished. Sometimes the beetles and roaches are so thick that the ground seems to be moving.*

*This means that the scarcity of food is now surpassed by a greater problem: disease. The subfreezing temperature had performed one vital service: it had frozen all the corpses that fill the cities and towns. The stories we hear from survivors of the towns are terrifying; whole regions belong only to the dead, and to the rats, which have grown as big as cats and dogs – and far more numerous than the human populations ever were. Efforts to burn the areas where the dead bodies are thickest have produced all sorts of unpredictable and horrible side effects. In one town, thousands, perhaps millions, of rats poured out of the flames and attacked settlements of survivors in the surrounding hills.*

But the rats, the roaches, and the fleas are only one way in which disease is spread. Drinking water is everywhere contaminated because of the staggering amounts of putrefying flesh and the chemicals carried in the air by the constant fires. Add to this the fact that we are all weakened by radiation damage to our immune systems and by the nearly complete lack of nourishing food.

Our lives, Nikolai's and mine, now have only one meaning and one goal: keeping Misha alive. If I could breathe for him, I would do it.

He sleeps in my lap. Sometimes at night I stay awake to watch him breathing. I make sure that his little chest is moving softly up and down, I put my hand in front of his face to feel the warm breath, in and out.

We make him walk as much as we can; I fight with Nikolai, who is old-fashioned and would keep the child ridiculously bundled up and overheated. It is important to try to build his endurance and resistance to temperature and physical exertion.

We use a good part of whatever decent water we are able to obtain to keep him clean, and ourselves as well, because we must touch him. Nikolai has grown a scraggly beard; I myself must look like a madwoman, although I do not know what I really look like because I have not seen a mirror for weeks now.

My hair has grown quite long – I keep it braided. Some stupid fear prevents me from cutting it all off with the hunting knife. I had asked Niki to do it, but as he stood over me with the knife, my braid in his hand, I began to cry and would not let him. Can I still feel some absurd vanity, some irrational need to signal myself as a woman and not a mere primate, a person who once wore silk dresses and had pretty fingernails, who danced and cried at the opera? Niki, to his credit, stood there with perfect dignity, trying not to let me see him laughing.

But tomorrow I will have to let him cut it; long hair is a luxury that requires the sanitary benefits of civilisation. Without those civilised attentions, it is merely a poor fur,

338

host to all the disease-ridden, fur-burrowing parasites that prey on animals.

Typhus, cholera, diphtheria, smallpox – these I was familiar with in the shelter. But now our lives have become dominated by a disease the name of which is enough to kill one with fear: plague.

All over the countryside people wander, escaping the towns and villages. We avoid each other, our faces wrapped in rags to try to lessen the possibility of breathing in the bacillus. It happens often that coming out of a stand of trees, or around the bend of a road, we will spot, farther along, another little group of people, similarly swaddled, their heads grotesquely swollen by the wrappings, their forms distorted by all the various things each of us carries on his back. Then we all stop; we look across the distance at each other, and each of us turns to take another way so that we will not meet. Sometimes news or warnings are shouted back and forth – this is our primary means of social contact.

There are three forms of the plague. In the first, the most common, the lymph nodes swell to make walnut-sized lumps called buboes. Once these lumps appear, death will follow in a few, perhaps three, days. In the second form, the lungs fill with bloody secretions. After perhaps only a few hours of malaise, the victim usually has sharp, spontaneous nosebleed. Then you know that he is going to die in a little while and there is nothing you can do to help him.

But in the third form, there are virtually no symptoms. The bacillus attacks the brain directly and death can occur without warning within twenty-four hours.

Is it any wonder that the ignorant peasants of the Caucasus make bonfires and pray to the devil? It does seem not a disease caused by micro-organisms and carried by fleas, but a divine curse. I do not mean that we have retreated to pre-Pasteur days – though many people in the countryside never knew of, or believed in, bacteria anyway. What terrifies me are the educated people who, confronted by the random and hidden devastation of the disease, are able to

339

*believe that behind its ostensible scientific cause is the hand of a furious God.*

*Thus I have heard of merciless and incredibly energetic (given all of our physical limitations) persecutions of Jews and other helpless innocents whose different culture or colour or language becomes the focus of a virulent and primitive form of scapegoating. Everywhere people are victimised by maniacal prophets who turn the universal terror and grief to their own incomprehensible ends. In one rural town, where, miraculously, a mental hospital was left standing, the local population was incited by a deranged truck mechanic to go in with torches and burn the poor and probably very much less insane in their beds.*

*Perhaps I felt the fear of these mad ones inordinately, for now we have all been confronted with acts of cruelty and destruction on a scale to defy human understanding. How much of our ability to live was based on the idea that death should have a meaning? I imagined them in their white-and-blue state pyjamas watching their own burning without knowing what they saw. It is said that some of the patients eagerly took up torches and helped to raze the place, thinking that they were finally winning their liberation. But in the end they were all trapped.*

*I have also heard that in the large shelter complexes scattered under the ground beneath us, the authorities use the very same tactics to keep their absurd and tenuous power over the healthy survivors who are now little better than slave labourers. It goes without saying that the sick have been turned out wherever and however the* nomenklatura *could get away with it. How incredible, in the face of the most total transformation the earth has ever known, that they have not changed at all.*

At the McDonough house, Kate was alone in the kitchen.

'Where is Dad?' Ian asked.

'He's napping,' she said. 'Please let him. Things have been very difficult in Washington. He's exhausted.'

It amazed him that his mother was still so protective towards his father. He kissed her.

She held on to him for a moment. 'Would you like anything?' she asked.

He shook his head and collapsed into a kitchen chair.

Kate came and stood over him; she put her hand gently on the top of his head.

'You have some mail here,' she told him.

She opened a drawer and handed him five coloured postcards of Paris: Montmartre, the Eiffel Tower, a houseboat on the Seine, the Arc de Triomphe, a flower stall. One postcard a week for five weeks, all from Lilianne.

'Why didn't you tell me these were here?' he said.

'I did,' she said. 'I told you that you had some mail, and you said you'd get it when you came out.'

The cards did not say anything in particular. They were casual, affectionate, just a way, it seemed, of being in touch. They made him afraid.

He had received, at least once a month until quite recently, a package or letter from Christian. In each sublet he had rented he had carefully put up and taken down Christian's paintings, collages and valentines. But in all that time he had not heard from Lilianne.

The reason for this, he knew finally, was not her recklessness; quite the opposite. She knew how hard, how agonisingly hard, it would be for him to be reminded of her.

Since the Fourth of July, so much had happened that he had neglected to write to Christian as regularly as he had been. Finally, he had called Paris. Lilianne had been quite warm. After a few minutes he sensed that she was hiding something from him. It turned out to be that Christian had run into his room when he heard that it was Ian and would not come to the phone. Ian realised that she had not wanted him to know this.

'How is Anna holding up?' Kate asked softly.

He shook his head again. He didn't want to talk.

'Does she know about her son?'

'She knows what she reads in the paper, just like the rest of us,' he said.

He saw Anna carefully taking Seriozha's piece out of her pocket. It had been folded and unfolded a thousand

341

times. It looked like a document that someone had been saving for years; it had been published two weeks before. She had wanted to talk about it with him, but instead they had sat not speaking for their entire half hour together. As the guard escorted her back to her cell, Anna's hand had gone restlessly to her pocket two or three times, touching it to make sure it was still there.

George came into the kitchen quietly.

'How do you feel?' Kate asked him.

'Better,' he said. His voice was low and Ian looked at him closely. His father came over to him.

'How is she?' George asked him.

Ian swallowed hard. 'I don't think she . . .' he said. He stopped and swallowed again. 'It's killing her.'

George remained standing next to him and Ian was conscious that his father's hand had stayed on his shoulder.

'Would you like a drink?' George said.

Ian nodded.

Kate sat down at the table with him and George went and took out a bottle of scotch. He put ice in three glasses and poured the liquor at the table. They touched glasses. No one spoke.

Ian took only a small sip. The scotch immediately warmed him. Now instead of a cold, clotted feeling inside, he felt as if he were bleeding. He wondered if he could get through everything he wanted to say.

'I know you want to talk to me,' George said. 'Do you want to go in the other room?'

'No,' Ian said. 'What I have to say, Mom can hear.'

Both his parents looked down at their drinks. Ian took a sheaf of papers out of his briefcase.

'You know they're trying to pin conspiracy charges on her,' Ian began. 'Do you know what her lawyer intends to counter with?'

His father did not respond.

'He intends to charge that the conspiracy is in fact on the government's side. That Anna was recruited and manipulated by certain interests in the government from the moment she left the Soviet Union. That when her

342

activities became too radical and it was apparent that she would not take a pro-administration direction, these interests turned against her, pressuring her publisher to drop her book, supporting – inciting – the anti-Soviet groups who heckled her and ultimately exploiting an industrial espionage case that has nothing to do with her in order to destroy her and discredit the movement she stands for.'

George looked at Ian and then at his wife. He spoke in a reasonable, measured tone.

'You can hardly maintain that she has nothing to do with the espionage case; by her own admission, she met with two of the principals on more than one occasion.'

In a second Ian was on his feet and had grabbed his father by his shirt. His father was stunned; his immediate reaction was to shield his face.

'When I met you in Paris a little more than a year ago,' Ian said, 'you knew that she was in the country before the press did. You were already there, ready with all the hospitality the fucking Naughton Foundation has to offer.'

'Ian!' His mother was struggling with him, prying his hands from his father.

Ian let go.

'This' – he slapped the papers in front of his father – 'is what you might call a sceptic's chronicle of Anna's rise and fall. I don't know what you know, but I don't have to. I suggest you read this and show it to whoever asked you to give her a grant in the first place.'

Liquor had released the agony inside him like a thaw; like a brook full of broken ice in the spring, pain strained and eddied into rapids, then burst forward to flow into the larger river of his anger. He picked up the chair he had been sitting on and slammed it into the wall.

His mother put her face in her hands and cried.

'You better do what you can,' he said, 'because if we can't expect justice from the courts, I'll destroy you and the people behind you like you destroyed her.'

He felt his heart pounding as though he had been running

after a thief. He realised to his amazement that he had not broken into tears and had no desire to.

His father stood up and took the papers.

'Ian,' he said.

But just hearing the sound of his voice incensed Ian.

'There have been times,' he told George, 'I've had to remind myself that you are my *father*. Through everything – so many things that I could not understand, not as a child and not now – I said to myself: he is my *father*. But this – this is too much. If you can sit there and watch them persecute her – kill her – then I don't know who you are.'

'I *am* your father,' George said quietly, and left the room.

'I don't know who *you* are,' his mother said to Ian.


George called a car to take him to the airport at 5:30 A.M. He had not slept during the night and he did not trust himself to drive. Kate had insisted on getting up and making him coffee before he left; one swallow of it seemed to burn a hole in his stomach, to burn a hole in his being, through which all the anxieties of the world could bore. On the plane to Washington the stewardess had given him more coffee. His whole body stung with tension.

He knew that Arthur Orr would not give him an appointment and so he got to Orr's office at 7:30 A.M. Orr's secretary knew him and smiled.

'I'll just be a minute,' George assured her. He saw her waver for a moment over the intercom. On the wall above her head a serene blue yacht crested over dark, dramatic waters. A small brass plaque proclaimed it the *Maribou* – Arthur's boat. There was something obscene, he thought, about a man making icons of his own possessions. It made him think of teenaged pharaohs, embalmed with their gold and agate toys.

'George,' Orr said, jovially but slightly unsure. 'What can I do for you at this hour? I hate to rush you but I'm expected on the Hill at eight-thirty.'

'What I want to say will take only a minute,' George told him.

He took out Ian's article and handed it to him.

Arthur Orr quickly scanned the first page.

'How the hell did you get this?'

'Under highly unpleasant circumstances that are none of your fucking business,' George said. 'I'm giving you what is known as a chance.'

Orr laughed. 'This is only the first of many.'

'An innocent person is being destroyed,' George said.

'Innocent? How can you be so sure? Maybe you should go on the stand as a character witness.'

'I may,' George said.

'I wouldn't advise it,' Orr said.

'You could be subpoenaed yourself.'

Orr sat down and began to read Ian's article more carefully. After a few moments he looked up at George and smiled.

'I can think of a few people who should have a look at this,' he said.

'The gentleman who gave it to me,' George told him, 'gave me to understand that he felt a certain urgency in publishing it. I think whomever you show it to should bear that in mind.'

'McDonough,' Orr said, 'this is cute – persuasive – but hardly conclusive. None of this can be proven.'

'Will that really matter?' George asked. 'If this hits the *Times*, you're going to have to answer some very difficult questions.'

'Listen,' Orr said. He was beginning to colour and his voice rose a bit. 'The person who gave this to you ought to bear in mind that I can have his fucking balls.'

'I don't think he was thinking of himself,' George said.

George noticed that the Atmos clock on Orr's desk read 7:59.

'I don't know what you can possibly be thinking,' George told him. 'There are laws in this country.'

Orr handed him back the article.

'You fucking son of a bitch,' he said.

'I think,' George said, 'you'd better hold on to that.' He

put the article down on Orr's desk and left without saying goodbye.

It had taken a week to reach the nine trustees of the Naughton Foundation; only five said they would come to New York, but this was a quorum. His secretary had sent each of them substantial briefs by courier.

He was conscious that he had never gone so far out on a limb during his tenure with the Foundation. He made sure that the upholstery in the boardroom had been brushed and that his secretary had ordered flowers; something discreet, he instructed her, perhaps lilies.

They were coming from all over, from Palm Beach and Palm Springs, from Washington and Denver and Phoenix. Three were professional philanthropists – an oil couple from Colorado, the St Phillipses, whose high lifestyle was reputed to be the model for a television serial George had never seen, and Scott Haller, a young man whose great-grandfather had been a railroad baron, whose grand-father had been an autocratic southern senator and whose father had once been a drummer with Benny Goodman. Haller IV ran a consumer advocate office in Washington. He had recently led a campaign against a major automobile manufacturer that had resulted in a record-breaking dam-ages award; until this, George had not been inclined to take the young man too seriously. Another trustee was a Naughton, and another, a retired lawyer like George.

As a young litigator George had occasionally recom-mended rash and idealistic modes of operating, but he did not feel that that was what he was doing now. He surveyed the boardroom before they came; they always sat at a fine old green baize-covered table. There were two sterling decanters of ice water and six Waterford glasses. Outside, the fragile urban maples of Sixty-ninth Street let a fragile yellow light through their leaves, and occasionally the hoofbeats of a hansom cab could be heard.

He loved it – he loved the very office and window where he sat – because it was just that much apart from the world, apart and above. He had never hoped for such a position

346

at his age; it had pushed retirement entirely off his horizon precisely at the moment when it had seemed most final and oppressive. When it had been offered to him, he had felt, in some way he could not describe, honoured, and that feeling of honour never failed to start up in him like some moral adrenaline each time he walked through the Foundation's doors. There was something old-fashioned and Irish in him that had been grateful for the opportunity, at the peak of his career, to return some of the privilege and benefits he had acquired to the social well from which they had been drawn.

But it was not always easy to feel grateful at his age. He had deserved the honour, he felt. He had worked hard.

There was no pretending that the influence and affluence of his position at the Foundation did not thrill him. It was something like the fantasy he had had as a very young man of eating dinner in a chic restaurant with a beautiful woman whose extravagant jewels he had obviously bought. But he had seen enough to be cynical of chic restaurants; the kind of women he admired would never wear ostentatious jewellery; he himself preferred to invest in the market. At least he had until recently.

In the past several weeks – or was it already months? – the insecurity of the fluctuating market had disturbed him uncontrollably. It wasn't that the market was wilder than usual; it was that the routine instability of events was catching up with him. He found himself eyeing real estate prospectuses, even considering buying gold. Late at night, when he couldn't sleep, these ruminations became enmeshed with others. He wondered how much Mary Ellen weighed; he wondered if Ian would ever marry; he wondered if Sarah had been able to pinpoint the exact date when her father's mind had begun to go; he wondered how it was that Kate could still fall into a deep, relaxed sleep beside him though they slept together but infrequently now.

There had been, and still occasionally were, nights of tears and tension, both he and Kate stalking the house in their nightclothes. They did this with a desperation that they had never been able to express when there were children sleeping in the house. He would read in the living room, then walk around, finally returning to the ghostly living room with a glass of brandy. Kate tended to sleep in the children's beds, but perhaps only for a fitful hour or two here and there. In the morning, all the beds in the house would have been slept in by one or the other of them.

The night of Ian's outburst, George had returned to the kitchen at about two in the morning to find Kate sitting on the floor with a tube of epoxy in one hand and a piece of the broken chair leg in the other.

She was weeping, but when she saw him, she laughed.

'I always hated these damn chairs,' she said. George had bought the chairs, six country George III chairs, at an auction once. At the time he bought them, he had been seeing a young woman who was a museum curator, and Kate had regarded the chairs as if they were pieces of that other woman's clothing.

'Why are you trying to fix it, then?' he asked.

She put the piece down and stared off, away from him, into the empty black window. He could see them both reflected there – she white in her blue nightgown, he looking stooped in his hastily tied robe. He straightened up.

'For Ian, really, I guess,' she said.

The two of them had sat on the floor and struggled to put the chair back together again. By four in the morning it stood, shakily and listing slightly to one side, and they had without a word gone to their bedroom together.

Kate had slept for an hour. George had remained awake, his body dead and heavy with exhaustion, but still floating on the surface of sleep, buoyed by guilts and other torments that seemed to flutter inside his chest like bats.

For the longest time, he had felt so alone that he had experienced only his own feelings. Those of others were removed from him, behind a transparent wall of his own pain. He saw the consequences of his actions; but he had not felt them. No one came close enough to him to feel his anguish – how could he touch anyone else's?

He had been able to deal with Mary Ellen's illness; so many girls her age had it. Even when Ian had grabbed him, his own reaction had been immense hurt – Ian's anger was so wild and unfair. But when he had seen Kate sitting there, diligently trying to repair the chair that she loathed, something had trembled inside him. The thick glass wall of his private sorrows had begun to craze and crack and it felt as if it were cracking along the lines of his veins and arteries. His hands still shook.

The trustees would arrive in less than a half hour. He did not want to leave his office, but he longed to be somewhere else.

He dialled Mary Ellen at school, where she was making up her lost semester. It was ten in the morning and there was no answer. He dialled the number again just in case he had made a mistake, but he knew she was in class.

He placed the receiver back gently and leaned forward on his desk. Then he dialled Ian.

Ian's answering machine picked up. Ian's voice, sounding bored and distant, said something to the effect that he was working and would return calls later. George waited for the beep, but the tape was worn and he wasn't sure if it had sounded.

'Hello?' he said. Nothing.

'This is your . . . dad,' he said. He waited for a moment, then he hung up.

In the pristine and polished stillness of his office he heard the dry leaves scraping against the outside of the window. It was a very gentle sound, almost soothing; it pierced him like the gasp of someone he might have inadvertently hurt in conversation. That autumn had been the warmest on record; the sky the driest blue, the ailanthus the tenderest orange. There was something about this gift of weather, he thought, that made everything seem too fragile. He resigned himself to sitting and clearing his mind until the meeting.

\*     \*     \*

When they sat in front of him – five of the busiest people he had ever known – George thanked them for coming.

'I'll make this fast,' George said. 'You know why you are here. Anna Khameneva, an exceptional person and one of the full fellows of the Foundation, has been arrested on espionage charges. In the past it has been the policy of the Foundation to steer clear of the personal travails and tribulations of any individual fellow. We have generally asked for the resignation of any fellow who became involved in anything questionable and occasionally we have requested the return of the grant where warranted.

'I've never hidden the fact that my personal political feelings are conservative; the Foundation as an organisation has been consistently aligned with the present administration. But I think this is an unusual situation.

'You have in front of you briefs prepared by an independent law firm. Cal' – he spoke to the trustee whose law firm had in fact done the research – 'I think you can vouchsafe for the respectability of the presentation.'

'What you are suggesting is a clear misuse of the Foundation's monies,' objected Mrs Van Allen, the oldest member of the board and daughter of the original Naughton.

No one said anything; not for Mrs Van Allen or for George.

George seized the silent opportunity.

'I think this is a historic moment,' he said. 'A Watergate, if you will, and I think it is that important that we be right about this.'

'I propose,' said Scott Haller quietly, 'that we support Mrs Khameneva in the press and that we post bail but do it privately, without using the Foundation's endowment.'

'You can't expect us to go along with that,' Deirdre St Phillips said.

'You've read the material,' Haller told her. 'I personally have no qualms about agreeing to Mr McDonough's motion. But I feel I cannot – and should not – impose my feelings through the Foundation structure.'

Deirdre St Phillips's husband, Peter, disagreed categorically.

'It's not the business of the Foundation to take sides politically, much less to take sides in an ongoing trial. It's in the courts; that's where it belongs. I don't understand you, McDonough. I think you have let personal and family considerations cloud your judgment this time.'

George looked down at the table. He noticed that the green felt covering of the old oak table seemed worn; not venerable and antique but merely old.

'This is and will be a very public case,' he told the trustees. 'It is my business to look out for the fortunes of the Foundation with regard to public opinion. This is not something, in my opinion, that we can step back from. We have to decide for or against. To maintain our traditional stance in this situation is to decide against. It is my contention that the proper and politic thing to do is decide for. I feel so strongly about this that I am prepared to offer my resignation if the board feels that it cannot so decide. When Khameneva is acquitted, as I believe she must be, if the Foundation has not stood up strongly beside her, it will be a matter of great embarrassment to the board.'

Calvin Rawlings sat back in his chair and looked at George.

'Although you make me feel that perhaps we ought seriously to consider your resignation, I hereby move that we table any discussion of support for the Foundation fellow in question and any discussion of your resigning for two weeks. If you still feel the same about this in two weeks, then we'll resurrect the latter discussion.'

'Second,' said Peter St Phillips.

George adjourned the meeting, and the trustees, with the exception of Scott Haller, left with the barest of personal salutations to him. He heard Deirdre St Phillips tell Cal Rawlings that she couldn't believe that George had brought them to New York for this.

When they were gone, Haller steered the conversation away from the polite amenities he had essayed while the others were in the room. He brushed a straight hank of hair off his forehead – his hair was too long and boyish, George thought, to be so grey.

351

'George,' Haller said, 'I've been waiting a long time to see this organisation put its money where its mouth is. I think you did something very important today and I want to shake your hand.'

'Thank you,' George said. He tried not to sound as defeated as he felt.

'I want to work with you on this,' Haller told him. 'I think we can arrange it personally.'

George hesitated.

'You have nothing to lose,' Haller said. 'If you're right, they'll love you and think you saved their asses; if you're wrong, the Foundation will dump you anyway.'

George looked at the young man and noticed for the first time that he was wearing an elegant crimson foulard bow tie.

Haller looked at his watch. 'I've got to cancel an appointment.'

'Let's move into my office,' George said, nodding to his secretary. For the first time in more than thirty years he felt the exhilaration he had felt as a young lawyer newly admitted to the bar. He remembered distinctly the first time he had tried a case in the Federal Courthouse of the Southern District – looking at the hard round pillars that seemed made to hold up the weight of the earth, and thinking, somehow, that it belonged to him.


Ian was only mildly surprised that night when he played back his father's message from the tape. The surprise was not that his father had called him – he had expected the call for several days – but that his father's voice sounded so worn.

Then he knew he was lying to himself. The sound of his father's hurt voice on the answering machine tore him apart in one swift motion, like a piece of fabric that has been notched to rip easily from the bolt.

Since he had attacked his father, he had felt bruised and shocked himself. He had never struck a woman; he didn't think he ever could. Yet there was something more awful about raising your hand to your own father, he thought. It was bestial, Freudian, obscene.

That night he had lain in bed, his sinuses blocked from crying, breathing through his open mouth with a wheezing sound like an old man dying of emphysema. He tried to bring Anna's image to mind, but he could not. He saw instead Christian's silver-blond head, his translucent skin.

The child had trusted him; how often had he dropped off to sleep in Ian's arms as Ian told him a story? And Ian himself, as he held that light sleeping bundle, had felt entrusted with life itself. Until he had made love to Anna, nothing had ever felt so alive in his arms as a dreaming child.

Why was it only when you loved someone that you noticed that life was so fragile? In the middle of the night, for several moments, he could not remember why he was so angry with his father, he wanted only to feel his arms around him, to hear him say: you are my son. I am your father. He wanted his father to forgive him; he wanted to forgive his father. He wanted to hold Christian; he wanted Christian to forget that he had neglected to write. He wanted him to trust him again, to come up on his lap and fall asleep in his arms.

When he had awakened that following morning, he had immediately written to Christian. He enclosed ten American baseball cards in the envelope. They had that old, marvellous smell of pink bubble gum; he wondered if Christian could love them the way he had.

He had not, however, written to his father. He had remembered why he had been so angry; he had woken up with the image of Anna waking up in her grey prison cell, the prison odour of Pinesol, urine and cigarettes ripe in his mind.

He was again imagining Anna in prison, the circles under her eyes bluer against the depressing steel-blue clothes she wore, when his father came to the door.

'I tried to call you,' George said when Ian let him in.

'I just got the message,' Ian said.

They stood, a few feet apart, in the hallway.

'Come in,' Ian said, and motioned his father into the small apartment.

His father sat in the one large armchair, which was covered in a loud fifties chintz of cabbage roses. But he was immediately conscious that he had done so and asked Ian if he preferred to sit there. Ian shook his head and did not sit down.

'Would you like something to eat or drink?' Ian asked him.

'What have you got?' George asked with deliberate warmth.

'Not much, actually,' Ian said. 'I think there's a bottle of Old Bushmills around here somewhere, maybe some wine. As far as food, I think I have some peanut butter. I haven't had a chance to do any shopping for a while.'

'Would you like to go out?' George offered.

'I don't think so,' Ian said. A moment passed during which George looked away from Ian and Ian felt an overwhelming desire to go to sleep. 'I think the Bushmills is your best bet. Okay?'

His father nodded. Ian went into the kitchen and came back with the bottle and two etched sherry glasses.

'Sorry about the glasses,' he apologised. 'This sublet is from an actress who's touring with a revival of *Mame*. All the stuff is a little kitschy.' He poured the whisky into the delicate glasses, which he and his father touched together with a wincing crystal clink.

'You should think of buying your own place; pay off a mortgage instead of rent. Save you on taxes,' George said.

Ian laughed. 'Do you know how much income I declared last year?' he asked. 'Eight thousand dollars. If magazines didn't pay my expenses, I'd probably be eligible for food stamps.'

'I didn't realise,' George said. 'I had the impression you were doing quite well.'

'I'm not complaining,' Ian said. 'In Europe it was a lot easier to sell stories; since I've come back I've been rethinking the kind of thing I want to write, so I haven't really written that much.'

'What is it that you want to write?' his father asked.

354

'I don't really know,' Ian said. 'I know I want to get out of writing news – topical things. I want to deal with things that are, well, enduring. You know, something that can't be used to wrap fish.'

But his father did not smile. He held his pretty little glass of whisky up to the light. 'I can understand that,' he said.

'Ian,' he continued, 'there are two things I came to talk to you about.'

'The old good news and bad news?'

George smiled but he did not laugh.

'Kind of,' he said. 'I showed your piece to the person who suggested giving Anna a grant, Arthur Orr. First of all, I have to point out that it was my decision to propose Anna to the board; Arthur only made a suggestion. He did not direct me to do it.'

'Would anyone turn down a request that came from so close to the White House?' Ian asked.

'Perhaps not,' George said. 'But it was still my responsibility.'

Ian did not look into his father's eyes, but at the absurd atomic rosebuds of the armchair.

'I can tell you that he was visibly affected by the article,' George told him, 'but I can't tell you that it will do any good to publish it.'

Ian laughed again, but this time the irony of his laugh was hard.

'What I would suggest,' his father said, 'is that you hold on to it for a while and see if they react. You can always publish it later if things get worse.'

How can they get worse? Ian thought. It was a staggering idea, one he had not even considered.

'There is some good news, though,' George said quietly.

Ian looked up at him.

'Principally through the good graces of the Foundation's youngest trustee, a man named Scott Haller –'

'I've heard of him,' Ian said. 'He's been active in that big GM suit.'

'That's right. He is going to post bail, Ian.'

Ian stared at him.

His father smiled. 'The rich are different from you and me,' he said. 'They can write cheques for a quarter of a million dollars.'

He stood up and embraced his father. He kissed him on the cheek again and again

When the US marshals turned Anna over to the Defence Committee that Miles Harding had arranged, mostly through funding by Haller, cameras were arrayed on the steps of the Federal Courthouse.

Kate McDonough had had to buy her new clothes; her apartment had been sealed by the court lest she or anyone else destroy evidence. Kate, perhaps instinctively understanding how Anna had been sickened by the dinginess and grime of prison, brought her a white sweater and a white wool skirt.

Her first sensation as she emerged from Metropolitan Correctional was the harsh autumn wind of lower Manhattan. She saw newspapers swirled in the air, and heard the strangely organised cacophony of taxi horns – she saw and heard, not through the thick wire mesh of a prison window, but there on the street, in the free air.

A jubilant yell went up from the crowd of supporters who had gathered in front of the courthouse. She felt that yell in the roots of her hair, indistinguishable from the bracing air, wonderfully cold after the stagnant, disinfected funk of the prison corridors and cells.

'How did they treat you in the slammer?' a reporter shouted at her.

'Very well,' she shouted back above the din

'How was the food?' someone else asked.

She laughed. 'Terrible.'

Questions flew at her. As they became more legal and more detailed, she put up her hand.

'I can't comment on that right now,' she said. 'But I want to thank everyone who is here today. You are really present at a celebration; all of you who have worked for my freedom, all of you who witness it, share it. Today I am free because you are free; you have been able to exert your freedom for me.

'Do you feel it?' she asked at the top of her voice. She was exhilarated. 'Do you feel what it's like to be free?'

The cheering started up again. Even one or two reporters grinned and raised their fists in the air. She waited for quiet, smiling.

'In the Soviet Union,' she went on, 'my son is in prison, and the whole country shares in his imprisonment.'

There were a few expressions of solidarity here; she nodded and acknowledged them.

'That those with power manipulate and harass those without it is nothing new or unique. It is our duty to resist this manipulation wherever it occurs, in this country or any other. We will not be victims. We will not have our minds made up for us. We will continue to dedicate ourselves according to the dictates of our consciences. No one, anywhere, can take that away from us '

'Oh yeah?'

Anna was not sure whether the comment had come from someone in the press. She looked around for the speaker and decided to answer though she did not know who had spoken.

'Let them put me on trial,' she said. 'I am ready to be judged by the consciences of twelve of my peers. I will be vindicated.'

Miles helped her down the steps. Perhaps forty cameras pressed towards her like weird, snake-nosed animals. But for the first time in her life she felt like reaching out and touching them. She liked these inquisitive animals and welcomed their curiosity. The oppressive lack of privacy she had been subjected to in prison had reminded her more than any other experience of life at home; the violation of privacy by the state was in no way comparable to the loss of privacy that is publicity.

Miles opened the door of a taxi for her. Ian was waiting inside.

She let him take her in his arms. She did not ask him why he had not stood on the steps with the others.

*Every night I dream that Misha dies.*

*I dream he dies in Niki's arms. He is carrying him – we have to cover too much ground every day for the child to walk. It is only when we stop to rest that Niki realises the child is warm only with the warmth of his own body, and seems to breathe only because Niki is breathing hard and the child in his arms moves up and down with his own chest.*

*I cry. He was my child, I think, Olga gave him to me. For us, he was the last child in the world. I can't move.*

*Niki stands up to take the body into the woods.*

*'Don't take him away,' I sob. 'Take me.' I cling to his legs and prevent him from walking.*

*'Anna,' he says, 'it is better this way.'*

*And then, with all the little strength I have left, I try to kill Nikolai.*

*I wake up because I feel Nikolai holding my fists – in my sleep my hands clench into fists. The Nikolai in my dream and my real Niki always look at me with the same calm face – the one because it would be a pleasure to die; the other because now that I am awake he will take me in his arms.*

*'Shh,' he says, 'you will wake the child.'*

*He calls Misha 'the child', as if it were a title, like the general, the archbishop.*

*What would we do if he were not here for us to take care of?*

*We have become so inventive – so brilliant – in our struggle to keep Misha alive. I felt like a genius when I was able to make a strong, glutinous soup out of acorns – I gathered them, ground them and cooked them myself by heating stones and then immersing them in the soup, which had to be made in a waterproof canvas bag for lack of any pot. The bag would have burnt directly on the fire, but this method worked well. Can I tell you what it means to us to know that we can have soup – a real and nourishing gruel – as long as we can find acorns? Our sense of well-being is*

*intoxicating; we laughed for the first time in weeks. Every-
thing seemed funny and wonderful and our laughter gushed
up like water in a spring. I fell asleep that first soup night
with an exhausted giddy feeling in my stomach and the
forest floor felt delicious against my tired face.*

*For once it was me and not Nikolai who woke up to
watch during the night. I awoke because suddenly in my
sleep I became conscious that I was not dreaming. It was a
blessing, a physical relief. God, I thought, a deep dreamless
sleep – as if night were nothing but healing. When I opened
my eyes, a tattered piece of cloud trailed off from the thick
cloud mass and revealed a slice of the clear sky.*

*When I saw the stars, all I could think was: they're still
there! And though I have despised those who saw God's
judgment in the holocaust, who saw a terrifying apocalyptic
hand raised against us instead of the reality of our own folly
towards nature, when I saw the stars I believed that it was
a miracle. Why should these beautiful lights still be there, I
thought – why should I of all people see them tonight of all
nights – unless there is a God and he has given them to me?*

*I have believed since that moment Misha will survive –
whether I do, or whether Niki does.*

*The child began to whimper in his sleep; the soup, or
maybe just such a quantity of any food at all after being
hungry so long, had given him pains. Niki was awake in
an instant. We took Misha to lie between us and after a little
while he forgot his stomachache and chatted and laughed
with us – that lovely silly laughter that children have, high
and trilling like a flute, for no reason at all. I know he was
probably still in pain, but because he was with us it didn't
matter to him anymore. How could it be possible to want
more power than that?*

*When he had fallen back to sleep, Niki and I whispered
above his head. There are rumours that somewhere to
the south there is a valley where the inhabitants of an
underground shelter rose up against the nomenklatura and
took it over. They cannot be much better off than anywhere
else, but they have water filters, electric generators – and
they live according to law, not according to the whims of*

359

*the leaders, but according to real human law which is
enforced by an elected tribunal. There are children there;
they have made a school. There is a hospital there, and they
take care of the sick.*

*It seems like a dream.*

'Do you want to see the papers?' Ian asked Anna.

She looked at him. He had been getting up very early
each day, making tea in a china teapot which belonged to
the actress who owned the apartment and going through
the papers before Anna had a chance to see them.

Almost every day there was something about her case.
The New York *Times* coverage had been restrained but
had given detailed portraits of the life of KGB pseudo-
diplomats. The New York *Post* used every opportunity to
vilify her, even having a photographer follow her and Ian
on the street and commenting on the difference in their
ages. When the prosecution had refused to publish a full list
of witnesses because revealing their names would endanger
US agents in the field, they had started referring to her
openly as 'alleged Red Spy'. The word 'alleged' was generally buried in the text; the words 'Red Spy' featured in
the headline. When Seriozha's piece had appeared in the
*Times*, they had started calling her 'Spy Mom.'

Several magazines had entered the fray as well, notably
*The Nation* and *The National Review*. A piece in the former
magazine had defended her quite forcefully. It had touched
off an avalanche of criticism in the conservative press. Ian
bought all these journals, and read them so avidly that she
expected to see the pages burn to ash under his concentration like a piece of paper under a magnifying glass.

His old terry robe was untied and his hair was rumpled.
His face looked soft and relaxed when he had just woken
up; she wanted only for him to come to bed and fall back
to sleep next to her. Let the two of them sleep forever.

He handed over the pile of papers.

'Well, today's the day,' he said to her. 'I'll bring you
breakfast in bed.'

'Don't you dare. I'd feel like an invalid.'

'Too bad you aren't sick,' he said. 'Then you wouldn't have to go.'

'What a thing to say.'

He looked at her; his eyes were small and tired. 'I'm sorry. You know I don't mean it; I just wish it didn't have to be.'

She kissed his hand. 'It has to be.'

He sat down with her, and as he always did, he pointed out the articles that pertained to her case. That morning the New York *Times* had decided to do a profile on the Justice Department's special prosecutor – Stephen J. Alther. A brilliant lawyer, still young, he had successfully prosecuted – and obtained maximum sentences in – two previous industrial espionage cases. He had been educated at the University of Chicago and Stanford Law School. His undergraduate degree was in American literature; he had done an honours thesis on Walt Whitman. And his mentor in the Justice Department had been a man named Daniel S. Davidoff, best remembered for his early and startling repudiation of the President during Watergate.

'Is that who —' Anna asked.

'Yes,' Ian said.

'And who is Walt Whitman?'

Ian shook his head. 'I can't get over that. He's a poet,' he said.

The courtroom was very beautiful – high, moulded ceilings, polished oak wainscoted walls. The high desk behind which the judge would sit was proportioned like an altar.

When the judge had come in, and the jurors had been seated, for a moment everything was breathless. The first ballet Anna had ever seen, as a child, had been a contemporary choreography of a Shostakovich piano concerto. The dancers had been motionless onstage when the curtain went up and had waited there for nearly a full minute until the first chord was struck. Now, on this American morning, thirty years later, the memory of that dance hung precise in front of her mind's eye and she understood why live theatre startles the way it does.

She was not afraid. It was strange, she knew, that confronted with the awesome power of the American government, and the equally awesome momentum of great bureaucracy, able to grind its own mistakes into the same fine powder as true criminal grist, she felt light, almost transparent. It was not courage; it was simply lack of fear. She had nothing to hide, there was nothing she could do for Seriozha – he had taken his life firmly into his own hands. She understood him; she herself had once earned the incredible release that comes from realising you are powerless.

She also understood what it was to stand alone in front of the Castle walls, looking up at those who held fate in their hands; even a pebble dropped from such heights was enough to kill a man. But this time, it was not the same.

She had never been in prison in Russia. She had had as much freedom as it was possible for an ordinary citizen to have – basically a limited physical freedom to live in one place and take care of one's needs. There was not much question of travel, not outside Russia anyway. There was no question at all of intellectual freedom: the freedom to think, to write, to speak her mind. She had waited a long time for this, she had dreamed about it without understanding what it was. Here, even in prison, they could not take it away from her.

Now Stephen Alther stood up to make the prosecution's opening statement, presenting their theory of the case and what they intended to prove. Anna was struck by the openness of his face. It was a clear-eyed American face, his features were all medium-sized, averagely handsome, he was grey around the temples. He had the only slightly individualised good looks of a newscaster. He spoke in an entirely reasonable tone of voice.

Do your best, she thought, because the deeper you try to drag me, the higher I shall rise.

He began with the simple, and obviously heartfelt, assertion that wisdom has it that the government never 'loses' a case. If the jury convicts the defendant, then he is

362

punished, and if it finds for the defendant, innocence has been protected and justice has been done.

Having made this point, he went on to define the charges.

'Under the law,' he said, 'when persons agree to a conspiracy, each one becomes liable for the act of any other. Common sense assures us that in fact it would be impossible for all the conspirators to do the dirty work; naturally this is done only by some or even one. Each conspirator performs only his own particular task, for that is the nature of such a network. But under the law, if there is a crime, they are all partners in it. If you believe that Mrs Khameneva was in agreement with persons who committed crimes against the United States, then you must find her guilty also, for each conspirator acts on behalf of the others.

'The charge of harbouring is yet simpler. If you believe that Mrs Khameneva knew, or even had reason to know, that someone she opened her home to and protected was involved in espionage against the United States, then you must convict. If you find her guilty of harbouring, you must additionally determine whether it was a unique act or whether she did so because she was a conspirator.'

Anna watched the jury listening to him. They were serious; he treated them seriously and with respect. He did not fawn on them; he did not make his explanations simplistic, only clear. He gave them the impression that he felt his responsibility to uphold the Constitution of the United States very keenly. She knew that this sincere conscientiousness would lend weight to every lie he told about her.

Up until the last few weeks there had been some question about whether or not the government would continue to press the conspiracy charges, as well as those of harbouring a spy, since the case was not strong. At the eleventh hour, they had been told that the government would proceed with the full case. Miles was not unhappy about this; he reasoned that the prosecution was worried about weaknesses in the harbouring case that it relied on the conspiracy case to buttress. A house of cards, he kept telling Anna.

But a house of cards can be dazzling in and of itself. She watched as Alther built layer upon layer of a structure of kings and queens, knaves and aces, and told a striking narrative of intrigue, conspiracy, ambition and zealotry.

The Anna in the story had been a simple housewife and academic in the Soviet Union. Her husband's heroic rise to fame had changed her life; it had made her vulnerable to the KGB in an extraordinary way and when they had offered her an equally extraordinary route to safety – a route involving wealth, international travel, fame in her own right and even the opportunity to work for the cause that had dominated her and her husband's lives – she had not been able to turn it down.

Alther was a genius in fitting every sliver and dust mote of her life into this structure. Her book had brought her to the brink of prison in the Soviet Union, he said, but its fame came to be perceived as the first link in a chain woven by State Security propagandists who knew just how to be most persuasive to the West. They knew exactly the kind of career her dramatic expulsion from the Soviet Union would bring her.

Perhaps her rise in the United States was not the direct result of a brilliant and calculated duping of idealistic and trusting Americans – but was it not interesting that it brought her into direct contact with some of the most outstanding scientists and businessmen in the country? Contacts she could never have hoped to make on her own?

Alther never questioned her dedication to disarmament; it was perfectly consistent with the interests of her alleged superiors – the Soviet Union, after all, had no greater aim than to see America militarily weakened.

And if she showed signs of breaking her link in the chain, if life in the West or dedication to her cause began to overwhelm her, there was always her son. He was admitted, even by the defendant, to be a kind of hostage. It was unfortunate, but concern for her son had to be considered a cogent motive for espionage. Concern for family held in the Soviet Union would be shown to have been the motive for more than one of the witnesses for the prosecution – conspirators who had already pleaded guilty.

He ended by exhorting the jury to listen very carefully to the witnesses since it is the province of the jury alone to judge their credibility.

'And as you listen to them,' he suggested, 'look at them closely. Keep in mind George Orwell's book 1984 – for the world of Russian diplomatic espionage is a world of doublespeak and doublethink. Almost nothing in this case is as it appears to be.'

Miles was on his feet in a second. He moved for a mistrial.

'The prosecutor's statements amount to an instruction to the jury to be prejudiced,' he said.

The judge did not hesitate in his response.

'The charge here is conspiracy to commit espionage, the espionage being the harbouring of a spy; it is not whether or not the defendant is Russian or Communist. If the government intends to establish that the defendant has an overriding interest in or love for Russia or Communism as a way of establishing motive, I will in due course rule on that point.'

'That is what I intend to establish,' Alther said.

'The defendant excepts to the Court's statement,' Miles said.

'Your exception is noted,' said the judge.

Miles's statement was briefer, simpler and to the point. He stood for a moment in front of the jury, as though still thinking. Then he straightened up. When he began to speak, it was obvious that that moment's stillness had been an effort to control his anger, for his quiet voice was laced with the sense of affronted dignity.

'You have heard Mr Alther tell you what he intends to prove or, I should say, what he intends to persuade you to believe, for there can be no proof in this case. This is not something, should you ever sit on a jury again, that you are likely to hear in the opening statement by the defence. When a defence attorney stands in front of you at the beginning of a trial, he keeps his words few and his promises fewer, for he does not know what evidence the government has, or how strong their case is.

'There will be no surprises in the case of Anna Khameneva. There has been no conspiracy – for conspiracy is a meeting of the minds like a contract. There is no meeting of the minds possible between Anna Khameneva and those in control of her native country; that is why she was expelled from that country and stripped of her Soviet citizenship. It may be that the meeting of minds that the government is concerned with is between the defendant and her fellow Americans who protest an insane and suicidal arms race; but that I cannot comment on, as it does not bear directly on our purpose here.'

'I'm glad you said that,' the judge said. 'You will please confine yourself to the matter at hand.' His voice was stern but there were titters of laughter in the courtroom. Anna felt the atmosphere relax slightly and she smiled at Miles. She noticed that some of the jurors had slightly eased their rigid postures; they had been sitting on the edges of their chairs as Alther spoke. She hoped that this meant they trusted Miles.

'There was no conspiracy to commit espionage; there was no harbouring of a spy. That is the overt act which the government must prove beyond a shadow of a doubt. If Anna Khameneva had no idea that espionage was being committed then she cannot be guilty of harbouring.

'I don't have to tell you ladies and gentlemen to keep in mind any book, any idea or any philosophy when you listen to the witnesses. I tell you only to use your own intelligence and common sense. The witnesses the government will produce will be desperate men and women, already convicted of espionage, and facing many years, perhaps the rest of their lives, in prison. There is little doubt that people in such a position will cooperate in any way with their captors.

'I don't have to paint a dramatic picture for you, of villains and victims, as Mr Alther has done, though the picture I could paint is a harrowing one. I, too, could paint a picture of cynicism and manipulation, of disinformation and lies. My victims would also be the American people but my villain would not be Anna. The villains would be American officials who hide behind the sometimes spurious defence of "national security interests". Ladies and gentlemen, though it is more than a decade since Watergate, let none of us forget that such disgraces are possible.'

Mr Alther objected.

'Your honour,' he said, 'this is complete and scurrilous speculation. It is totally without merit or relevance.'

'If he can speak about the defendant's motives, I can speak about the government's motives,' Miles said. 'And anyway, that is all I intended to say on the subject. I will not bring it up again in the course of the trial.'

'You certainly will not,' the judge said.

'I am only a lawyer,' Miles said, 'and it is my client's wish simply to refute the charges as they stand. I am not as gracious and forgiving as she is. But it is my duty to serve her according to her desire and within the scope of my professional responsibility. We are all here for only one reason – to assure the defendant a fair trial. We all have a stake in Anna Khameneva's freedom.'


Ian's head was reeling. As soon as they had shut the door behind them, he kicked the grotesque and rosy armchair. It retained a dent in its mouldy chintz in the rough shape of his foot.

'You've killed it,' Anna said. There was a little smile on her lips. He was amazed.

They had just spent the last four days listening to a man named Mikhail Kirillenko – a.k.a. Alexander 'Sasha' Whittmore – tell the jury how he had operated from the centre of a ring of Russian nationals with diplomatic immunity, disseminating disinformation and recruiting Americans – more than one of them a naturalised émigré – to steal indexed technology from the universities and corporations where they worked. His recruits had a variety of motives, mostly money, but sometimes a stark and even attractive idealism.

Though Kirillenko told a tale of calculation and coercion, he was young and blond and sometimes looked at the prosecutor as a puppy looks at its master. He maintained that his Soviet superiors held numerous threats over him, including the health and welfare of a wife and two young children back in the Soviet Union; he was cooperating now, he said, because he had been caught and his only hope in the world was that the State Department would intercede for him to protect his family. He had no expectations of any kind for himself. He seemed so undone, so ingenuous that Ian wondered how in hell Miles, during his cross-examination, would show him to be the cold, venal apparatchik they knew him to be.

And today, after hours of painstaking reconstruction of a network involving nearly a dozen committed conspirators, a number of them employed in laboratories or otherwise connected to the sciences, he had alleged that his superiors had come to the conclusion that the fame that Anna Khameneva's book had won in the Soviet Union would be a windfall in the West.

'How can you be so calm?' Ian asked her irritably.

'I never expected him to tell the truth,' she said.

'But you sit there and listen to him slander you – how can you?'

'It's not me he is talking about.'

There were moments when she created a stillness all around herself, like a dark icon in a church in front of which one candle flickers down to its wick. Her face was pale, her hair darkened by the evening shadow; her eyes were not enormous but they were deep. Looking into them was like looking into a tidal pool; there were layers of life there – the immediate happy and sad and ordinary things of the day flitted across their surface; beneath was a clear, profound suffering, and beneath that, something that no one could ever disturb – not a calm, but a silence.

'Forgive me, Anna,' he said.

Now her smile was only in her eyes; if he hadn't known her so well, he would have mistaken it for sorrow.

'Would you like to go out to dinner?'

She shook her head. 'Let's go to sleep,' she said.

'It's only six o'clock.'

'I know.'

She came and pressed her face against his chest. He held his hand under her hair, the way one holds a newborn whose neck cannot yet support the weight of his head.

When the phone rang, Ian thought he was asleep on his feet. He picked it up and said hello groggily.

It was a call he had been expecting for some time; it was Lilianne. There was static on the line, she sounded far away. But she was calling from midtown.

'Who was that?' Anna asked him.

'Do you remember my little boy?' he said.

She looked at him without answering.

'That was his mother.'

She put her hand on his cheek and then got up quietly and went into the bedroom.

He let her go. She left him sitting in the old armchair; its springs were stiff and broken, he could not lean back. He sat rigid, nervous, suddenly almost hysterical. Anna closed the bedroom door gently.

Lilianne arrived quite promptly. She had taken a cab all the way – or rather they had taken a cab, for she was not alone.

With her was Christian and a tall man in a linen suit. All Ian could think of was how studied the man's wrinkled clothes were, for his hand was disturbingly soft and clean when Ian shook it and his manner was so vague and distracted that Ian could not believe that the man could manage to accomplish very much in a day.

Lilianne was much more beautiful than he remembered, softer, blonder. He extended his hand to her; she kissed him tenderly on both cheeks.

But it was Christian who took his breath away. He no longer looked like a child. He was tall and thin for a

369

six-year-old, and wearing the most horrible eyeglasses Ian had ever seen, currently chic in French children's fashion magazines – perfect round black circles that made him look like a cartoon owl.

'Christian,' he said softly to the boy. He crouched down to hug him, but Christian stepped back towards his mother.

Lilianne looked at Ian despairingly.

'Come in,' he said to her. The three moved slowly into the apartment.

'*Très mignon*,' she said, taking in the little room.

He shrugged.

'Won't you sit down?' Ian said to the man. He still did not know if the man spoke English. He smiled uncomprehendingly and remained where he was standing.

'Stanni,' she said to the man, '*attends-moi dehors, s'il te plais*.' Her tone was low and sweet; it reached inside Ian and twisted something he didn't know still existed.

The man smiled at Ian again and backed out the door.

'He is Polish,' she told Ian. 'He comprehends English very bad.'

'Badly,' he corrected her.

'You are right.' She smiled. 'No one speaks English to me anymore.'

'Sit down,' he told her. 'Christian, would you like a Coke?'

She sat down but Christian remained standing, slightly apart from both of them, silently staring at the floor. Lilianne looked at her son and Ian knew that he had never seen her so unhappy.

'He is always like this,' she said. Her eyes filled with tears. 'I can't do anything.'

Ian took her hand.

'Stanni and I will go to California,' she told him now. 'He will make a movie there; he is invited.'

Ian felt that she was holding on to his hand more tightly.

'What will Christian do there?' he asked her.

'I hope I will find a special school; they pay Stanni,' she said.

He knew her too well not to understand the logic of her

370

non sequitur. Man = money = career = child care. The only flaw in this was Lilianne herself; somehow there was never very much of her left over for her son.

'Come on,' Ian said to the boy. 'Sit over here.'

But Christian would not even look at him.

'He is impossible,' Lilianne said. 'Very destructive. Since you left, he has been so bad.' Her voice was barely audible. Ian was not sure if this was because she did not want Christian to hear or because her voice failed her.

She looked at Ian hopelessly. 'I thought he would be happy to see you,' she said. He felt the strength go out of him; it was so obvious that Christian was terribly unhappy – and that Ian was making it worse.

Lilianne pressed her cheek against Ian's; it was cold.

'Sometimes,' she whispered, 'he is so quiet that I am afraid that he is dying.'

'Shhh,' he said. 'You're just distraught. I can't blame you.' The child's hostile silence had exhausted Ian in only a few minutes.

'I don't know what to do,' she repeated.

'Lili,' he asked. 'Do you want to leave Christian with me?'

Lilianne looked so far into his eyes that he involuntarily shut them.

'I couldn't possibly,' she said.

He was struck that she did not say no.

'When could you come back for him?'

She turned aside. 'A few weeks.'

'Just a moment,' Ian said. He went into the bedroom and came back out with Anna. He introduced her to Lilianne, who shook her hand coldly. But he knew that the *froideur* covered embarrassment, and it hurt him. Lilianne humiliated by the thought of leaving her child with another woman was the Lilianne he had only glimpsed but never known.

Anna turned to Christian and smiled gently.

'Do you remember me?' she asked him.

Ian saw Lilianne's jaw tighten momentarily.

Christian continued his tragic, triumphant silence. Three

371

adults gazed down on him ready to give in to him in every way. Ian finally crouched down and took Christian's chin in his hand.

'Do you want to stay with me for a while?' he asked him.

Now Christian was looking into his eyes. He still loves me, Ian thought; he had seen it in his eyes at once.

'I hate you,' Christian said in perfectly good English.

He must have overheard it more than once, Ian thought.

'Paddington,' Lilianne said to her son. '*Soi sage.*'

'I'll take him,' she said. 'It's better this way. But thank you.' He had never seen her look so lost, not even when he'd left her. He did not touch her.

The child looked at her finally, but he stood stock-still. She embraced him, but his arms remained stiff at his sides. She opened the door.

When will I see him again? Ian thought.

They stared at each other, the boy and the man. Lilianne shook Anna's hand again.

When they were gone, Ian stood with his back to Anna facing out the window. There weren't many children on the street; the neighbourhood had grown too expensive.

'He doesn't forgive me,' he said.

'Ian,' Anna said softly, 'he is a child.'


Sarah sat quite still, holding her gloves in one hand. Her gloves were of new black kid. She thought again and again of the famous line of Anna Akhmatova's in which, as the poet parts from her lover, she distractedly puts her glove on the wrong hand. The whole texture of the meeting was like a glove forced on the wrong hand.

'Do you remember meeting me?' Stephen Alther asked her.

'Yes, of course,' she said. 'I was not a child. I was nineteen years old.'

He laughed. 'I was probably the same age you are now,' he said. 'Now I'm an old man.'

She did not laugh. She waited for him to be honest with her. She knew that he interpreted her waiting as hostile.

'Your father was the best man in the world to me,' he said.

She looked down at her gloves again. She had stuffed such black kid gloves in her mouth at her father's funeral; they had tasted salty and she'd realised to her horror that leather gloves are made from killed animals.

'I've followed you a little since he died,' he said to her. 'You've really thrown yourself into your cause, haven't you?'

'I have the impression that you're something of a work-aholic yourself,' she said.

'What else? Couldn't have survived around your father if I wasn't dedicated, could I?'

She smiled. 'What do you want?'

He looked tired.

'I did not want to see you involved in this,' he said. 'From the moment I heard that you were so close to the defendant, I scrupulously kept you out of it, got them to steer a clear path around you.'

He sat on the edge of his desk. He had taken his jacket off and his shirt sleeves were rolled up. It was a sincere impression of hard work that he made, but she could tell that his shirts were hand-finished and she knew that the office was a very large one.

'She's going to be sent down,' he told her. 'There's no question about it. And a lot of people with her.'

'What do you mean there's no question about it?' Sarah asked angrily. 'You've got a jury in there.'

'Sarah, there's no limit to what they have on her. They have informants in the Glen Cove compound; this whole case is lousy with information that comes from nowhere. And that nowhere happens to be protected – classified.'

'You're telling me that you were told to bring back a body,' Sarah said, indignant.

'Sarah,' he said; his voice was flat and unhappy, 'I'm trying to offer you the opportunity to save some of what you've worked so hard for.'

'How dare you drag me down here and speak to me of

373

my father and then offer me some shitty deal? Are you out of your mind? I don't understand how you could have gotten so far.'

'You are deliberately misunderstanding me,' he said. He had stood up and was very close to her. He held out his hands in front of him in a very un-Waspy gesture of beseeching. She recognised that gesture instantly; it was her father's.

'There are some fights worth fighting,' he said quietly. 'Your father was a genius at picking them.'

She stared at him.

'Don't be a child,' he told her. 'This is the reality. Do you think your father would have survived Watergate as such a big hero if it wasn't already known that Nixon was on his way out?'

'My father denounced the President because he loved the law,' she said.

'The law is a living thing,' Alther said, 'no better than the people who apply it.'

She put her face down. He handed her a tissue from a box on his desk.

'I'm sorry,' she said. 'I'm just tired.'

'Why don't we meet in a few days,' he said kindly, 'when you're feeling better.'

Anna came in at five minutes to midnight. She could see Ian sitting on the edge of the cot that had been set up in the tiny office. In the bedroom one light burned; their own bed was rumpled and an open book lay facedown next to her pillow.

She sat down quietly in the kitchen so as not to disturb them. She was grateful for the dark and the deliberate silence of the apartment. The atmosphere was the delicate and cosy one adults create for children to fall asleep in, she reflected; if only adults could treat each other as they treated their children.

But that was a folly, too, she knew. People did not automatically love children. Perhaps human beings did not automatically love at all.

What am I? she thought. Is it I who am human or is it they?

Ian came quietly into the kitchen.

'I was with Miles,' she apologised.

He nodded and put his hand over his eyes. She could see even in the dark how exhausted he was.

'How did it go?' he asked her.

'The same,' she said.

He looked for her eyes in the dark.

'What's wrong?'

'Nothing, really. I'm just tired.'

'Tell me,' he commanded her. 'Why did Miles keep you so late?'

She turned away from him to look out their little kitchen window. It faced an inner courtyard with an ailanthus tree. The leaves were withered and shook on their branches, making a sound like water, like the little brook that used to form each spring behind her parents' wooden house in Moscow.

'He told me that Sarah has had a private meeting with the prosecutor,' she said.

'What does that mean?'

Anna shrugged. 'I don't believe it.'

'What does Miles think?' Ian pressed her. 'I don't get it; the prosecution can just subpoena her as a witness.'

'Apparently,' Anna said, 'Miles is afraid that because of Alther's close relationship with Sarah's father, Sarah might wittingly or unwittingly reveal information to him that is crucial to us. He says I must not see her or talk to her under any circumstances.'

Ian shook his head. 'I was afraid of that.'

'She is my friend,' Anna said.

'Life is so complicated,' he said.

'But you don't understand,' Anna said to him. Life was complicated, she would be the first to admit it; but certain things cut through everything else. Love, honesty, family, friendship.

'Sometimes I don't understand human beings period,' Ian said.

375

'But you understand me?'

He looked into her face. She felt him reading all the doubts he found there.

'Yes,' he said.

The day that the government turned Mikhail Kirillenko over to Miles for cross-examination, Ian sat with the press. Every day that Kirillenko testified the courtroom was packed with reporters – it was not that seeing a KGB agent on the stand was in itself unusual, though it was; it was that Kirillenko was also a diplomat and was privy to a slice of Soviet life that Americans were not aware of. Ian looked enviously at those who held a yellow pad or small computer on their laps; he longed for something to do with his hands that would relieve the unending tension.

But he knew he could not have taken his eyes off Anna. They belonged to each other really only late at night now. Then they would lie with the covers drawn up to their faces and whisper. He knew that no matter how many people rallied around her – and though her supporters had diminished, the ones who remained were staunch – she missed him in the courtroom. He knew how much she needed him.

It was hard to think, looking at her sitting next to Miles, her oval face severely beautiful, intelligent, judgmental, that this was the woman whom he held at night – who sometimes cried in her dreams, making a weak sound like a young animal. How strange to expend the whole power of the American government to crush this small, fragile woman. Why?

One would have thought, perhaps, that she would face Kirillenko as though he did not exist. But she sat there every day examining him closely, and not with contempt, but with intense inquiry. She was asking herself, he knew, if any combination of circumstances could make her into him.

When Miles stood up to cross-examine Kirillenko, though he was tall and dignified, seeming heir to the august surroundings, he came up close to the witness and made

376

eye contact with him. His behaviour, like Anna's, seemed rinsed of contempt. He did not smile, exactly, but Ian felt his expression indicated to Kirillenko something on the order of 'we're all in this together, so let's try to make the best of it'.

Miles opened his questions as the prosecutor had, seeking general information about Kirillenko's life. He seemed to be taking the same direction the government had, drawing out a portrait of the lifestyle of the Soviet elite – the *nomenklatura* – which Kirillenko had claimed to aspire to not only out of the envy of an ordinary man but as a means to better provide essentials like health care and education to his family.

Perhaps because the questions were so similar to his friend the prosecutor's, or perhaps because he was speaking about something he knew well, the witness began to relax and his testimony began to flow freely. Miles did nothing to inhibit him.

Out poured minute – in fact, marvellous – descriptions of parties at lavish country estates outside Moscow, of military jets commandeered for the use of private individuals, of a standard of privilege that far exceeded that of all of the jurors. Indeed, Ian thought, amused in spite of himself, even in Greenwich you wouldn't find people living quite that high.

Now Miles began to direct the questioning more precisely. Ian noticed that the questions were phrased differently. The difference, which at first was almost imperceptible, was that increasingly less information was required of the witness. Kirillenko began to give yes and no answers.

'One of the benefits, one might presume, if one went into the service of the KGB, and was able to rise up the ranks,' Miles suggested, 'is a better standard of medical care. Is that not so?'

'Yes,' Kirillenko said. He was emphatic. 'It is most important,' he offered, 'since the standard of state medicine is very poor.'

Miles nodded.

'Perhaps,' Miles said, 'since most of us here are not familiar with Russian life, you might give us a description of, say, one of your trips to a state clinic before you were in the KGB and a visit to a *nomenklatura* doctor after you had, as we say in America, made it. You don't have to say much, just what your personal impressions were.'

The witness hesitated for a fraction of a second.

'*Nomenklatura* doctors are just like Western doctors,' he said.

'But what about going to a regular clinic? How were you treated there?'

'They are rude,' the witness said. His voice seemed to have fallen off slightly, inexplicably. 'It is crowded.'

'Tell us more,' Miles said. 'When was the last time you went to a clinic?'

'I don't remember. A long time ago,' Kirillenko said.

'What was wrong with you?'

The witness paused.

'Did you have a bad experience there?' Miles asked.

'Yes,' the witness said immediately.

'Were they rude to you? What did they say?'

The witness seemed to be searching mentally for something.

'But it was a bad experience?' Miles asked again. 'You are definite about that?'

'Oh yes,' Kirillenko said.

'Then why don't you remember what was wrong with you when you went there? Presumably you were ill or in pain to go to a clinic – why don't you remember what they said to you while you were ill and in pain?'

'It was a long time ago,' the witness stammered.

Stephen Alther now rose to his feet. 'I object,' he said. 'Mr Harding is badgering the witness with a useless and trivial line of questions.'

'Your honour,' Miles said, 'if I may, I'd like to point out that I have a very definite purpose and relevance in mind here.'

'What is your purpose, Mr Harding?' the judge asked.

'To show that the witness has never been in a public

378

clinic. And he has never been in a public clinic because he has always been – from birth – a member of the elite which he has described. I think it is important in establishing the character of the witness to know whether or not he was an ordinary man lured by reward and concerned with the safety of his family, as he claims, or whether he was a rich man's son, seeking only to more deeply entrench his privileged lifestyle.'

'You may proceed,' the judge said. 'But I will stop you if I think you are roaming too far afield.'

'Thank you, your honour,' Miles said. And he went on to demolish Kirillenko's 'recollection' of doctors, dentists, schools, even grocery stores.

By the end of that day, everyone in the courtroom had quite a different feeling about Mikhail Kirillenko than they had begun with.

Ian leaned forward, his chin on his fists, his elbows on his knees. His skin tingled.

'Miles is a genius,' Ian told Anna over supper.

'It was my idea,' Anna said. She sat back in her chair and smiled at Ian. She had not felt as good since the opening of the trial. She leaned forward and kissed him happily.

'Well,' Ian said.

'It will work out,' Anna said softly to Ian. 'Everything will work out.'

'Anna, don't take this the wrong way, but it worries me to see you so happy. We're not out of the woods yet.'

She took his hand. 'You worry when I am unhappy and then you worry when I'm happy. I know this means you love me.' She looked at the lines around his mouth, which were hardening. She couldn't explain herself why she felt so supernaturally buoyant and carefree.

'I just don't want you to get depressed. There's a lot left to go through.'

'Do you remember,' she asked him, 'when you said they'd get me if they wanted to?'

He nodded, the worry darkening his face further.

'Do you still believe that?' Even to her, her voice sounded brittle and gay.

'I don't know,' he said. He laughed. 'I was going to say, "The jury's still out on that," then I realised that there really is a jury.'

When Sarah called, it was Ian who answered the phone.

'What do you want?' Anna heard him say. 'She's asleep.' Anna was standing right there. She guessed at once who it was.

'Let me speak to her,' Anna said to Ian.

'No,' Ian said to the woman on the phone.

He hung up.

'Anna, don't take a chance,' he said. 'Imagine if Alther had known in advance how Miles planned to attack Kirillenko. You just cannot risk it.'

'I don't believe it,' Anna said. She remembered her first meeting with Sarah, how she had understood Anna's distress and called the *gebisti* lice. She remembered countless other moments as she and Sarah worked together. Sarah had been able to watch Anna struggle silently for a word in English or in Russian and known instinctively what word it was that Anna wanted. It had been a wonderful feeling to open one's intellect so intimately to another person; Sarah was the only real colleague Anna had ever had. Such an uninhibited collaboration would not have arisen in the Soviet Union.

She called Anna her muse; no night was too late to sit up and drink strong tea and work on the book, if Anna happened to get an evening free from her public appearances. She had laughed at Anna's late-night solemnity in her lighthearted American way, which became both lighter and more heartfelt the more serious the discussion. She quoted Akhmatova to her:

'"Are you the one who came to Dante and dictated the pages of Hell?"'

Anna had turned to her in the most tragic, muse-like fashion she could muster and answered the verse:

'"I am."'

How could one reconcile the friend who quoted Akhmatova in firelight with a spy who might betray one at the most delicate and most dangerous moment of one's life? A woman who was also a traitor would have been poisoned by Akhmatova's words, as if she had touched cyanide to her lips.

'Ian,' Anna said, 'there must be something we don't know.'

'Do you want to take that chance?' Ian said.

'They won't put Kyrstov on the stand,' Miles told Anna as they met during the luncheon recess.

'Why?'

'Well, they say that he is ill, but I am certain the reason is that he could not confront you successfully in court.'

She felt her heart grow smaller inside her.

'Both are true,' she said.

She thought of Kostia, so old and so far from home, in a prison hospital. The food would be strange, the language strange. He would have no friend; he would know that he would die there.

'This means,' he told her, 'that only his statements to the FBI will be admitted into evidence. As you know, those statements are basic reiterations of the facts of his involvement as a courier, which, naturally, he says he was forced into – and his friendship with you. It verifies the government's informants' story that you went to Glen Cove –'

'But I don't dispute that,' Anna said.

'Unfortunately,' Miles said, 'Kyrstov was the only one who could have been relied on to testify to your version of that day. Or the day in your apartment, which is most at issue.

'What I am saying,' he continued, 'is that it brings it all down to whether the jury believes in Kirillenko or in you.'

She saw the depth of concern on his face; it was not worry but something more abstract. It was a contemplation, she thought, of justice – two equal possibilities in conflict, both sides so strong that the tension between them creates a stasis, an illusory immobility.

'I'm afraid I'm going to have to put you on the stand, Anna,' Miles said.

'I'm not afraid,' she told him.

She looked at her hands; because of not working in a lab, because of the easy availability of high-quality American skin-care products, her hands seemed to belong to a woman younger than she herself. But nothing is ever truly still, she thought. Reality has a certain weight to it, and pulls you in its own direction.

'I know you have almost looked forward to it,' he said, 'but you've got to be prepared for how difficult it will be. Government prosecutors are the best and the brightest lawyers this country produces.'

'Not better or brighter than you,' she said.

'You don't have to worry about me,' he said. He gave her a smile.

'You don't have to worry about me, either,' she said. 'People know the truth when they hear it.'

His smile became old, almost rhetorical.

'If only that were so,' he said.


The last day that Miles had Kirillenko on the stand he attacked his story as to why Konstantin Dimitrievich Kyrstov had been sent to Anna's apartment.

The account developed by the government was a clear-cut description of harbouring. According to Kirillenko, at the last moment before Kyrstov's departure, there had been some problem and his visa was being questioned. Worried and knowing that it would be dangerous for him to try to contact Kirillenko, Kyrstov had gone to Anna for help.

Obviously, Kirillenko could not be taken in by Miles twice, but the government was not taking any chances. Miles had prepared Anna to expect that Kirillenko's performance would be polished but he was so well coached that she felt exhausted after listening to Miles hammer at him for only an hour.

'Wouldn't it have been unusual, not to say stupid, of Mr Kyrstov,' Miles pressed, 'to turn to someone so visible and therefore vulnerable as the defendant? Wouldn't you, as his superior, have to say that?'

'Yes, I would,' Kirillenko admitted. It was the first time the wind of the cross-examination had blown in Miles's direction all day. Anna felt her hope expand like a spinnaker.

'But he was old and confused,' Kirillenko volunteered, 'and he was her friend.'

'Objection,' Miles demanded. 'Strike that from the record. It has no bearing on this testimony.'

'Overruled,' the judge said.

A sharp spot of pain penetrated Anna's forehead like a tack and she knew that the jury saw it.

Moments before the court was adjourned for the day, one of Miles's assistants was passed a note, which he read and passed on to Miles. Miles nodded.

Anna sat quietly, formally. The judge gave his standard charge to the jury not to watch television or read the newspapers, and not to talk to the press; Miles had consistently striven for as well-educated and successful jurors as could be found and, knowing that sequestering the jury would inhibit such people from serving, had indicated to the judge that the defence would be satisfied with the jury being given the traditional instructions. Every night the jury went home to their families, just as Anna went home to Ian.

Every night court adjourned and it was as if time stopped; it made her feel the need to protect herself. Other people lived in the world where time moved; it seemed somehow dangerous to try to move among them – she felt clumsy, vulnerable. She was overcome with a physical gratitude and safety when she closed the door of the little Village apartment behind her and took her place at the supper table.

'Anna,' Miles whispered to her, 'listen to me.'

She realised then that fatigue was making her vague and inattentive.

'It's just come out that your son and his friend have been on trial for the last four days. This morning they were convicted of what's being called "defaming Soviet reality", and sentenced to four years of internal exile in the East.'

*Bozhyemoy*, she thought. At least not labour camp.

'Another friend, Anatoly Krelnikhov, also named in Seriozha's case, was sentenced to six years in a labour camp.'

She shut her eyes.

'You're going to have to face a lot of reporters when you walk out,' Miles said.

'I can't,' she said suddenly. 'Please, don't make me.'

Miles was not quick enough to hide his shock from her; he had, she knew, become used to her being strong.

'Oh God, Anna,' he said. 'I'd give anything to protect you from them. If you were anyone else, we could issue a statement and take you out downstairs. But you cannot let this opportunity pass. You've got to keep the press on your side, and that means giving them what they need.'

She put her hand in front of her mouth and pressed hard to keep the agony inside and silent.

'Write something,' he said. 'You know what to say; when you go out you can just read it.'

He put his hand on top of hers. But she shook her head; if anyone touched her she would crumple.

She took a pencil and a yellow legal pad. She thought for a moment, staring past him. Then she wrote quickly.

'My son has just been sentenced to four years of exile after four days of a "trial" the outcome of which had been decided before he was arrested. The press was barred from the courtroom; no friend was allowed to stand up for him, even as a spectator.

'In spite of everything that has happened to me, I must reaffirm today my love for the country which has adopted me. As I face a jury of twelve of my peers, nothing can more clearly point out the value of the freedoms guaranteed by the Constitution. I stand by the promise I made to protect and defend the Constitution when I became a citizen of the United States, and I state again my willingness to be judged by the jury. They will vindicate me, for everyone, in his heart, knows the truth when he hears it.'

'Good,' Miles said.

'Do you believe it now?' she asked.

'We have no choice but to believe it.'

She put her hand on his.

'Come,' she said. 'I'm ready.'

*Niki goes ahead every day to scout. We are determined to find the valley where survivors live free.*

*I make my way slowly behind, since the child cannot possibly travel so much in one day. Niki and I each have a compass made of a piece of paper and a needle rubbed on a magnet. In one settlement we visited there was a man with a magnet and people paid court to him as if he were a king.*

*But by the end of each day, I am almost hysterical with worry that I shall never see Nikolai again. Imagine the ludicrousness of wandering in the semi-dark in the mountains with a paper compass that is really no better than a child's toy.*

*How he finds us in the evening is a miracle. I believe not in the compass but in the human heart – he finds us because he belongs to us. Let anyone laugh at me, but I believe he finds us because our love and need for him is so strong it draws him to us infallibly.*

*And when the child sees him! His face is like a time-lapse photograph of a flower opening. He runs to him and hugs Niki's legs so that Niki walks towards me awkward and stooped like a bear. With me, during the day, Misha drags his feet and seems always tired. I think he is only really alive when Niki holds him and we are all together. I know how he feels.*

The defence began with the appearance of character witnesses. A number of the people that Miles had approached – especially those who were elected officials – declined to

385

become involved. This did not surprise Anna, though it couldn't help but depress her. It was too reminiscent of her colleagues at the Institute; most had avoided her and avoided fulfilling their 'duty' to denounce her. But some had not.

Of those who took the stand in her behalf, James Bradford was the one she knew best. He, like Miles, was dressed and carried himself in such a way as to seem to actually belong in the noble, neoclassic courtroom. He was, by virtue not only of breeding and background but as well by the eminence he had achieved as a scientist, as close as anyone could come to American aristocracy.

He handled himself in a relaxed but dignified way. He did not smile, but rather gave the impression of cooperating wholeheartedly with a very serious business. He let Miles lead him through direct examination easily.

'When did you meet the defendant, Mrs Khameneva?' Miles asked him.

'I met her on Christmas Eve a year ago,' Bradford answered.

'Would you tell us about that meeting – where it occurred, the circumstances and surroundings?'

'It was at the Kennedy Center in Washington, DC, at a benefit for the Smithsonian Institution. Mrs Khameneva and I were both featured speakers on the programme.'

'Would you tell us, briefly, what you spoke about and what Mrs Khameneva spoke about?'

Bradford now smiled broadly.

'I spoke theoretically, saying that human beings are social animals, and like all socially organised species, have a tendency to fascism – biologically speaking. That is, an innate propensity to submit themselves to authority, whether that authority is an actual leader or an abstract ideology. I gave my opinion that wherever people put themselves at the service of ideas they do some violence to their human spirit.

'Anna – Mrs Khameneva – took me to task in front of nine hundred people. She said that just because we do have this tendency to want to live by ideas does not mean

386

that all ideas are equal. She went on to say that some ideas, like the ideas embodied in the Constitution of the United States, are life-giving, life-protecting ideas, worth dedicating one's life to. As I recall, she was given a standing ovation.'

Anna wished she could hug him. She sat by Miles's assistant, joyous tears brimming in her eyes.

Miles continued with Bradford at the same pace, developing the theme of Bradford's high respect for Anna as an individual, their close relationship, the time she had spent with his family.

In the afternoon, Bradford was turned over to Alther for cross-examination.

'When was the last time that the defendant came to visit you at your home?' Alther asked.

'February last,' Bradford said.

'What was the occasion?'

'We had just finished attending a conference of scientists concerned with the atmospheric effects of thermonuclear war at Stanford University, which is only two hours from my home.'

'Were there many other eminent scientists present at this conference?'

'Yes,' Bradford said.

'How did Mrs Khameneva come to be included in the group?'

'I invited her; I am on its board.'

'Would she have been able to attend this conference if she didn't know you?'

'I don't know; quite possibly.'

'How would that have been possible?'

'She would have to know another of the scientists in the group.'

'Did she know any of these ladies and gentlemen before you introduced them to her?'

'I don't know.'

'Your honour, the government would like to submit into evidence exhibits numbers 67 through 115, signed depositions demonstrating that the defendant had never met any of the eminent scientists present at this meeting before the witness introduced them to her at said meeting.'

There was a quiet rush of words in the courtroom; reporters typed quickly on their miniaturised keyboards.

Alther continued to push Bradford in the same direction. Bradford fought him off well, with wit and poise, but Alther was pursuing a line of questions that was just impersonal enough to stay outside of Bradford's reach.

However, after a while, the prosecutor changed his tack. 'Do you have any children?' he asked Bradford.

'Yes,' Bradford said. 'I have two children.'

'How old are they?'

'My boy is ten and my girl is four.'

'Do you carry their pictures in your wallet?'

Bradford looked at him strangely. 'Yes.'

'Would you show them to us?'

Bradford did this, holding open his wallet and turning towards the jury.

'When Mrs Khameneva was in your home, did you ever think she was, well, homesick?' Alther asked him.

'I can't say that, no.'

'She never spoke about her life in Russia, or her son?'

'Well, at that time, her son was reported to be a political prisoner in a mental hospital, so naturally we tried to keep abreast of the news.'

'Did you have the impression that she loved her son?'

'Yes, of course,' Bradford said. He was clearly getting angry.

'Did you have the impression that she was a good mother?'

'Yes.'

'How did you get that impression? Did she talk about her son?'

Bradford's light eyes grew dark and furious.

'Actually,' he told the prosecutor, 'she almost never spoke about him. What could she possibly say?'

Alther shrugged. 'Then how did you know that she was a good mother?'

388

'Mostly by the way she treated my children. She adored them. And they adore her, by the way.'

'Did you have the impression that she missed her son?'

'Yes, of course.'

'Did you have the impression that she missed Russia?'

'Not really, no.'

Miles finally stood up, exasperated. 'I object to the amount of time Mr Alther is taking to develop a line of testimony which is self-evident and proves nothing relevant to the charge.'

The judge turned to the prosecutor. 'Please come to the point,' he said.

Mr Alther turned back to Bradford, unperturbed.

'Did Mrs Khameneva ever speak of Russia at all?'

'I'm sure she did,' Bradford said curtly. 'I think I remember her describing the Kremlin or Red Square or some such thing to my wife and the children.'

'Did you have an impression that she was proud of these monuments, or that she felt nostalgia for them?'

'Mr Alther,' Bradford said in a withering tone of voice, 'I love Venice, but I have never been tempted to betray the United States for the benefit of Italy.'

There were a few guffaws in the courtroom. Anna looked in triumph at Miles, but his face was motionless.

'Where are your children, Dr Bradford?' Alther asked.

'California,' Bradford answered.

'The government is through with the witness,' Alther told the judge.

All that week, Anna listened to the character witnesses describe her in the highest terms of praise. Then she listened to Stephen Alther riddle their testimony with doubts as mercilessly as machine-gun fire as he forced them to testify, truthfully, that she loved her son and missed her home.

The morning that she was to take the stand, Miles took her to breakfast at the Mayfair Regent Hotel. It was quiet and stunning, a small marble courtyard of deep armchairs and potted palms.

'Why have you brought me here?' she asked. She was trembling too much to eat.

'Because it's pretty,' he said. 'Because I want you to remember that you had a life before this trial and that you will have a life after it.'

She sat back in her chair. She held her cup of tea in both hands like a child. It was hot and her hands were cold.

'You are a fine man,' she told him. 'Thank you.'

'Anna,' he said, 'your direct testimony is your chance to give your story in your own words. This is not only the best chance you're going to get during the trial, it is the only chance. I know we have gone over everything and that you are prepared, but I want you to keep one thing in mind.

'The jury will be listening to how you speak perhaps even more than to what you say. I know this sounds impossible, but try to be yourself. Leave it to me to ask you questions which give you the opportunity to state your case. Do not be tempted to volunteer anything I have not asked for. Do not become upset or defensive with Alther; if he gets your back up, he will get the better of you. You've seen that again and again here. When he is finished cross-examining you, I will be back to clear up any messes he makes.

'You and I are two halves of the same coin now,' he told her.

'What you leave undone, I will do, either today or in the summation. Don't forget that the summation is still to come; then I will take everything you have said and present it in the most polished and persuasive way. And so if there are things you feel I haven't gotten to, don't try to get to them yourself from the stand. Tell me later and I'll work them into the summation. We've got to work together like, like – well, like something even better, more organic, than clockwork.'

'We must create a synergy,' Anna said.

'Fine,' Miles said. 'But on the stand try to avoid scientific terms. Just speak normally.'

*     *     *

390

As Anna stepped up to the witness box to be sworn in, she was conscious of two things: that this was the most important moment of her life, on which her freedom depended; and that after it was over, Ian would be there.

Miles approached her and touched her hand gently. She had not expected it and she shot him an inadvertent look of intense gratitude and trust.

'Are you all right?' he asked her.

'Yes,' she said.

'You better speak louder,' he said. 'It is important that everyone hear everything you have to say.'

He began by asking her where she was born, and when; he drew out the story of her parents and her father's persecution under Stalin. As she spoke of these things, she relaxed. She even took some pleasure at that stricken moment, in remembering the warmth of her childhood home, the simplicity and love of both her father and her mother.

By the time she came to speak of her marriage to Pavel Leonidovich Khamenev, she was so deeply immersed in the past that, though she was hardly aware of it, her voice was cracking.

'Your husband was an idealist, was he not?' Miles asked her.

'Yes,' she said, 'he was.'

'Would you have loved him so much had he had a different set of ideals, or none at all? If he had been an ordinary kind of man who merely did his work, ate his dinner, spent time with his family?'

She laughed a low, tired laugh.

'I prayed to God to make him an ordinary man, that he might have been spared even one moment of what he suffered.'

'Are you an idealist?' he asked her.

'I don't know,' she said.

'What do you believe in?'

She looked at him blankly. He had never told her that he intended to ask such a question.

'Take your time,' the judge told her.

She realised that the courtroom had fallen absolutely silent. Everyone looked at her.

'I believe that life is good,' she said to Miles. She said it haltingly, holding out her hands, as if she wished that she could possibly make that simple statement into something more. 'I believe that life is good and that we should protect it.'

'Anna, are you a Communist?' Miles asked her.

'No,' she said. 'I had a Party card in Russia in order to work but I was never an active member. I never even went to the routine Wednesday-night meetings in my department, which meant nothing and which everyone went to.'

'Why? You could have gotten a promotion at the Institute, could you not? You might have been allowed to travel, isn't that true? Why didn't you do at least the simple, pro forma things?'

She thought for a moment and then gave a little laugh. 'The truth is that it was very, very boring. I would sit in a meeting and think: my husband is at home alone, my son needs me to mend his sweater for the morning, I might have finished writing up my lab notes. I'd look out the window and see that it was April or May or whatever and that Venus or Mars was visible in the northeast – there just always were a thousand other things that I wanted to do more.'

She noticed that several jurors were smiling. It suddenly struck her that it might be very, very boring to be a juror. She smiled back.

'If you could sum up in a sentence what it is that you want, personally, your desires and dreams, what would you say?'

She sat still for several long seconds. She stared at the spectators; she realised that they were all asking themselves the same question.

'I am ashamed to say,' she said.

'Speak up,' the judge ordered.

'I want to be safe,' she said.

Miles looked at her tenderly. The judge recessed the court for lunch.

During the afternoon, Miles took her meticulously through her three meetings with Kostia, concentrating on the day at Glen Cove. He asked her every question that the prosecutor might ask her, seeking to defuse the damage by her candour.

'Why, if Mr Kyrstov was the person who dismissed you from your job – which you tell us was an act of political persecution – were you happy to see him?'

'He was a person from the old days,' she said. 'He was the only person I have spoken to since I left Russia who knew my husband and my son. At the time I met him in Washington, he told me that he would try to find out information about Seriozha.

'How did you think he would find this information?'

She shrugged. 'In Russia, one never knows where information comes from. Only rumours are reliable.'

'Did you think that one of his sources might be the KGB?'

'I knew that it was possible,' she said.

'Why did you go to Glen Cove?' he asked her. 'Did you think that you would encounter persons in the employ of the KGB there?'

'Yes,' she said. 'I knew I would encounter such persons. I went because Kostia told me that there was additional information about my son which he was unable to tell me on the phone.'

'What was in your mind when you went there, knowing that, essentially, you had been invited by the KGB?'

'I thought that in all probability I would never be heard from again. I saw many people disappear as a child. The Chekists called them in for questioning and they never came back.'

'Then why did you go?'

'I didn't even know if my son was dead or alive.'

'Did you meet Mr Kirillenko there?'

'Yes,' she said.

'What did he tell you?'

She reported her conversation with 'Sasha Whittmore'; she told how he had strung her along with details of her son, revealing for the first time that he was exiled. But when she came to tell about the death of her grandchild, she stopped.

'It's all right, Anna,' Miles said. 'Just say it.'

'He said that in the city where my son and his friend, Katerina – she is really like his wife – were exiled, there was not decent medical care.'

Anger was hardening between her shoulder blades. She held herself very erect.

'What did he mean, Anna?'

'He meant –' she began.

'Louder,' the judge interrupted.

'He meant that when it was time for Katerina to give birth to their first child, my grandchild, they were not seen by a doctor in time and the child's life was lost. He meant that this was not an accident. The doctors knew who they were and refused to treat her properly.'

She clutched her hands in front of her; she was shaking. But she was not shaking from grief – she was shaking with hatred.

'What did you do then?' Miles asked quietly.

'I left,' she said.

'You just stood up and left?'

'Yes,' she said.

'Why?'

'Because I knew then for sure what I had felt in my heart since I left. I knew that Russia was dead for me, that my son was dead, the same as dead.'

'Why?'

'Because if I allowed myself to feel even one thread of connection back to my home, they would use it to torture me and the people that I love. That it would be, in effect, as if I had never escaped from them at all.'

Alther zeroed in on details.

'When you left Glen Cove,' he said, 'you took with you an envelope. What was in that envelope?'

'It was a list of statements that they wanted me to work into the English translation of my book.'

'Why did you take it?'

'At first I thought it was a letter from my son.'

'Why did you keep it when you saw that it was not? That in fact it was a directive from the people you supposedly hated more than anything in the world.'

'I thought,' she said, 'that there might be clues about Seriozha hidden in it. They are like that. Every bit of information is held in front of you, ambiguous, tantalising. I wanted to read it carefully to see if, in trying to get me to do what they wanted, they would tell me more.'

'But you just said that after Mr Kirillenko supposedly told you about the death of a grandchild, you wanted nothing at all to do with them.'

'That's true,' she said.

'Then why didn't you just get rid of the letter?'

'I don't know,' she said. 'I kept thinking there must be something more I can find out.'

'Isn't it possible that you held on to it because you were considering doing what they asked in order to gain the information you were looking for?'

'No,' she said.

'It never crossed your mind?'

'Mr Alther, my book had already been delivered to the publisher by that time. I have made no changes in it since then.'

'Naturally not,' he said. 'Konstantin Kyrstov was arrested a few days after the material was given to you and you were subpoenaed by a Senate committee within a week of that date. And to date your book has not been published in its entirety in this country.'

He hammered at her. His questions came so quickly that she had no opportunity to say much more than yes or no. Her back ached, she was continually cold. Miles nodded at her gravely whenever she looked towards him. His face betrayed no emotion whatsoever, only that he was there in the same room with her, and that she must go on.

'Why did Konstantin Kyrstov come to you on the afternoon of July fifth?'

'To say goodbye,' she said.

395

'Could he have come to you without someone in the KGB knowing where he was?'

Miles interrupted. 'I thought it was the government's contention that Mr Kyrstov sought out the defendant because he could not establish contact with Mr Kirillenko. The government cannot have it both ways.'

'Just because Kyrstov didn't know where Kirillenko was doesn't mean that Kirillenko didn't know where he was,' Alther responded.

'What's your purpose here?' the judge said to the prosecutor.

'I beg your pardon,' Miles said, 'but I must respectfully object to your honour trying to help Mr Alther out of this.'

'My purpose is to show that the defendant took in Kyrstov knowing that he was from the KGB,' Alther said.

'You may proceed,' the judge told him.

'Could Kyrstov have come to you without the KGB knowing he was there?' Alther repeated to Anna.

'I don't think so,' she said.

'Didn't he come to you with another request from them?'

'We did not speak of it.'

'What does that mean – you did not speak of it? Did he come with a request, yes or no?'

'He had been told to ask me to cooperate with them, but since he knew I would not do it, we did not talk about it.'

'So you knew that Kyrstov had come from the KGB?'

'Mr Alther, all Russian citizens travelling abroad can be expected to be under constant scrutiny and direction from the KGB – dancers and opera singers as well as scientists. It did not mean that he was a spy.'

'Answer the question. You knew that he had come from the KGB?'

'Yes,' she said. She knew her voice sounded dead.

'Your witness,' Alther said to Miles.

Miles approached her for redirect.

'What did you and Kostia talk about that day, Anna?'

'Nothing much,' she said. 'He brought me elderberry jam from a gourmet store, we talked about the fact that

396

there are no elderberries in America. We talked about Seriozha. Kostia suggested that since I was an American citizen I should try to bring him here.'

'What did you say to that?'

'I said I knew they would never let him go.'

'What else did Kostia say to you?'

She thought it over.

'He told me that he liked my apartment but he thought that the intercom was used for surveillance – that the CIA must be watching me.'

'What did you say to that?'

'I laughed. I told him this was America.'


On her way out of court, the photographers pressed around her so hard she was afraid of falling. She felt Miles grip her arm hard.

'Keep breathing,' he told her.

She answered questions; she breathed. When they finally began to clear away, she saw Sarah Davidoff standing against a wall. She wore a black coat and her face was white. Her hair fell around her shoulders and reminded Anna of Katinka. Anna's instinctive reaction was to smile at her, to step towards her.

But Miles held her back.

'We have nothing to say to you,' he said to Sarah.

Sarah was shaken. 'Please,' she said. 'I must talk to you.'

'We have nothing to talk about,' he repeated.

Anna felt the anxiety of the day suddenly take possession of her; her shoulders went rigid as if someone had grabbed her. She began to shiver.

'Please,' Anna said to Miles.

He looked at her, commanding her to be quiet; but he saw how shaken she was and instantly relented. He turned to Sarah.

'I'm going to take her home. Be at my office at nine this evening,' he said. Sarah nodded thankfully.

Anna felt Miles propel her towards the door. She looked over her shoulder to see her friend still standing there, ashen. She remembered how tenderly Akhmatova had written about Lot's wife, who gave up her life for one look back.

*The stars are not eyes; no God sees us. We are finally alone.*

*My eyelashes feel like pinpricks. The child stares as if he is blind. I cannot warm him.*

*Yesterday, Niki came back while it was still light. He walked quickly, but strangely, as though he were following something he couldn't quite see.*

*'I know how to get there,' he said. 'We are not as far as we think.'*

*He took both my hands in his; he was nearly weeping with exhilaration.*

*Then suddenly he sneezed – and he was covered with blood. My hands were drenched, my dress.*

*'Oh my God,' he said.*

*I couldn't speak; I clutched him.*

*'No!' he said He pushed me away from him.*

*The child began to cry.*

*'Stand there,' he commanded Misha. I have never heard a voice like it. His voice came from hell. Misha did not move.*

*'Listen to me,' he said. Blood poured over his lips as he spoke.*

*'Go east until you come to tall white cliffs; you will find chalky rock and pebbles on the ground when you are near it. From there, go northwest until you find a small river. When you have found the river, follow it. Did you understand? Repeat it to me.'*

*I stared at him. The front of his shirt was soaked with blood. He was beginning to stagger.*

*'Repeat it,' he said. This time he did not order me. His voice was gentle and I know that it took everything in him to speak so softly.*

*'My darling Nikolai,' I said. I felt my tears run back down my throat. God, I thought, let me bleed, too.*

*'Anna,' he was whispering now, 'don't.'*

*Misha edged closer to me and pressed his face against my legs.*

*'Go now, go,' Niki said.*

*'I won't leave you alone,' I told him.*

*'You must take the child,' he pleaded.*

*God forgive me, for one instant the child did not exist. Niki began to back away towards the woods.*

*'Niki,' I screamed, 'don't go!'*

*'Use all the water,' he said. 'Wash. Burn your clothes.' He moved farther away as he spoke.*

*I started to run after him; Misha clung to me. In the moment that I looked down to try to tear the child away from me, Niki was gone.*

*I washed his blood from my hands and arms slowly; it was him, his life. But when my hands were clean and cold, I saw Misha. His face was smeared from touching me; his clothes, too, were ruined.*

*I scrubbed him, I burned his clothes with mine. Now I hold his naked body to mine for warmth; only the blanket is left.*

'Oh God, Anna,' Ian said. 'Don't cry.'

He had awakened because he heard her sobbing and then realised that she was asleep. He'd touched her and she had opened her eyes and stared at him in terror.

Then she clung to him and cried so that he thought he would have to call a doctor.

'It was just a nightmare,' he said. He wished that they could all wake up now, and find that the trial had never taken place.

She shook in his arms and would not be still.

'I dreamed you died,' she said.

He stroked the top of her head. It was the closest she had ever come, he thought, to speaking of how her love for her husband still affected her, affected both of them.

'Shhh,' he told her.

She looked at him and shook her head.

'Is this me,' she asked him, 'here with you?'

'I hope so,' he said.

She laughed, though she was still crying, and he held her until she fell back to sleep.

\* \* \*

One of Miles's assistants took her aside before court in the morning.

'Things are looking up,' he said.

'Why?' she asked.

'I can't talk about it now,' he said. 'You'll see.'

The first thing that she noticed when she went in was that Stephen Alther was not present. The session was delayed for fifteen minutes because he was late.

Miles had filed a motion to put a new witness on the stand; someone had come forward with evidence not previously known. The motion had been granted.

The defence called Sarah Ruth Davidoff to the stand.

She came in, tall, pale, beautifully dressed in a dark suit with a lace jabot. As she was sworn in, her voice was high and clear. But Anna could tell that she was nervous.

Miles asked her where she had grown up, where she had gone to school. He asked her who her father was.

'Daniel S. Davidoff,' she said.

'Did he work for the Justice Department?'

'Yes,' she said. 'He was in the Internal Security Division. He was one of the people responsible for preparing the case against Richard Nixon, had he gone to trial.'

'Do you know the prosecutor?' he asked.

'Yes,' she said. 'He was one of my father's assistants.'

'Did you know him then?'

'I was introduced to him.'

'Have you seen him since then?'

'Yes,' she said.

'Tell us when and where.'

'He asked me to come to his office after the beginning of the trial.'

'Why?'

'Because, as he put it, Anna was going to "be sent down . . . and a lot of people with her". He said he didn't want me to go down with her.'

'Did you have the impression that he said this merely because he was an old friend of your father's?'

'No, sir,' she said.

'Why did he say it, in your opinion?'

'I am Anna's translator and have worked more closely with her than perhaps anyone else.'

The prosecutor objected.

'Your honour,' he said. 'The conversation Davidoff is describing is not unusual in seeking the cooperation of a witness and the government objects on the grounds that it is prejudicial.'

'Objection sustained,' the judge assented. 'Did the prosecutor ask you to perjure yourself?' he asked Sarah.

'Of course not,' Sarah said.

'Mr Harding,' the judge said, quite annoyed, 'why are we listening to this witness?'

Miles did not answer the judge. Instead he turned to Sarah.

'Did the prosecutor ask you to testify in court?' he asked her.

'No, not at all,' she replied.

The judge was fuming.

'Then why did he want to see you?' Miles pressed.

Alther was on his feet. 'This is a gross misuse of the court's time. It's obvious that Ms. Davidoff would be among many prospective witnesses we would wish to interview. I interviewed her myself because I know her family.'

'Sarah,' Miles said, 'you know something about government trial procedures. Was this an average interview?'

'I don't think so,' she said. 'I hope not.'

'What are you trying to say?' the judge demanded.

'I am trying to say that I feel Mr Alther wished to use me as a spy in the defence camp, as it were. He wished to exploit my close personal relationship with the defendant to the advantage of the government's case.'

'Did he directly ask you to do anything that would imply a violation of ethics or professional responsibility?'

'Not directly,' she said.

'It is our contention,' Miles said, 'that the government gave Ms. Davidoff the impression that if she did not cooperate, she might also be prosecuted, even though there is absolutely no basis for any suit.'

The judge paused.

'Is this accurate? Did you have such an impression?' he asked Sarah.

'Yes, your honour,' she said.

'Your witness,' Miles said to Alther.

As Alther passed Miles on the floor, he looked at him coldly. 'I'll sue you for slander,' he said.

He stood for a moment facing Sarah. His face glowed with insult.

'Ms. Davidoff,' he began, 'you are the defendant's translator, are you not?'

'Yes,' she said.

'You have occasion to work with her, travel with her, have access to her almost all the time, is that correct?'

'Yes, sir.'

'Were you in Washington with her last Christmas for the Smithsonian benefit at which she spoke?'

'Yes.'

'May I have exhibit number 29?' the prosecutor asked the clerk. The clerk found and handed to him a photograph of Konstantin Kyrstov.

'Have you ever seen this man?'

Sarah stared at the photograph and faltered.

'Yes,' she said.

'When and where?'

'He was at the benefit.'

'Did you just notice him, or did he happen to be talking with someone else you knew?'

She looked at him with fear.

'He was talking to Anna,' she said.

'Did the defendant introduce you to him?'

'No,' Sarah said.

'Did she tell you who he was?'

'No.'

'Did you ask?'

'I don't remember.' She was red. 'I may have.'

'What did she say?'

'She said he was someone she used to know.'

Anna knew how Sarah was suffering; she tried to catch

her eye to show her that she knew it was not her fault. But Sarah was being very careful to look straight at the prosecutor; she obviously did not want to do Anna any worse damage.

'Yet you are very close to her; not only that, you speak Russian and presumably have a good understanding of Russian society and culture. Why, of all people, wouldn't she confide in you?'

'I don't know,' Sarah said.

When Miles finally took the floor to make the summation, everyone was quiet. It was not the normal quiet that had usually prevailed in the courtroom, Ian thought, but a self-conscious silence. Perhaps there was a certain speech-lessness that affected people in the presence of the Big Abstracts – love, beauty, truth, justice. There was no whispering among the press with whom he now sat; the only people who were writing anything down at this point were the few poetic souls who wanted to capture the atmosphere. He felt that they violated it.

Anna looked as she had looked throughout the trial; serious, placid, innocent. This was not just Ian's bias; Miles continually told her to sit facing the jury.

There was some graciousness in her expression. He wondered if it would have been better for her if she could have shown her suffering more. She did not look as though they were crucifying her. She did not look injured; it was, he knew, because she tried to be forgiving.

But as he heard the word in his head, he grew angry. Don't forgive them, Anna, he thought.

Forgiveness was an unnatural thing. He could see no reason to forgive Alther, Orr, all the ignorant or, worse, evil people to whom human lives were pieces in a game. Make them things, he prayed, turn them into meaningless objects with no ability except the ability to feel their own powerlessness and pain.

His heart beat strangely. He was aware that he was no longer listening to Miles. He tried to calm himself by thinking of Anna's hands, of the soothing sound of dead leaves on the little tree in their courtyard, of Christian's satiny hair, thicker now that he was older, but still straight and fine.

What was Christian doing at that very moment? Was he at the beach? Had he already turned a soft brown in the sun? Ian looked at his watch. If it was 9 A.M. in New York, it was 6 A.M. in Los Angeles. Christian was still asleep.

Tears clawed delicately at the back of his throat. If forgiveness was unnatural, why did he crave it so much?

He looked at his own family, his mother, father, and Mary Ellen, sitting on the other side of the room with the spectators. He couldn't see it, but he bet that Mary Ellen was holding his father's hand. He wondered if this bothered his father or whether, actually, George had always liked being the father of a fairly fragile girl more than being the father of an unbending, troublesome boy.

His father watched Miles intently. Obviously, he was judging his performance as a lawyer. The set of his father's mouth was hard and sad; Ian realised that his father was also judging himself.

'There is a singular lack of evidence in this case,' Miles was saying. 'And that is the nature of the charges. No one can get inside Anna Khameneva's head and verify whether or not she agreed to be part of a conspiracy, whether or not she suspected that Kostia Kyrstov was a courier of classified information.

'You, the jury, must decide what the facts are. You must decide whom to believe – whose story makes sense, whose motives are compelling, who is wrong and who is right. Today you have no better example of why a court will never be able to merely read testimony into a computer which is programmed with the infinite measurements of the law, and derive an answer. Judgment is a human faculty and demands all – all – that we can give it. Not only intelligence, not only common sense, not only the wisdom of experience.

'You are here to put yourself in the shoes of every witness you have heard, of the plaintiffs, of the defendant. You must use your human capacity for empathy – not of sympathy; you need not feel sorry for anyone – to identify yourselves with each of the players on this stage. Imagine speaking their words, performing their actions. Only by doing this will you feel inside yourselves that indescribable sensation by which we know the truth.

'And you are in a yet more unusual position. For do not forget that in effect you are all the plaintiffs in this case. It is on behalf of the people of the United States that Anna Khameneva is accused. It is you that the government wishes to protect by taking away her liberty.'

Ian smiled. Miles's words hung in the air for a moment; could anyone really be afraid of Anna?

Miles continued, toting up the evidence that the government had offered and emphasising that nowhere could a direct proof be offered of Anna's complicity. Judgment, he kept repeating to the jury; it's all up to you.

'I asked Anna,' Miles said finally, 'if there was anything that she particularly wished me to stress in my remarks to you. She thought about it and said only this: "Tell them to decide according to their consciences. There's nothing else to say. If they do not feel free to look into their own hearts and speak out as they feel, then there is no difference in my being free or going to prison – there is no difference between my living here and being sent back to Russia."

'Ladies and gentlemen,' he concluded, 'I couldn't have said it better myself.'

He sat down. The quiet remained intact for a few seconds and then people began to stretch and whisper. The judge adjourned court until the following day.

Ian saw his family go up to Anna and speak to her as the crowd broke up. His father's face still looked grim. Ian tried to catch his eye, but he was too surrounded by others. He had wanted to smile at him.

At home, Anna was distant. They ate silently in front of the television. The news was a catalogue of wars, holy and unholy. At one point the camera zoomed in on huge unidentified boxes on the deck of a ship. It was said that they were fighter planes en route to Central America. The

Secretary of Defense told reporters that the next time America intervened in a foreign conflict they would do so at full force and with the intention of winning.

Anna stopped eating. Ian had never seen her look ugly before; she looked almost as if she would smash the glass screen.

'Do you want me to turn it off?' he asked her.

'I don't care,' she said.

'Anna,' he said. 'You really have no good reason to be so depressed. Miles did a brilliant job. The jury was completely on your side.'

She shrugged.

'Of course they're on my side. Today was my day. Tomorrow is the government's day. The state always speaks last. Tomorrow they will be on their side just like they're on my side today.'

'Annichka,' Ian said. 'You don't sound like yourself.' She sounded now, he thought, the way he used to sound – cynical, despairing; and he himself sounded like her. He realised that he believed absolutely that the jurors would recognise the truth and exonerate her.

'I'm not myself,' she said bitterly. 'I haven't been for a long time.'

For the first time in all the time they had been together, she went to bed alone, and was asleep when he lay down next to her.

*I am exhausted; we walk until dark every day. I have made a kind of poncho out of our blanket and I carry Misha underneath it, next to my skin. We will die of exposure unless we can find other people who will share what they have with us.*

*I don't know if the needle of my stupid compass is still adequately magnetized. Sometimes I am sure that I have passed the same tree or rise more than once. The ground beneath my feet – that is what I mostly look at, since Misha's weight draws me down – is unchanging. We have come to no country of white rock.*

*If we can only get that far! I have become increasingly*

*convinced that the chalky stone Niki spoke of may herald*
*a gem gravel: the ravines of the Caucasus were once full of*
*them. If I can find such pieces of stone, I will build a house*
*out of these pebbles, one by one, a corundum and beryl*
*house, which no radiation will ever penetrate. I see it daz-*
*zling in my mind's eye: a round house of dark, oily uncut*
*diamonds, repelling the ultraviolet, warming us inside like*
*embryonic chicks inside a stone egg.*

*We will crouch in there, safe, enjoying the strange refrac-*
*tion of our even stranger daylight. No one will find us.*

The morning of the government's summation, the crowd
of her supporters assembled on the steps of the Federal
Courthouse was larger than it had been on any other day
of the trial. There were cheers when she got out of the taxi
with Miles. She forced herself to smile. Then she saw Mary
Ellen.

The girl stood, unnaturally thin but vibrant, her collar
turned up against the cold, with a group of students. When
Anna walked past her, Mary Ellen smiled and she and a
friend lifted a white bedsheet on which had been spray-
painted: *Remember Hiroshima*.

During all of Alther's concluding remarks she saw war;
she saw people holding their own skin in their hands like
dresses, she saw people running as they burned, lighting
up the smoky dark around them like grotesque human
lanterns. She heard the sound of thousands of voices
weeping; it was not a human sound at all, but something
like wind which precedes a hurricane, or the groaning that
the earth emits before an earthquake. She smelled the
odour of fire doused with blood, human tissue rendered
like animal fat for soap. She held her hand up to her face
and thought that she already smelled slightly of prison,
and therefore death, in a way that the lissome lemony
scent of her hand cream only made more obscene.

Miles leaned towards her. 'On this day, of all days,' he
whispered, 'you should not let the jury see you looking so
dejected.'

She drew herself up. It was out of her hands; there was

nothing she could do except face the jury's deliberations with dignity.

But a prisoner has no dignity, she knew. That was the first thing you learned.


Miles brought Anna home that night and stayed to have a drink. He told Ian to turn on the television news as soon as they came in the door and the three of them stood in front of it, waiting for the report on the end of the trial. When it came on, Anna went into the kitchen.

'Keep her next to you tonight,' Miles said to Ian.

'I'm all right, Miles,' Anna said to him. She saw Ian look at her unhappily.

'Hey, look at this,' Ian said to her, pointing at the screen. The Defense Committee, which Miles chaired, was hosting a rally at the Statue of Liberty. Perhaps one hundred and fifty people stood beneath the dark statue, its form obscured by webs of scaffolding, holding lighted candles.

'Are you watching, Anna?' Miles asked.

She nodded.

'We've told everyone who believes in your innocence to light a candle tonight and every night that the jury remains out.'

The candles flickered in the wind and illuminated the faces of the people carrying them so that their eyes seemed to appear and disappear in the darkness. She was aware that they did not stand there still and silent with their candles – they talked and laughed.

Miles took a second scotch, but try as he might, he could not get Anna's mind off the jury. He finally made his apologies and left.

Anna did not look at Ian. On the kitchen table was a large postcard of Disneyland. Lilianne had written something, which Anna did not permit herself to read, but the boy had obviously signed his own name.

'Christian,' she said. 'What a name for a child.'

Ian shrugged and then smiled. 'Why? I thought you were a true believer.'

'I believe in God,' she said.

408

'Then what's so strange about the name Christian?'

'I have been wondering if there ever was a Jesus Christ,' she told him, 'or whether he is a myth we made up to console ourselves over the way we eternally sacrifice our own children.'

'Annichka,' he said, 'come here.'

She shook her head. But he insisted; she got up and went to him. He pulled her down on his lap.

'You are exhausted,' he told her. 'You should go to sleep.'

'How can I?' she said.

'Try,' he said. 'I'll sit with you.'

They went into the dark bedroom. Anna lay down and Ian kept her hand.

'Imagine that you can just go to sleep for the whole time, and when you wake up everything will be over. You'll be free,' he said.

She stared at the shadows on the ceiling. They seemed alive.


'Who can believe that all this could happen?' Kate said. The shadow in the dining room palpitated with the light of a dozen candles that she had placed on the table and in all the windows. 'Where has the time gone?'

George leaned forward and put his elbows on the table. He was conscious that he was doing it and he thought for one instant that that was what was good about family: you could be a slob at home and no one cared, they still loved you.

The dining room was still. He heard the furnace click on and he wondered what the thermostat was set at; there was no end to the prices that the oil companies extracted.

'Why aren't you wearing a sweater?' he said miserably to his wife.

'I am,' she said. 'But it doesn't matter. I can't feel a thing.'

He looked at her more closely. She did indeed have a soft blue sweater over the blue dress she wore.

'I'm sorry,' he said, 'but why does everything you wear have to be blue?'

She shrugged. 'Put your glasses on, and leave me alone.'

'I'm sorry,' he said again. 'This is awful – waiting. I wonder how they're doing.'

'Call them,' Kate said.

'I don't know if that would be right,' George said. 'This kind of thing is very delicate.'

Suddenly Kate was angry – or was it only that the candlelight enhanced her impulsive way of speaking?

'Delicate be damned,' she said. 'If you want to know how your son is, call him.'

He was silent for a moment. The candlelight soothed his eyes.

'You're right,' he said. 'But let's wait a little longer.'

*I woke up because I felt the child's small hands on my face. It was as if he were trying to make me listen without awakening me.*

*'Mama, Mama,' he whispered over my lips; he had never called me his mother before. He knows I am not.*

*I opened my eyes to see three other women bending over me.*

*'Bozhyemoy,' one said, 'she is so cold I thought she was dead.'*

*I felt her take my feet in her hands and warm them.*

*The other women held Misha and wrapped him in a man's shirt; they wound rags around his hands and feet.*

*'Try to sit up,' the first one said to me. Her face was weathered and grey like the bark of a tree, her hair was wild. As a child I would have been terrified and thought she was a witch; as an adult I would have shunned her as mad. Yet her eyes were the kindest eyes that have ever looked at me – a cloudy amber colour like honey stirred into tea.*

*'Eat this,' she said. She withdrew a piece of dried meat from inside her own shirt. It was warm from the heat of her body.*

*'It's all I have,' she said, 'but you need it more than I do.'*

*'Is this the valley we have heard of?' I asked her. She shook her head.*

*'Eat,' she told me. 'If it exists, we'll find it in the morning.'*

*I ate because I couldn't stop myself.*

*'I can help you,' I said. 'I am a scientist.'*

*She just smiled.*


Anna woke up because the phone rang.

'She's asleep,' she heard Ian say. After a few moments she realised that he was talking to his parents. Then she heard him hang up and walk around in the dark in the living room.

'Ian,' she whispered, 'what time is it?'

He came and stood in the doorway.

'About nine,' he said. 'Feeling better?'

'Thank you,' she said.

'Get up,' he told her. 'I want to show you something.' She got up, but having just awakened, she shivered with cold. In the dark, she pulled the blanket off the bed and wrapped it around herself.

'This way,' he said. He was standing outside in the hall. She followed him and he led her upstairs and out onto the roof. The air was clear and cold and smelled of chimney smoke. The stars were lucid and near.

'Look,' he said. He pointed down West Tenth Street.

In almost every one of the crooked little Federal town houses of that old street, at least one candle burned.

'They're not for me,' she said.

'Why do you say that?' Ian asked. 'Everyone knows you live here.'

She looked again.

'Why?' she said. 'Why should they care about me?'

He made her face him.

'It's what you yourself said,' he told her. '"Life is good." It feels good to love something good, it is rewarding, renewing.'

She touched his face. 'You are good,' she said.

Her face was cold in the night air, but inside the blanket,

411

at least, she felt warm. Ian came behind her and put his arms around her. They looked out on the tiny lights together.

'I can't get warm,' she said.

There was nothing he could say that he hadn't already said, many times, since morning. They had never gone to bed, but held each other on the couch during the night. He had dozed several times; he was ashamed of it – he knew that she had never once closed her eyes. She was hard and tense and cold in his arms.

The phone had rung at least twenty times. Miles had called twice. But not with the news. The jury was still out. They were still waiting. Anna's eyes were small with exhaustion, her expression was so empty that it frightened him.

'I wish I could cry,' she said, her voice suddenly very loud.

'Cry,' he said. He felt as though his lungs had contracted into fists; he wanted her to cry, to scream, so that the tension in him could break, too. His own tears would not have done it.

'I can't.' Her voice was down again.

'Then talk,' he said. 'At least talk.'

'There's nothing left to say.'

'Nonsense,' he said. He knew how angry he sounded. She recoiled.

'Ian,' she whispered, 'stop it.'

'No,' he said.

She turned away from him.

'Talk,' he commanded her.

'Leave me alone,' she said. Her voice was so low and so harsh that it was almost a howl.

'If everything's been said, then what are you afraid to say?'

She suddenly faced him and brought her fist down hard on his chest. He gasped.

'Say it.'

The blankness on her face broke; every nerve shivered.

She put her head down and sobbed like a drowning person who has managed to fight to the surface.

'I don't want to go to prison,' she cried. 'I'd rather die.'

He put his arms under her arms. There was no tension left in her body. He pulled her back to the couch and held her until she was quiet. He watched her breathe.

Once her whole body started; he kept his hands firm on her.

'Did I fall asleep?' she asked him.

He nodded.

'How long?'

'About eleven minutes,' he told her.

Miles's call came at a quarter to ten. The jury had been out for over twenty hours altogether and had now notified the judge that they had reached a decision. In order 'not to prolong the agony', as Miles quoted him, the judge would reconvene court at 11 P.M. Anna's hands felt inanimate with cold when she put down the phone.

'They say,' she said to Ian, 'that the longer the jury is out, the better it is for the defendant.'

'It seems to me,' Ian said, 'that they've been out forever.'

In the cab, they huddled together.

'This is like the first night I met you,' Ian told her.

She looked out at the wide-awake streets of New York, littered with coloured light.

'This is like no other night of my life,' she said.

He held her hand tightly.

Miles was waiting on the courthouse steps. Behind him stood twenty or thirty people holding lighted candles. The little flames were so frail, she thought; she wanted to touch them, to warm her fingers on their fragile heat.

They watched her go in – tonight no one cheered, no one spoke. They had come only to be near her.

When the court had reassembled, each of them in the place he had come to own in the last several weeks, the judge summoned the jury back into the box.

'Will the jurors please answer as their names are called,' said the clerk.

The roll call was taken.

'Mr Foreman,' the clerk said, 'have you agreed upon a verdict?'

Anna could hear her heartbeat.

'Yes, we have,' the foreman said.

'How say you?'

'We the jury find the defendant, Anna Khameneva, not guilty on either of the charges brought.'

She felt her voice escape from her throat and Miles threw his arms around her.

After most of the guests had left the McDonoughs' house, the nucleus of the group relaxed in front of the fire.

Sarah, in a pink sweater, seemed to be dreaming; her eyes were half closed and she leaned against Anna the way Anna leaned against Ian. Ian was smoking a pipe and the musky smoke of his tobacco seemed to swathe Anna in a bluish forgetfulness. She watched over his shoulder as he played Trivial Pursuits with Mary Ellen, whose new boyfriend was being politely drawn out in conversation by Kate. Ian eyed them coldly and Anna quietly laughed at him.

'Try this,' George said to Miles, offering him a brandy. 'It's nearly as old as you are.'

'But that's much too young for a really fine brandy,' Miles said.

George laughed and offered a glass to Anna and she held it in front of the firelight, watching another deep, warm fire form in the glass. 'I've never tasted anything like that,' she said. She remembered the night in Paris when George had taken such pleasure in showing off the food. The pleasure had been real, she didn't doubt it.

'Neither have I.' George laughed. 'My very extravagant son gave it to me for Christmas. I would never have bought it myself.'

Anna was aware that George had been watching her all evening; how odd he must find her, she thought, so much older than his son.

As if Ian had read her mind, he put his arm around her shoulder.

George cleared his throat. He looked at Anna again.

'I have something for you,' he said. 'I was saving it until things were quieter.'

He took out his wallet and from it produced a small snapshot.

'This came from our Vienna office,' he told her. 'I don't know exactly how, but they were very proud of themselves.'

She took the photograph. It was a poor, blurry candid of a bearded Seriozha and a fat Katinka. They were at a train station and stood beside the sign that marked it: Ussugli, a small town in Siberia, not far from the Chinese border.

'When was this taken?' she asked him.

'I don't know,' he said, 'but I assume it's recent.'

'Let me see,' Kate said. Anna handed it to her.

'Is she pregnant?' Kate asked. 'Or is it just the heavy coat?'

Anna looked to George. He shrugged. Then Anna looked back at Kate and smiled. Kate kissed her.

Sarah took the photo from her hand.

She studied it. 'What kind of life awaits that child?' she asked.

'What awaits any of us?' Miles said.

'Enough,' Anna said. She stood up and took George's hand.

'Thank you,' she told him.

'Tonight is a night to be happy,' she said to the others.

*First we found the river, and the water was clear. We stood on the edge bathed in a light that was so much like the light we remembered from before that for whole, hot moments we were able to fully forget. We washed ourselves, we were naked, and we laughed.*

*Then we found the others, and they turn no one away.*

*We sleep with many other women and children in what was once a barn. But it is blessed to wake up in the morning*

415

to that live noise, to belong to it. And to see Misha disappear among the other children and play with them, never looking back to make sure that I am there! Soon he will go to the school.

As for myself, I have been able to begin experiments on the soil.

Who knows but that this may be the place where something will grow?